T0328864

Visconti

In this study, the first in the English language to consider Luchino Visconti's entire oeuvre, Henry Bacon examines the films of one of Italy's preeminent filmmakers, against the cultural, historical, and biographical contexts in which they were made. The author focuses on three fundamental themes of Visconti's cinematic output: his varying styles and strategies of audiovisual narration, which create enthralling images of individuals and societies at a given moment in their development; his ability to take literary works and other cultural influences into his possession and recreate them as a highly individualized cinema; and the interplay between the filmmaker's intense feeling for life, art, and beauty and his critical detachment, disillusion, and painful awareness of death and decay. In Bacon's analysis Visconti emerges as a twentieth-century inheritor and renewer of the nineteenth-century narrative tradition, especially that of the novel and the opera.

Henry Bacon is Associate Professor of Film and Television at the University of Helsinki, Finland.

Visconti

EXPLORATIONS OF BEAUTY AND DECAY

Henry Bacon

CAMBRIDGE
UNIVERSITY PRESS

PUBLISHED BY THE PRESS SYNDICATE OF THE UNIVERSITY OF CAMBRIDGE
The Pitt Building, Trumpington Street, Cambridge, United Kingdom

CAMBRIDGE UNIVERSITY PRESS
The Edinburgh Building, Cambridge CB2 2RU, UK   http://www.cup.cam.ac.uk
40 West 20th Street, New York, NY 10011-4211, USA   http://www.cup.org
10 Stamford Road, Oakleigh, Melbourne 3166, Australia

First published 1998

Typeset in Bauer Bodoni 10.5/13.5 pt, in QuarkXPress ® [RF]

*A catalog record for this book is available
from the British Library.*

Library of Congress Cataloging-in-Publication Data
Bacon, Henry.
Visconti : explorations of beauty and decay / Henry Bacon.
p.   cm.
Filmography: p.
Includes bibliographical references and indexes.
ISBN 0-521-59057-4. – ISBN 0-521-59960-1 (pbk.)
1. Visconti, Luchino, 1906–1976 – Criticism and interpretation.
I. Title.
PN1998.3.V57B34   1998
791.43'0233'092 – dc21   97–19635
                                                           CIP

Transferred to digital printing 2002

*Dedicated to the dear memory of my late father,
Walter Bacon, who used to be the first reader of
my English texts, including this study.*

Contents

Visconti

Introduction

Sandra is hosting a cocktail party when she suddenly becomes aware that someone is playing César Franck's *Prelude, Chorale and Fugue*. The piece used to be in the repertoire of her pianist mother, and now it fills her mind with bitter memories. As the film – *Vaghe stelle dell'Orsa (Sandra)* – progresses, she is forced to redefine her relationship with her family and her husband, her past and her future. When she finally decides to sever her ties with the past, she pays a high price for her freedom.

The problems of relating to time and history constitute one of the most pertinent themes of Luchino Visconti's (1906–76) artistic output. He could remember how as a small boy he could hear his mother play that piece after bedtime. The main theme of Franck's *Prelude* has much the same function in *Sandra* as the tea in which Marcel soaks his "petite madeleine" in Proust's *Remembrance of Things Past*. There the mere sensation of the warm liquid on the lips produces "an exquisite pleasure" that makes "the vicissitudes of life . . . indifferent, its disasters innocuous, its brevity illusory."[1]

Both Visconti and Proust were keenly aware of the perpetual sense of loss that is an inextricable feature of life, but as Mikael Enckell has pointed out, the perspective of both also emphasizes "the continuity of existence: What appears to be irrevocably lost returns through its very passing, as memory, imagination, and works [of art]."[2] Sandra is unable to gain strength from her painful memories and perhaps reaches a sterile peace of mind by rejecting her past. Visconti, like Proust, transformed the pain and the sorrow into restless creative energy. Resignation enabled them to view their characters both from within and without, in sympathy with the burning immediacy of their passions, yet with the tender, ironic detachment, as if viewing their own follies from a sufficient distance in time. This is the foundation of the deep resonance of their works. As

Youssef Ishaghpour points out, in Visconti's films it takes the form of a constant dissonance between the pursuit of an ideal and reality, between aspiration and immanence:[3] "Aspiration toward something else, like a glance, carries beyond phenomena, toward that which illuminates them from yonder, a light which reveals beauty in them, but only as a path. Immanence is attached to the here and now, it wants to possess immediately the absolute and take the phenomenon for a complete 'reality': in passion."[4]

Visconti's characters are often caught in the mesh of their past, dissatisfied with their present and unable to assume responsibility for the future. They may be driven by aspiration, but their attempts to realize their most cherished hopes are often crushed by their own spiritual limitations, their social condition, or the historical circumstances of their lives. Many of them would like to free themselves of all responsibility, find a quiet pool of rest beyond the relentless stream of time. But no one can escape that inexorable flux: what has passed cannot be regained; life deprives us of all that we hold dear. The struggle against the fugacity of things, the attempt to create a haven of peace and pleasure for oneself by ignoring all other commitments can all too easily lead a person to betray ideals, friends, a loved one, and be crowned by self-deception. In depicting this struggle Visconti assumes the role of witness and accomplice:

Again and again Visconti returns in his films to the phenomenon of betrayal. . . . We can see this as an expression of his basic and passionate striving to cover everything. He who wants to represent both the past and the future, both to give shape to his own traditions and belong to youth, faces the danger of betraying one or the other, probably both. This mighty aspiration, this tremendous passion to be everything Visconti expresses in film after film.[5]

Visconti's need to become a "master of time" grew from the conflict between his aristocratic background and the marxist view of life and society that he adopted in his thirties. He attempted to find a balance between emotion and intellect, between the private needs and the public demands imposed by the past and the future. His work was imbued with two opposite temporal perspectives, which together enable him to study and depict characters in their historical and social milieu with intellectual rigor and deeply felt compassion. This duality is not restricted to Visconti's historical films but can also be seen in those with a contemporary setting. In these there also emerges the reverse side of temporal experience, immutability and stagnation, as opposed to fugacity and transition. Workers and fishermen face the inexorable laws of nature and the almost equally fixed structures of power in their pursuit of happiness. At times they seek to change things, but the time is not yet ripe; at times they find it difficult to cope with the changes imposed on them.

In short, Visconti's view of life and society is conflict-ridden through and through. His characters are torn between mutually incompatible desires. Money and love, cynicism and idealism, loyalty and betrayal are the ever-present alternative means of survival or pursuit of self-interest. Such conflicts create a burning desire to return to some kind of peace, to reach a final synthesis. Visconti's starting point was an all-encompassing social vision rooted in marxism, but when working on a given subject, he would never let himself be confined by dogma or theoretical analysis. Instead, he created a complex, multilayered, equivocal, and rich image of the interrelationships between the individuals and the society he was depicting. The interaction of the subject matter with the expressive means at hand, the resistance of material that all artists encounter in their work, is an essential part of the creative process. It can even be seen as a metaphor of human interaction with the world. An artist can succeed only by being in a dialectical relationship with his material and the world he lives in.

As Visconti grew older, his artistic work acquired a tone of resignation. An almost oversensitive feeling for time and place eventually led him to concentrate on the questions of old age and decay. Though even at this stage he could hardly be described as an idealist, his concern with fugacity led to an understanding of permanence, and to an almost reverse perspective of the world. The gradual transformation in his work reflected a heightened sense that art itself is the ultimate manifestation of immanence, aspiration, and their interdependence. In Thomas Mann's words:

Conceiving the world as a colourful and turbulent phantasmagory of images through which the ideal, the spiritual glows is something eminently artistic and allows the artist to find his true nature. He can be sensuously and sinfully attached to the world of phenomenon and appearances, because he knows he belongs to the spheres of both ideas and the spirit, as the magician who makes appearances transparent for them.[6]

This book examines Visconti's films against their cultural, historical, and social backgrounds. The sometimes tortuous production histories and practical problems that shaped certain films as well as Visconti's personal life are treated here only insofar as they shed light on the formation of his films or offer a key to richer interpretations of them.

The approach is auteuristic in a fairly broad sense of the word, the basic assumptions being that the maker of the fourteen feature-length and three short films discussed in this volume is to a meaningful extent Luchino Visconti and that his central role must be taken into account to fully understand the connection between his films and the society and the ideological context from which they emerged. This is not to ignore the contribution of all the other people involved in making these films, nor the economic, social, and practical factors that influenced their production. The point is, it was Visconti who organized this process and gathered round him a team of faithful collaborators whose efforts would add up to a single artistic whole. He taught his collaborators not only to recognize what he wanted but also to contribute actively to the creative process and to extend their limits in doing so. Without the "workshop" that he instigated, his last film, *The Innocent*, would probably not have been completed with the loving care that it deserved, and *Ludwig* would certainly not have been posthumously restored to its full four-hour beauty. The strength of Visconti's vision can be seen also in his ability to coax his actors to give the best performances of their lives. This has often been noted, for example, of Alida Valli and Farley Granger in *Senso* (known in the United States as *The Wanton Contessa*), Helmut Berger in *Ludwig*, and Laura Antonelli in *The Innocent*.

Rather than follow a strict chronological order, I have grouped Visconti's films according to their most interesting and relevant characteristics. This classification is by no means "pure," of course. For example, most of Visconti's films are adaptations. To varying degrees, I have treated them as such, although I deal specifically with Visconti's relationship with literature only in connection with the three films discussed in the last chapter. The treatment of the films within each chapter follows the order of their making. Because the first chapter deals with neorealism and the second with the Risorgimento films, the discussion follows Visconti's early career chronologically all the way up to *Senso*.

Many people have encouraged and helped me in shaping my ideas and locating material for this study. Among them are Dudley Andrew, Peter von Bagh, Peter Bondanella, Francesco Bono, Satu Kyösola, Satu Laaksonen, Lino Micciché, Jarmo Mäenpää, and Elina Suolahti. Interviews with Guido Aristarco, Gian Piero Brunetta, Suso Cecchi D'Amico, and Enrico Medioli, in particular, have helped me gain an understanding of how Visconti's works evolved and how they related to Italian society at the time of their making.

This study might not have come about had I not been invited to present a paper at the enormously inspiring *Convegno internazionale di studi viscontiani* held in Rome in December 1994 and chaired by Professor Lino Micciché. At this meeting Millicent Marcus and Roy Armes recommended that I translate my book in Finnish on Visconti, *Tiikerikissan aika* (1992), into English. Instead, I decided to rewrite that work extensively in the light of recent research both by myself and by many other scholars. Above all, I have incorporated ideas that I developed in my doctoral dissertation, which benefited enormously from the feedback of Professor Dudley Andrew, who acted as the so-called opponent in my public defense at the University of Helsinki in May 1994.

1

Visconti and Neorealism

An aristocrat and a filmmaker

The early 1930s were a thrilling time for a handsome, restless young aristocrat to be in Paris. A successful career as a horse trainer had not been enough for Luchino Visconti. He knew he had the potential for something greater. But to realize that potential he needed more stimulation than his native Milan of the Fascist era could possibly provide. And so, after about 1932, Visconti's visits to Paris became increasingly frequent. Soon he became acquainted with the latest intellectual and artistic trends. He participated in riotous society life and met Coco Chanel, who fell for him and introduced him to many of Paris's leading artists. He got to know people like Serge Lifar, Jean Cocteau, Henry Bernstein, Kurt Weill, and Marlene Dietrich, and their art. He also saw many controversial films that were banned in Italy, ranging from the avant garde works of Luis Buñuel, Cocteau, and Man Ray to the revolutionary works of Vsevolod Pudovkin and Sergei Eisenstein.[1]

The period in Paris was a formative one for Visconti. On a personal level, although it would be sometime before he could fully acknowledge his homosexuality, living amid the emancipated members of Parisian high society helped considerably. He formed a close relationship with a young German, Horst P. Horst (Horst Paul Bohrmann), who had just embarked on a spectacular career as a photographer. Visconti developed a greater political awareness as well. Fascism had come into fashion in Paris, but Horst, with his openness and frankness, helped Visconti see through it and distance himself from false nationalistic pride, Fascist rhetoric, and his habit of emphasizing his aristocratic background.[2]

Visconti's values changed even more markedly in 1936 after Chanel introduced him to film director Jean Renoir and his colleagues, all of whom were members of the Popular Front or were at least sympathetic to it. The time was propitious: the Popular Front had just won a major election victory – although the sense of optimism it generated would soon dissipate as the new government turned out to be ineffective and downright reactionary in its cultural policy. Getting to know Renoir's group must have been somewhat disconcerting for Visconti, who had been brought up to think of communists as a major threat to civilization. The feeling of strangeness was reciprocal: he was unable to downplay his aristocratic manners, and he came from a fascist country.

The aesthetic influence of Visconti's associates was equally significant. Renoir was on his way to becoming one of Europe's most prominent directors of the thirties. His *Toni* (1935) heralded a change in French as well as European film in general. There had been other films shot in alfresco style, but, in the words of Raymond Durgnant, this was "the point at which the whole documentary movement of the French cinema achieved its fullest coalescence with the fiction film."[3] As Renoir himself put it:

I think I may say that what characterized *Toni* is the absence of any dominating element, whether star performer, setting or situation. My aim was to give the impression that I was carrying a camera and microphone in my pocket and recording whatever came my way, regardless of its comparative importance. Nevertheless, I had given myself a framework. *Toni* is not a documentary; it is a news item, a love-story that really happened in Les Martigues. . . . I scarcely needed to adapt it for the screen.[4]

Toni foreshadowed neorealism in many ways: the characters are ordinary workers or peasants depicted without resorting to sophisticated psychology, the actors were provincial amateurs expressing themselves in their accustomed way, and the film was shot on location.[5] Visconti probably saw it as being close to Giovanni Verga in its depiction of the lives of uneducated (Mediterranean) people by means of emotionally charged realism. Visconti's eventual adaptation of Verga was to be quite different in style, but Renoir served as a general model, particularly with respect to some of his aesthetic principles:

From the moment when I realized the importance of unity I tried never to shoot a scene without some background movement more or less related to the action. . . . Another of my preoccupations was, and still is, to avoid fragmentation, and by means of longer-playing shots to give the actor a chance to develop his own rhythm in the speaking of the lines. To me this is the only way of getting sincere acting.[6]

Similarly, Visconti's art was to be closely tied to the actor, to his or her ability to incarnate a character in a given setting. And like Renoir, he was willing to use a literary text as his starting point and to adapt it according to his own expressive needs and sociopolitical concerns.

It is not quite clear at what stage Visconti got to know Renoir. According to some sources, it happened as early as 1934, in connection with the shooting of *Toni*, but if so he was probably a mere observer.[7] In any case, that year Visconti had his first taste of filmmaking. Horst had taught him the basics, and he made a Buñuelesque amateur film about a young man who first has an affair with a young girl, then a prostitute, and finally an ideal woman. Then he kills himself. The film has not survived but apparently it was not a particularly promising start for a filmmaking career.[8]

Visconti must have gained his first professional experience in filmmaking as the third assistant director of Renoir's *Une partie de campagne* (A day in the country, 1936; released in 1946). His actual task was to design and supervise the making of costumes. This he did with enthusiasm. He studied the collections of the Musée des Arts Décoratifs and went through a considerable amount of relevant literature. But he derived his greatest pleasure and benefit from following how Renoir directed actors.[9]

Later in many interviews Visconti said that he became politically conscious and decided to start making films while working with Renoir. Yet it appears that his anti-fascist convictions were not particularly strong, at least at this stage He did not take a stand on the Spanish civil war or on any other major political event before the Second World War.[10] At the same time, all the influences he had come under during his sojourns in Paris gave him a far broader view of the world than his aristocratic upbringing on its own could possibly have done.

For a while he thought of becoming a writer, and two drafts for novels survive from this period. The first was a vaguely autobiographical work titled *Angelo* (Angel), the second an almost gothic horror story, *I tre, un esperimento* (The three, or the experiment). The drafts are interesting only because they foreshadow some of the themes of Visconti's mature output.[11] On the surface, there are some obvious connections between *Angelo* and Visconti's first film, *Ossessione:* "The same social class, the same poetical digressions, the same geographical setting: the Po valley, Piacenza in *Angelo*, Ferrara in *Ossessione*."[12] These features also connect *Angelo* with Verga and verism, while the theme of sickness links it with the decadent movement. Together with the intensity of the mother–son (or daughter) relationship, these themes were to become important in the second half of Visconti's cinematic oeuvre. The draft also reveals Visconti's obsession with details, which at times make the text quite burdensome. This passion he was later able to turn to his advantage in films. There the phenomenal world in all its richness could be conveyed through what Seymour Chatman has called "tacit description," which refers to the power of the cinematic image to convey information about the diegetic world (that is, the fictional world created in the film) without having to halt the narrative flow.

Before his first serious attempt to make a film, Visconti tried his hand at working in the theater. He had had some experience with amateur stage production in his early youth in the small theater inside the Visconti family residence in Milan; now he approached it as a professional. After returning to Italy, he designed the sets and costumes for a production of Giannino Antona Traversi's *Carita Mondana* (Mundane charity) at Teatro Sociale in Como in 1936 and for Jan Mallory's *Sweet Aloes*, produced in Teatro Manzoni in Milan the same year. Immediately after the latter he went to Hollywood, where he saw the studio system at its peak. Apparently the trip was not particularly successful, however, and he never talked much about it.[13]

An opportunity to return to filmmaking arose when Renoir came to Rome to direct a film version of *La Tosca* (1940). In a prime example of the inconsistency of its art policy, the Fascist Italian government had actually invited Renoir to teach and direct in Italy. Although his *Grande Illusion* (1937) had been banned in Italy, Mussolini had acquired it for his private collection, and it was his idea that Renoir should come. Renoir was an officer in the French army, and France had already declared war on Germany, Italy's ally at that time. Renoir had the support of the French government, which hoped that keeping up cultural relations with Italy might help to sustain its noninvolvement.[14]

Renoir's aim in *La Tosca* was to combine features of both documentary and crime films. Visconti took him around Rome, and they chose locations for shooting. They prepared the script together with the second assistant director, Carl Koch.[15] But as the presence of Germans in Rome became increasingly apparent, it was obviously unwise for the French members of the team to remain there. Renoir returned to Paris only shortly before Italy declared war on France and Great Britain. Koch, who had a German passport, stayed and with Visconti's assistance completed the film. The result was somewhat uneven. Visconti later described it as "a horrible film – it was all we could do."[16]

The collaboration with Renoir helped Visconti establish contacts in the

Italian film world, above all with a group of critics who had gravitated around *Cinema* magazine, notably, Gianni Puccini, Giuseppe De Santis, Michelangelo Antonioni, and Pietro Ingrao. Many of them were communists dreaming of the overthrow of the Fascist regime. It was most probably at this stage that Visconti himself adopted a marxist outlook and thus felt drawn to these young intellectuals.[17] Politics could not be discussed openly, of course, particularly as the chief editor of the magazine was Vittorio Mussolini, the son of Il Duce himself. Vittorio did not take much part in the actual running of the magazine, but thanks to his position it almost had the status of an official publication. This did not prevent it from printing articles that criticized national film policy and mainstream productions.

Indeed, Italy's Fascists never exerted the sort of control over cinema exercised by the totalitarian regimes in Germany or the Soviet Union. According to Martin Clark, at least, "In general, intellectuals were tolerated and flattered, indeed bought off, rather than persecuted."[18] Apparently Mussolini believed that intellectuals producing art and exchanging ideas would have little impact in a country run by a party of the masses and entertained by a blossoming film industry. And so, though it was wise for critically minded writers to exercise a degree of self-censorship, they were not completely silenced. A few were deported to remote corners of the south, where they actually expanded their understanding of the squalor behind the facade of "official" Italy. When they returned, they were even allowed to write about what they had experienced.

Only in the mid-thirties did the government begin to exert sterner measures in the form of preliminary censorship. At the same time, it began promoting a national film culture. In 1934 films became a part of the Venice Art Festival. The following year the Centro Sperimentale Cinematografico film school opened its doors under the highly competent direction of Luigi Chiarini. Also in 1935 the government established a fund to finance film production as well as a national film production company, Ente Nazionale Industrie Cinematografichelle (ENIC). ENIC was given a monopoly on importing films. This led the big Hollywood companies to withdraw from the Italian market for the time being, thus considerably improving the prospects of domestic films. In 1937 Mussolini himself came to open the Cinecittà studios, and the Centro launched the ambitious *Bianco e nero* (Black and white) magazine, which was to gain worldwide recognition. Most of these institutions are still in operation.[19]

Sterner measures were not needed in part because the film industry –

in good capitalist fashion – responded to the same sentiment that had
brought the Fascist party to power in the first place, and so the government had little to worry about from these quarters. Though only a few
films had an overtly fascist content, most were supportive of the traditional family and the established social order. However, the films also
reflected an almost involuntary admiration for everything new and American. James Hay has defined these two opposite trends as "essentialist
pride" and "epocalist hope." There was a distinct ideological tension between the two, but it was usually left unresolved. Films adhered to traditional values even in the context of modern society, although they also
depicted exciting and/or amusing adventures, often connected with tem-
porary social mobility: typically a handsome but poor young man would
try to have an affair with an upper-class lady, only to realize that his true
happiness lay among the members of his own class. These light social
comedies were nicknamed "white telephone" films.[20]

The Fascist regime did not try to quench the enthusiasm that things
American generated. Although the regime wanted to develop Italian culture and therefore in principle opposed everything foreign, American culture as such was not disparaged but rather involuntarily admired. Vittorio
Mussolini, for one, was quite open about his feelings toward American
cinema. He thought it was youthful and energetic – traits that according
to official propaganda were also the distinguishing features of fascism –
and thus it was a much better model for Italian audiences than the decadent European cinema. The trouble was that American films posed an
obvious threat to the domestic film industry. The Cinecittà studio, "Hollywood on the Tiber," was thought of as a means of boosting national
self-respect in the face of foreign media imperialism.[21]

The attitudes of the filmmakers toward American films was equally
ambivalent. On one hand, the films of Frank Capra, John Ford, William
Wyler, and King Vidor, in particular, were held in high esteem. On the
other hand, leftist-orientated directors sought to counterbalance this influence by also studying the works of French and Soviet directors, insofar
as copies of their films were available. The French connection was especially important and generously acknowledged. Visconti was not the only
aspiring Italian to work under or be influenced by the French masters.
Antonioni served as Marcel Carné's assistant on *Les visiteurs du soir* (The
devil's envoys, 1942) and thought of him as "a sort of phenomenon, a
man who had broken the barriers in the name of a true freedom."[22] It is
telling that the term *neorealism* was probably first used by Umberto Barbaro in 1943 to describe certain French films of the thirties, and that in

1945 Guido Aristarco used it in reference to the works of Renoir, Carné, and Julien Duvivier. According to Roy Armes, what the French did for Italian neorealism was to communicate "the complexities of cinematic style and an appreciation of the artistic possibilities of stylization, both of which were later to provide a vital counterpart to the purely documentary impulse to record the surface of war-torn Italy."[23]

Another important development occurred among the radicals who had gathered around *Cinema* magazine. They severely criticized the white telephone films for being mere escapist entertainment. Gianni Puccini, Giuseppe De Santis, and Michelangelo Antonioni argued that Italian cinema should go to Verga and other turn-of-the-century veristic writers for their inspiration. At the time, this was quite a revolutionary idea, not only in terms of cinema but Italian cultural history in general.[24] Verism was the Italian version of French naturalism. Verga was its greatest master and Luigi Capuana its major theoretician. The aim was to describe objectively the life of peasants and other poor and oppressed people in order to elicit a moral response in the reader. Capuana also explored psychological processes through descriptions of external, objective things. This was a kind of positivism that often degenerated into fatalism, as the descriptions of reality conveyed a sense of something unbearable and immutable, dictated by nature. According to G. M. Carsaniga: "To be 'defeated by life' is a natural subject for bourgeois *verismo*. . . . [U]nable to free himself from his class ideology and to understand and express reality, the *verista* can achieve nothing more significant than to celebrate consciously and conscientiously his own defeat by chronicling the defeat of his characters."[25]

However, someone like Verga did not restrict himself to mere surface realism and was able to circumvent the pessimism. In any case, the criticism delivered by the verists was sharp enough to generate fierce opposition among the representatives of "official Italy," who were loath to admit that such squalor as described first by the verists at the turn of the century and then by the neorealists a half century later actually existed. Yet the verists were unable to hold the attention of the reading public for very long, and soon many of them changed direction. Although they continued to pursue a certain degree of realism, they also sought greater popularity through melodrama spiced with off-color material. Neorealism was also to follow a similar pattern of development in this respect.[26]

Though both trends were relatively short-lived, they proved to have an immense effect in creating a whole new conception of what art could be about. In the view of *Cinema* contributors in the early forties, in addition to their social commitment, the verists provided an aesthetic ideal. It was seven years before Visconti had an opportunity to start realizing his ideas about adapting Verga in his *La terra trema* (The earth trembles), although he had been looking for models even earlier. He wrote in his essay *"Tradizione e invenzione"* (Tradition and invention):

It may sound obvious but I have often asked myself, as there is a solid literary tradition which in hundreds of novels and stories has realized in fantasy such genuine and pure "truths" about human life, why should the cinema, which in its more exterior access to life could actually be documentary, complacently accustom the audience to petty plotting and pompous melodrama the mechanical logic of which protects the spectator from the risks of whim and invention. In such a situation it becomes natural for those who sincerely believe in the cinema to turn their eyes nostalgically to the grand narrative structures of European literature and to think of them as the truest source of inspiration of our time. It is good to have the courage to say "truest" even though some people might label it as impotence or at least as a lack of cinematic purity.[27]

At this stage Visconti apparently already had a clear idea of the kind of cinematic realism he was after. He took as his starting point the ability of the film to create an illusion of a fictional world. But he was also aware that in order to make a statement about reality he needed a firm narrative structure. The way the story evolves and the characters develop was to play a major part in creating the all-important sense of verisimilitude in his films. To achieve all this, the acting had to be deeply felt and carefully executed down to the smallest gesture in meticulously (re)constructed environments.[28] This was the core of what Visconti referred to in his essay *"Anthropomorphic cinema."* He drew some of these concepts from his literary idol, Marcel Proust. According to Jean-Francois Revel:

What human beings feel, want, their inner states which they think they have concealed can be read in their mimicry, their intonations, their facial expressions, and their verbal habits. Proust is among the most impressionable of literary witnesses of behaviour, or rather it never occurs to him to separate behaviour from feeling. His writing is a demonstration of the inanity of the theoretical and abstract distinction between the psychological and the objective novel. . . . He does exactly what each of us would do in similar circumstances: he only interests himself in the sight of gestures in so far as he has a simultaneous perception or presentiment of their psychological significance without which he would not even see what was in front of him, would not even be aware of it.[29]

Visconti, too, wanted to convey the internal life of his characters through their behavior and their relationship to the environment, to capture their essence by showing them as an organic part of a certain social

reality, which in various ways constantly conditions and guides their behavior, their thoughts, and feelings. In his article *"Il cinema antropomorfico"* (Anthropomorphic cinema) published in *Cinema* in 1943, he
expounded his ideas about the relationship between acting and reality:

Of all my duties as a director the one that I find most fascinating is working with
the actors; human material from which I construct those new people, who, when
asked to live in it, generate a new reality, a reality of art. This is because an actor
is above all a human being. He has the key human qualities. On these I seek to
base my work, to grade these in constructing a character: up to the point where
the human-actor and the human-character become in a certain sense one. . . .
The most humble gesture of a human being, his steps, his hesitations and his
impulses alone give poetry and vibrations to the things that surround them and
within which they are confined. Any other solution to this problem appears to
me like an attempt to destroy reality as it opens to our eyes: made by men and
continually modified by them.[30]

By the time the article appeared, Visconti had begun realizing his ideas.

The making and reception of *Ossessione*

After *La Tosca* was completed, Visconti decided to make a film of
his own. Together with Giuseppe De Santis, Pietro Ingrao, and Mario
Alicata, he drafted scenarios for several films. Among them was an adaptation of a Verga novel, but like so many of the ideas of the *Cinema*
group, it was rejected in the preliminary round of censorship. There was
a note written in red on the first page: "Enough of brigands!"[31]

While shooting *A Day in the Country*, Renoir had given Visconti a
present that was to provide a decisive impulse to his creative career. It
was a typewritten translation into French of James M. Cain's novel *The
Postman Always Rings Twice* (1934). Renoir had received it from Julien
Duvivier and perhaps contemplated directing it himself. Duvivier also
gave a copy to Pierre Chenal, who based his *Le dernier tournant* (1939)
on it. Visconti prepared his script with the help of Alicata, Puccini, and
De Santis in 1941–2. As the project proceeded, various other people also
participated in shaping the text, including Alberto Moravia. The script,
at this stage titled *Paluda* (Marsh), passed the preliminary censorship
probably because the story was thought to be a melodrama with the message that "crime doesn't pay."

The screenwriters saw the subject quite differently. There has been
some debate as to which features of *Ossessione* arose from Visconti's
treatment of the material at different stages and which were the ideas of
the co-writers. According to Alicata, he, De Santis, and Puccini developed

most of the original political allusions, although Visconti changed some
of them. The other writers apparently wanted to make *Ossessione* a man-
ifesto, whereas Visconti steered it firmly toward a passionate yet critical
melodrama set in a definite social context. His fierce determination in
pursuing his artistic ideas and visions together with his aristocratic background kept his friends in *Cinema* at bay.[32]

For the male lead of *Ossessione*, Visconti chose Massimo Girotti, whom
he had come to know and admire during the shooting of *La Tosca*. The
other writers preferred Andrea Girotti, who would have been better suited
to portray the Italian type they had in mind. The main female part was
eventually given to Clara Calamai, who had previously played mainly
high-society women. Everyone knew Visconti was a beginner in filmmaking, but he had absolutely no inhibitions in directing established film
stars. According to Calamai, he beha7ed like a medieval prince with a
whip. He ordered Calamai to be made up to look scruffy and dishevelled.
Calamai and Girotti were rising stars of Italian cinema, but by deter-
minedly stripping the glamour and polished mannerisms from their performances, Visconti was able to capture the rugged quality of Cain's novel
and to use it for his own purposes.[33]

Visconti could be dictatorial on the set also because, although the nom-
inal producer was Industrie Cinematografiche Italiane (I.C.I.), he produced and to a large extent financed the film himself. He also astonished
the film crew with his enormous store of energy and ability to control the
shooting situation. Although he had no formal education in this field and
not that much experience either, he was able to make decisions about
composition, camera location, and length of shot without the slightest
hesitation. He also handled little details on the set with loving care – this
was to be a hallmark of his art throughout his career.[34] Mario Serandrei,
who was editing the film, had some difficulty in comprehending that Visconti was aiming for a style quite different from that of standard Italian
films, for a rhythm generated by shots of considerable duration. Visconti
himself completed the editing.[35]

All the while, political pressures were rapidly increasing. In December
1942 Alicata and Gianni Puccini and his brother Dario were arrested.
Visconti and his crew were being observed, but their work was not inter-
fered with. The premiere of *Ossessione* took place at a film festival hosted
by Vittorio Mussolini in May 1943. Visconti no doubt thought this showing would be a mark of official approval and thereby hoped to circumvent
bureaucratic and censorship problems. According to De Santis, the film
was a success among the intellectuals who had gathered to see it, in ad-

dition to which Vittorio Mussolini passed along to Visconti the favorable opinion of his father. Visconti himself, however, has related that the invited spectators, in their furs and diamonds, were shocked. The most well-known and commonly accepted version is by another *Cinema* group member, Aldo Scagnetti. According to his account the audience did applaud enthusiastically, but that Vittorio Mussolini dashed away shouting: "This is not Italy!"[36]

The critics were on the whole positive. Most of them thought that the film had truly captured something of the material and spiritual reality of Italy. Even the review in the Fascist *Primi piani* magazine agreed that the film captured certain national sentiments. So at least the Italianization of Cain's novel had been successful. But as the reported cry of outrage from Vittorio Mussolini suggested, this also caused the film some problems.[37]

In each of the handful of cities where it was initially shown, *Ossessione* was sharply attacked. Fascist officials refused to accept its depiction of immorality and squalor as reality. The film's social realism, especially its overt pessimism, was the exact opposite of the optimism espoused by Fascist propaganda. Although the film was not actually censored, several officials impeded its distribution. In Salsomaggiore, the archbishop was invited to cleanse through his benediction the cinema in which the film had been screened.

In Rome, the first public showings did not take place until May 1945, although there had been a special screening in June 1943, in the same theater where it had its premiere. The film had no sooner begun than it was interrupted by the police, who took down the names of everyone there.[38] Not long after the Fascists confiscated the original negative and carried it to their film studio in Venice, where they edited it into a forty-minute version. Subsequently the negative was either mislaid or destroyed. Thus the extant copies of *Ossessione* have been made from a duplicate negative, which according to Visconti's own statement is incomplete. The original version that had its premiere in May 1943 is reputed to have been 140 minutes long, whereas 135 minutes appears to be the maximum length of the copies.[39]

Melodramatic realism

The plot of Cain's novel is much more complicated than that of Visconti's film. The main dramatic irony – a man is acquitted of an actual murder, then finds himself charged with murdering a mere accident victim – and the arbitrariness of jurisdiction have been left out or kept in the background. The events have been transferred to the Po Valley, the characters have been thoroughly Italianized,[40] and certain important details have been added. With all these changes, the crucial themes became aligned with Visconti's pervasive concerns.

The most obvious change is in the character of the protagonist. In the book, Frank is quite active and shrewd, but at times the complexity of the situations in which he finds himself overwhelms him. The story is laconically narrated by Frank himself. In the film, Gino, no longer in the position of the narrator, drifts with the tide of events and constantly submits to the will of others, unable to think of alternatives for himself. Although Cain's protagonist cannot be called evil, he does not appear to be heavily endowed with moral scruples. Driven by his passion for Cora, a young woman married to an older man who owns a "sandwich joint," he plots to kill the husband. His plan fails and he leaves. But after trying in vain to forget her, he returns, hatches yet another plan, and this time succeeds in carrying it out. All this he does apparently without any qualms. In Visconti's story, Gino would probably not have killed the husband had he not been goaded by the woman, Giovanna. And toward the end of the story, whereas Frank goes to Mexico with another woman to have fun, Gino goes to a prostitute for consolation and to confess what he has done. Despite sudden and at times violent bursts of anger, he is a gentle man deeply tormented by the situation he has let himself be driven into.

As the film begins, a lorry arrives at an out-of-the-way trattoria that also functions as a petrol station. The driver discovers a vagrant sleeping in the back and wakes him up. The vagrant wanders off to find some food while Bragana, the owner of the petrol station, starts filling the tank of the lorry. The vagrant's attention is suddenly caught by the voice of Bragana's young wife, Giovanna, singing in the kitchen. He goes to the kitchen door, and we see his back and beyond it, her legs. There is a cut to the first shot of her face as she notices him and interrupts her song. A countershot brings us the first glimpse of the vagrant Gino's face. The moment is further emphasized by a slight track-in to a close-up and a momentary lack of ambient sound. The erotic tension between them is immediate; from their first gaze, they communicate in the language of their bodies. They will soon find in each other a chance to realize some of their innermost hopes and desires, as well as an incarnation of their worst fears.

For Gino, it is a chance to assuage the loneliness that comes with his vagabondish freedom. He yearns for human contact but is unable to tie

himself down and form stable relationships. For Giovanna, the encounter
suggests a way out of her stagnating life. As she herself remarks, earlier
on she had "to let men offer her supper," implying some degree of prostitution. Bragana rescued her from that by marrying her, and she has no
intention of ever returning to it, however much she might be repulsed by
her obese and somewhat loud husband. Passion apart, Giovanna's and
Gino's situations and needs are thus mutually incompatible and this fact
guides their relationship to the very end. If they want to stick together,
they have but two courses of action open to them: either Giovanna must
leave with Gino or they must get rid of Bragana and stay at the trattoria.
This is the basic conflict in the film: between insecure freedom and secure
confinement. In Youssef Ishaghpour's words, the painful tension between
aspiration and immanence appears as the basic opposition of Visconti's
oeuvre right from the beginning.

Money and economic relationships are immediately posited as a crucial
factor controlling human and sexual relationships. After having something to eat, Gino leaves the trattoria, but Giovanna hides the coins he
has put on the table and tells her husband that he left without paying.
Bragana runs after Gino and insists that he pay for the food by doing
some work around the place. Gino recognizes this as Giovanna's love call
and agrees to return and repair Bragana's car. Gino tricks Bragana into
going into town to buy a spare part for the car, and while he is gone
Giovanna and Gino make love. Gino stays on for a while working for
Bragana, and soon he and Giovanna are so deeply involved with each
other that they are forced to choose between their two alternatives. They
first decide to leave, picking a day when Bragana happens to be away.
But exhausted by the walk in the sun, Giovanna quickly realizes that she
is not prepared to pay the necessary price for this kind of freedom. Her
choice is made easy by Gino, who takes no notice of the difficulty she is
having in keeping up with his stride. She returns to the dull economic
security of life with her husband. But after they part company, Gino is
unable to forget her.

Before turning to the other way out of his predicament, yet another
possible course of action appears to open up to Gino. An itinerant vendor
who calls himself Spagnuolo (Spaniard) pays Gino's train fare and they
share a room in Ancona. Spagnuolo's act might at first be interpreted as
an act of solidarity, but in a scene in their bedroom the way he looks at
Gino together with some of his remarks betray a homosexual interest.[41]
Gino does not appear to respond to Spagnuolo's implied offer of an alternative to the destructive attraction he feels toward Giovanna. Gino is

aware of the danger Giovanna poses for him, but when they happen to meet again he is unable to curb his passion. Gino spots Giovanna and Bragana at a market square where Spagnuolo is putting on a show to sell his junk to people. Gino is carrying large sandwich boards advertising a singing contest. Bragana is there to enter the contest.

The film now reaches its turning point. On the way back to the trattoria, Giovanna and Gino kill Bragana and stage it as a car accident. All that the audience sees, however, is their nocturnal drive through the Po Valley – with Bragana extremely drunk after celebrating his victory in the contest. This is immediately followed by a police investigation at the scene of the crime. Gino and Giovanna are not apprehended, but they remain under suspicion and are closely watched. All too soon, their aspirations turn out to be illusory. Gino had thought they would be able to sell the trattoria and move somewhere else, but he was obviously deceiving himself. As Giovanna points out, they will either have to meet people face to face or stay on the run for the rest of their lives.

And so Giovanna's life continues to be one of humdrum toil while Gino starts behaving like a caged animal. His anxiety reaches a high pitch during a party Giovanna has arranged to boost sales at the trattoria. Just then, Spagnuolo happens to pass by, and he and Gino enter into an increasingly heated discussion. It ends with Gino punching Spagnuolo – who appears to be criticizing him as much for the suspected crime as for betraying their male comradeship by shacking up with a woman. Gino tells him a bold-faced lie – "I am fed up with traveling life" – which is too blatant to pass even for self-deception.[42] Soon after this Spagnuolo is seen arriving at an office at the police station, perhaps to betray his friend. His silhouette in the window of the door echoes that of Giovanna and Gino when they left the same room.

Yet another incident intervenes before the trap closes on them. During a visit to Ferrara, Gino makes an attempt to break off from Giovanna only to discover that he is tied to her more closely than ever before. While waiting for Giovanna in a park, he encounters Anita, a pretty young woman who turns out to be a prostitute. A little later Giovanna arrives and tells him she has just collected the insurance money.[43] Gino is infuriated to think they are profiting from their crime. He heads off in a rage to Anita's lodgings. Money never meant much to him anyway, but now he is obviously eager to dissolve his devastating relationship with Giovanna. Anita, however, cannot offer a genuine alternative for Gino, even in the way Spagnuolo could. Giovanna sees them on the street as they go out to do some shopping and in a fit of jealousy threatens to turn him in.

Gino silences her by hitting her and returns to Anita. When, shortly afterward, he realizes he is being shadowed by a plainclothes policeman, he jumps to the erroneous conclusion that Giovanna really has betrayed him. He succeeds in escaping and heads back to the trattoria.

The last episode of the film depicts a desperate attempt to conflate mutually incompatible needs and wishes, dreams and reality. Giovanna succeeds in convincing Gino that she did not betray him and then tells him that she is pregnant. For a moment a new positive dimension appears to open up in their relationship. There is an almost dreamlike sequence on a desolate beach that calls to mind another, more tranquil world. But there is no escape from the threat of punishment. They leave the trattoria in Bragana's car and with tragic irony end up having an accident similar to the one they staged earlier on. Giovanna dies; the police arrive and arrest Gino.

The themes of the film do not develop as they would in a typical crime story. The police sequences, in particular, appear to be inserts and make the otherwise steadily unfolding narrative hobble slightly. After the inquest report has been signed, the police investigations continue in two short sequences. In the first, Spagnuolo is seen arriving at the police station apparently to betray Gino. Or perhaps he has just been invited to answer some questions – there is very little of an incriminating nature that he could possibly tell the police. The episode does not fit comfortably with the otherwise linear narration, and it has to be thought of as the film's only flashforward. But the idea of betrayal is extremely important thematically. Because Spagnuolo's appearance at the police station follows soon after his and Gino's fight, the connection between the rejection of friendship – and possibly homosexual love – and the threat of punishment is strongly underlined. The police appear as an impersonal force whose task is to punish not only a judicial but also an existential crime: the inability to control destructive drives or to remain loyal to one's friends and perhaps even to some of one's innermost desires, however much it might be a question of trying to satisfy mutually incompatible needs.

As a depiction of an existential situation, Giovanna's and Gino's scene at the desolate river bench foreshadows Antonioni's films of the early sixties.[44] There is no apparent motivation for them to be there.[45] But whereas the desolate landscapes in Antonioni's films reflect the alienation of his protagonists, in *Ossessione* the desolation offers Giovanna and Gino a moment away from society and its pressures and thus also a possibility for displaying genuine tenderness. The scene functions to balance both

the literal and figurative darkness that has become increasingly oppressive throughout the film. Particularly in the first half of the film shabby
interiors have gradually become a metaphor for Giovanna's suffocating
situation, whereas open air has been the realm of Gino's freedom. Bragana's murder takes place in the open air, and it is as if this act would
force Gino to confine himself inside the trattoria. When Gino does come
out during the party scene, he ends up giving Spagnuolo a punch, which
in turn serves to spring the trap on him.

The Ferrara sequence in turn represents an unsuccessful attempt to
get away from all this. Gino encounters Anita outside in the beautiful
sunshine, but he soon finds himself escaping to her apartment. In contrast
to the trattoria, it is quite cozy, but because the police are already on his
heels he cannot stay there for very long. After this the trattoria appears
even gloomier than before, for it can no longer be a safe haven for the
guilty couple. Finally, the scene on the riverbank serves as a reminder of
how illusory calm and tranquility have become to them.

Van Watson has pointed out that, as opposed to standard cinematic
practice, in which – as analyzed by Laura Mulvey in her famous article
"Visual Pleasure and Narrative Cinema" – the female is subjected to the
male gaze, in *Ossessione* Gino is subjected first to Giovanna's feminine
and then to Spagnuolo's homosexual gaze. Gino walks through most of
the first half of the film in a sleeveless vest, and his broad shoulders often
feature conspicuously, particularly when he is being watched by Giovanna or Spagnuolo.[46] All this emphasizes his passivity and Giovanna's
active role. In contrast to the swanlike acquiescent Anita, Giovanna is
prepared to trespass both law and morality in order to improve her lot.
On the other hand, Lino Micciché sees in her an image of the "feminine
condition" in Fascist Italy. Her marriage to Bragana stands for family
relations that have degenerated into institutionalized prostitution
propped up by a capitalist ethos, embodied in the bloated body of Bragana.[47]

Anita, just like Giovanna before her marriage, makes a living through
prostitution. Displaying such characters on the screen infuriated those in
power not only in Fascist but also in postwar Christian Democratic Italy.
There are a wealth of other details in *Ossessione* that the contemporary
Italian audience might well have interpreted as references to the situation
in their country. Spagnuolo was so named because he had worked in
Spain – this might well have been understood as an allusion to the Spanish
civil war. Gino in turn tells Giovanna that he once worked in Trieste. This
could be a reference to a dispute over the ownership of the docks in Trieste

and to their being bombed after Italy had declared war on Great Britain.[48] In the Ferrara scene, a troop of boys marching through the park resembles a Fascist youth squadron, and on the street scene in front of Anita's home invalids and alcoholics can be seen as the camera follows them briefly.

Certain details in *Ossessione* have subtle symbolic and often ironic functions. The Ferrara scene opens with the camera showing a swan-shaped ice cream cart just before Gino encounters Anita, and it can be easily associated with her. As they talk and flirt with each other, a dragon-shaped cart appears. Later it crosses Giovanna's path as she comes to the park and its black color matches her mourning dress. Thus the two carts form a clear, slightly amusing parallel to Gino's view of the two women. Some details foreshadow dramatic moments, such as the razor seen when Bragana alludes to the life insurance he has taken out. More serious and melodramatic is the scene in which Giovanna and Gino, after having made love for the first time, converse next to the mirror of the wardrobe. As they move back to the bed in a passionate embrace, the wardrobe door swings open, revealing Bragana's suits and other clothes. Sometimes these devices are also infused with irony. Just before the party at the trattoria, Gino says: "Watching the house of someone who has died is not a proper job." Just then a tall, stout woman dressed in black appears at the door. Half in shadow with a large scythe in her hand, she seems to be a comic image of the grim reaper.

Yet more important than such realistic or symbolic details, is Visconti's ability to create an organic relationship between the characters and their environment. De Santis, who together with Antonio Pietrangeli worked as the assistant director, recalled in later years:

I inherited the longed-for duty of caring for the film's backgrounds – i.e. of all that which occurred behind or on the periphery of the foreground action: life, to put it briefly – life which continued flowing on its own, with its daily cadences in spite of the tragic feelings expressed by the actors. . . . The major achievement of one who presided over this task consisted of forcing the background to play a role of counterpoint so as to obtain a kind of visual and aural conflict yielding a disagreeable effect but one, nevertheless, which gave the spectator a sense of life as lived and therefore a sense of the complex realism enacted in front of the camera.[49]

The contrast with contemporary Italian cinema, which had neither much background activity nor any social or historical depth, was considerable. *Ossessione* may be compared with two other major Italian films made at the end of the Fascist period: Blasetti's *Quattro passi fra le nuvole* (Four

steps in heaven, 1942) and De Sica's *I bambini ci guardano* (The children
are looking at us, 1943). In one way or another, all three treat the dissolution of the "sacred institution" of the family. But whereas the other
two films look backward aesthetically and hang on to conventional morality, Visconti's films present an open challenge on all levels. To a considerable extent, thanks to the thoroughly assimilated influence of Renoir
and other contemporary French directors, Visconti was able to deviate
from certain standard patterns of representation that characterized Italian cinema of the time. In Micchiché's words: "As regards sex the ethereal
spiritual sublimation became a dense physiological carnality; as regards
the family the cell of society became an inhuman prison; as regards the
people, the beautified unity changed into the sour solitude of an aggregate
of individuals; as regards the world of peasants the site of unity became
a site of fragmentation; as regards the landscape the idyllic backdrop
became a turbid scenery." It was a film that would destroy "all the existing stereotypes."[50]

The charting of a certain human situation had become at least as important as the telling of a story, action had become less determined by
plot requirements than, say, in classical Hollywood cinema or its Italian
equivalent of the Fascist era. On the level of the shots, in Gilles Deleuze's
words, "Objects and settings [*milieux*] take on an autonomous, material
reality which gives them an importance in themselves."[51] After Giovanna
and Gino make love, for example, she tells how she ended up as Bragana's
wife. Gino's attention, however, is focused on a sea shell, which he presses
against his ear. The gesture reveals his lack of interest in Giovanna's story,
which motivates his actions in what follows. Nevertheless the gesture appears random and free from any direct plot function.

Such lingering on scenes as if to explore how the characters behave in
a given situation – spatiotemporal, historical, social, psychological, and
existential – became one of the ideals of neorealism and started a line of
development that led to the films of Rossellini in the 1950s, those of
Antonioni in the early 1960s, and through them to the New Wave in
France. In a slightly different way, it also became one of the most crucial
elements of Visconti's own style. In *Ossessione* the situation the protagonists find themselves in imposes certain severely limiting conditions on
them. Their passion is pitted against their intellectual limitations and
inability to conceive any viable alternatives for themselves. This severe
realism keeps the melodramatic gestures under strict control without,
however, even so much as subduing it. On the contrary, the realistic
framework ensures that the melodrama appears meaningful and relevant,

as a way of evoking reality in its flesh and blood with maximum emotional and existential intensity. Such *melodramatic realism* in ever differing patterns is one of the distinguishing features of Visconti's art.

The camera work in *Ossessione* is fairly restrained, maintaining just a slight sense of detachment and observation rather than thorough involvement with the characters, as in conventional film melodrama. At times, however, the camera plays a crucial role in conveying feeling and passion. The best example is Gino's entrance to the kitchen described earlier. Immediately afterward the erotic tension between Gino and Giovanna remains strong, as they almost playfully compete for control over the situation and exchange looks every time Bragana turns away. As the positioning of the camera is often quite surprising – for example, boldly flaunting the 180-degree rule – it is at times difficult to follow the movements of the characters in the small kitchen. Later on, after Gino decides to stay in the trattoria, the lovers embrace as Bragana goes out to kill a howling cat. There is a dramatic cut that throws the camera to their opposite side, suddenly reversing their left and right positions.

Because there are only a few shots defining the different rooms of the trattoria as a whole, it is difficult to get a clear picture of the layout of the building. An altogether new view opens up even at the end of the film as a little girl is unexpectedly seen in a corridor that presumably leads to the bedrooms above the trattoria.[52] All this enhances the atmosphere of claustrophobic disorientation. It reaches its peak in the scene in which Giovanna and Gino return to the trattoria after the investigation: the movements of the camera surround them and make Gino's anxious wandering around appear like the pacing of an animal in its cage.

There is a full range of camera work from conventional shot/counter-shot sequences to some quite elaborate shots. Particularly memorable are certain exceptionally long and mobile shots in which space and situation are displayed extremely well. The first of these introduces the cafe in which the singing competition is held and shows the arrival of Bragana, Giovanna, and Gino, then shows them sitting down and Bragana entering the contest. Even more masterful is the way the investigation at the site of the accident is captured in a single shot. The length of the shot reflects the pressures that the protagonists experience. Also the street scenes in Ferrara are shown in fairly lengthy shots, and through them the social reality of the town becomes apparent.

Giuseppe Rosati's background music is fairly typical of its time, emphasizing dramatic moments, at times almost to the point of being inadvertently amusing. Diegetic music has a more crucial role in characterization. Right at the beginning, as the truck stops in front of the trattoria, the aria "Di provenza il mar, il suol" from Verdi's *La Traviata* is heard. The singer turns out to be Bragana. As Gino steps inside, his attention is first caught by Giovanna's song, "Fiorin fiorello, l'amore è bello vicino a te" (Flower, little flower, love is beautiful near you), and this is the song she uses to call Gino to her after Bragana has gone off to buy the spare part. Later on, Gino expresses his sense of freedom by playing jolly tunes on his mouth organ. The music of each of the characters reflects their initial situation and aspirations. The operatic numbers during the singing competition, particularly Gilda's and Duke's duet, "É il sol dell'anima" from Verdi's *Rigoletto*, sung by a couple grotesquely inconsistent with the characters they are portraying, form an ironic parallel with the protagonists of the film. After the competition there is very little diegetic music, except when the orchestra plays at the party at the trattoria. The absence of song emphasizes the sense of isolation and loss of hope.

BACKGROUND, THEORY, AND PRACTICE OF NEOREALISM

Birth of a concept

Initially, immediately after the war, one of the major distinguishing features of neorealism was its anti-fascism. The current political situation and the memories of the resistance fighters provided a stock of compelling stories that were of great relevance to the audience and that could be shot on location, which was important since most studio facilities had been destroyed in the war. An important connection was felt to exist between this new aesthetic movement and the multiparty government that had taken over after the fall of Fascism. At this time most Italians agreed that it was essential to create a new anti-fascist Italy. But the country was soon divided in the debate about how it was to be cleansed of fascism. Some saw the entire Fascist era as a mere aberration that should simply be forgotten; others demanded that the entire period be thoroughly analyzed and that the government and society be purged of the people and institutions that had made it possible for the Fascists to gain power and to maintain it for twenty-two years.

After all the pompous nationalistic rhetoric, many artists sought to create a style that would make possible the rebirth of a genuine art of the people and that would plumb the depths of the nation's tormented soul.

It was a call for a new kind of realism that the cinema appeared particularly suited to portray. According to Alberto Lattuada:

After the last war, especially in Italy, it was this very need for *reality* which forced us out of the studios. It is true that our studios were partly destroyed or occupied by refugees, but it is equally true that the decision to shoot everything "on location" was above all dictated by the desire to express life in its most convincing manner and with the harshness of documentaries. The very spirit of walls corroded by time and full of the tired signs of history, took on an aesthetic consistency. The actor's costumes were those of the man of the street. Actresses became women again, for a moment. It was poor but strong cinema, with many things to say in a hurry and in a loud voice, without hypocrisy, in a brief vacation from censorship; and it was an unprejudiced cinema, personal and not industrial, a cinema full of real faith in the language of film, as a means of education and social progress.[53]

The period after the war was felt to be a "springtime": it was as if new buds were emerging in all fields of cultural life after a dreary winter. This attitude led people to forget or ignore the fact that many fine films had been made during the Fascist regime and that in many ways these films foreshadowed neorealism and provided it with models. The attitude toward *Ossessione* provides an example. Because it had been made within the Fascist production system, it did not fit the concept of neorealism as a total renewal of Italian cinema. In their anti-fascist fervor, the most ardent of the propagandists of neorealism explained that Fascism should have been condemned more clearly in *Ossessione* for it to deserve the accolade of neorealism.[54]

The anti-fascist ethos did not survive the war as a politically unifying factor, and this had an immediate effect on the cinema. The neorealist movement was soon at loggerheads with the Christian Democratic party, which was to govern Italy on its own for the next few decades. Neorealist films were condemned as attempts to smother the international reputation of the nation, and through indirect measures the film industry was in effect placed largely under state control. After the so-called Andreotti Law was passed in December 1949, an official body called Direzione Generale was established through which all government loans and subsidies were issued to films considered "suitable." The government could also ban public screenings of films and their exportation on the grounds that they were not "in the best interest of Italy." Prime Minister Mario Selba made the attitude of the government toward the film industry perfectly clear: "Film is merchandise. If the government has the right to control the export of vegetables and fruits to make sure that they are not rotten, it also has the right, and the duty, to prevent the circulation of films infected with the spirit of neo-realism."[55]

Leftist critics in particular saw all this as a post-Fascist reaction against all kinds of social criticism. After all, no actual policies were proposed in the neorealist films. The measures exerted by the Christian Democrats also appear exaggerated, considering the small number of these films and the meager success that most of them were able to achieve. Of the 822 films made in Italy in the years 1945–53, only 90 can be considered neorealist. Roberto Rossellini's *Rome, Open City* (Roma, citta aperta) was the most popular film in Italy during 1945–6, his *Paisà* was the ninth in 1946–7, and Vittorio De Sica's *The Bicycle Thief* (Ladri di biciclette) the eleventh in 1948–9. But most neorealist films failed to make a profit and were often torn apart by the critics.[56] Success came mainly abroad, and the most eloquent proponent of the movement was France's André Bazin. Neorealism had nothing to do with mainstream Italian cinema. Most audiences went to see melodramas, adventures, and comedies, as they had done before and everywhere else in the world. The significance of neorealism sprang largely from the aesthetic and ethical ideal it provided, as well as the theoretical debate that it prompted. These made it a crucial part of film history.

Theory and ideals

Few movements or trends in the history of cinema have given rise to as much theorizing and explanation as neorealism has. Many lists have been compiled of the basic criteria of neorealism, but there is no consensus as to which of these would define its essence. Hardly any films thought to be neorealistic meet all the criteria. Together, these criteria simply characterize in a general fashion the direction certain Italian directors took after the war.[57]

The founder of *Biancio e nero* magazine and its long-time editor, Luigi Chiarini, has defined four characteristics of the movement:

(1) men derived from the audiences' own reality replaced the pre-conceived characters in conventional narratives of the past; (2) the chronicle (if we can call it that), events and facts culled from the daily existence of men, replaced the pre-fabricated adventures of novels and comedies; (3) the throbbing photographic document replaced pictorial and figurative virtuosity; (4) the cities and countryside, with people effectively living there, replaced the *papier-maché* scenery of the past.[58]

Chiarini also thought that neorealism was born out of an inner need to express thoughts and sensations that were not tied to conceptual systems but that arose from reality itself. It depicted the social reality of man as well as his relationship with "nature, his immediate environment, and society."[59] The veracity of representation was to be further enhanced by the use of real people from the streets to play roles that were supposedly close to their own lives. This never became common practice, however. De Sica used nonactors for the leading roles of *The Bicycle Thief* and *Umberto D* (1952), but Visconti's *La terra trema* (1948) was the only film in which the entire cast consisted of "ordinary people." Even in these cases the directors succeeded in pulling out great performances from their actors within a strong narrative structure.

Most filmmakers and theorists saw neorealism essentially as a moral stand rather than an aesthetic position. According to theoretician and screenwriter Cesare Zavattini, the goal of neorealism was to promote the love and understanding of others as they actually are. This meant mainly poor people, as "misery . . . is one of the most vivid realities of our time." This was to be achieved in large part by eliminating plot, at least in the conventional sense. Zavattini did not mean that there should be no narrative structure at all, but rather that a film should concentrate on situations taken directly from the lives of ordinary people.[60] The crucial point was that ordinary people should recognize themselves in a film instead of identifying with the characters of escapist fantasy. According to Chiarini, the audiences of the first neorealist films saw on the screen their own tragedy: "No longer following a mere story, but history, the audience saw life reflected on the screen."[61]

These objectives were rooted in the idea that the medium of film enjoys a privileged relationship to reality. The major lines of film theory until about the early 1960s can be roughly divided into realist and formative traditions. The former emphasizes the way that the cinematic apparatus can be used to register and convey an image of the phenomenal world photo-mechanically; the latter focuses on film as an artifact, a construction of images and sounds. Controversy raged as to which is the true vocation of cinema until a more balanced view emerged in the work of scholars such as Jean Mitry, who in his monumental study *Esthétique et psychologie du cinéma* (1963–5) fused the extremes. Modern film theory emerged as approaches such as structuralism, semiotics, and certain branches of the social sciences and psychology led scholars to pose new questions often far removed from the earlier essentialist theories. But before all this, neorealism was seen by many as the strongest manifestation

and vindication of cinematic realism. To some of the more extreme of its
proponents, cinematic apparatus provided a way of approaching reality
to the point of dissolving all the constraints of the medium. Felix A. Morlion, for example, claimed:

Neo-realism's thesis is that the screen is a magic window which opens out on to
the "real"; that cinematic art is the art of recreating, through the exercise of free
choice upon the material world, the most intense vision possible of the invisible
reality inherent in the movements of the mind. The basis of every good work of
art is not what people *think* about reality, but what reality actually is. Through
a shared vision of existence, both artists and audiences forget with pleasure those
artistic inventions which merely served as means for the creation of that new-
born thing.. . . .The neo-realist school has taken a great step forward. It has for-
sworn vanity to reach the true aim of cinema: to express reality.[62]

A vestige of positivism can be seen in this rather naive idea that reality
can be captured as it "actually is." A phenomenological approach made
the idea of cinematic realism far more resonant. French film critic André
Bazin, in particular, pitted what he thought was the true, "phenomenological" realism of cinema against "the traditional dramatic systems and
also [against] the various other known kinds of realism in literature and
film with which we are familiar." In his opinion, Italian neorealism differed from naturalism and verism in that it rejected "analysis, whether
political, moral, psychological, logical, or social, of the characters and
their actions." His goal was to look "on reality as a whole, not incomprehensible, certainly, but inseparably one."[63] Certain cinematic means
were more conducive to this visual exploration than others. Bazin com-
mended the deep focus and long shots, which, in the films of someone
like William Wyler, helped to achieve "a cinematographic universe, not
only rigorously consistent with reality, but also as little modified as possible by the optics of the camera."[64] Such means allowed reality to
"shine" through the cinematic apparatus.

Also Bazin would like to have done away with the plot, as it is always
likely to divert the filmmaker from reality. He pointed out that "reduced
to the plot, they [neorealist films] are often just moralizing melodramas,
but on the screen everybody in the film is overwhelmingly real." He, too,
thought that the chief merit of these films was their deep humanism.[65]
He emphasized that the aims of all the leading neorealists were basically
the same. They all wanted to give a unified picture of humans that would
not separate them from the geographic, historical, and social situation to
which they belong. This could be achieved when the action is no longer

just a skeleton but an integral part of what is being depicted in the film, when it emerges from the very pattern of life.[66] Similarly, though many other theorists felt uncomfortable with plot structures, they were basically arguing against the kind of narration which, in neoformalist terms, proceeds more on the basis of compositional and transtextual motivation rather than realistic motivation.[67] What they wanted was action generated by the psychology of the characters, which would be shaped by the relationship between individuals and their social situation and environment. This view approached what Visconti himself had proposed in his essay "*Anthropomorphic cinema.*"

In effect, the neorealist filmmakers were after what Hungarian literary scholar Georg Lukács called typical as opposed to average characters, that is, characters who in their rich individuality would exemplify the general. Yet this kind of realism can by no means do away with clear narrative structures. On the contrary, the notion of the realism of the cinematic image has to be complemented by Aristotelian poetics, according to which the plot universalizes the characters, not the other way around. From this point of view, the fact that neorealist films – as well as all mainstream films and most so-called art films – rely on various plot structures is not a flaw with respect to their realism. On the contrary, it could be argued that narration is *the* way of articulating the concerns of human beings as temporal creatures.

To understand how fiction relates to reality it is necessary to reexamine Aristotle's conception of mimesis. The traditional translation of this word as "imitation" is misleading, says literary scholar Paul Ricoeur, as it tends to suggest naturalism in the sense of copying reality. But mimesis is constituted by *mythos*, the the plot, the crucial element of which is *configuration*. The configurational dimension opposes the episodic dimension and thus transforms "the succession of events into a meaningful whole."[68] Because it involves composition and construction, mimesis does not consist simply of duplicating reality. Rather it is a way of modeling the basis, possibilities, motivations, and consequences of human action: "a tension is revealed at the very heart of mimesis, between the submission to reality – to human action – and the creative action which is poetry as such. . . . The creative dimension is inseparable from this referential movement."[69]

In the case of film, this implies the need for a conceptual separation between the indexical relationship the cinematic image has with the profilmic event and the organization of the cinematic discourse in terms of mimetic configuration, that is, plot. The indexicality and iconic quality[70] of the photographic image in cinema derives its meaning from its context, since it is incorporated into a discourse, usually a narrative. This in turn has its place in the *realm of narratives*, that is, all the accounts both factual and fictional through which the human world is rendered for a given community in its historical and social conditionness. In this sphere the claim of realism of a given film narrative is negotiated in respect of and possibly in contradiction to the prevailing codes of realism in that community.[71]

Ricoeur's conception of mimesis connects with the notion of classical realism in fiction, the ideal of which is to capture the essence of reality through emplotment guided by the laws of necessity and probability. Reality is understood as a dynamic process that human action might help to move in a better or a worse direction. Naturalism, on the other hand, which arose in France in the nineteenth century in the wake of positivism, seeks to present reality objectively without taking any kind of moral stand. The ideal there is to relate *how* rather than *why* things happen as they do. In practice however, the French naturalists no more than the Italian verists in their best works did not adhere rigorously to the principle of detachment. Similarly, when the group that gathered round *Cinema* magazine in the 1940s turned to the verists for inspiration in their pursuit of a new kind of Italian, anti-fascist, and humanist film, they were looking for a socially committed narrative tradition rather than a positivist mode of objective observation. As Giuseppe De Santis and Mario Alicata noted:

At any rate, it is necessary to make clear that the cinema finds its best direction in the realist tradition because of its strict narrative nature; as a matter of fact, realism is the true and eternal measure of every narrative significance – realism intended not as the passive homage to an objective, static truth, but as the imaginative and creative power to fashion a story composed of real characters and events. It remains evident that when the cinema began to create characters, and to examine the change in men's souls in relationship to their concrete environment, it was necessarily influenced by Nineteenth Century European realism.[72]

The writers end up summoning Verga, who "miraculously stark and real, . . . could give inspiration to the imagination of our cinema which looks for things in the space-time of reality to redeem itself from the easy suggestions of a moribund bourgeois state."

Visconti realized this dream of translating Verga to the screen in his second feature film, *La terra trema*. He never embraced the most far-reaching ideals of Italian neorealism, even if his *Ossessione* can be considered an important precursor of that movement, as can his *La terra trema* as its peak. He certainly had no desire to do away with the plot, even if in his later films the dramatic tempo could slow down considerably. In the last instance, Visconti's realism is based not only on his celebrated meticulous (re)constructions of settings but also on using the plot as a means of modeling human behavior in given circumstances. *La Terra trema* is a prime example of how to articulate social criticism by means of tragic *mythos*.

LA TERRA TREMA

Realism after the war

In 1943 Italy became a battleground. Mussolini was deposed in June and a government headed by Marshal Pietro Badoglio took over. After the Allies made a successful landing in Sicily in July and August, Badoglio sought to sign an armistice with them. But by then the Germans had occupied the country and were in control everywhere except in areas the Allies had not yet reached. At the same time, an anti-fascist partisan movement that transcended all party boundaries had sprung up and was growing rapidly.

Among those assisting the partisans was Visconti, who offered them shelter in his apartment in Rome. But he was disappointed when they would not accept him for active duty and give him a chance to be a hero in battle. The main reason was probably that he was well known and therefore thought to be of more use as a contact person. It is also likely that his aristocratic background and known homosexual tendencies had built up some prejudice against him. In March 1944 he was imprisoned as part of a retaliation for the explosion of a partisan bomb that killed thirty-two and wounded many members of a German detachment. He was beaten and locked in a filthy lavatory without food for twelve days in order to make him talk, but he remained silent. He was released shortly before the Allies arrived in Rome. Later on he would exaggerate his experiences in the resistance movement, but at least he had been more active than most Italian intellectuals.

After Italy was liberated, Visconti helped film one of the few Italian documentaries made immediately after the war, *Giorni di gloria* (The days of glory, 1945). The project was headed by Mario Serandrei and supported by the Allies' Psychological Warfare Branch. It covered the German occupation of Rome, the activities of the resistance movement, the liberation of Italy, and the events that followed. Visconti shot many

events on the streets of Rome, among them the lynching of Donato Carretta, the governor of the Regina Coeli prison in Rome. From Visconti's
point of view, the most interesting episode was the trial and execution of
Pietro Koch, the governor of the prison where he had been held. The
strong feelings that emerged after the fall of Fascism, above all the hysterical thirst for revenge, were captured relentlessly in the lynching and
the trial episodes of *Giorni di gloria*. In contrast, the executions appear
plain and undramatic.

Like many other creative people at the time, Visconti felt the need to
express his feelings about the war in fiction. Already in June and July of
1944 he and the *Cinema* magazine group had begun planning a film titled
Pensione Oltremare. It was to be based partly on his own prison experience and was to be about a young man summarily imprisoned and tortured by the Fascists. Eventually his political consciousness begins to
grow, but in the end he is executed by the Germans. Later Visconti drafted
two scripts with Michelangelo Antonioni. One of them was about an all-
female orchestra assigned to entertain soldiers at the front. The other was
titled *Il processo di Maria Tarnowska* (The trial of Maria Tarnowska). It
was the story of a Venetian beauty who persuades two of her lovers to
kill her fiancé. She is subsequently imprisoned, but because she captivates
all men, her guards have to be changed daily. The producer, Alfredo
Guarini, insisted on having his wife, Isa Miranda, in the leading role, but,
at least according to Antonioni, Visconti soon got fed up with her child-
ishness and mannerisms and withdrew from the project. Nevertheless, the
story was close to Visconti's heart, and apparently the idea of filming it,
with Romy Schneider as the *femme fatale*, haunted him even in the
1960s.[73]

Although Visconti had begun writing and planning novels and plays,
he soon decided to channel his creative energies into theatrical productions. *Les parents terribles* had its premiere at Rome's Eliseo theater on
January 30, 1945, and it established Visconti's reputation as an artist.
Few had seen *Ossessione*, and up to this point he had been dismissed as
an eccentric aristocrat who entertained himself by making films. Now he
proved that he was a professional. The play was an enormous success,
made all the greater by occasional protests from the audience. The production was a landmark in the history of stage productions in Italy. The
unwavering realism in particular kept the audience nailed to their seats.[74]
His next production, Hemingway's *The Fifth Column*, caused a political
scandal. The reason was partly that the play treated the Spanish civil war
from the point of view of Italy's enemy at that time and partly that the

performance concluded with the *International*. The furor was one of the many indications that Italy had not yet been purged of fascism, and it was only a prelude to the problems Visconti was to encounter because of his marxist outlook.[75]

During the next few years Visconti directed in rapid succession a host of plays in various styles, but with uneven success. The productions were noted for their "tendency towards theatrical exaggeration, violent visual effect," and Visconti was observed to have developed "an almost obsessive devotion to exact truth of detail." But what at least one critic found to be most significant was "the director's ability to build up atmospheric tension by every means." At the same time, many of the productions drew a great deal of attention because of the explicit manner in which they treated various forms of sexuality. There was an aura of incest in Jean Cocteau's *Les parents terribles*, homosexuality in Jean-Paul Sartre's *Huis clos* (No exit) and Marcel Achard's *Adamo*, and brutality and amorality in Erskine Caldwell's *Tobacco Road*.[76]

The production of Pierre Beaumarchais's *Le mariage de Figaro* at Teatro Quirino in 1946 was the first spectacle Visconti staged. The production appeared to prefigure the fall of Italy's monarchy in the election held that same year. Visconti took a stand on this issue in an article published in the communist newspaper *Unità*. He claimed that monarchist institutions had been a vehicle of Fascism and gave his full support to parliamentary democracy, "as is clearly stated in the programme of the Communist party."

Actually, Visconti's relationship with the Communist party was always fraught with problems. The party found it hard enough to accept his background, but his homosexuality proved particularly difficult to tolerate, for the communists were even more puritan about sexual matters than the Church. The situation was made somewhat easier by the fact that Visconti never appeared to extol homosexuality. Rather, he showed how it could, because of social and psychological pressures, be almost a curse. In any case, the general secretary of the Italian Communist party, Palmiro Togliatti, courageously demonstrated his support for Visconti by visiting him after the premieres of his productions. Togliatti and Antonello Trombadori, who was responsible for the party's cultural policy, were among the few whose opinion mattered to Visconti. To him they probably represented moral responsibility, without which he might have succumbed to vacuous aestheticism and adoration of beauty.[77]

Visconti was now on the verge of discovering his own artistic line, which would draw from his background, his political views, and his aesthetic inclinations. There was also some interchange between his work for the stage and for the screen. The cinematic influence led him to aspire to a more natural form of vocal expression in the theater, to greater wealth of detail, more variety in the scenery, and challenging texts. Visconti also demanded unprecedented discipline and accuracy from the actors. All this could create an intensive theatrical experience, although at times he would emphasize the visual aspect at the cost of the dramatic effect. By concentrating on objects, he often enticed audiences to imagine they were seeing a close-up on film. Correspondingly, theatrical experiences enriched Visconti's work as a filmmaker by giving him a sense of dramatic form that would help him keep the elements of melodrama and spectacle in check.[78]

Working in the theater did not dampen Visconti's desire to make films. The opportunity came when the Communist party commissioned him to make a documentary about fishermen that was to be used as propaganda in the 1948 election campaign. Apparently the party expected the project to be completed quite rapidly, especially since it had only limited financial resources to allocate for this purpose. In any case Visconti had something more ambitious in mind. For sometime he had dreamed of adapting Verga's *I Malavoglia* (The house by the medlar tree) for the screen, and he had even acquired the rights for it in 1941. A little later he had made a trip to Sicily, to the fishing village of Aci Trezza, in which the events of the novel take place. The village had hardly changed since Verga's day. From this grew the idea of shooting the film on actual Sicilian locations and of using the people of Aci Trezza as actors.[79]

Visconti directed the fishermen by explaining to them the scenes that were to be filmed and then letting them improvise the dialogue. Franco Zeffirelli, the second assistant director, made notes and showed them to older natives, who then spoke them in their more ancient dialect, which even the urban Sicilian population of the time found it difficult to understand.[80] Extracts from *I Malavoglia* also went through this treatment.[81] Finally Zeffirelli coached the actors to speak these new lines. There has been some debate about how authentic the result really is. Decades later Agnese Giammona, who played the part of Lucia, recalled: "Zeffirelli, how he pretended to know Sicilian better than we do."[82] The opening titles state that "Italian is not the language of the poor in Sicily," but Pio Baldelli, among others, has pointed out that neither is the language heard in Visconti's film. In contrast to Verga, who in accordance with veristic ideals used a natural, spontaneous, and clear language, Visconti sought a language that would sound archaic and mix well with the other, equally controlled, sounds in his film.[83] The resulting dialogue has been described by Stefania Parigi as "more expressionistic than naturalistic." But in its own way, it is drawn, just like Verga's language, "both from literary high culture and the expressive universe of the people."[84]

In any case, mainland Italians found the dialogue incomprehensible. This was a shock in a country where most foreign films are dubbed and where sound is seldom recorded while shooting. Yet Visconti cherished the musicality of the sound track and, wanting to keep it intact, even contemplated using subtitles to guide the audience through the film. In the end the film was made more accessible by adding a voice-over commentary written by Antonio Pietrangeli.

The use of local people as actors caused many other problems during shooting. Visconti stated in an interview for *Cahiers du Cinéma*:

I worked hours and hours with my fishers while making *La terra trema* [The earth trembles] just to make them say a little bit of dialogue. I wanted to obtain from them the same result as from an actor. If they were talented – and that they truly were (above all they had one special trait: their lack of inhibition in front of the camera) – they reached this stage very quickly. The real task with actors is to get them to overcome their inhibitions and modesty. But these people weren't modest at all. I got what I wanted from them much quicker than I would have from actors.[85]

Elsewhere, however, Visconti talked about how ridiculous it was to talk about "actors taken from the street." In his mind the only reason for using nonprofessional actors in a film was that they could bring into play the truth about themselves as opposed to assuming roles. This was one of the governing ideas in the making of *La terra trema*.

Fate and alteration

In the planning stage, Visconti's second major film project went far beyond either the idea of a documentary about fishermen or the adaptation of *I Malavoglia*. He conceived an entire trilogy, the first part of which was to be a story about fishermen, the second about peasants, and the third about miners. The title *La terra trema* originally referred to this concept, and thus the final film carries the title *Episodo della mare* (The episode of the sea) in its opening credits. Once it became apparent that the last two episodes would not be shot, *La terra trema* became the name of the single episode that was filmed. And even this part went through many changes in the script stage. Among the original ideas was that a big motor trawler would exploit the fish resources and thereby constitute a threat to the whole trade. But for the sake of dramatic concentration and in order to make the social comment more pointed, the wholesalers were made the principal opponents of the protagonists.

The second episode would have told about miners who form a cooperative in order to excavate an unused sulphur mine. When the vein gives out, their enterprise seems close to failure, but they find a new vein and are able to continue. Even so, life remains hard. The third episode would have been the most optimistic. It was to show a group of peasants waiting for a man who is to instruct them in cultivating previously unused land. Upon his arrival he is shot by the Mafia, before he even has a chance to get started. However, he is replaced by a man who leads the peasants into battle against the semifeudal order. In a show of unity and power, they organize a cooperative. The Mafia tries to frighten them by firing machine-guns at them at an open air festival, but the funeral of the victims becomes a mighty display of solidarity. The peasants take over the land and meet official resistance, but workers from towns and cities arrive to support them. Victory is finally theirs when fishermen, farm laborers, and industrial workers join together to oppose the exploitation and repression.[86]

The first episode would thus have ended in defeat, the second in a stalemate between the exploiters and the exploited, and the third in a triumph of solidarity of the oppressed. The three stories would have proceeded in parallel in four phases. This would no doubt have enhanced by turns both the optimistic and the pessimistic aspects of each story. There would also have been a fourth story, which Lino Micciché has called "the episode of the city," running through the three main episodes. It would have helped emphasize that urban and nonurban workers needed to join together. But as the weight of the "episode of the sea" increased in its association with Verga, the remaining plans were gradually abandoned. This, of course, had a substantial effect on the implied political content of the film: instead of ending in miraculous victory, the film concludes on a note of resigned defeat. It is not even clear whether Visconti actually intended to realize the entire project. Francesco Rosi, who was an assistant director, together with Franco Zeffirelli, has stated that "Luchino always knew that we would make only one of the three episodes."[87]

La terra trema can be divided into a prologue, three main phases, and an epilogue. The prologue introduces the social structure and economic constraints surrounding the characters, central relationships, and the general atmosphere within the community as a whole and within the Valastro family. The first phase tells of the fishermen's attempt to improve their economic circumstances. Led by 'Ntoni, the eldest son of the Valastro family, they demand a better price from the wholesalers for the fish they catch. The attempt ends in a brawl during which 'Ntoni, in a powerful rhetorical gesture, throws a pair of scales into the sea. In Millicent Marcus's words: "When 'Ntoni seizes the scales and uses them as his call to arms, he counteracts the wholesalers' betrayal of justice and reinvents the original icnography [of the scales as the traditional symbol of distributive justice] by consecrating their symbolism to the fishermen's cause."[88]

'Ntoni and his colleagues are imprisoned, but the wholesalers, realizing that their profits have plummeted, argue that the fishermen are of more use at sea than in the prison and have them released. 'Ntoni, however, now tries to get the others to form a cooperative. When they refuse, the Valastros decide to try to do it on their own. They have to mortgage their entire ancestral home, but since the first catch is big, their prospects look good. The sequence ends in a festive mood with the villagers joining the Valastros in salting the fish.

In the second phase, the vulnerability of the Valastros' enterprise becomes apparent. Being heavily in debt, they have to go to sea even in storms and end up losing all their fishing equipment.[89] The wholesalers and even some of the fishermen mock them, now more convinced than ever of the immutability of the prevailing social order. During the third phase of the film, the social and psychological consequences of the Valastros' attempt to change things are gradually revealed. No one wants to give them work, and the wholesalers are able to set the price for their fish. They lose their home, and the family's unity breaks down: the grandfather dies (as so often happens in Visconti's films, the father died even before the story begins); 'Ntoni's brother Cola leaves to seek his fortune on the continent; their sister Lucia loses her reputation by yielding to the temptations of Marshal don Salvatore; 'Ntoni starts drinking. Only the elder sister Mara remains strong, although she loses all hope of ever getting married. Finally, in the epilogue, 'Ntoni swallows his pride and returns with his two younger brothers, Vanni and Alessio, to work for the wholesalers, who in their prosperity have bought new boats and need all the labor they can get.

The film draws on Verga's *I Malavoglia* in a somewhat complex way. In his 1941 essay *"Tradizione e invenzione,"* Visconti described the impact that Verga's works, particularly *I Malavoglia*, had had on him. He emphasized its aesthetic value and described its suggestive power as being supported by "an internal and musical rhythm":

Perhaps the key to a cinematographic rendering of *I Malavoglia* is to attempt to feel again and to catch the magic of the rhythm, of the vague yearning for the unknown, the realization that things are not right or that they could be better, which is the poetic substance of that play of destinies which cross . . . without ever encountering [one another].[90]

A couple of years later Visconti spelled out more precisely the kind of film he wanted to make, emphasizing the role of the actors and their innermost qualities, which he felt should be the source of the characters they portrayed, so that the "actor-person" and the "character-person" (l'uomo-attore e l'uomo-personaggio) would become one. The first step was to get rid of all the accumulated acting clichés and to uncover the instinctive expressive ability of the actor. Only this, a genuine human presence, could animate and poeticize a film.[91] But this was just one side of the coin. Visconti also wanted to show how nature and society control the way people live their lives. Visconti's wartime experiences and his involvement in the subsequent political struggle waged under the aegis of marxism gave form to his ideas about how "genuine human presence" is conditioned by a given environment and social situation. All these ideas played a crucial role in the way he used material from *I Malavoglia* to develop a story line and a genuinely cinematic aesthetic strategy for his *La terra trema.*

In Verga's novel the events are structured around the character of the grandfather. He believes that fate has determined the course of things, and that the social hierarchy in which he finds himself is a direct continuation of the natural order. This also appears to be the message of the (in Seymour Chatman's terms) implied author.[92] However, Verga's social analysis does not stop there. A single storm is a catastrophe for the Malavoglias as they lose the load of beans they have bought on credit, but this probably only adds to the fortunes of old Cippola, who can afford to keep his boat safely ashore. During the course of the novel, the members of the Malavoglia family experience a series of misfortunes, many of which are a direct result of their ever-increasing poverty. They lose not only their wealth but also their social status. Eventually 'Ntoni loses his faith in his prospects in life as well. He starts drinking and soon gains a bad reputation. In utter desperation, he thinks of joining a band of smugglers but is only too aware of the dangers involved:

And then there was that other outrage, which meant that to land foreign goods you had to pay a tax, and don Michele and his policemen had to stick their noses in! They could lay their hand on everything, and take what they wanted; but the others, if they risked their lives trying to land their goods, were regarded as thieves, and were hunted down worse than wolves with pistols and rifles.[93]

As for the other villagers, they cannot think of a better reason for duties and taxes than "to pay the soldiers, who cut such a dash with their uniforms, and we'd devour each other like wolves if we didn't have soldiers."[94] The Italian kingdom is such a remote concept to these people that it could well be a part of the natural order. There is not the slightest hope that things could be any different from what they have always been, and it seems the only way to achieve personal prosperity is through marriage. In such fatalistic circumstances, rebellion against one's condition is nothing more than the inability of a weak character to accept the basic facts of life, rather than a heroic struggle to make things better. Again and again 'Ntoni vents his bitterness. At one point when the grandfather accuses him of loitering, he responds:

You lot don't know the world, and you're like kittens with your eyes still closed. Do you eat the fish you catch? Do you know who you're working for, from Monday to Saturday, worn away to such a state that not even the hospital would want you? You're working for people who don't do anything, and have money by the spadeful![95]

Yet the grandfather's conservative fatalism does not prevent him from engaging in financial speculation, which begins a chain of events that lead to the family's ruin.

Visconti's *La terra trema* can be taken as a modern critical reading of Verga's novel. The film begins with the words:

The events represented in this film take place in Italy, or to be more precise in Sicily, the village of Acitrezza, by the Ionian Sea a little distance from Catania.
The story which the film tells is the same all over the world and is repeated every year everywhere that people exploit other people.
The houses, the streets, the boats, the sea are those of Acitrezza.
All the actors have been selected from among the inhabitants of this country: fishers, girls, laborers, bricklayers, wholesalers.
These people know no other language than Sicilian to express their rebellion, sorrows, hopes.
The Italian language is not the language of the poor.

As Micciché has pointed out, each of these statements makes explicit a poetic choice and implies a theoretical position that coincides with the main ideals of neorealism. The first statement places the events in a specific location and emphasizes *representation*; the second announces that the *story* to be told has universal validity. The third and fourth statements indicate that the locations are authentic and that nonprofessional actors are being used to play parts that could be lifted from their very own lives. The last two statements stress the authenticity of the language of the film and indicate that its use can be taken as a form of social protest.[96]

Although the film transfers the events to the contemporary world, as indicated by details such as references to the Fascist era that has just ended, this has not necessitated many changes in the story material: life in the village of Aci Trezza has changed but little between the time that Verga wrote his veristic novel and that Visconti shot his neorealistic film. But, for the purposes of conceptual clarity and narrative concentration, the story line has been simplified, certain events have been combined with others, and their narrative and thematic function has been changed. Only the characters closely related in one way or another to the Valastros have been picked up from the motley crowd of the novel. The downfall of the Valastros, in particular, is depicted with marvelous dramatic economy in a series of scenes in which one event, one blow, inexorably follows another. Just as 'Ntoni is about to enter the tavern where the "man with American cigarettes" is talking Cola into leaving for the continent, Vanni comes to tell him that the representatives of the bank have arrived to examine (and eventually take over) their ancestral home. After this Cola is seen leaving, grandfather falls ill and is taken to a hospital, and Lucia brings shame on herself by becoming don Salvator's mistress. We never learn what happens to them; one by one, all three simply disappear from the story.

As opposed to Verga's gossiping and bickering villagers, Visconti's characters display a stoic nobility that gives 'Ntoni's fall the dignity of tragedy. Renoir's *Toni* comes closer to Verga in this respect. *La terra trema* is structured around 'Ntoni's courageous attempt to change the fortunes of his family. He fails, but it is not because of some immutable fate or because the laws of nature are against him. He knows he is fighting against an oppressive social and economic order. This becomes apparent particularly in the scene in which the Valastros are forced to sell their fish to the wholesalers: the latter know the family is in trouble and that they can dictate the prices of fish. Gradually 'Ntoni becomes aware that the social order is not a fixed entity. It can be changed, but only through collective action. This point is made explicit when, close to the end of the film, 'Ntoni receives sympathy from a little girl, and he tells her that change can only take place when all the fishers are ready to unite in a collective effort.

In the film, economic factors determine the way most human relationships are structured. For a brief moment it appears that 'Ntoni will be able to reach his beloved Nedda, the daughter of a rich family, but as his fortunes change, he cannot even get to see her. Toward the end of the film she is seen in the arms of the successful wholesaler Lorenzo. Mara's beloved Nicola feels that as a poor bricklayer he is not worthy of her after her family launches a private enterprise. After the Valastros' downfall, Mara in turn feels that since she is a woman without a dowry, she is no longer a suitable candidate for marriage.

The Valastros' struggle against the prevailing social conditions and prejudices also leaves them at the mercy of nature. Because the community lives in close contact with nature, the two are not very far from each other. The Valastros' attempt to introduce change is in effect an attempt to impose a linear concept of time as opposed to the predominantly cyclical time that governs life in the village of Aci Trezza. In the present scheme of things, the only way the inhabitants can escape the wheel of cyclical time is to leave the village, as 'Ntoni's brother Cola does. Linear time manifests itself only in wear and tear, in growing old, in the loss of possibilities.

Partly because of the voice-over ("As always the day in Aci Trezza begins . . .", "Every night the boats leave . . ."), there is a strong iterative sense at the beginning of the film, but it quickly becomes what Gérard Genette has called "pseudo-iterative" in that although something is presented as iterative, it displays details that are unlikely to occur repeatedly. When we first see the Valastro girls, Mara and Lucia, the latter is looking at the family photograph and the memories it evokes in her serve as an exposition of the family's past. The act itself is obviously not likely to occur too often, and thus it helps to change from iterative to singulative, from general (the fishermen of Aci Trezza and their morning routine) to the particular (the Valastros on the morning when the story starts). Soon the chain of events that forms the backbone of the film begins with the singular event of 'Ntoni's rebellion. As Marsha Kinder has pointed out, in many neorealist films, the "slippage" from iterative to "singulative" mode suggests that the singular events are representative and typical rather than something exceptional emerging from ordinary life. What happens to the Valastros is, of course, extraordinary, but the iterative aspect of the beginning emphasizes that they are ordinary people seeking a solution to the basic problems of their lives.[97]

As things grow worse for them, the relics of stability gain new significance. Millicent Marcus has focused on how the family photograph seen in passing at crucial moments during the film serves as an image of continuity and family unity. Yet because the picture is strongly characterized by studio artifice, it also emphasizes the illusory quality of stability, once the family has chosen a path of change. In its stillness, the photograph is an image of escapist fantasy outside the realities of linear time.[98] At the end of the film, as the men once again leave for the sea, Mara in a sad gesture of hope hangs the picture on the wall of their new home.

The weight of the oppressive conditions is felt strongly also because the camera never leaves Aci Trezza, except in the scenes at sea at the beginning and end of the film. The outside world appears only indirectly when 'Ntoni is taken off to prison, when the family goes to sign a contract with the bank, when a strange man offering American cigarettes appears to tempt the youngsters to move to the continent, and when the old baroness honors the inauguration of the new boats with her presence. There are also allusions to modern Italian history. An image of a hammer and sickle can be seen on the wall of the restaurant. Raimondo, one of the wholesalers, says: "The country is full of communism!" And his colleague answers: "Raimondo is always right," in a parody of the Fascist slogan, "Il Duce is always right." At the end of the film, a faded text can be seen behind Raimondo: "Go with determination toward the people. Mussolini."[99]

'Ntoni has lived on the continent for some time, and apparently that is where his mind has been opened to new thoughts. He is now in charge of the family because his father has died at sea and his grandfather is old. 'Ntoni feels that he belongs to Aci Trezza, that this is where he has to fight his battles. His thoughts take shape gradually, mainly in the open air, at work. Cola does not have such a strong relationship with his work or nature, and, above all, he is not responsible for the family. He can escape. He is seen taking a number of photographs out of 'Ntoni's trunk, images from the big world outside Aci Trezza. In one of the film's visually and psychologically most complex scenes, the brothers are seen in front of a mirror on which Cola has put a photograph of 'Ntoni in his army uniform and which reflects his own face. The next shot captures the photograph and 'Ntoni's image in the mirror until the camera pans to 'Ntoni's sad face in the tightest close-up of the entire film, as he says: "Everywhere in the world the water is salty, if we go beyond the Faraglioni [the rocks in the sea that guard the port of Aci Trezza], the current can carry us away." The different images – photograph, mirror, the cinematic image itself – reflect and represent the past, the present, and the future, the tension between immanence and aspiration at the core of Visconti's art.[100]

As 'Ntoni proceeds on his *via dolorosa*, he exhibits almost a touch of saintliness. When he and his brothers Vanni and Alfio bow their heads and approach the wholesalers for work, they take the sting out of Lorenzo's mocking laughter with the simple dignity of their stare. And earlier on, when the wholesalers offer a ridiculously low price for the Valastros' catch of fish, as is so often the case in neorealist films, the faces of the children register amazement at the cruelty of the adults, which in this narrative context can almost be seen as the first signs of awakening consciousness. Similarly, just when 'Ntoni is about to recognize the true cause of the problems of his kind and his class and see the need for collective action, the sympathy shown by the little girl Rosa helps him overcome his pride and seek work from the wholesalers as a day laborer.

The sense of nobility is enhanced by the visual style, a crucial feature of which is the use of fades to separate and mark transitions from one main sequence to another and dissolves to connect/separate subsequences with/from one another. In his *Visconti e il Neorealismo*, Lino Miccichè has made a thorough study of the use of fades and dissolves (as well as almost every other conceivable formal aspect) in *La terra trema* and demonstrated how they too have a definite function in creating a distinct narrative rhythm in the film. Furthermore, he points out that this cinematic strategy has a precedent in Verga's *I Malavoglia*. In ten cases out of fourteen, a new chapter begins with the same subject and sometimes almost a paraphrase of the last sentence of the previous chapter, as can be seen at the end of chapter 10 and the beginning of chapter 11: "Come quel 'Ntoni Malavoglia là, che va girelloni a quest'ora pel paese!" and "Una volta 'Ntoni Malavoglia, andando girelloni pel paese" (Like that 'Ntoni Malavoglia there, loitering round this beautiful country!/Once 'Ntoni Malavoglia, loitering round the beautiful country . . .). Similarly, within the chapters Verga's narration runs fluently from one topic to another.[101] A name might emerge in the course of the dialogue and the next paragraph will tell something about that individual and what he or she happens to be doing at that time:

"I have not found a husband," snapped back la Vespa waspishly. "I'm not one of those women who bring a string of men after them right into church, with polished shoes, or big paunches."

The one with the paunch was Brasi, padron Cipolla's son, who was the darling of mothers and daughters alike, because he owned vines and olive groves.

"Go and see if the boat is properly moored," his father said to him, making the sign of the cross.

No one could help thinking that that wind and rain were pure gold for the Cipolla family; that is how things go in this world, and once reassured that their boat was well-moored, they were rubbing their hands in glee at the storm; while the Malavoglia had turned quite white and were tearing their hair, because of that cargo of lupins they had bought on credit from zio Crofisso, Dumb bell.[102]

The text is full of such "literary dissolves," as Miccichè calls them. It gives the impression of a lively flow of events and characters constantly gossiping about each other. In the film, however, the use of fades and dissolves creates an almost solemn effect of time passing while people are engaged in their various tasks.

There are several long takes in deep focus, the pans are serenely slow, the camera is involved with but slightly distant from the characters.[103] Particularly beautiful is the first fish market scene, in which the camera follows closely the way Vanni moves among the noisy men haggling over prices. The shot conveys the urgency of the trading, which looks like a fight for one's daily bread, and one has the sense that this same scene is acted again and again, every morning, with more or less the same results. In contrast, the trading that takes place the next morning when 'Ntoni tries to negotiate better prices consists of fairly short shots, mainly confused images of fighting men.

As long as the Valastros prosper in their enterprise, the loving couples are seen in fairly lengthy takes. The second half of the scene between Mara and Nicola after the Valastros have started their enterprise is captured in a long take, a continuous movement as they push her cart forward. The scene changes through a dissolve and 'Ntoni and Nedda are seen in a particularly beautiful and long take as they return to the village from the sunny cliffs by the sea. The length of the takes helps to convey the feeling of tranquility; the sun and light give at least 'Ntoni and Nedda a chance to exchange gestures of tenderness. But after the family's economic downfall, toward the end of the film, instead of showing bustling crowds and loving couples, the long takes reveal lonely figures in desolate environments or people in confrontation with one another.

There are also many long takes in the scenes inside the Valastros' home. At first most of the doors of the house are open, and the family members move effortlessly from room to room, from outside to inside, and vice versa. The length of the takes, together with the deep focus and the polyphony of space with the two rooms and the yard outside, emphasizes the organic relationship between the characters and their environment. This is where they and their predecessors have lived as long as

anyone can remember. At this stage the Valastros are still an integral part
of the community. The point is made even more manifest in the scene
after the Valastros return from the big city where they have completed
the necessary bank transactions to start their enterprise. As the camera
pans and the angles change in an inspired and mobile shot/reverse-shot
pattern, neighbors are seen at various distances from the camera observing and commenting cordially on 'Ntoni's high spirits. This marks the
peak of his relations with the community, made apparent by an ingenious
cinematic realization. As Marcus has put it, "Visconti's staging provides
spatial analogues to Verga's multilayered chorality."[104]

Although a sense of open space is conveyed in some scenes, more often
the characters are framed by doors, windows, mirrors, and the like. They
all define social spheres and indicate limits. Sexual transactions, for example, are negotiated through windows: Mara and Nicola have a coy
conversation over a pot of basil (the traditional sign indicating that there
is an eligible young woman in the house) resting on the window sill discreetly between them, while don Salvatore almost penetrates the house
in order to lure Lucia into a relationship. As the Valastros fall into misfortune, doors and windows tend to be closed, the people inside become
isolated, and the house begins to appear like a trap in which they are
caught. The camera follows the characters relentlessly as they pace
around like caged animals. But even at this stage, leaving the house means
uprooting the whole family. They rent a house, but very little is seen of
it, almost as if its individual features were entirely irrelevant.

The scenes inside the ancestral home are also shown in long shot/coun-
tershot sequences mainly in connection with conversations about the fate
of the family. The earlier scene with the salting of the fish from the Valastros' first big capture in turn has sometimes been compared with Eisenstein's montage technique.[105] This is a slight exaggeration as the shots
are not arranged in the kind of counterpoint that Eisenstein thought to
be the essence of montage, but the pace of editing is at its highest and
certainly reminiscent of the Russian style of the 1920s. After the downfall
of the Valastros has begun, there is a brief return to rapid montage editing
as a series of shots of the faces of the members of the family – men and
women, of three generations – emphasizes their silent desperation as their
fish are being sold at an absurdly low price. But however long the shots,
the images, with their careful compositions and contrast of light and
shadow, both give the milieu and the fates of the characters a sense of
serene beauty and a mythical aura. There is a connection with the heroic

proletarians of early Soviet films, but here the images evoke pity rather than admiration.

A vast majority of the shots are no closer than medium shots. According to Miccichè's count, one-fifth of the shots are medium long shots and three-fifths range from full shots to medium shots. The rest tend to be long shots. There are only about a dozen close-ups. Only in one shot is the framing tight, though not yet an extreme close-up, namely, the scene in which 'Ntoni tries to assuage Cola's burning desire to leave Aci Trezza. Apparently this style was chosen in part because of the use of nonprofessional actors, who could not be expected to act with the precision required by a more character-centered camera style. In any case, the characters move around within their space as if guided by a spontaneously invented choreography. Already in his second film Visconti showed himself to be a master of mise-en-scène, having an impeccable sense of how objects and characters need to be distributed in space in order to achieve maximum clarity of expression. The impression is that the people and the things are there not for the camera and for the plot, but because they belong there. Visconti could achieve this effect because, as Ishaghpour has pointed out, he "thinks in terms of scenes, as opposed to Murnau or Eisenstein who think of the take or montage."[106]

The use of a camera style that keeps the spectator at a slight distance from the characters and events is both an aesthetic and an ethical choice, a gesture of respect for the life of the people of Aci Trezza. Together with the calm pace of the film, it prevents the ideological objective and the need to formulate it as a story from taking over the documentary or anthropological aspect of the film. Together with the commentary, this makes Visconti's narrative strategy much more detached than Verga's, which, with its abundance of direct and free indirect discourse, gives much more of an inside view of the life of the villagers. Visconti gives Aci Trezza and its people enough space to establish their individuality and their particular situation, as opposed to the universalizing aspect of the plot. The two have to be in balance so that an event can be appreciated both in its uniqueness and universality.

Georg Lukács would have approved of the way Visconti treats his subject matter. As Guido Aristarco has pointed out, "Naturalism stops at describing phenomena in the present; realism of phenomena reveals the essence, it indicates the 'from where' and the 'where to.' "[107] In other words – as was argued earlier in connection with the theory of neorealism – cinematic realism is not just a question of reproduction, it is also an attempt to penetrate beyond the superficial to the underlying structures. The most effective means to do so is, in the Lukácsian sense, through a typical as opposed to an average character, a figure who embodies some of the relevant contradictions of his age. An average character can be used in describing situations, but through types it is possible to analyze those situations and embody the relevant social, moral, and psychological oppositions of a given historical situation.[108] Pursuing this line of thought, one may see in *La terra trema* a movement "from chronicle to history, from phenomena to their essence, from the average to the typical."

However, Lukács's idea cannot be separated from the narrative mode he is discussing. In his *The Historical Novel* he writes that "both drama and large epic, to give a faithful image of human life, must reflect correctly the dialectics of freedom and necessity." According to Lukács, drama focuses on individual initiative, and thus "it is only in the collision and its consequence that the human deed is shown to be restricted and limited, to be socially and historically determined." In contrast, the vast epic emphasizes necessity, "those general objective forces which are necessarily stronger than the will and resolve of the individual."

In *La terra trema*, Visconti appears to steer between these two forms of narrative. On the one hand, individual initiative does occupy the foreground; on the other hand, "the circumstances which . . . give rise to this initiative" are indicated more than just "in their general outline" and "the element of necessity is present and prevalent throughout," as is typical of the epic. So although in terms of cinematic tradition *La terra trema* can conveniently be classified as an epic – primarily because of its length, leisurely pace, and cyclic features, which together create the feeling of time passing solemnly, irrespective of all human activities – there is also a sense in which the film has a distinct dramatic quality, namely, the tight organization of the plot. The dramatic and epic features, together with the purely cinematographic, give the film a rich sense of both the natural and the social environment, as well as an aesthetic quality that is in perfect harmony with the underlying social analysis and psychological sensitivity.

Within this scheme Visconti also realized his ideal of that "internal and musical rhythm" that already in 1941 he thought would be the key to adapting Verga for the screen. He and Willy Ferrero took the nondiegetic music from Sicilian folk melodies. On the whole music is quite sparse in the film, but it increases toward the end to emphasize the fate of the Valastros. There is an abundance of diegetic music in the form of songs, don Salvatore whistling tunes from operas, and the poignant melodies played by uncle Nunzio on his oboe. Furthermore, the sounds of the wind and the sea, of ships returning to the harbor, cries from the streets, and the musicality of the Sicilian dialect create their own archaic atmosphere.

Much of the debate surrounding *La terra trema* has centered on the question of its realism with respect to its considered aesthetic quality. Millicent Marcus quotes Visconti's "*Tradizione e invenzione*":

if it is the musical treatment that will elevate the story from the level of "peasant chronicle" to that of ancient tragedy, we realize how far we are from a critical realist perspective whose means would be rigorously intellectual, and whose end would be the cinematic equivalent of the historical novel, as Lukács defined it.[109]

But the film does have a critical realist perspective, and even the wordless passages can be seen not as mere aesthetic indulgence or documentary description, but as meditations on time and space. The point is that here time and space emphatically constitute *the* environment that the characters inhabit. Whereas in Antonioni's films the desolate urban surroundings can be seen as a metaphor of alienation and spiritual emptiness, in *La terra trema* the characters live in very close relationship with nature. In the storm sequence they almost become one with it as the women are seen in their black garments among the equally black rocks anxiously gazing at the sea, waiting for signs of their menfolk returning from nature's vehement embrace. The tone and atmosphere of the scene is stoic and unsentimental. The indexical potential of film, its capacity for "phenomenological realism" within a narrative structure, is exploited to the full to make a profound and moving statement about the severe conditions imposed by nature on those who have been ostracized from their community. Nature is strongly present in the images while the relationship of the characters to the community is shown through the plot.

Some confusion has arisen in assessing this film owing to the use of the voice-over commentary, which was added after the film was completed. Apparently even Visconti himself thought of it as a compromise. Nevertheless, it serves to make an important point, regarding the film's opening statement about Italian not being "the language of the poor." Since the commentary is in Italian, it reminds us that the analysis has been provided and the film has been conceived by non-Sicilians, foreigners from abroad.[110] But the commentary also has important narrative and thematic functions in the unfolding of the story. The poetic quality of the voice and the words are a part of the classical unity of the film. The commentary repeats or resumes some of the dialogue – partly for the benefit of most of the Italian audience, to whom the dialect is incomprehensible – but it also mediates between the particular and general spheres by pointing out the factors that govern the behavior of the characters and the community as a whole, particularly its traditions.[111] The commentary is thus a crucial part of the structure, which in Micciché's words "determine[s] the greatness of this film . . . the perfect fusion between anthropological discovery, lyrical contemplation, ideological enunciation and narrative practice."[112]

There is yet another, even more basic reason why *La terra trema* can be called a realistic work. Visconti has often been accused of betraying his ideals in making this film. As already mentioned, the film was at one point going to be a documentary about Sicilian fishers. The idea may have been to show that Italy was in a revolutionary situation in the marxist sense and that a film about the poverty of the south might make people more aware of the contradictions between the south and the north. The way the film turned out reflects, or at least is curiously parallel with, the changed political circumstances in Italy. After the defeat of the left in the election of April 1948, the prospects of a socialist revolution (or evolution) probably seemed increasingly utopian. Visconti's art is anything but utopian. Making the film was a continuous interaction with the subject matter at hand, and thus reality imposed its own conditions on the film. The poor of the south were not prepared to rise against the prevailing order, and the only protest they engaged in was to support rebels such as the bandit Salvatore Giuliano. Thus Visconti could not depict collective action according to the marxist ideal without blatantly distorting the actual situation.[113]

This cannot be seen as a betrayal unless loyalty to an ideology is understood to require blind dogmatism. Visconti could hardly be accused of distorting reality and its richness by sticking to an ideologically burdened interpretation of it. For him marxism was not a way of explaining the world in its entirety, as it was for many of its supporters in the heat of the cold war. To Visconti, it was more of an ethical stand and a way of analyzing certain features of society. In *La terra trema* the reasons for the Valastros' failure are carefully spelled out in the narrative structure, which clearly portrays economic relationships as the all-important factor governing the activities of individuals and the community as a whole. The subjective point of view conveyed through the characters enables the spectator to experience the human significance of the social relationships depicted.

La terra trema offered Visconti an opportunity for once to side unequivocally with his characters. As Youssef Ishaghpour points out, it is one of the few films in the history of cinema in which "poverty is neither a degradation nor the source of miserableness made comforting by bestowing on it the halo of sanctity."[114] Instead, as Visconti had already hinted in his essay "*Il cinema antropomorfico*", the aesthetic quality of the film, its poetic formalism, the austere beauty of its images, and its solemn tempo give the characters the quality of Homeric heroes. To some extent, this might appear to subscribe to the fatalistic notion of human affairs, but at least man is shown to have had a hand in shaping his destiny. The aesthetic – as well as the passionate and melodramatic – quality in Visconti's films is always kept in check by the underlying analysis and ideological commitment.

La terra trema was very poorly received when it premiered at the Venice film festival. A group of protesters pronounced it an artistic failure. Zeffirelli became enraged and got into a fistfight with them.[115] The shouts, whistles, and fights were in response not only to the film, but also to the political scene. The Christian Democratic government had just launched an attack against the entire neorealistic movement, and the bourgeois audience at the festival was probably strongly prejudiced against the homosexual communist aristocrat who, on top of everything, dared to direct films. Furthermore, many leftist critics accused Visconti of formalism and of indulging in aestheticism. Togliatti, for example, could not understand why Visconti's film had not depicted the activities of the party and the trade unions. Visconti replied: "There are no parties, not to mention trade unions [in Aci Trezza]." On the whole, Italian critics remained cool, and it was only after the premieres in Paris, London, and New York that the film began to be appreciated.[116]

BELLISSIMA

In search of a style

After Visconti completed *La terra trema*, he resumed his career as a theater director. Now he wanted to create something grandiose, to take some distance from realism. In a production of *As You Like it* he explored theatrical possibilities to their fullest. He asked Salvador Dali to design the sets, the rococo-style costumes, and the lighting. The music for Shakespeare's texts was by Thomas Morley, Henry Purcell, Thomas Arne, and William Boyce. Visconti himself described the production as "a fantasy, a dream, a ballet-like fairy-tale, variations from the theme of love." The

audience loved the production, but some leftist critics accused Visconti
of betraying neorealism. In reply, Visconti protested that neorealism
should not be reduced to "a confinement, a law," but that it should be
understood as "a method, an approach." He called for "neither realism
nor neorealism, but fantasy, complete liberty of display."[117]

Visconti's next production, Tennessee Williams's *A Streetcar Named
Desire*, was easier for the proponents of realism to stomach, and it was
favorably received. According to critic Silvio d'Amico, Visconti now
succeeded in combining his "ultra realistic" and his "existentialist"
approaches. Gianni Rondolino recalled these productions in his study on
Visconti: "The crudest naturalism was transfigured into a dramatic tension that made the spectacle not only a slice of life but a grand metaphor
of human existence."[118] Visconti's next projects were Vittorio Alfieri's *Oreste* and Shakespeare's *Troilus and Cressida* at the Maggio Musicale festival, which gave him another chance to produce grand spectacles.

Although many of his productions at this time, particularly the grand
spectacles, were successful and helped Visconti become internationally
known, they were an artistic dead-end. Despite his love of fantasy and
his skill in creating it on stage, his true strength lay in charting the human
social and spiritual condition through fictional characters studied as the
agents of carefully constructed plots set in meticulously (re)constructed
environments. This kind of emphatically mimetic approach proves awk-
ward in the theater as compared with the cinema. Nevertheless, throughout his life, particularly in the 1950s, Visconti remained active in
directing for the stage.

Visconti also tried his hand at staging ballets. When he met one of his
greatest literary idols, Thomas Mann, Visconti asked his permission to
adapt the novella *Mario and the Magician* (1930) into an opera-ballet.
Mann consented and encouraged Visconti and the composer Franco Mannino to develop the idea. Their aim was to create a new form of drama
in which the symbolic and caricatural elements would form the basic
structure but would be counterbalanced by realistic and critical elements.
The choreographer was Leonide Massine, who had for some time worked
with the renowned ballet producer Sergei Diaghilev. Mann was eager to
see the results, but in a manner typical of La Scala, the production was
postponed repeatedly. By the time the premiere was finally held in 1956,
Mann was already dead. The production won the Diaghilev prize, but it
was never featured again in the repertory.[119]

This considerable activity in the theater did not diminish Visconti's
desire to make films. But things had changed since the heyday of neo-

realism. After the Christian Democrats had won the 1948 election, the Vatican excommunicated all those who voted for the communists or who sympathized or collaborated with them. There were strikes and political unrest. Socially committed films were a risky investment in this context for they could not be expected to obtain government subsidy. In fact, the film could even be confiscated.[120]

Although by no means were all neorealist directors leftist – Roberto Rossellini, for example, was never far removed from the Christian Democrats – the entire movement was branded as being socialist. Giulio Andreotti, at that time undersecretary of state, attacked De Sica's *Umberto D*:

We ask people of culture to recognize their social responsibility, which should not be confined to criticizing the malpractices and miseries of a certain system and a generation. . . . [E]ven if it were true that evil can only be fought by bringing into light its most miserable aspects, it is also true that De Sica has done a disservice to his country if people around the world begin to think that Italy in the twentieth century is the same as *Umberto D*.[121]

According to the Christian Democrats, a good film should offer the possibility for relaxation. By controlling production grants and the exportation of films, the government effectively exercised a preliminary censorship with the intention of directing production away from unpleasant subjects.

At the same time, not all dogmatic marxists approved of neorealist films. Vsevolod Pudovkin, speaking at a conference on cinema in Perugia, encouraged filmmakers to concentrate on content instead of form and to depict "positive heroes." This message was echoed by Umberto Barbaro, who as a teacher at the Centro sperimentale di Cinema during the Fascist era had helped shape neorealism. Now he criticized *Ossessione* for its eroticism and *La terra trema* for its lack of a clear idea.[122]

To make matters worse, the film industry was hit by an economic crisis. Whereas in 1946 Italy produced sixty-five films, by 1948 the number had dropped to forty-nine. American films controlled the market, and in the years 1945–50 they commanded a 60–75 percent share of the cinemagoing audience. Government attempts to restrict the importation of foreign films and to encourage the export of Italian films to the United States were by and large unsuccessful. The assumed low production costs of neorealist films was of little help either, in that most of these films did not reach a wide audience. Also, in practice the technical difficulties encountered in shooting on location often meant that the time required for production had to be extended, and so the possible savings were easily eaten away.[123]

Thus the pressures both from the side of the audience and the political parties were great. More and more features of American gangster films and sex began to creep into neorealist films. Another way to attract attention was comedy, and this gave rise to *neorealismo rosa*, or pink neorealism. Its roots were in the light comedy of the Fascist era, and the message was the same: everyone should stick to his or her place in society. Poverty and misfortune were romanticized. Often the comedies offered the further attraction of a sexy Gina Lollobrigida or Sophia Loren. These films, more than the actual neorealist ones, helped to create a fairly wide audience for Italian cinema.[124]

Visconti's *Bellissima* belongs to this strain of comic neorealism, but in a way that is consistent with the director's ethical commitment. The initiative for the film came from Salvo d'Angelo, who had lost money in financing *La terra trema* but not his faith in Visconti. The director himself was enticed by the possibility of finally having a chance to work with Anna Magnani.[125] The idea and the first synopsis were Cesare Zavattini's, but the script went through many changes that departed considerably from his original plan. In any case, the script was more or less put aside when Magnani entered the picture. She tended to improvise and follow only the substance of the text. Visconti knew that the best way to get a good performance out of her was to give her as much freedom as possible and to concentrate on keeping the other elements together and focused on her.[126]

Illusions of art and reality

The central themes of *Bellissima* are introduced during the opening credits. The audience first sees different sections of an orchestra, and after the first few shots the entire orchestra appears. A soloist and a female choir join in. The music is from scene II, 4 of Donizetti's *L'elisir d'amore*, and it turns out to have a certain symbolic function in the film. The opera is about the charms of love and money and the exploitation that they both invite. Visconti in turn treats the illusions of the film world and does it in a somewhat ironical way.

The music heard at the opening of the film is part of a radio broadcast announcing a competition to find the prettiest little girl in Rome for a part in a new film, "Oggi, domani, mai" (Today, tomorrow, never), to be directed by the famous Alessandro Blasetti. A throng of mothers is seen pushing their way into the Cinecittà studios. One of them, Maddalena

Cecconi, moves away from the crowd because she has lost her daughter, Maria. She is found playing by a pond. This scene immediately establishes conflict between her own needs and the wishes and ambition of her choleric mother. A young man, Alberto Annovazzi, appears and offers his help. He turns out to be a typical opportunist who hangs around the studios in order to further his career and make a little money whenever possible. He does not seem truly unpleasant, however. (Visconti would always have sympathy for the young scoundrels he depicted.)

After Maria passes the first screen test, the film moves to episodes in the daily life of the Cecconi family and Maddalena's attempts to turn her daughter into a film star. Her husband, Spartaco, has grave doubts about the project but knows he has no hope of restraining his tempestuous and energetic wife.[127] First, Maddalena is seen earning a bit of extra income by helping to give injections to the diabetics living in the neighborhood. The Cecconis are fairly poor and have difficulty saving enough to buy a new flat. The money Maddalena spends in training her daughter thus represents considerable loss for the family.

Next to the building they live in there is an open-air cinema. About halfway through the film, Maddalena and Spartaco follow a screening of Hawks's *Red River* through their bedroom window. She is quite taken by what she sees, whereas he dismisses it as just fiction and says she should forget about films altogether. The cattle-driving scene of the Hawks film dissolves into a scene at the gate of Cinecittà, where a herd of mothers can be seen ushering their daughters to the screen test – with sound of the cattle continuing until the next shot. *Bellissima* contains several such ironic parallels between reality and fiction. Many employees of the Cinecittà play themselves in this film. Among them is Blasetti, who plays the part of the director of the film to be made. Apparently he was not aware of the ironic aspects of his role or the fact that the theme from *L'elisir* in his scenes in the film is associated with the charlatan in the opera. When he discovered this connection, he was furious, but Visconti succeeded in calming him down by suggesting that

we are all charlatans, we directors. It is we who put illusions into the heads of mothers and daughters. It is we who take people from the streets and that is where we do wrong. We sell a love potion which is not a potion at all: [as] in the opera, it is just Bordeaux wine. The theme of the charlatan doesn't refer just to you but also to me.[128]

Blasetti was satisfied with this explanation, and they were reconciled. It is easy to agree with Nowell-Smith, who emphasizes that Visconti did not

consider himself to be above the film world he was depicting and criticizing. He, too, is in the line of fire.[129] At the same time, as Michèle Lagny
has pointed out, inasmuch as the film pleases us, it "suggests that as
dangerous as they may be, illusions are indispensable to us."[130]

Before Maddalena finally discovers how the film industry works, she
devotes all her energy to making her daughter a star. An opportunity to
improve Maria's chances then appears, in the guise of former actress who
has heard about Maddalena's ambitions. She offers to teach Maria the
basics of acting. The two wander into the garden while Maddalena stays
inside and vents her doubts about this quaint old lady. This is one of
Maddalena's bravura arialike soliloquies in which Magnani displays to
the full her acting talents and charm. These solo parts also reveal that
Maddalena is completely immersed in her own world and unaware of the
true needs of her little daughter. Meanwhile, Maria appears to join in the
game of the old actress and to enjoy herself, but the scene, like so many
in this film, ends in an argument, because Maddalena cannot stop inter-
fering with the "lesson."

The subsequent visits to the photographer, the ballet school, the
clothing store, and the barber are comic episodes that illustrate how
much money and effort can go into creating a superficial effect. Yet
these are mere bagatelles compared with the trick that Annovazzi
plays on Maddalena. She gives him money to use his "influence" to
help Maria get the part. It soon becomes clear that he has spent the
money on a new motor scooter and on entertaining his girl friend.
This does not upset Maddalena to any great extent since her plans appear to be proceeding in the right direction anyway. An alleviating
factor is no doubt Annovazzi's charm, to which Maddalena is certainly
not immune. He considers her a desirable woman and starts flirting
with her. It looks as though she might even be succumbing, but then
he starts talking about not wanting to have illusions and disappoint-
ments in life and pits this against the ideal of living for the moment.
He is inadvertently guiding Maddalena toward a more mature attitude
toward life, something beyond the pursuit of both illusions and pleasure. Maddalena eases herself out of the situation with a hearty laugh,
and Annovazzi makes an embarrassed retreat. As he leaves, he suggests that Maddalena should visit his friend Iris who is working at Cinecittà. She could show the screen test that was made of Maria.

Iris turns out to be a friendly young woman, and Maddalena recognizes her as the star of Castellani's film *Sotto il sole di Roma* (Un-

der the sun of Rome, 1948). Iris – played by Liliana Mancini herself but going under the name of the character in Castellani's film – tells Maddalena what has happened to her since that film was made: after acting in a couple of films, she had no more roles offered to her, the illusion wore off, and she ended up as an ordinary employee at the film studio (which was roughly what actually happened to Mancini). Maddalena is shocked but nevertheless succeeds in persuading Iris to let her and Maria into the projection room as Blasetti and his assistants are watching the screen tests. The test film shows Maria bursting into tears, and members of the film crew laugh cruelly. Only Blasetti remains calm and appears slightly annoyed by the reaction of his assistants. In the projection room, Maddalena is devastated. The moment is particularly touching because her crying face is seen in close-up, the only one of the entire film. From that moment on, she will not try to substitute dreams and illusions for real life.

Perhaps an even more important theme in *Bellissima* than the conflict between illusions and a sense of the real world is the notion that the practices of the film industry lead to the misuse of people. In the end, Maria is offered the part in Blasetti's film, but Maddalena refuses to accept it, even though it turns out that Maria has made an impression because of her natural behavior and not the mannerisms cultivated in acting and dancing lessons. Life with Spartaco may not be particularly exciting, but he represents the security and human warmth without which life would be meaningless. The ending, with its reaffirmation of family unity, is unique among Visconti's films.[131]

Bellissima can also be interpreted as a critique of the use of nonprofessional actors in neorealist films – Liliana Mancini's fate was in no way exceptional. *La Magnani* in the leading role was a major step away from this policy. Her strong presence gives Maddalena's line, "I too, could have become an actress, had I wanted to," a delightfully ironic flavor. Equally comic is the instruction she gives to her daughter. "To become an artist one mustn't speak Romanesco," while Magnani's own torrential speech flows throughout in this Roman dialect. On the whole, Magnani amply demonstrates how theatricality and stylization can be used to reveal aspects of reality that might otherwise remain hidden. Though Maddalena is hardly a typical mother, in her own peculiar way she embodies all the aspirations that mothers with scant knowledge of the big world might have for their little daughters. The typical is concentrated in the extraordinary.

OUR WOMEN

Just as lovable as Maddalena Cecconi is the second character that Magnani and Visconti created together, in the episode film *Siamo donne* (Our women, 1953). Again the original idea came from Zavattini. This time he wanted to tear down myths built around great stars and to give certain ones an opportunity to make a sincere personal confession. Again, the final result was far from what he was aiming for.

The film begins with an introduction directed by Alfredo Guarini, in which some girls and young women arrive for screen tests. The situation is reminiscent of the corresponding scene in *Bellissima*, in that these girls, too, walk past a row of men who have the power to choose them for further tests or reject them. Again there are mothers present, but they are soon ignored and the girls' own aspirations are brought into focus. Some lines refer to the film itself even more directly than was the case in *Bellissima*. One of the girls dreams of starring in films with Ingrid Bergman, Alida Valli, and Isa Miranda, that is, with the stars of the other episodes (directed by Rossellini, Gianni Franciolini, and Luigi Zampa, respectively), and the actress chosen in this screen test, Emma Danieli.

Visconti's episode is arguably the most amusing and charming. Magnani is again at her best as a Roman singer with a fierce temperament and little control over her feelings. The humor is derived mainly from her excessive need to make a display of herself and attract as much attention as possible. The story unfolds when a taxi driver demands that Magnani pay extra fare for her dog, arguing that the small creature is not a lapdog, which would be entitled to travel free of charge. Magnani soon treats this as a matter of principle, and they end up sorting it out at a police station. Before the dispute is resolved, it is discovered that she has failed to pay her dog tax and has to do it there and then. Because the driver charges her for driving her to the police station and then to the theater where she is to perform, she ends up paying thirty times more than she was charged originally. But at least the police are on her side and agree that her pet is a lapdog.

The theater at which Magnani performs appears almost as chaotic as Magnani's state of mind, but in the end everything works out fine. A particularly amusing detail is the entry of the chorus girls: the moment they walk onto the stage they put a smile on their face and make a ludicrous dance gesture. Finally, we hear Magnani singing her confession of love for Rome. The film is a mere anecdote and is based almost exclusively on Magnani's exuberant personality. But thanks to her, it is one of the most innocently funny works in Visconti's cinematic oeuvre.

The Risorgimento Films

SENSO

Opera and realism

In addition to *Bellissima*, Visconti shot a short documentary in 1951 titled *Appunti su un fatto di cronaca* (Notes about a news item). It was part of a film put together by Marco Ferreri and Riccardo Ghione, with De Sica, Carlo Levi, and Alberto Moravia in charge of the other parts. Visconti's contribution was based on a news item about a girl who had been raped and whose body was discovered in a well. A man had been arrested and he had confessed, but in the trial he withdrew his statement and claimed he had given it under torture. Visconti began his film by showing images of children playing and ended it with shots of the well and the girl's grave. By concentrating on the external factors, he apparently sought to demonstrate the effect of environment on human behavior. The documentary was banned in Italy, but it was fairly well received in France.[1]

The next year Visconti worked with Suso Cecchi D'Amico in preparing a script based on Erich von Stroheim's *Wedding March* (1928). Because the film might have been interpreted as a comment on the debate over the question of divorce raging in Italy at the time, Lux Film rejected the script, probably intimidated by the uproar De Sica's *Umberto D* (1952) had just caused. Thus for a while Visconti concentrated on theatrical productions. One of them was Chekhov's *Three Sisters*. Chekhov was a relatively late inspiration for Visconti but turned out to be among the more important. He once stated: "Stendhal wished his epitaph to read: 'He adored Cimarosa, Mozart and Shakespeare.' I would like mine to read: 'He adored Shakespeare, Chekhov and Verdi.' "[2]

Chekhov was extremely critical about the social conditions in Russia.

He conveyed his political insights through the total pattern of psychological and social relationships he depicted, rather than by bringing forth an
explicit message through an individual "positive hero." As an evolution-
ist, he believed in the possibility of progress. However, social development
often does not coincide with the wishes of his characters, who prefer to
look backward in time, but it appears to be the only alternative to a
numbness that reduces life to eating, drinking, and sleeping.[3] They might
be intelligent and sensitive yet unable to build a future for themselves
and to adapt to the inevitable changes that take place around them.[4]

Chekhov created a dramatic framework in which by depicting only a
few moments in the stream of time he could create a sense of change – a
feature that Visconti was to adopt and treat in different ways in many of
his films. Chekhov also had an ideal of stage expression that enabled him
to convey feelings without resorting to melodramatic gestures. In this new
style, the characters had to be not only round but also types whose behavior would reflect both their internal life and the part they played in
the social fabric. The characters are not just individual cases, but an entire
social structure and situation are crystallized in them.[5] In a sense, Chekhov introduced to the stage a principle that Lukács thought to be characteristic of the historical novel.

As has been pointed out, similar ideas can be found in Visconti's concept of anthropomorphic cinema. In the early part of his career, his social
psychological treatments, particularly in his theatrical productions, appeared to be separate from the trend toward melodrama and spectacle.
Gradually, however, these two aspects of his art began to complement
each other until together they gave rise to one of the most crucial tensions
in his art. The production of *Three Sisters* was a landmark from this point
of view. A new kind of realism emerged through the union of spectacle
and a critical analysis of reality.[6] It allowed Visconti to give artistic form
to the tension between his emotional attachment to the past and his intellectual commitment to the future, between his aristocratic background
and his marxist ideology, between his decadent and his progressive traits.[7]
This duality is, of course, particularly evident in the historical films, not
only in the treatment of the subject matter but also in its relationship with
the medium: the most characteristic means of expression of the twentieth
century fueled by the art of past centuries; mechanical reproduction
transferred into the aura of art.[8]

The Chekhov-like quality becomes increasingly apparent in Visconti's
later films. It takes the form of resignation to social ideals and attachment
to one's own class, which he considered doomed to destruction because of

historical inevitability, but toward which he felt an ever-growing nostalgia. Visconti always depicted the past through a combination of involvement and detachment, often through the double perspective of nostalgia and irony, Verdian melodrama coloring the former, Chekhovian atmosphere the latter. Some of the most powerful moments in Verdi's operas arise from merciless conflicts between the public duties of the protagonists and their private aspirations, the ultimate expressions of which can be found in *I due Foscari*, *Simon Boccanegra*, *Don Carlos*, and *Aïda*. The characters are relentless in their feelings and passions, but they are destroyed by the grinding wheels of fate or the inexorable march of events. Visconti's characters are destroyed because their feelings and passions blind them, prevent them from understanding and/or accepting the objective factors that condition their lives. By closing their eyes to unpleasant reality, Visconti's "heroes" lose whatever ability they may have to affect the course of events. In this respect, their feelings and attitudes appear slightly ridiculous, much as the emotional reactions of Chekhov's characters do.

Hardly any of Visconti's characters fail to be touching in their frailty. They drift with the tide of events because they are so intensely human. Even at their cheapest, they are pitiable in the way they desperately stick to whatever they think is valuable or irreplaceable in their lives. This, if anything, is what makes them "operatic" characters. Over time, Visconti moved increasingly toward depicting the loneliness of people caged in the ideals of the past. This change of focus can be seen in his two films set in the time of the Risorgimento, the struggle for Italian unity and independence. One of these is *Senso*, a still predominantly Verdian work. The other is *The Leopard*, which is essentially Chekhovian. The protagonist of the latter is the first great resigned hero of Visconti's cinematic output, a man who looks into the past but who has the strength and courage to face the present and adapt to it. In Visconti's later films the characters are often frustrated, embittered, secluded by their loneliness. They are exceptional people – a composer, a king, an aesthete – but even at their most extraordinary they embody certain basic questions about humanity.

Visconti told Henri Chapler in 1958:

I love melodrama because it is located at the borders of life and theatre. . . . Theatre and opera, the world of the baroque: these are the motives which tie me to melodrama. I am intrigued by the idea of a "diva." This rare creature, whose role in the spectacle should be reassessed. In the mythologies of our time the diva is the incarnation of the rare, the extravagant and the exceptional.[9]

Visconti's somewhat obscure statement becomes clearer when compared with his ideal of anthropomorphic cinema, according to which the "actor-person" and the "character-person" had to become one for either of them to find their essence. The aim is to reach a level of intensity at which an intuition of what it is to be human and an intellectual view of the world can be combined and revealed on both the level of lived experience and understanding. This is how the extraordinarily singular can stand for the universal; this is something that can be achieved by means of a strictly controlled "diva."

Visconti had indeed moved some distance away from the idea of using an entire cast of nonprofessional actors. He had a chance to test his theories when in 1954 he was invited to produce Spontini's *La vestale* for La Scala, with Maria Callas in the leading female role. Callas and Visconti shared not only a deep love for opera but also an artistic passion and integrity that could not tolerate any obstacles. For Visconti she was "a marvelous instrument which I could play according to my will and who reacted with inspiration."[10]

La vestale also offered Visconti an opportunity to evoke the spirit of a certain period. This was not that of the setting of the opera, imperial Rome, but that of the first Napoleonic Empire. His intention was to remind viewers what Napoleon had meant to Italians: not a conqueror but a liberator whose accomplishments inspired the Risorgimento. To get ideas for the sets and costumes, Visconti turned to the paintings of that period. He was out to revitalize opera as an art form and to explore the psychological and social depths of works obscured by stale conventions of performance. Thus he was making a way toward a wholly new kind of operatic production. But his production of Verdi's *La traviata* in 1955 made some critics accuse Visconti of reducing the music to a mere accompaniment of a "brutal, veristic, and vulgar" drama. Others, however, realized that Visconti had given new life to these works and that in fact he had been much more faithful to Verdi's dramatic aspirations than had become customary over the long production history of this beloved work.[11] During his career, Visconti produced more than twenty operas and works of musical theater. In particular, his production of *La traviata* at La Scala in 1955 and of *Don Carlos* at the Royal Opera House, Covent Garden, in 1958 are considered to be among the highest peaks with modern staging of opera.

The formation of *Senso*

Visconti's love of opera is apparent also in many of his films, above all in *Senso*. The project started when Lux Film, after having rejected the

script for *Wedding March*, commissioned Visconti to create a "spectacle
of high artistic level." He and Cecchi D'Amico proposed five ideas, one
of which was based on Camillo Boito's novella *Senso*, which had just
reappeared in a collection edited by Giorgio Bassani. The events related
in the novella take place at the time of the Risorgimento. Many of Visconti's immediate family and other relatives had taken an active part in
Italian unification and thus he felt he had a personal connection with that
period in history.[12]

As a boy, Visconti had often seen the brothers Camillo and Arrigo Boito
in the audience at La Scala. The latter was a notable composer and the
librettist of, among other works, Verdi's *Otello* and *Falstaff* and Ponc-
chielli's *La Gioconda*. According to Colin Partridge "Each brother found
the nuances and deployed the resonances of words. They were careful
craftsmen of language and not major literary artists."[13] They belonged
to a generation disillusioned by the political and social development in
Italy after the Risorgimento, particularly by the so-called *trasformismo*,
the policy of endless cynical compromise that characterized Italian political life after the unification – and that has continued even to the present
day. Arrigo belonged to a group of artists known as *Scapigliatura* (the
dishevelled). They sought to renew Italian artistic and spiritual life but
in practice were paralyzed by their pessimism, which extended from politics to metaphysics.

From the point of view of the prudent producers, *Senso* probably appeared innocent enough as a basis for the film since the historical setting
is used merely as a backdrop. An Italian noblewoman, Livia, tells the
story of a love affair she has had during the war for Venice. Her tone is
cold and cynical and the story centered entirely on herself. It is told in
the manner of a confession, but with aggressive self-justification. All the
other characters are merely supernumeraries. Even Remigio Ruz, an Austrian officer and the object of her mad passion, does not emerge with any
degree of personality in Livia's narration. This emphasizes Livia's merciless egocentrism. She herself states at the beginning of her story: "They
say the sum of philosophy consists of knowing oneself: I have studied
myself with such apprehension for so many years, hour by hour, minute
by minute, that I believe I know myself through and through and can
consider myself to be a perfect lady philosopher [*filosofessa*]."[14] And she
certainly is under no illusions. She describes her feelings for her lover:
"His lack of fidelity, of honesty, of delicacy, of restraint appeared to me
as signs of arcane vigour, real might under which I was happy, proud to
submit myself as slave."[15]

The war is merely an obstacle for her to overcome in her pursuit of sensations and emotional experiences. The war breaks out soon after she falls in love with Remigio, and she gives him money to obtain a false doctor's certificate relieving him of military service. The war separates them, but she travels across the battle fields to join him, only to find him in the arms of another woman. Having denounced him, she attends his execution. It stirs in her memories of their embraces, and she experiences a moment of remorse, but as she sees his new lover throw herself on his dead body, she collects herself: "Seeing that disgusting woman made my scorn emerge again and with that scorn also my dignity and force rose. I was conscious of my rights; I left calmly, proud of having completed a heavy duty."[16]

Boito shows no interest in the Risorgimento or its political and social consequences and concentrates on his single cynical protagonist. This very omission, of course, can be seen as a comment on the supposed glory of the historical events. Visconti's view of the Risorgimento could also be described as cynical, but at least he was not apathetic about it. The adaptation took a long time, and numerous changes were made both before and after the shooting. Visconti and Cecchi D'Amico first wrote a synopsis and then a script together with Bassani, Giorgio Prosperi, and Carlo Alianello.[17] In this first version, the story proceeds in three flashbacks that Countess Livia Serpieri and her cousin Ussoni relate to each other in a Veronese hospital after the battle of Custoza. The war and the political changes are carefully outlined. The Custoza battle scene, for example, brings out clearly the reluctance of the official army to cooperate with the voluntary soldiers and the traumatic effects of the lost battle.[18]

A second version written by Visconti and Cecchi D'Amico under the title *Uragano d'estate* (A summer storm) soon followed. This was to be the final version. Many scenes relating to the military and political activities were left out, and Ussoni lost his status as a narrator. Livia does not appear as cynical as before, and new themes emerge in the love scenes. At this stage the idea was to begin with the execution of a lieutenant called Franz, and then to relate the story as if from Livia's point of view. The story would have begun in St. Mark's Square with Ussoni challenging Franz to a duel, followed by a scene at the La Fenice opera house. As in the first version, Livia would have in the end encountered Franz in prison, but Franz would have hidden his fear behind a mask of cruel irony. The role of the opportunist Count Serpieri was considerably reduced. For example, the scene of his dishonorable death while trying once more to switch sides when it appeared that the Austrians might still win the war

was deleted. Serpieri's behavior was perhaps conceived as a metaphor for
Italy's conduct in the two world wars, sitting on the fence until it was
clear which side was to be the victor. In the context of the film as a whole,
however, it might not have been effective.

Because both Lux Film and Visconti wanted to use foreign stars, the
next stage was to translate the new version into English. Visconti asked
for help from Tennessee Williams, who recommended the services of his
friend Paul Bowles. Bowles, however, did not appear to be able to write
sufficiently concise dialogue for cinematic purposes, so in the end Williams was enlisted anyway. The translation is quite faithful to the Italian,
but some of Livia and Franz's dialogue, their conversation in their lovers'
nest, and some of their scenes at the Serpieri country mansion in Aldeno
were added by the translators.[19]

Visconti wanted Ingrid Bergman and Marlon Brando to take the leading roles. According to Gaia Servadio, Roberto Rossellini, Bergman's husband at that time, did not allow her to make the film and the Lux came
to the somewhat discredited conclusion that Brando was already passé
while Farley Granger was the great star of the future.[20] The leading female role was eventually given to Alida Valli. It is difficult to imagine
what Senso would have been like had Visconti been able to use the actors
he originally wanted. In any case, he succeeded once again in squeezing
excellent performances out of the actors he did use: both Valli and
Granger reached the peak of their careers in Senso.[21]

The story was altered in many ways in the shooting stage as well. The
opening scene, at St. Mark's Square, was deleted, and so the film begins
with the scene at La Fenice opera house. In addition, many scenes that
were not related to the love story between Livia and Franz were left out.
Livia's voice-over was almost omitted but eventually it remained.[22]

The visual style was greatly affected by the death of the director of
photography, Aldò Graziati (known as G. R. Aldò) in a car accident during the shooting. He had been using all his talent experimenting with the
Technicolor stock in order to create colors and hues that would give depth
and intensity to the film's characters, emotions, and themes. He was now
replaced by Robert Krasker and Giuseppe Rotunno.[23] The scenes in Venice were shot by Krasker, the execution by Rotunno, and all the rest by
Aldò. It has been estimated that the opening scene at La Fenice, for example, would have been very different had it been shot by Aldò. He would
probably have sought to create the effect of candlelight of the period.[24]

In the original closing scene that was actually shot, Livia, after having
betrayed Franz by informing his military superiors about his false doc-

tor's certificate, walks among the drunken Austrians celebrating their victory. According to Visconti:

One left Franz to his own affairs; we threw away Franz's story! It did not matter whether he died or not! One left him after the scene in the apartment during which he showed how repugnant he is. There was no point in seeing him executed. So we were left with her who ran to denounce him and rushed to the street. She passed among whores and became a sort of tart herself, going from one soldier to another. Then she fled shouting "Franz! Franz!" and we panned on to the young soldier, symbol of those who paid for the victories and really cried, shed hot tears while shouting: "Long live Austria!"[25]

Lux thought this ending was too "dangerous" and burned the negative. It was replaced by the scene in which Franz is executed.[26]

In the editing stage the producer suggested altogether fifteen cuts, and Visconti had to fight fiercely to preserve the unity of his film. The requests were apparently made to avoid censorship and to cut the film to a commercially suitable length, rather than to bend to ideological or moral scruples. Visconti, however, stressed the need to maintain the narrative clarity and coherence of his film.[27] Many of these changes reflected the film's political explosiveness: Risorgimento was a sore point for official Italy and its army.

Risorgimento as history and mythology

One of the first articles to discuss the censoring of *Senso* was aptly titled "The Fear of History."[28] All nations mythologize their past, particularly their birth and formation. Because Italian unification took place at a time of fairly advanced historiography, an outright distortion of events was needed to make possible a nationalistically respectable history of the birth of the Kingdom of Italy.[29]

In 1860, after Italian unification was more or less completed, the next target became the annexation of Venice, which at that stage was still part of the Austrian Empire. Negotiations with Prussia were started. Bismarck's aim was to guarantee Prussian hegemony in the German areas and keep Austria outside the German union that was to be formed in the near future. When the Austrians realized that they were caught between a hammer and an anvil, they offered to cede Venice in exchange for neutrality.[30]

But the Italians wanted to win Venice by military means. Statesman Francesco Crispi delivered a speech in Parliament and received a tremendous ovation when he demanded that the new born kingdom be baptized in blood. General Nino Bixio, a member of Parliament at that time, assured the nation that its army was splendid, the navy incontestably superior, and Italian commanders the envy of Europe. He also stated that it would be better to have 100,000 men die in battle than to see Venice won by peaceful cession.[31] A few days after the declaration of war, however, a battle was fought near Custoza in which the Austrians, despite being outnumbered, routed the Italian advance forces. Italian casualties were relatively small, but the military leadership was unable to take control of the situation and the Italian offensive ended in panic and retreat. Subsequent Italian maneuvers were also poorly conducted, and the war was brought to a conclusion with an overwhelming victory by the Prussians at Sadowa.[32]

Giuseppe Garibaldi, an ardent patriot acting independently, had gathered an army and was prepared to march to Venice, but the king and the army kept them in the south. Even after the decisive battles were fought, the patriots were sent to a remote sector of South Tyrol, whence they advanced slowly to the gates of Trentino. Most of these areas were returned to Austria in the peace negotiations. But what angered Garibaldi even more was that the Venetians had done precious little to liberate themselves. In certain areas they had even fought against their "countrymen."[33]

In the peace negotiations, Austria agreed to cede Venice to France, which would then hand it over to Italy. The idea of Venice being treated as a gift from France was obviously humiliating for the Italians, especially because they could not really explain away their losses as heroic defeats, as the press had already suggested.[34] But the embarrassment was soon forgotten, and the war for Venice became part of Risorgimento mythology and official rhetoric. Historians tried to put the best face on things, for example, by playing down the disastrous role the king had played at Custoza.[35] People were certainly not unaware of Italy's humiliating and unnecessary defeats, but it was just something that could not be openly discussed.

The version of events that thus emerged was not allowed to be questioned as it would have shaken the very foundations of the nation. The Risorgimento had not been the kind of social revolution to forge a new nation. For most Italians, it was just another chapter in history. Nor was it given much scholarly attention until Antonio Gramschi, during his imprisonment in the Fascist years, started rewriting Italian history. Gramschi's main conclusion was that the Risorgimento was not a true people's revolution, and that the rhetoric about unification being a result of the will and activity of the people was simply untrue. In many provinces the people actually resisted being subjected to the Piedmontese king; the only groups really interested in the unification were the industrialists and the intellectuals, who for once had found a common interest.[36]

Gramschi's ideas took root after the Fascist period, when Italians felt a great need to affirm their national identity and to settle their accounts with the past. One result of the ensuing debate was twelve films, made in 1949–54, in which the Risorgimento featured in one way or another. Most of them garnered little attention. Visconti's *Senso* was an exception. The director himself told of the difficulties his film encountered with the officials:

The historical aspect was my original guideline. I even wanted to name it *Custoza* in accordance with the major Italian defeat. But there was an uproar: Lux, the Ministry [of Defense], the censors. . . . The battle was originally supposed to be much more important. My idea was to create an overall picture of Italian history from which the individual story of Livia Serpieri arises, a Countess, who is basically just a representative of a certain class. What interested me was to tell a story about a mismanaged war, fought by a single class and ending in a disaster.[37]

Although many of the scenes that were related to historical events had actually been dropped in the script stage, the result was nevertheless political dynamite. The political Right (Christian Democrats and the like) accused Visconti of stirring up the dustbins of history, while the leftist critics (but not the Communist party) complained bitterly once again about what they considered betrayal of neorealism. And the army was greatly offended to see its defeats, even if almost a century old, on public display. Perhaps the military also felt that some of th' events Visconti depicted had a connection with more recent events.[38]

When fighting broke out in Italy toward the end of the Second World War, the Allies refused to have any official dealings with the partisans. Instead, they negotiated an agreement with the High Command of the Italian armed forces. This protected the military – which had little to show in the way of successful action or political integrity – from having to face postwar trials. Not only was the resistance movement ignored, "official Italy" had once again changed its allegiance at an opportune moment.

Although anti-fascist values were incorporated in official rhetoric at the end of the war, the partisan movement had as much difficulty gaining political recognition, despite its role in the liberation of Italy, as had Garibaldi and his men, despite their role in the overthrow of the Bourbon regime in the south of Italy in 1860 and in the battle for Venice. Many civil servants of the Fascist period continued in office as if nothing had happened. The Anti-Fascist Sanction Committee was soon disbanded and its tasks transferred to ordinary courts chaired by the same men as in the Fascist period.[39] Although the Communist party had participated in the Committee of National Liberation and in the cabinet after the fall of Fascism, party cooperation came to an end after the 1948 election, when Christian Democratic Prime Minister De Gaspieri formed a new cabinet without including Communists or Socialists. The entire Left felt it had been betrayed. Its members had fought against Fascism and helped establish the republic, but now the fruits of their victories were taken from their hands.[40]

Yet some would say that simple comparisons should not be drawn between the Risorgimento and the Resistance. Some leftist intellectuals, for example, see the liberation in large part as a people's revolution. In Guido Aristarco's opinion, too, there is an essential difference between the two events:

While the Risorgimento was a movement of the elite, the partisan movement was a genuine people's movement, which is something quite different. The partisans came from all parties, including the Christian Democrats. The Risorgimento never had such popular support. It is a part of a certain rhetoric to claim that the partisans were a second Risorgimento movement.[41]

Where the two are similar is that in both cases Italy lost the opportunity to change social structures because the ruling class or party was primarily interested in securing its own economic and political power. And in both cases the government and the armed forces, despite their conceit and arrogance, had succeeded only in further destroying the country while winning hollow and undeserved political victories.

Suso Cecchi d'Amico, when asked whether she and Visconti conceived their film as a comment on the political situation in the late war and postwar years, stated: "I don't think so. . . . We really thought about the story itself."[42] Whatever the filmmakers' intention, the military was not prepared to accept that kind of criticism, at least not from a communist celebrity. In the final version of the script for *Senso*, there is a scene in which Ussoni offers the army the help of the volunteers he has recruited. He reminds an officer that all Italians have been summoned to amass a collective effort for the fatherland. The officer, however, claims that experience has shown volunteers to be of little use to the regular army. Bitterly disappointed, Ussoni replies that the entire army, from General

Lamarmora on down, are nervous about volunteers and simply want to keep them out of battle.[43]

Before the release of *Senso*, apparently some officials who had seen a prescreening requested certain changes in the dialogue, and Visconti had agreed. But after the premiere the army demanded that the entire scene be deleted. Lux Film did as it was told. It also agreed to certain changes demanded by the Office of Censorship before distribution copies were made. Then the censors suddenly demanded up to twenty more cuts. At this point, Lux Film, fearing that the commercial viability of the film was in jeopardy, protested. After a long battle, the number of cuts was reduced to four, which were then made separately to each distribution copy. The cuts were short, sometimes just a line such as Livia's "Oh Franz, I beg you to stay" in the scene at Aldeno, and Franz's ironical "She [Livia] is an Italian aristocrat" at his lodgings in Verona. It is difficult to understand the point of all these cuts. As Visconti stated: "Why cut half of a love scene and leave the rest? Why delete just a certain number of kisses?"[44]

Because part of the censoring took place at this late stage, at least some of the cuts could eventually be restored to most copies once the uproar subsided – in fact, some copies were left intact. But most of the earlier cuts are probably lost forever. In addition to the scene with Ussoni and the officer, the most important loss is probably the first half of the scene in which Livia walks through the streets of Venice searching for Franz. She becomes aware that Italy is preparing for war and the effect of this on people's lives as she sees newspaper headlines blaring the news and people being evacuated. The scene would have emphasized Livia's betrayal of her ideals and made the connections with the political events much stronger. Another scene that is still missing from many copies of the film is the one in which the count goes to the granary before leaving with the laborers to help put out the fire, as well as the scene in which Luca, one of Ussoni's trusted men, comes to Livia to collect the money left to Livia's safekeeping.[45]

Melodrama as criticism of history

What did Lux Film expect? Visconti's political leanings were publicly known and his ability to represent them by cinematic means had been made obvious in his two first films. Apparently the company wanted a spectacle that would be easy to market and that could win a critically favorable response, combining the grandeur of a star-studded Hollywood-style spectacle with the prestige of an art film director. The melodramatic topic was probably thought to be politically neutral, and as the script was processed stage by stage it might have appeared that Visconti was willing to concentrate on the love story. What was not understood was that Visconti was going to use melodrama as a metaphor for a radical re-interpretation of history and the historical background to put the melo-dramatic gestures into critical perspective. Perhaps this simply could not be foreseen. Visconti's irony is less apparent in the plot than in its au-diovisual realization. In particular, by moving away from the literary first-person narration to a more objective narration typical of what is considered to be realistic style in cinema inevitably resulted in a drastic rethinking of Livia's motivations, and in a major change in the balance between the four main characters in the film, who act as foils to one another in the subtle interplay of irony and melodrama.[46]

A clue to the narrative strategy is already provided in the opening credits. The third act of Verdi's *Il trovatore* is just about to reach its conclusion at La Venice theater in Venice. Writing appears on the screen explaining the time, place, and political situation.[47] The performance has reached the point where the tenor hero, Manrico, has decided to attack his enemies. As if to spur his men to battle, he sings the rousing aria "Di quella pira." He advances toward the audience, and the camera turns to reveal the spectators for the first time. Manrico's aria is clearly a message also to the audience. On one level the tenor playing Manrico obviously wants to win over his audience, but he is also evoking the nationalistic sentiments of his compatriots. As his men join in the call "All 'armi!" (to arms), we see men mingling among the audience who in their dark tail-coats can be clearly distinguished from the Austrian soldiers in their white cloaks. As the performance ends, the audience explodes into applause and patriots on the balcony begin to shout their slogans. Suddenly the air is filled with green, white, and red propaganda leaflets and bouquets of flowers in the same colors.

The scene has a definite basis in history in that opera houses were the most important sites of demonstrations in many of the peninsula's eight states before the unification. Foreign rulers were often unable to curb bursts of nationalistic sentiment in performances of the inspiring works of composers such as Verdi. Even his name became a slogan of the royalist supporters of the unification: *V*ittorio *E*mmanuel, *R*e *D*i *I*talia (Victor Em-manuel, the king of Italy). Right from its premiere, *Il trovatore* became one of Verdi's most popular operas despite its confused libretto. Regard-ing its contradictions, Vincent Godefroy has aptly commented:

But a sort of obscurity does pervade this opera, partly because it seems to be historical yet it is not the history we are taught at school; and partly because in its clash between a just establishment and a selfish rebellion law and order are represented by the baritone villain, while the heroic tenor is on the side of the trouble makers. So we get a topsy-turvy picture of events; our loyalties are misdirected; our comprehension misled.[48]

The protagonists of *Senso* appear to be as confused about the historical situation as the passionate characters of *Il trovatore*. But the point is not simply that they are presented as melodramatic heroes in conflict with reality. The world of opera and of *Il trovatore* in particular soon become parts of the web of metaphors through which the political and the social upheaval is depicted.

As the performance of the opera resumes, it turns out that Ussoni has ended up in jail – just like Manrico at the beginning of Act 4 of the opera. Thus the counterpart of the heroic tenor in this film is not Franz, the comely lover, but this hotheaded idealist. Now he has got himself into trouble because he recklessly challenged Franz to a duel after hearing his comment about Italians: "This is the kind of war that suits the Italians; showers of confetti to the sound of mandolins." As a leader of the patriots, Ussoni has no business exposing himself to the enemy. As Millicent Marcus has pointed out, the event "represents in a germinal form, the military future of the entire story: Franz will flee combat later on while Ussoni will seek out battle against all military-bureaucratic odds."[49] Later on, Ussoni's heroics on the battlefield of Custoza prove to be as Manrico-like as his opening folly. The fact that *Il trovatore* helped boost nationalistic sentiment in Italy before the Risorgimento gives the irony yet a further twist.[50]

Livia and Franz first meet after the performance has finally resumed; on stage, Manrico's beloved Leonora is singing in front of the jail where Manrico is awaiting execution. For a moment, Livia, Franz, and Leonora are seen through a mirror, the frame of which disappears beyond the frame of the screen as the camera tracks forward. The relative positions of the three are thus reversed, and stage and reality briefly appear to change places.

Livia says she likes opera, "but not when it takes place outside the stage, or when people behave like the heroes of a melodrama, without thinking of the consequences." It sounds as if she is criticizing Franz, but the description would obviously suit her cousin Ussoni much better. As the story progresses, it turns out that she might as well have been talking about herself. This is hinted at by presenting Leonora's love for Manrico as a metaphor for Livia's feelings for Ussoni: the two women are paralleled both by juxtaposition within two shots and a cut from Livia to Leonora just as Franz has mentioned Ussoni's arrest at the very moment when Leonora is singing about her feelings for the imprisoned Manrico.[51] But the real irony lies in the fact that she is unable to live up to the standards set by the romantic heroine. She soon forgets about her Manrico as she becomes irresistibly charmed by Franz. This implies that she is forsaking her public allegiances for private concerns.

Livia is then seen saying farewell to Ussoni, who is being carried into exile. As she leaves, Franz follows her. She makes weak attempts to get rid of him, but they happen to discover the body of an Austrian soldier. Just then a group of Austrian soldiers appear, and Franz is able to act as Livia's protector by hiding her from his countrymen. Thus instead of serving as a reminder of the political situation that should separate them, the event serves to bring them closer together.

Livia still tries to resist, but as they walk through the Venetian night she gradually yields to temptation. She suddenly mentions that Ussoni was not her lover. Franz might well be aware of this, but right from the beginning almost everything they say to each other has a different function from what their words suggest. Franz quotes Heine: "Tis the judgement day/ the dead rise to eternal joy, or to eternal pain./ We still embrace, heedless of all, both Paradise and Hell." But whereas Livia really lives, feels, and behaves in accordance with melodramatic models, Franz's references to the romantic sentiments of Heine are hardly more than part of his seduction strategy. He lives for the pleasure of the moment.

Before long Livia and Franz are seen together in a rented room. The scene charts the perpetual game between the wish to possess the other and the need to maintain one's independence, which is a feature of most intense human relationships. A part of the pattern is that Livia's words constantly contradict her innermost wishes about the need to terminate their affair. Franz knows Livia's needs better than she herself and is not impressed by such talk. Their relationship is very similar to that of Giovanna and Gino in *Ossessione* in that it shows the weaving of a web of betrayals and self-deceptions. What Livia – like so many of Visconti's characters – would really like to do is to step outside time, history, and all of life's responsibilities. She says: "If I was told: 'You have only this moment, no tomorrow' I would feel as if a doctor had told me: 'You are about to die, you've got only a few more hours to live.' I know it is true. We have only this moment, no tomorrow."[52] In other words, she would like to be like an operatic heroine singing an aria, separating herself from all action and the external world in order to concentrate on her feelings.

Livia is given precious few moments of this kind. Ussoni has scarcely been turned out of Venice when her affair with Franz begins. And this affair does not last long either. After not hearing from him for a few days, she goes out to the streets of Venice to find him. She fails. Finally, having returned home in a state of exhaustion, she receives an anonymous message "from a young man" telling her to come to a certain place. In her excitement she tells her chambermaid she intends to leave her husband and rushes to the meeting place – with Count Serpieri following her and catching her just as she knocks on the door of the meeting place. Livia confesses her adultery and swears she will leave Serpieri for her lover. The door opens, and the film reaches its first ironic climax, for it turns out that the message has come from Ussoni, who has secretly returned from exile. Serpieri thinks Livia has simply tried to protect the patriots, and perceiving an opportunity begins to negotiate with them in order to secure his position in case the Italians should win. Thanks to the misunderstanding, Livia's multiple betrayal is not exposed, and a large sum of money that the patriots have collected for their cause is left in her safekeeping. Together with her husband, she moves to their country mansion in Aldeno.

She thinks she has recovered from her feelings when Franz suddenly appears and successfully rekindles her love. His aim, however, is to obtain money from her in order to bribe a doctor to forge a certificate that would relieve him of military duty. Fully conscious of the extent of her betrayal, Livia hands the patriots' money over to Franz. Later on, as the fortunes of war appear to separate them, she abandons her husband, her friends, and her status in society and goes to Verona to be with Franz. She finds a dirty, drunken man who has lost all his self-respect, accompanied by a pretty young prostitute, Clara. The scene creates vivid contrasts with many earlier ones in the film. For example, Franz tearing the veil from Livia's face is in contrast to an early scene of them together in which he gently lifts her veil. Franz tying the laces of Clara's corset recalls an earlier scene in which he tied Livia's corset in their love nest. Also, Livia's black dress is contrasted with Clara's white negligée. After a cruel settling of accounts, Livia goes to the Austrian headquarters and denounces Franz – the very opposite of what the self-sacrificing Leonora does at the end of *Il trovatore*. Franz is immediately arrested and executed. Livia is left in the streets crying his name.

The most immediate effect of audiovisualizing any first-person literary narration is that it opens up all the characters so audiences can see and assess them for themselves. The expressions on Farley Granger's face have a particularly important function, not just in rounding out his character but also in conveying the themes of the film. Nor can Livia find refuge behind her narration and control the audience's impression of her. The change is further emphasized by the fact that Alida Valli's appearance and performance depict a totally different kind of person from that in the novella. She looks much older than her twenty-two-year-old literary counterpart. She is still beautiful, but being married to a somewhat less than charming opportunist she has little hope of romance in her life. Thus her romantic aspirations easily gain at least some sympathy from the spectator. This is enhanced by her voice-over, which for its part directs the audience to identify with her. As Livia's actions become increasingly questionable, the voice-overs gradually disappear.

In the film, Livia's love affair is put into perspective by her siding with the patriots at the beginning of the film. Her betrayal of their cause sets the tone of her story and creates the major metaphor of the historical interpretation that is being put forward. Her betrayal of their cause is at first "only" metaphorical – she falls in love with an enemy soldier, who has just had a confrontation with a patriot, the previous object of her admiration. This leads her along a path of lies, which ends up in the literal betrayal of the patriots when she hands their money over to her new lover.

The way many of the scenes have been shot gives further ironic emphasis to the game of betrayals the protagonists play. *Senso* does not have many shot/reverse-shot sequences. During the most important dialogues, the interlocutors are seen together in most of the shots. Often they do not face each other but instead offer the audience a privileged view of their facial expressions. Above all, in the Aldeno scene Franz's face reveals his true feelings to the spectator as he gradually coaxes Livia to give him the money. As he speaks, he does not look at Livia; at most, he glances at her to check whether his words are having the desired effect. As he finally elicits from her the suggestion of bribing a doctor, Franz asks: "Do you think I could do something so despicable?"[53] The spectator almost expects Livia to answer: "Yes." The expression on Franz's face suggests that he might well accept this as the right answer.

The way Visconti tells this story reflects both a genuinely sympathetic and a severely critical view of the protagonists and is undoubtedly connected with his background as a marxist of aristocratic descent. He had a unique ability to present as understandable and lovable even those characters whose selfishness, betrayal, and exploitation of others are the tar-

gets of his criticism. Livia and Franz's betrayals are paralleled by the
revelation that the values they are supposed to be fighting for – national
pride, military glory – turn out to be false. All this cynicism is complemented by the story's audiovisual features. On one level, the reconstruction of a historical era serves as an excuse to revel in the sheer beauty of
the images, the glowing colors, and the gorgeous music, all of which are
tightly integrated into the overall discourse. Youssef Ishaghpour has suggested that for Visconti, color is "a way of creating a different world and
revealing its 'flavour,' its internal tonality."[54]

The music in the film, extracts from the first and second movements
of Bruckner's Seventh Symphony, emphasizes Livia's feelings. The opening of the symphony is heard as she walks through the Venice night with
Franz hot on her heels. The theme on the French horn, rising from a
string tremolo, leads to the main theme of the symphony, a warm, broad
melody on the cellos, sensuous and full of longing. The same extract is
heard at the end of the Venice sequence, as a gently ironic comment on
Livia's romance as Ussoni says: "We have no rights, Livia, only duties.
We have to forget ourselves, Livia. I do not hesitate to sound pompous,
as Italy is at war. It is our war, our revolution."[55]

First when Livia decides to leave her husband and again when she
decides to forget about the patriots – at the end of the Venice and the
Aldeno sequences – a dramatic passage from the development section of
the first movement can be heard, starting with the inversion of the opening bars and leading to a turbulent treatment of the material of the main
theme. In the Venice scene, as she and the count enter the patriots' hiding
place, the music dies out completely. Her feelings, too, have died – or so
she thinks. Other extracts from the first movement of the symphony are
also heard in scenes in which Livia is alone with her feelings. After she
leaves Aldeno for good and travels in her closed carriage through the
military lines, a series of short extracts is heard, which could be interpreted as an expression of her state of mind – although the fragmentation
might just be a consequence of the extensive cutting the film suffered.

The extracts from the second movement of Bruckner's symphony are
connected almost exclusively with the moments that Livia and Franz have
together. The first is heard in the "night in Venice" scene, after they have
escaped being noticed by the Austrian guards. The conflict between the
nobility of the music and the depraved motives of the protagonists is one
of the major structural components of the film. The music brings out
Livia's feelings and helps the viewer identify with her romantic longing.
The tension between the nobility and the degradation reaches its peak in

the scene in Aldeno. One night Franz suddenly appears in Livia's bedroom and gradually starts seducing her again. The gently caressing music, together with the romantic setting, evokes feelings that for Livia appear to offer a genuine alternative to the decency of her marriage as well as to her now emotionally irrelevant allegiance to the patriots. Gradually the music moves through each succeeding extract toward the tremendous climax of the movement. It explodes at the moment when Livia finally decides to give the patriots' money to Franz. The same extract is heard again during the closing titles, just after Franz has been shot.

Visconti's style has often been characterized as "operatic" or "melodramatic," often using the words loosely, without much consideration of what is actually at issue. In almost all of Visconti's films, at least some of the characters indulge in melodramatic gestures with which the audience is, to a degree, invited to identify. At the same time, the characters are illuminated by the floodlights of irony and thereby shown in the clear perspective of the given historical and social situation. In *Senso*, the carefully composed color scheme and the music create an atmosphere of sensuality and emotion that gives credence both to Livia's private and to Ussoni's public aspirations. Yet these melodramatic features are kept in check by the sense of detachment created by the camera work – there are only a very few point-of-view shots and no actual close-ups – and above all by the antiromantic story line with all its ironic twists. The tension between the haunting visual beauty and the sordid story is a part of the strategy, which turns a plot involving a few characters into a metaphor for certain historical events. In this way, Livia and Ussoni's aspirations are made to appear intensely utopian and deceptive.

Just how blatant Livia's self-deception is becomes apparent when Franz coaxes her to give him the money he needs to bribe a doctor. The expressions on his face, seen by the audience but not by Livia, put the melodrama in a farcical light. The farce almost overcomes the melodrama after Livia decides to give him the patriots' money. As Franz crawls on the floor near Livia's feet to collect coins and jewels dropped from the box, he babbles: "Oh my poor, desperate beloved, treasure, treasure, poor treasure." Livia's anxiety, however, prevents the scene from dissolving completely into farce.

Melodrama and irony as aesthetic categories are often seen as polar opposites. As Zdzislaw Najder has put it, "While melodrama blows up, irony deflates."[56] Albert Bermel makes a similar distinction: In a tragedy the protagonist consciously or unconsciously wills and causes his own destruction whereas in melodrama his downfall is caused by an antagonist. The difference between melodrama and farce is that in the latter the disparity between a character and his or her surroundings is laughable, whereas in the former it is distressing. Shifts from one mode to the other may easily occur both intentionally and inadvertently.[57]

Visconti's mastery, particularly in *Senso*, lies in his ability to modulate constantly between these different tones, to superimpose irony and melodrama so that neither is overwhelmed by the other. In a sense, this can be seen as the joint influence of Verdi and Chekhov, the Verdi-inspired melodrama being constantly constrained by refined Chekhovian irony. Chekhov, too, moves adroitly between melodrama and farce. When Voinitsky, at the end of the third act of *Uncle Vanya*, tries to shoot Serebriakov, his melodramatic gesture almost dissolves into farce when he shouts "Bang" upon pulling the trigger and pathetically misses his target. Yet the sincerity of his desperation prevents the farcical aspect from taking over entirely.[58] In *Senso*, Livia behaves like the heroine of a melodrama, which leads her to be the dupe in a farce until she finally becomes the agent of Franz's and finally of her own tragic destruction. Meanwhile Ussoni's heroism is denied the dignity of tragedy and is reduced to pointless and silly farce on the battlefield at Custoza. As in the Chekhov example, their melodramatic desperation prevents the irony from turning into cruelty. The result is what could be referred to as *melodramatic realism*, a mode of presentation that gives full credence to the feelings and passions of the characters, allowing the viewer to identify with the character while keeping the intellectual, the critical mode in constant operation.

Youssef Ishaghpour has pointed out that the inherent tensions in the style of representation in *Senso* grow from the opposition of opera and novel, both as related to history:

Opera appears in it clearly as a superstructure; it is the imaginary of a prosaic life which it reveals and enveils at the same time. The relationship between that life and the imaginary, the auditorium and the stage, history and its ideological vision, makes opera something quite different from a slightly picturesque overture or a place for political manifestations.[59]

Ishaghpour sees nineteenth-century opera as a bourgeois art form, which in the last instance is denied by history guided by bourgeois revolutions. Opera gave fire to a development that made that fire appear illusory. As the century wore on, the chasm between "ideology and reality, magic and disenchantment" grew ever wider, a development that was to an extent recorded in the great European realist novels.

All in all, the opposition between melodrama and realism is used as a "creative potential" to produce a cinematic answer to the hermeneutical problem of reconstituting the temporal horizons of a past era in a way that will be accessible and meaningful in terms of our own temporal horizon and sensibilities. The meaning of the battle scene in the film – as it exists – can also be appreciated from this point of view. Its "novelistic" attention to detail, the setting, and action hardly carry the plot forward but they do provide a spectacle in which idealism in the public sphere taken into melodramatic extremes clashes violently with the reality of death, disaster, and defeat.[60] It is immediately followed by a similar conflict in the private sphere as the meeting of Livia and Franz demonstrates the emptiness of both emotional and hedonistic egocentrism, of intellectual dishonesty and cynicism, which either knowingly or through self-deception negate all communal values. All this amounts to a refutation of the world of opera in the most lovingly operatic manner conceivable.

In contrast to Ussoni's idealism, Franz's cynicism allows him to see beyond the official values of his class and society, to criticize the *realpolitik* of nation-states, and to see with clarity the human suffering they cause. It also helps him to see beyond romantic illusions. He is prepared to exploit those myths, but he sinks into total nihilism and is destroyed from two quarters. When we first meet Franz, he is convinced that living for one's own pleasures is the right thing for a man of his charms to do. At the end of the film, having relinquished the code of honor of his class and rank and having prostituted himself, he has lost both his social standing and his self-respect as a man. Unlike Livia, he is unable to hide his degradation from himself. During his last hours, however, Franz at least appears to understand the entire historical situation. He points out to Livia that the victory of his countrymen at Custoza is futile as "they will lose the war anyway. And not only the war. In a few years, the whole of Austria will come to an end. And an entire world will disappear, the one in which you and I belong."[61]

In their different ways, both Franz and Livia have attempted to step outside history and to blind themselves morally, either by decision or deception, to the way they exploit other people in dedicating themselves to hedonism on his part, to romantic fantasies on hers. Paradoxically, this shameless pursuit of self-interest epitomizes the very nature of the historical events inexorably moving along in the background. On the strength of this metaphorical tension, the film transcends both the historical context it depicts and that of its making and opens the possibility of viewing it from ever new horizons of expectation.

Ussoni is in many ways Franz's counterpart in this pattern. In his romantic idealism and national sentiment, he represents a rising tide in European history, the final stage of the formation of the nation-states before the First World War. But the raging war is about a much more acute struggle for power and economic interests. Ussoni's energy could well serve as a driving force on one side or the other in this conflict, were it not for his blind idealism, which leaves him without powerful allies. Much like Livia, he finds his actions pathetically at variance with the factors that ultimately govern the situation.

Thus the only one who survives the historical events unscathed is Count Serpieri. In the beginning, he is seen courting the favor of the Austrian rulers; evidently he is a respected member of the establishment. When Livia accidentally leads him to the patriots, he has a new chance to reveal his true nature. In blatantly opportunist fashion, he starts to negotiate a deal with Ussoni should Venice actually become part of Italy. It is left to the spectator to rely on his or her knowledge of history to grasp the full irony of the setting: Irrespective of the efforts of the idealists, a new Italy will be formed for the benefit of opportunists such as Serpieri. Like the politicians of his country, he intends to sit on the fence until the winner emerges. Interestingly enough, though he is a crucial figure from the point of view of the historical interpretation put forward in the film, his role is fairly small – Visconti was always more interested in the vanquished than in the victors.[62]

The juxtaposition of the two melodramatic characters, Livia and Ussoni, reveals that the great flourish and the grand gestures with which the Risorgimento was conducted were a mere veil over the avarice of people like Serpieri and the vanity of the military. It is a way of articulating by cinematic means Gramschi's view that the Risorgimento was a takeover by an elite, not by the people. In the scene behind the lines during the battle, peasants are seen working despite the military maneuvers taking place around them. According to Guido Aristarco, this small detail is extremely significant: "Politics of power continue but it doesn't bother them. It is as if they were saying: 'You do what you want, gentlemen; it does not concern us. It is not our war.' "[63]

Guido Aristarco was one of Senso's most ardent supporters in the debate in which Visconti was accused of betraying neorealism. The story was not taken from contemporary reality, and the film was audiovisually splendid, particularly in comparison with neorealist films. Leftist intellectuals still associated historical themes and operatic mannerisms with Fascist cinema, something that neorealism had expressly sought to counter. Aristarco argued that *Senso* was an instance of neorealism developing into realism, with surfaces deepening into analysis. But he was unable to convince the most vocal critics of this view, especially Césare Zavattini and Luigi Chiarini. The former claimed that only contemporary and socially relevant subjects could educate the public and stir its political consciousness. The latter thought that an excessive cinematic style would drown out any political or moral message a film might be conveying.[64] There is a degree of moralism in these arguments: faith in asceticism as a prerequisite of fidelity to reality. But *Senso*, which is really a merciless critique of melodramatic gestures, is effective precisely because the spectator, too, gets to share the lure of feelings and sensations.

THE LEOPARD

Reassessing the Risorgimento

Despite the enthusiasm for unification in certain quarters, it was not easy to achieve a political and social union of the eight, highly diverse states of the Italian peninsula. Their stages of social development varied from the fairly advanced north to the basically feudal Bourbon government of the Kingdom of the Two Sicilies. Territorial claims, as well as the complexity of ethnic backgrounds, gave rise to endless debates about which areas belonged to a unified Italy. There were also disputes and prejudices among the parochial-minded provinces.[65]

Most of northern Italy joined the Piedmontese Kingdom in 1860 as a result of the insurrections sparked by the war between France and Austria the previous year. The decisive events leading to complete unification began when Giuseppe Garibaldi, with some thousand men known as the Redshirts, landed in Sicily in 1860. Though humble, perhaps even quite simple, this charismatic man was able to raise an army that during its brief existence was almost invincible. Garibaldi's fiery spirit might have led to permanent results had the Piedmontese prime minister, Count Camille Cavour, not forged these republican victories into royalist conquests. Using an uprising that he himself had engineered as an excuse, Cavour conquered the Papal state with the exception of Rome and its immediate vicinity. The annexation was confirmed by a referendum, the result of which was 99 percent approval of a "unified and undivided Italy." Roughly the same pattern was repeated elsewhere in the peninsula. The election results were ensured by suppressing the press behind the opposition and by using election functionaries who had sworn an oath of loyalty to the king and who did not even pretend to be impartial. In the face of a civil war, Garibaldi handed his victories over to the king of Piedmonte. This gave many revolutionaries and republicans an excuse to switch to the royalist side.[66]

For the royalists, who formed "official Italy," Garibaldi now became a mere nuisance. By the end of the unification process, his achievements were more or less denied. Former enemies such as the Neapolitan royalists were treated better than Garibaldi's volunteers, whose successes had been an embarrassment to the Piedmontese generals. Soon the main function of the army was to quell internal unrest, and in this respect the Neapolitan henchmen had better credentials than Garibaldi's troops. By the time the situation was finally brought under some control in 1865, more soldiers had died in this turmoil or as a result of disease than in the actual war for unification.[67]

Risorgimento did not result in any significant social change. Whereas the old society had been governed by the aristocracy, they were now equaled by the *haute-bourgeois* enriched by industrialization. The most important classes of the new state were the big landowners – increasingly the bourgeois – and the more senior civil servants. Although some of the most glorious victories of the Risorgimento had been won by peasant folk rebelling against the landowners, the new political situation was solidified by securing the power of the landowners. In the south, poverty was as rampant as ever and eroded the sense of national unity just as it had done during the Bourbon regime.[68] In fact, even at the beginning of the 1960s – indeed, even today – the division between the north and the south was still as deep as it had been at the time of the Risorgimento. Sicily's land reform of the 1950s had failed, and more and more people were moving from rural areas to the cities, from the south to the north, and from Italy to other countries. All this created ever new social problems.[69]

Whatever the past or the current problems might have been, Roberto Rossellini was commissioned to make a film celebrating the first centenary of the Risorgimento. And so, though *Viva l'Italia* (1960) contains some elements criticizing the way the conquest of Sicily turned out, political controversies are tactfully sidestepped by mythologizing Garibaldi, presenting him almost as a Christ-like figure. He hands out bread on a mountain, he displays endless understanding and mercy, the peasants venerate him. Instead of questioning or deconstructing these features, the narration keeps a respectful distance from him.[70]

In turn, Visconti's *The Leopard* can be seen both as a criticism of the official view of the Risorgimento and perhaps also of Rossellini's film. The actual starting point, however, was the novel by Giuseppe Tomaso, the duke of Palma and prince of Lampedusa, an amateur historian with a special interest in the Risorgimento. Before writing his novel, Tomaso di Lampedusa had spent years collecting material, going through archives and interviewing people who had known his grandfather, Giulio. He was to serve as the model for the main character of the novel, don Fabrizio, the prince of Salina. The grandfather's nickname, *Il gattopardo* (The leopard), had come from the leopard in the Tomaso di Lampedusa coat of arms and thus was an apt name for the title character.[71]

The basic story line is remarkably simple in view of the richness of the themes that Tomaso di Lampedusa explores within its boundaries. As news of Garibaldi's landing reaches the house of Salina, the prince's nephew, Tancredi, leaves to join the rebels. Later the family moves to its summer residence in Donnafugata, where they are able to follow the turbulent events at a safe distance. One is reminded of the outside world mainly by the vote for an "undivided and unified Italy" and the appearance of a certain Chevalley, who comes to ask the prince to join the new Senate in Turin – he flatly refuses.

In Donnafugata, Tancredi meets the beautiful Angelica, daughter of the *nouveau riche* don Calogero. They appear to be a perfect match, not only because of their personal charm but also because they complement each other's social and economic aspirations – all which is of little consolation to the prince's daughter, Concetta, who has always been in love with her comely cousin. Eventually the family returns to Palermo and attends a grand ball at which signs of the social change that is taking place are already apparent. The penultimate chapter describes don Fabrizio's death in 1883, which is about twenty years after the ball. In the last chapter, which takes place in 1910, his unmarried daughters burn an array of family relics. The widowed Angelica visits them and revives painful memories in the two spinsters. Her marriage to Tancredi has served its social function, but emotionally and physically it died long before Tancredi.

The manuscript was completed in 1956, but not a single publisher was interested in it. After Lampedusa's death, the manuscript ended up in the hands of Giorgio Bassani, who took it to Giangiacomo Feltrinelli, a rich, eccentric, and anarchistic publisher who was immediately taken by it. Still, no one thought it would achieve much success, and the first edition was limited to 3,000 copies. To the surprise of all concerned, it became Italy's all-time best-seller and was awarded the Strega prize for literature. Visconti was among the enthralled. He thought the novel complemented well what Verga, Pirandello, and De Roberto had written about Sicily at the time of the Risorgimento. He also admired Lampedusa's ability to interweave the inner life of his protagonists with the social milieu he was describing, something that in his view struck a good balance between Verga's folksy yet artful realism and Proust's sophisticated art of memory.[72]

Georg Lukács has noted that, by revealing the corruption of bourgeois realist novels often offer greater insight into social reality – and thus also a more effective weapon for marxism – than works that strictly observe the codes of socialist realism. Similarly, Tomaso di Lampedusa's personal view of the Sicilian aristocracy during the turmoil of the Risorgimento offered Visconti an opportunity to express his own marxist views with only slight adjustments. Although the result appears less cynical than *Senso*, the view it presents of the birth of the Italian nation is just as free of illusions. There were many who seriously doubted that Visconti would be able to adapt Tomaso di Lampedusa's intimate novel into a big budget spectacle. But in addition to its grandeur, the film was able to convey the humor, warmth, and insights that are not far from Tomaso di Lampedusa's novel.

For his historical films, Visconti chose topics with which he had some familiarity thanks to his aristocratic background. This is one of the reasons why his meticulous cinematic reconstructions of past eras have seldom been matched. In *The Leopard*, the marriage between the poor young aristocrat and the rich bourgeois girl parallels that of Visconti's own parents, the Duke of Modrone and the heiress of the Erba industrial fortune. The precision with which Visconti attended to the smallest detail on the set for *The Leopard* became legendary. For example, the shirts of Garibaldi's men were rinsed in tea, dried in the sun, and buried in the ground for some time to make them look appropriately worn. Carriages were discovered in funeral parlors and the stables of half-ruined palaces. Local people who played the Bourbon soldiers were taught to ride in the stiffly upright manner of the 1860s in the Kingdom of the Two Sicilies. The great ball sequence was shot in the Palazzo Gangi in Palermo, one of the town's few palaces in which relatives of the original owners still lived.[73]

Despite the grandeur of the project, Visconti for once succeeded in remaining within the budget he had been given. But while *The Leopard* was still in the script stage, the budget of another film also produced by Titanus (Robert Aldrich's *Sodom and Gomorrah*, 1963) had jumped from two to six million dollars. Consequently, American funds were needed for

Visconti's film. Although 20th Century Fox was interested, it demanded that the film be made in English and that the leading role be played by an international star. It eventually went to Burt Lancaster. In the end, Fox contributed two million dollars in exchange for the distribution rights.[74]

Even so, Visconti was very reluctant to accept English as the language of his film, and in the end it was decided that both an Italian and an English version would be made. However, 20th Century Fox made many changes to the latter version, mainly by cutting it from the original 205 minutes (cut eventually by Visconti himself to 185 minutes) to 161 minutes. Fox also scaled the film down from 70 mm to 35 mm and transposed it from a Technirama format shot on Eastman Color, and processed originally by Technicolor, to Fox's own CinemaScope system processed by their subsidiary De Luxe. All this resulted in a film of considerably inferior technical quality. In an open letter published in the *Times* of London and the *Sunday Times*, Visconti wrote: "[*The Leopard*] was in my view badly cut and dubbed with ill-chosen, unsuitable voices. . . . When I saw the film in New York I had difficulty following the plot. Moreover, the film has been processed as if it were a bright piece of Hollywoodiana. . . . It is now a work for which I acknowledge no paternity at all."[75] Fox announced that it was considering legal action against Visconti, "who seems intent on harming his own picture with statements which seem to damage the film."[76] The English-language version seemed unable to touch audiences in the United States. It was not until the film was rereleased in the subtitled Italian version twenty years later that it was greeted with almost unanimous praise.

In Europe *The Leopard* was fairly well received both by the public and the critics, although reactions on the political Left were mixed. Writers such as Mario Alicata, Guido Aristarco, and Pier Paolo Pasolini criticized the film for not suggesting a positive alternative to the Risorgimento history. However, the leader of the Communist party, Palmiro Togliatti, openly supported the film. In his opinion, *The Leopard* was a masterpiece, better than the original.

Stagnation and change

As an adaptation, *The Leopard* is almost the total opposite of *Senso* in that it is remarkably faithful to the original work, at least on the surface. The most obvious difference is that the last chapters of the book have been omitted and their major thematic concerns have been inserted into the dialogues and the imagery of the great ball sequence. Also, the basic approach is quite different. Whereas in *Senso* the key was the interplay of sympathy and irony, now it is the tension between tender nostalgia for a certain way of life and the bitterness in having to accept its inevitable loss. Although much of this is certainly present in the novel, the film intensifies it, especially the nostalgia, through a splendid historical reconstruction. Also the bitterness of the aging prince as he becomes increasingly aware of the price that has to be paid to extend the life of his moribund social class is further exacerbated when seen against this rich and sensuous background. The spectacle is thus balanced by elements that could be called Chekhovian: the relentless march of time and the stagnation of society; the shallowness of love and the arbitrariness of family relationships; life-promoting and destructive forces in a dialectical interplay.

The leitmotiv of Tomaso di Lampedusa's novel is expressed in words first uttered by Tancredi, the prince's beloved nephew: "If we want things to stay as they are, things will have to change." Echoed throughout the book as well as the film, and enhanced by long dialogues, particularly between the prince and Chevalley, a representative of the government of the new Italy, the statement gradually encompasses the condition of Sicily throughout its history. All attempts to change things merely start ever new cycles of opportunism. Men of the old regime, such as the prince, give way to men of the new age, such as don Calogero, who, in the prince's words, "are able to cover their private interests by public ideals." Their pursuit of personal fortune will at least keep the system going. But nothing will ever change because Sicilians do not really will it. Why should they change, the prince asks, since they are already perfect? Indeed, how can they change when "their vanity is stronger than their misery"?

The nature of the social change that does take place is made apparent by the fact that the lands the prince had to sell years ago are now in the possession of don Calogero. Thus part of the ancient Salina heritage is returned to the aristocrats in exchange for accepting the bourgeois into their company. The former have no alternative, and the latter are eager to overcome the inferiority complexes that have pestered them for centuries. The bourgeois do not want to destroy the aristocracy; they want to become like it. For the time being at least, don Calogero needs the prince of Salina to support him – as can be seen when don Fabrizio lifts him in the air and kisses him to seal their agreement concerning the marriage of Angelica and Tancredi.

On the political level, the next step for the aristocrats and the bourgeois is to band together in order to protect their interests by curbing
the forces unleashed by Garibaldi. He has to be stopped as soon as he
has done what had to be done: help overthrow the old regime. A member of Garibaldi's Redshirts at the beginning of the film, Tancredi later
appears in the uniform of the army of the Piedmontese king. He and
his comrade do not like to be reminded by the prince that just a little
earlier they were Redshirts. Now they denounce Garibaldi's men and
refer to them as a mob. This point is carried further when the prince,
strolling around in the ball sequence, hears a certain Colonel Pallavicino boasting that after the battle of Aspramonte Garibaldi thanked
him for helping him to see what an arrogant and cowardly lot his men
were. The Pallavicino scene has been expanded considerably from the
original to allow don Fabrizio to express his moral outrage. Furthermore, the very ending of the film is made bitter by the sound of a firing
squad: the men who actually started the process of unification are now
being executed. Don Calogero, Tancredi's future father-in-law, comments: "It's a good army, and they're serious. That's what's needed, for
Sicily. And now, there's no more to worry about."

The prince looks at all this as if from above – his hobby is, appropriately enough, astronomy. At times he appears to soar so high above all
the rest of the characters that they are almost reduced to puppets whose
main function in the film is to enhance his glory. No one, not even either
of the belligerent sides, questions his dignity and rights. He is allowed to
pass through roadblocks, for example, while ordinary mortals must stay
and wait.[77] The prestige the prince enjoys allows him to boss even the
family priest.[78] Thus it is easy for the prince to feel resigned and to let
things take their course. He will always be respected as a leopard, as
opposed to the bourgeois hyenas. He still represents what is felt to be the
best in Sicilian society.[79]

Yet the prince, too, has already entered on the path of compromise.
He knows all too well that Tancredi, whom he apparently loves more
than his own children, is poor and will have to marry into a rich bourgeois
family in order to maintain the standards expected of an aspiring young
aristocrat. The prince associates himself strongly with his nephew, a point
made right at the beginning as Tancredi – played by Alain Delon – is first
seen as a reflection in the mirror in front of which the prince is shaving.
This image gives notice of the metaphorical tension between the two men.
At the end of the film this scene is called up in another image of the prince

looking at himself in a mirror, now feeling old and alienated, and no longer discovering Tancredi's handsome face there.[80]

Although the prince sees Tancredi as his true successor, he also feels his nephew embodies the inevitability of change. He understands that Tancredi has done what a dashing young man of high ambition should do. Tancredi does not betray his ideals – he never really has any ideals to betray. He is always innocently loyal to himself, and that is a part of his charm, the charm that captivates even don Fabrizio.

The fact that Tancredi must marry below his own social class is presented not only as an economic and social necessity, but also as a biological one. There is some speculation in the film about aristocratic cousins marrying and begetting monkey-like progeny, while the sheer appeal of the new is represented in the beauty of Angelica, a rich bourgeois girl who becomes Tancredi's bride. And just in case the audience should fail to appreciate the looks of Claudia Cardinale, Angelica's first entrance is, as in the book, amply emphasized by the attention she draws to herself: the conversation is interrupted by an expression of wonder on the faces of the prince's family upon seeing her beauty, the intensity of the sequence of close-ups of their faces, and the gently caressing music. As with Livia in *Senso*, the audience is invited to sympathize with the young couple and the attraction they feel toward each other.

As the prince bids farewell to Chevalley, he compares himself and his race to leopards now being succeeded by hyenas. The point is made almost too obvious through the contrast between the handsome, dignified prince and Angelica's father, don Calogero, who, despite his shrewdness, acts like a silly little man. But there is a hyena-like aspect to Tancredi too, however outwardly charming he may appear. In the great ball sequence, Tancredi mentions in passing to Angelica and Concetta that the men who left the regular army to join Garibaldi are to be executed at sunrise – at which point there is an insert of dancing guests. Then Concetta reminds Tancredi that once he would not have talked like that. Her comment reflects her jealousy of Angelica, but then again, changes in Tancredi's relations to women are always in step with his political opinions. After some more bitter remarks, Concetta runs out and the young couple are left to enjoy each other's kisses. They join a chain of merry dancers.

The parallel between the prince and Tancredi, together with the fact that at least at the beginning of the film the prince still has sexual relations with women, suggests that had there been changes in the political scene in his youth he would have been as eager as Tancredi to exploit every interesting opportunity that life might possibly offer. The prince has succeeded in remaining a leopard partly because the historical situation has not offered him the opportunity or forced him to take sides in conflicts of loyalty. Besides, he knows only too well that being a leopard, in all its might and glory, is a costly business and that to create the necessary wealth when it can no longer be inherited requires moral compromise.

To make this point, Visconti glorifies the protagonists by having them played by beautiful actors, by focusing on the visual splendor of the palaces they inhabit, by backing this with Nino Rota's noble music, and then by counterbalancing all this with the sordid aspects of the political events that constantly loom in the background. In his novel, Tomaso di Lampedusa mentions several details that reflect the decrepit state of the Sicilian aristocracy. The way Visconti has chosen to visualize the book plays down this element, but he compensates for this loss by other means. At times the family appears to be posing in painterly and composed immobility, as if to imply the waning of the way of life they exemplify. Particularly during the mass at Donnafugata, as the camera tracks past the family members, covered by dust, it is as if they were merely a part of the decoration of the ancient church. Furthermore, the squalor of the lower classes is made apparent, if only in passing, as when Chevalley notices a poor, apparently famished mother with her child. The woman is sitting under a sign, "Viva il plebiscito" (Long live the plebiscite), a bitterly ironic reference to the meaninglessness of democratic gestures for those too low on the social scale to exploit changes in the political system.

Toward a novelistic cinema

The Leopard was a fairly easy book to adapt. Apart from a few remarks that reveal the true motivations of the characters, the narrator does not explore their inner life to any great depth. Nor are their outer appearances described in any detail. Therefore the actors, with their striking visual appearance and carefully executed performances, enhance rather than vie with the characterization in the novel. This holds true also for the settings, ranging from the battlefields to the palaces, which go far beyond what the book relates or suggests. Visconti uses to the full the cinema's capacity to be like the realistic novel as defined by Georg Lukács:

Since the novel portrays the "totality of objects," it must penetrate into the small details of everyday life, into the concrete time of the action; it must bring out what is specific to this time through the complex interaction of all these details.

Therefore the general historicity of the central collision, which constitutes the historical character of drama, does not suffice for the novel. It must be historically authentic in root and branch.[81]

Whereas Tomaso di Lampedusa does not provide many details about the settings of, say, the ball sequence, Visconti makes their realization a primary concern. He has accomplished this task with loving care, but as Youssef Ishaghpour has pointed out, there is nothing fetishistic or museological about Visconti's relationship to the objects that fill the places his characters inhabit.[82] In *The Leopard,* particularly in the ball and the battle scenes, the development of the story is almost completely replaced by thematic interest, and the setting becomes a kind of dramatic agent, the phenomenal form of a social structure in the process of a slow but inevitable transformation. It is left to the tactless don Calogero to comment on and draw attention to some of the more sumptuous details of the magnificent palace in which the ball takes place.

A realistic effect is once again created by the milieu as characters appear to exist and time to pass independently of the story's progression. There are a great many people in the prince's family and household whom we do not get to know but who appear to live their own lives somewhere in the background. They seem part of a much broader field of existence than is seen on the screen, and so it seems as if the film has been suspended between a mimetic plot (as understood by Paul Ricoeur) and a spectacular audiovisual reconstruction. The relative lack of action invites the spectator to assume a certain strategy of viewing: he or she is offered immediate sensuous experience, on the one hand, reflection on the other, with the two resonating rather than competing with each other.

In certain parts the adaptation has obviously been inspired by Marcel Proust's *Remembrance of Things Past.* The ball sequence, in particular, partly because of length and the kind of reflection it allows, is reminiscent of the parties Proust describes with such loving detail. In Tomaso di Lampedusa's book, the party chapter takes up about 28 pages out of a total 270 pages, while in the film the scene lasts about 46 minutes out of a total 185 minutes (which amounts to one-quarter of the film in the Italian version, and an even slightly larger fraction (40/154) in the American version).[83] But in Proust, as Gérard Genette has counted,

Guermantes: 525 pages for two and one-half years. But we must specify that this sequence itself contains very wide variations, since 80 pages tell about the Villeparis reception, which must last two or three hours; 110 pages tell about the dinner at the Duchesse de Guermantes's, lasting almost the same length of time;

and 65 pages tell about the Princess's soiree: in other words, almost half the sequence is for fewer than ten hours of fashionable gatherings.[84]

Proust uses the massive length of his work to cover a long period of time, not by narrating a great number of events but by describing certain events with extraordinary detail. Also, toward the end of the story the narration slows down as ellipses grow larger and short time spans are covered by ever longer scenes. Similarly, the leisurely manner in which Visconti's *The Leopard* evolves creates the feeling of epic sweep. The ball sequence begins, pointedly enough, with a dissolve from peasants working in a field. The little amount of story that there is in this long film evaporates almost completely as the characters wander around the palace. On the verbal level, there is a great deal of small talk, conversations about political events and musings about mortality, decadence, and degeneration. Most spirits are kept high, however, by the visual extravagance, the elegance of the music, the joy of dance.

About halfway through the ball there is a passage of almost 3 ½ minutes without any dialogue during which the prince walks around the palace and ends up alone in a library. There he sees a painting, defined in the novel as a copy of Greutze's *The Death of the Just Man*. He sees himself in the dying man and wonders whether his death will be like that in the painting. The sheets will be dirtier, but hopefully his daughters will be dressed more decently than the women in the picture. The dying tension between *eros* and *thanatos* is felt once more in him as Angelica and Tancredi enter and the young man asks casually: "Are you courting death?" As if responding to the pun, don Fabrizio turns his attention to Angelica and arouses the nephew's jealousy. But the prince indicates that there cannot be much competition on his side by reminding them to have the family tomb repaired.

The prince's thoughts about the painting, rendered in the novel through indirect quotation, are "dialogicized" in the film, in the conversation between the prince, Angelica, and Tancredi. Similarly many other reflections, sometimes the narrator's comments, sometimes the prince's thoughts, are inserted into the dialogue. Nevertheless, as Nowell-Smith has aptly pointed out:

The meaning is conveyed, not just by the words but by a permanent relationship between the man and his surroundings. There is no visual or rhetorical expressionism. Everything is real, but seen in a particular way, reflected through the consciousness of the Prince. Stylistically it is the perfect cinematic equivalent of Flaubert's *style indirect libre*.[85]

Thus, for example, the way Angelica and Tancredi are able to dismiss the idea of death suggests, in the narrator's words, that they are "unknowing actors set to play the parts of Juliet and Romeo by a director who had concealed the fact that tomb and poison were already in the script."[86] In the grander design, the eroticism incarnated in the young couple is subtly conditioned and constricted by the political and economic expediency that their relationship embodies. We can already see that what is sensuous about it is doomed to fade away, like the world the film so lovingly re-creates. Visconti's true mastery can be seen in the way this is hinted at in the attitudes, actions, and reactions of the characters. Even in the role Visconti gives to sensuality, he appears to tacitly assume a political stand: As Sam Rohdie says:

Visconti's *mise-en-scène* belongs not to nostalgia, but to sensuality and eroticism. While celebrating a reactionary world, or at least framing it in nostalgia, he places a fuse under the dullness of a progressive one. He does so not only because he celebrates a sensuality in the film (the objects), but by practicing a sensuality in the composition of the film (in the way objects are depicted and ordered). And he withholds from the new world the excitement and attractiveness he feels for the old.[87]

Visconti's politics, "which celebrates fiction, desire, sensuality," as Rohdie puts it, also serves to interweave the public and social sphere with the private lives of the characters. The introduction of Angelica and her father into high society marks the ball as a singular event, even if, on the thematic level, it stands for the rise of an entirely new class and even if it otherwise might be taken as just another party of the Sicilian aristocracy. The exhilaration of the individual debutante conveys the intensity of an entire historical moment and the social change it brings about.

The earlier dinner party at Donnafugata has a somewhat similar function. There are important dinner scenes in almost all of Visconti's films, always functioning as the place where social and psychological alliances and antagonisms are encountered at their densest. They show people in the midst of an activity that in its everydayness is highly revealing of time and place, class, and hierarchy. Conflicts between people often united by biological or formal ties rather than by love and mutual appreciation come to a head sometimes and produce drastic consequences (*The Damned, Conversation Piece*). In *The Leopard*, the dinner scene marks a turning point in the family history, as members of the bourgeoisie are for the first time present on (almost) equal footing with the aristocrats. Only Angelica's loud laughter at Tancredi's inopportune joke reveal that she has not yet fully mastered the codes of the class she is aspiring to join.

Not only the ball scene and the dinner party but most of the film, apart from the battle in Palermo, is in counterpoint to the historical events, the revolution taking place behind the quiet and untroubled life the esteemed prince and his household live throughout the turbulences. The only historical figure to feature in the film is Colonel Pallavicino – probably not generally recognized as such even in Italy – and he makes his only appearance in the ball scene. Garibaldi is mentioned every now and then, but he is also constantly present as if in the collective subconscious: despite all the small talk, all that he really represents is supressed. Attempts to understand him and take him into account only lead the characters into casuistry and new repression.

In contrast, the battle scene, an addition to the novel, might at first appear curiously detached from the narrative. Chaos reigns as the battle for Palermo is waged street by street, the fervor of battle overcomes all nobler instincts, brutal violence reigns, and summary executions take place on both sides. Gradually the Redshirts win the day. The spectacle of war provides a sensation of immediacy, of the life and death of individuals being at the mercy of chance, as opposed to the inevitability with which the unification will take shape. Partly because none of the main characters appear until the very end of the sequence, the events can be seen to stand for all the battles taking place during this stage of the Risorgimento. Only at the very end do we get a glimpse of Tancredi as a dashing young hero. Without this view of him, his blind opportunism later on would appear merely despicable; this way, there is a sad feeling of youthful exuberance lost, a synecdoche suggesting the overall interpretation of the Risorgimento being put forward in the film as a whole.

Tancredi is somewhat reminiscent of Julien Sorel in *The Red and the Black*. On the one hand, writes Dominick LaCapra, "his inner, private self is elevated, poetic, spontaneous, passionate, idealistic, even exuberant." On the other hand, "his manner is calculating, and it operates shrewdly to achieve worldly success and public acclaim."[88] The difference is that whereas Julien is a man "on the make," Tancredi is merely trying to secure what he takes without a cloud of doubt to be his natural rights. This almost childlike ability to constantly change his own horizon of expectation and to forget about the views he held only a little while before makes his opportunism appear almost charming.

Whereas Tancredi's portrayal is nothing if not critical, that of the prince is quite the opposite, and the audience is seduced into identifying with his point of view. This effect is further strengthened by the crucial themes of the film being either expounded by him (e.g., in the conversation with Chevalley, as in the book), or crystallized in him and his relationship with Tancredi. He is an embodiment of all that is supposedly good in the aristocracy, and in his figure this class is redeemed in the historical perspective that is being put forward in the film – or indeed, as this film. While the history evolves as a dialectic between changes that to a great extent are illusory and permanence that is slowly being eroded, the prince encounters the ultimate questions of temporality in his own private sphere. He is an observer and not a participant, not only because of his social standing but also because of his age: he is aware of his own approaching death and prepares for his succession in Tancredi. He soars high above all that is sordid and decrepit about his class and society, and in the last instance it is his approaching death, rather than having to accept a don Calogero or a Colonel Pallavicino into high society, that adds a touch of sorrow to the sense of irretrievable loss.

The death scene of the prince has been omitted from the film and the meditations on death made shorter, but the portrayal of having to come to terms with the finitude of life is no less apparent. In the film and the book alike, the prince is well equipped to succeed in this. His interest in astronomy is not only a metaphor for his aloofness but also for his awareness of the passing of time and the transience of human pursuits and concerns. In Mikael Enckell's words: "The descent has begun and can be accepted with sorrow as he knows that there are loved successors as well as admired predecessors. This insight, which invites humility, also gives us the capacity to perceive without unsurpassable bitterness the limits of our own existence and faculties."[89] History, Ricoeur has said, is "constructed on the fracture line between phenomenological time and astronomical, physical, and biological time."[90] On the one hand, there is temporality as subjectivity; on the other hand, there is the inexorable march of objective time. Both factual and fictitious accounts of history mediate between the two. Narratives are on the whole attempts to map out the events of the past in their full human significance. They are forms of explaining and understanding, ways of making sense of the evidence left from the past. But while all narratives exude a sense of being a structured tale about the past, in cinema this feature is combined with a strong feeling of audiovisual representation always being in the present tense, presenting us with the sensation of an immediate view of a diegetic reality.

In *The Leopard*, the rich texture of the audiovisual reconstruction provides the ground for representing a certain kind of being-in-the-world, the inexorably temporal character of which is made apparent in the prince's awakening into awareness of both transience and continuity, the dual nature of time as the creator and devourer of the phenomenal world. This insight enables him to come to terms with the historical process that consumes and tarnishes everything he himself represents, the world that he so fully embodies, as well as with his approaching death. His final address to the star ties together these themes, but the very last scene, with Tancredi, Angelica, and don Calogero discussing in a detached manner the execution of Garibaldi's men, is a reminder of the human costs entailed in the creation of the new historical circumstances.

One of the reasons for the psychological resonance of *The Leopard* is undoubtedly the fact that there is so much of Visconti himself in both don Fabrizio and Tancredi: on the one hand, there is the aristocrat viewing society with a certain detachment; on the other hand, the almost unscrupulous potential fascist. It is also interesting to notice that though the film can be seen to reflect certain social and economic concerns of the early 1960s,[91] there are hardly any self-conscious references to the future from the point of view of the fictional events, such as Franz's vision of the destruction of the Austrian empire toward the end of *Senso*. We may see in various details signs of the bottomless mire of compromises and opportunism into which the Italian kingdom will start to sink immediately after its birth, but among the characters only the prince is even vaguely aware of the illusory character of the revolution taking place.

Just as in *Senso*, although achieved by a slightly different cinematic style, the dialectic between identification and outside perspective mediates between the past depicted in the film and our own time. There is considerable alleviation of the ironic stance, and the audience is cued to assume a far less unequivocal attitude toward the characters. The characters are not as inclined to melodramatic gestures as in the earlier Risorgimento film, and thus the viewer is not invited to identify quite as strongly with their emotions. Nor are the characters depicted from different perspectives or in different modes. Instead, they are shown living their lives in self-sufficiency and even calm, considering the perturbing events taking place in the background. Though there are long shot/reverse-shot sequences, they do not particularly draw the spectator into the diegetic space. Nevertheless, the diegetic space appears to continue indefinitely beyond any framing, and this, together with the relative length of the shots, helps to create a sensation of observing the events from a slight distance.

The visual style is closely related to the fact that there is no tight plot development, which in turn corresponds to a resigned elegiac attitude toward history. Not only was there less need to make a political point than at the time of making *Senso*, but Visconti apparently discovered much of his own critical attitude toward Risorgimento in the book. Very little refiguring of the plot or rethinking of the characters' motives were needed. All he had to do was refocus some scenes and slightly change the emphasis. In the earlier Risorgimento film, the turns in the historical chain of events had immediate effects on the characters and their decisions, without them really being able to understand the situations or truly exploit them to their advantage – with the partial exception of Count Serpieri, of course. Now major events are taking place in the background as if automatically, and many of the characters simply let themselves be carried by the rising tide. In Ishaghpour's words: "People do not reveal the world through their actions any more; it is the world which explains the passivity of their existence."[92]

The Leopard is an important milestone in Visconti's career. For the first time, a more or less lonely, frustrated young man is replaced by a lonely, resigned elderly man as the male lead. Also the portrayal of the family is of considerable interest from the point of view of Visconti's cinematic oeuvre as a whole. Though this family turns out to be fairly hollow, it is nevertheless a factor that keeps people and the society together. Problems with the family were crucial to Visconti's personality, and he idealized his own family and youth despite the known facts. Although he expressly denied it, even *The Leopard* is a kind of idealized version of his own family. The temporal distance enabled him to give it an aura of nostalgia. In all his films in contemporary settings apart from *Bellissima*, the families are in a state of disintegration.

3

The Family and Modern Italian Society

Luchino Visconti was born on November 2, 1906, the fourth child of Carla Erba and Giuseppe Visconti, duke of Modrone. The Viscontis were distantly related to the medieval dukes of Milan. Through this connection, their lineage can be traced to Desiderius, the last ruler of the Kingdom of Lombardy and the father-in-law of Charlemagne. In the eleventh century the family acquired the hereditary title of viscount, which eventually became the name of the family itself. Gradually the Viscontis expanded their domain until it covered most of northern Italy. It is indicative of their might that Pope John XXII excommunicated them and preached of the necessity of a crusade against them.[1]

The male line of the Viscontis ended in the fifteenth century, but through their female members the family became related to some of the most important royal houses in Europe: the Valois, the Hapsburgs, and the Tudors. In the nineteenth century a distant branch of the family assumed the name and crest of the Viscontis. The title of duke of Modrone was granted by Napoleon, and gradually the family secured its position among the leading noble families in Italy. In Milan the new Viscontis maintained their high status by becoming patrons of the arts, particularly opera. Luchino Visconti's parents, don Giuseppe and donna Carla, belonged to the circle of King Victor Emmanuel III and Queen Helen. Don Giuseppe became a gentleman-in-waiting to Queen Helen, and the children of the royal family and of the Viscontis sometimes went riding together.[2]

Accounts of donna Carla's and don Giuseppe's family life do not always coincide. Monica Stirling in her biography paints a portrait of an ideal family. Both parents and children were exceptionally beautiful and "the love, admiration, and loyalty that the young Viscontis felt for their parents and for each other outlasted their childhood."[3] This description accords with Visconti's own statements about his family but with little else. According to Gaia Servadio, the parents had little in common, and both had extramarital relationships, don Giuseppe possibly also with members of his own sex. There were scandals in 1916, and in 1921 don Giuseppe threatened to expose facts about donna Carla's private life if the Erba shares that he owned were not given into his possession. The matter was settled in court, and subsequently the two lived apart. Luchino, who suffered from a mother fixation, never forgave his father and afterward gave all his love to his mother. This weighed heavily on don Giuseppe, who cherished Luchino perhaps more than any of his other children.[4]

Youssef Ishaghpour has pointed out that "from the origin of tragedy, familial conflict [was] conceived as the essence of the poetics of drama; not the battle against the other, against the outside, but civil war, internal battle."[5] The family crystallizes in human terms the most basic opposition: that between unity and individuality. A child is born into perfect communion with the world but is condemned to live in dissonance with it as the price of consciousness and personal identity. Thus the family can be seen, at least metaphorically, not only as the nucleus of society, but also as the womb of the internal dissonance that is the necessary complement of the consonance that holds a society together. When Visconti was asked why families have such an important role in his films, he answered:

Maybe for old reasons of my own, maybe because it is within the family that there still exists those unique taboos, the moral and social prohibitions, the last impossible loves. In any case the family nucleus seems to me very important. All our way of being, of living, derives from there, from the inheritance we carry with us, from the happiness or unhappiness of our childhood. Each of us is the product of this smallest social cell, before being the product of society. Often an unchangeable product, or capable of modifications only with great difficulty. So the family represents a kind of fate, of destiny, impossible to elude. The relationships, the contrasts, the intrigues, the upheavals within the family always interest me passionately.[6]

The problem of the family thus conceived is inextricably connected with the questions of the individual's relationship with temporality and tradition; Mikael Enckell writes:

Each generation repeats the fate and models of earlier generations and is bound to them by many apparent and by an even greater number of hidden ties – this observation, made repeatedly throughout the centuries, we stubbornly seek to forget. However, behind the fairly transparent veils of differences we can recognize those ancient themes on which we have been able to build our existence and of which our lives are only variations. Faithfulness and tenderness – when they dominate – appear to give to this perspective on being depth and sense of belonging. Hate and defiance bring out – when they in turn take over – something undeniably but thinly unique. In this eternal and unresolvable conflict we look for models which could show us a way out of this dilemma of repetition, faithfulness and defiant will for renewal.[7]

However much Visconti might have idolized his own family, he would surely have agreed with Chekhov's view: "Remember that in our day every cultured man, even the most healthy, is most irritable in his own home and among his own family, because the discord between the present and the past is first of all apparent in the family."[8]

Gradually Visconti was able to study the family institution also as an outsider. After having accepted his homosexual orientation, he must have been aware that he would never father a family. He moved from one love affair to another spending almost as much energy on them as in the making of his films. On the other hand, these relationships also served as a source of inspiration and incentive. Many of them, says Servadio, had a strong sadomasochistic element: Visconti could humiliate his lovers and/ or let them humiliate him.[9] However, Visconti's almost life-long friend and collaborator, Suso Cecchi D'Amico, thinks Servadio's image is wrong. She denies that Luchino was masochistic, although he could be cruel. In her opinion, Visconti drifted into homosexuality almost without noticing. In the manner of a Renaissance prince, he thought he could also have boys and was not aware that his interest gradually centered exclusively on men.[10]

But success brought with it a circle of friends and lovers who probably were a kind of substitute for family relationships. In any case, a princely court of opportunists, petty thieves, and mediocre persons gradually formed around Visconti. He was their idol for he appeared to combine success with a contempt for social restrictions and norms. Though Visconti was otherwise quite severe and patriarchal, he apparently was intrigued by this group of misfits. He was often slandered because of his sexual orientation, his love of luxury, and his political stance, which was often thought to be mere pretense, but apparently he did not care. He did not like to be called a homosexual, though, and could speak of homosexuals with contempt.[11]

The centrality of families in Visconti's films is marked by the conspicuous absence of fathers. The only truly positive father figure appears in *Bellissima*, and even he has a fairly small role. There is the prince of Salina, of course, but he prefers his nephew to the point of neglecting his own children. In *La terra trema*, the father is dead and the grandfather has a considerably smaller role than in Verga's novel. In *The Damned*, Konstantin has no connection with his son Günther, represents the worst elements in society (or even in humanity), and is brutally killed. Grandfather Joachim is murdered early in the film, and his son, father of the central character, Martin, is already dead when the story begins. In *The Innocent*, the author Filippo d'Arborio is the biological father of the baby born during the film, but his role is marginal, and he dies before the birth of the child. Tullio, the protagonist of the film – whose father is dead – assumes paternity, but only to kill the "intruder."[12] In *Rocco and His Brothers*, *Sandra*, and *Ludwig*, the fathers of the relatively young protagonists have died before the films begin. In the *Conversation Piece*, the one real father mentioned never appears; the youngsters have clearly become totally alienated from him, and the professor's attempt to pose as a father ends in pathetic failure.

Mothers receive only slightly better treatment. In *Bellissima* and *Rocco*, lovable but overcaring mothers almost suppress their children by sincere attempts to secure their success in life. In *Sandra*, the mother is severely disturbed and hates her children. In *The Damned*, the influence of Sophie on her son Martin grows into monstrous proportions and the film ends in matricide. She is counterbalanced by Elizabeth, the loving mother of two little girls, but they all perish in the power struggle between different Nazi factions that some of the other family members represent. In *Ludwig*, the mother of the young king appears to be interested only in the political role his son has to play. Neither does the mother in the *Conversation Piece* appear to be particularly interested in her children's activities. Finally, two tender mothers appear in *The Innocent*, but their relationship with their children is not at a critical stage. In any case, Giuliana loses her baby within months of his birth, and Tullio's psychological problems are an obvious indication of unresolved childhood problems.

The psychological implications of the absence of fathers from Visconti's films may be connected not only with his personal history but, more interestingly, with the melodramatic mode of expression in which the director so often indulges. Through its long history, melodrama has been mainly a conservative form of art; its function has usually been to maintain the values of the patriarchy and the bourgeoisie. It tends to depict society as a static entity and the main characters as being outside

its power structure. In this context, it overemphasizes the internal relations of the family, which comes to represent society in nucleus. The story
often climaxes in the restoration of family unity and the moral order it
represents. However, more perceptive writers could invert the entire pattern. In Balzac, family relationships tend to be based on exploitation. A
home presented at first in an idyllic light turns out to be distorted by
internal tensions and repressed conflicts. There soon emerges an interplay
of forces, some unifying and others tearing the family apart. The family
is presented as a direct outgrowth of the conditions that culture and society impose on individuals.

Visconti goes even beyond Balzac in depicting the family as a battleground between "individual lives and historical forces, between personal
and social necessity."[13] The young men in his films cannot rise to a symbolic mutiny against society by opposing their fathers because they are
almost always dead. Thus they end up opposing the norms of society as
a whole. But whereas in traditional melodrama the rebellions of the young
men are often mere rites of passage that end in the restoration of the
patriarchal order, the antagonism in Visconti's films invariably moves
beyond reconciliation. Only the conformists survive and prosper. But neither does the individualist stand up as a model of virtue. The price to be
paid for renouncing patriarchy is shown to be the loss of integrity, love,
friendship, solidarity, and honesty – both toward others and oneself. At
its most extreme, the rebellion is distorted into perversity. In *Sandra*,
Gianni's incestuous love has obviously hindered his relationship with the
rest of the world, while in *The Damned*, Martin's destructiveness manifests itself as pedophilia, mother incest, and sadism.

ROCCO AND HIS BROTHERS

Production and censorship

In *Rocco and His Brothers*, Visconti addressed an explosive social
issue: the mass migration from the poor south to the prosperous north. It
turned out to be one of his most difficult and dearest projects. Trouble
began at the shooting stage in the spring of 1960. The murder at the end
of the film was supposed to take place at Idroscalo, a large recreational
area on the outskirts of Milan, where a young prostitute had recently been
murdered. Several permits were applied for and granted, but just when
the shooting was about to start, civil servants from the provincial administration announced that these were insufficient. A new application was

made, complete with the requested excerpt from the script. In the end, permission was not granted on the grounds of "inopportune resemblance to reality" of the scene to be shot. This reference to the Idroscalo murder was obviously an excuse – many films had been shot in this area, and no one had come asking about permits. The most likely reason was the wish to hinder the activities of the politically and morally suspect director.[14]

A scandal erupted. The Associated Film Critics of Milan protested and claimed that the provincial administration's decision was an unconstitutional act directed against the freedom of expression. But the officials also garnered support. A well-known neo-fascist congratulated the provincial administration and said he hoped he would not have to see any more films about "prostitutes and bicycle thieves." While the debate continued, Visconti completed the shooting at a location near Lake Fogliano that resembled Idroscalo.[15]

But the filming problems did not end there. Cardinal Tardini requested that officials take action against "certain destructive films," and Milan's public prosecutor, Commendatore Carmelo Spagnuolo, was encouraged to view Rocco with a group of police officers and lawyers. They demanded that four scenes be cut or the film would be confiscated and the producer Goffredo Lombardo prosecuted for "disseminating an obscene object." After negotiations, Lombardo agreed to darken the critical scenes with filters. This in turn prompted the censors in Rome to demand that two of the darkened scenes be omitted entirely.[16]

It was Visconti's turn to seek the protection of the law. He succeeded in getting the earlier decision nullified by a legal declaration specifying that a film is a work of art that cannot be infringed upon – and since by this time the Venice Film Festival jury had awarded the film a special prize, it had at least indisputably reached the status of art. The deleted scenes were restored to Rocco, but on the larger front the battle continued. Apparently the decision had some adverse effects on later films. It is indicative of the prevailing paranoia at the time that together with Rocco, which at least contains fiercely violent scenes, films as innocent as Fellini's La dolce vita (1960) and Antonioni's L'avventura (1960) ran into trouble.

The whole question of freedom of speech in a conservative and clericalistic society was at issue. In the background there loomed political questions rooted in the ideological oppositions of the cold war as well as in the political situation in Italy. The Central–Right coalition government was in crisis, partly because the Socialist party had advanced considerably in the 1958 election. Social and political tensions had burst into

heated ideological debate. *Rocco* even became the subject of a parliamentary debate as some Christian Democratic and neo-Fascist members
asked why a film slandering the emigrants from the south was allowed to
be distributed. The leftist intellectuals saw the censoring of films as yet
further evidence that the Christian Democratic government was merely
the successor of the old Fascist regime. All this assured *Rocco* of tremendous box-office success.[17]

Social and literary background

Rocco became the figurehead in the battle for the freedom of expression largely because it addressed a social problem concerned with
Italy's very identity. The pressure to emigrate from the south was great.
The rate of unemployment in the south ranged from 33 to 50 percent.
Income per capita was only about half of what it was elsewhere in Italy,
and almost every fourth person was illiterate. In effect, the south had all
the distinguishing features of a developing country. Although the constitution granted Italians freedom of movement, an old Fascist law that
prohibited people from moving to another locality without having secured
a job was still in force. Although it was not strongly enforced, it did mean
that the poor who moved in masses to the big cities were in effect illegal
residents and therefore not entitled to social security or the right to vote.
Although the law was denounced as unconstitutional by the Constitu-
tional Court, it was not superseded by new legislation until 1961.[18]

Between the years 1951 and 1961, about 1.75 million people, that is,
about 10 percent of the population of the south, emigrated. In the 1960s
the flux even increased. Some moved abroad, but most of them found
their way to the industrial centers of the north, which were soon surrounded by grey housing areas deprived even of basic services. In many
places the immigrants lived in shantytowns. But despite the often appalling conditions, the people did not want to return to their former
homes. To make matters worse, they encountered prejudice and were
accused of causing all possible social problems. They were thought to
constitute a threat to the values of the north, whereas in fact they were
most eager to integrate and to become part of urban society.[19]

The fact that most immigrants had no wish to return surprised also
Visconti and Suso Cecchi d'Amico in their interviews of southerners who
had moved to Milan. Among those they spoke to was the famous Rosaria
T., an immigrant mother who, by squatting and harassing civil servants,
had succeeded in acquiring basic security for her family. She so delighted
Visconti that he modeled and named the mother in his film after her.[20]

In addition to this in-depth investigation of social reality, several literary sources influenced the making of *Rocco*. The name of the film is a combination of the title of Thomas Mann's *Joseph and his Brothers* (1933) and the name of Rocco Scotellaro, a poet whose works expressed the feelings of the peasants of the south. Particularly his *Contadini del sud* (Peasants of the south) inspired the screenwriters of *Rocco*, as did certain other works related to the south, such as Carlo Levi's *Cristo si è fermato a Eboli* (Christ stopped at Eboli).[21] They found more directly useful material in Giovanni Testori's collection of stories, *Il ponte della Ghisolfa* (The bridge of Ghisolfa, 1958). Although Testori's Catholic faith and interest in spiritual questions were not particularly close to Visconti's heart, Testori's image of the urban jungle that had grown up in Milan made him see his native city with new eyes.[22] The collection was the first part of Testori's series *I segreti di Milano* (The secrets of Milan), depicting the world of lonely women, prostitutes, budding artists, and disillusioned boxers. In one of the stories, *Cosa fai, Sinatra?* there is a scene between two brothers and a prostitute who earlier "belonged to" the elder brother. These characters became the models for Simone, Rocco, and Nadia in the film.

The relationship between Rocco and Simone also parallels that between Prince Myshkin and Rogozin in Dostoyevsky's *The Idiot* (1868). Just as Myshkin and Rogozin both fall in love with Nastasya Filippovnaya, both brothers fall for Nadia. For her, Rocco represents goodness and faith in life, in the manner of the almost saintly Myshkin, whereas Simone eventually makes her succumb to her miserable self-image. In both stories the woman inadvertently leads the men to compete for her, which in the end drives all three into misery. The women also die in the same way, stabbed by the more violent of their two lovers. And in both cases the two men meet after the murder and are joined in a brotherhood of pain that is beyond rational understanding.

Just before *Rocco*, Visconti had directed Arthur Miller's *A View from the Bridge* (1955) for the Teatro Eliseo in Rome. In the play, two brothers move from Sicily to New York. They, too, are driven to violence by jealousy, but an equally important theme is the conflict between the Mediterranean conceptions of honor and justice and the capitalist order of the New World. In the beginning of the play, the lawyer Alfieri tells of the immigrants' suspicions about him: "I often think that behind that suspicious little nod of theirs lie three thousand years of distrust. A lawyer means the law, and in Sicily, from where their fathers came, the law has not been a friendly idea since the Greeks were beaten."[23] This became one of the basic conflicts in the dramatic structure of *Rocco*.

The original treatment was worked out by Visconti together with Cecchi d'Amico and the novelist Vasco Pratolini. When asked whether the
script had gone through any major changes, Cecchi d'Amico replied:

From the very beginning Luchino was sure about one thing: That he wanted a
story of a mother with five sons. Like the fingers of a hand. So I kept saying, but
why five? We don't know anything, there may be four, three, six. No, there must
be five. . . . But we didn't make so many changes. There was the beginning in the
south, but it was never shot because the picture was too long. . . . We thought it
was useless to shoot it [and that] it was even better to start with the arrival in
Milan. And there was another, longer chapter on the boy [Luca]. . . . But no.
There were no big, big changes.[24]

It must have soon became obvious that not all fingers of the hand were
to be equally prominent. As the script was under preparation the triangle
drama of Rocco, Simone, and Nadia was gradually brought to the foreground while the more epic material of the five brothers trying to adapt
to their new urban environment became less prominent. Perhaps, as Nowell-Smith has suggested, this led to "changes . . . in the structure of the
film which Visconti did not fully foresee and which he would not necessarily recognize as having taken place."[25] The "working diary" does indeed give the impression that though the melodramatic element was
already present in the first treatment, all sorts of changes did take place.
And even in the last instance, of course, Visconti exercised his creative
powers during the actual shooting, not only in the composition and organization of images but also by deleting certain scenes and adding and
modifying others.[26]

Many screenwriters helped prepare various parts or "chapters" of the
film. The Simone chapter was written by d'Amico, the Vincenzo and
Rocco chapters as well as the unrealized prologue by Pasquale Festa Campanile and Franciosa, and the Ciro chapter by Enrico Medioli.[27] One
might think that such an approach would produce uneven results, but
Medioli is probably right in stating: "I don't think the audience realizes
that different hands have been working on the script. Besides, the one
who creates the unity is the director."[28] All of *Rocco*'s four screenwriters
have on different occasions emphasized the creative role Visconti played
in the script-writing stage. According to Festa Campanile and Franciosa:

The thing that struck us right from the beginning was the most intelligent dis-
cretion with which Visconti indicated the points in the story which had inspired
him, the way he knew how to invent without wrecking what had already been

achieved and to guide the collective effort: as did Suso Cecchi d'Amico's intelligent and modern ability to create the overall structure, combined with a quick and acute talent for invention.[29]

Apart from Nicola Badalucco, who worked on *The Damned* and *Death in Venice*, Visconti did not use other screenwriters during the rest of his career. His long working relationship with Cecchi d'Amico and Medioli, in particular, which was based on deep mutual respect, was a major factor in the evaluation of his cinematic style. At the same time, they have both emphasized the creative role Visconti played in the script-writing stage, and they soon learned what he wanted. At various times they have also remarked that the director is, after all, the final creator of the film.[30]

Five alternatives for five brothers

Rocco is divided into five "chapters" named after the five brothers. Actually, the chapters are not as distinct in terms of plot development as are the phases in *La Terra trema*, but they do correspond roughly to the strategies the Parondi brothers are seen to adopt in response to their new environment. As each brother tries to learn from the mistakes of their elders, the film creates a strong cumulative effect. Vincenzo (Spiros Focas), who has settled down before the others arrive, has kept a low profile both with respect to family ties and the new community he is gradually integrating into. Although he cannot escape the conflicts between the two worlds, he eventually succeeds in starting a home with the petit-bourgeois Ginetta.

Simone (Renato Salvatori), unimpressed by this sort of life, seeks adventure and glamour. He becomes a boxer and uses his sex appeal to get women to fuss over him. His physical abilities bring him success, but otherwise he is weak. When troubles emerge, he quickly becomes dissolute and resorts to theft and violence. Rocco (Alain Delon) follows Simone's career as if to make up for the way the older brother has let everyone down. He ends up with a successful career in boxing, a sport that was basically alien to his nature and that he took up just as a form of exercise. Ciro (Max Cartier) works his way up, step by step, to become a skilled worker at Alfa Romeo. Gradually he severs his ties with the past and partly also with the family and succeeds in integrating into his new environment.[31] Perhaps it remains for Luca (Rocco Vidolazzi), the youngest brother, to reach a better balance between the past, the present, and the future. He, too, may be able to carve out a future for himself, but without having to renounce the past, family tradition, and the south. Even his name suggests that perhaps the ties to their native Lucania do not have to be relinquished completely.

The major structural opposition in the film is that between Simone and Rocco. They both start out at much the same point and have similar early careers, but then they start catalyzing each other's spiritual development toward opposite poles on the moral scale. At the beginning of the film they are both simple country lads, but their ways of coping with the potentially corrupting influence of the big city are almost diametrically opposed. Whereas Simone wants to be a success, Rocco finds himself unable even to desire the sort of things one is supposed to strive for in the north. Above all, Rocco lacks the aggressiveness that almost makes Simone a champion. It is not that boxing as such would be unpleasant for Rocco, but it becomes a moral problem for him when he learns to direct his bitterness against his competitors.

As in so many of Visconti's films, there is a solid link between money and love. This is made manifest not only in the figure of Nadia (Annie Girardot), a prostitute who one evening storms into the Parondis' first home in Milan to escape the anger of her father (or so she says), but also in the way Simone and Rocco for their separate reasons have to sell their bodies in order to achieve what they desire, be it a woman or family unity. Vincenzo's former success as a boxer and Nadia's coaxing – the idea is that success will bring with it sexual favors – make Simone take up boxing seriously. His prowess is soon noticed, and he is accepted into special training. He wins matches and he wins Nadia. Everything appears to be arranged for him, but this becomes precisely the cause of his downfall. He never has a chance to develop the sense of responsibility and toughness that are required both in the ring and in real life. Easy and casual relations with women turn out to be equally fatal. Soon Simone begins to deteriorate both physically and morally and eventually loses everything he has gained. When he gives Nadia a piece of stolen jewelry, she leaves him.

A couple of years later, Rocco meets Nadia by chance just after she has been released from prison – where she served a sentence for prostitution. He succeeds in rekindling her faith in life, and they fall in love.[32] By this time, Simone is already on the decline, whereas Rocco's boxing talent begins to gain attention after he is seen sparring with Simone. The elder brother's fury foreshadows their bitter fight at the turning point of the film soon to follow. After Simone loses an important match, his manager demands that Rocco compensate for the financial losses Simone has caused. One blow follows another: Simone has hardly recovered from this defeat when he hears that his little brother is going out with his former girlfriend. He finds out where they are to meet, interrupts their tryst, and while his chums hold Rocco back, he rapes Nadia.

Although the rape scene is not explicit, it has a shocking effect as it conveys forcefully the spiritual destructiveness of physical violence. Immediately afterward, the two protagonists are seen in a powerful composition: Simone stands in the background with his back toward the camera; Rocco, in the foreground, also faces away, with the weeping Nadia between the two, neither of whom can offer her a genuine alternative. The brutal and selfish Simone can only destroy all that is beautiful and meaningful for her; the martyr-like Rocco does not have the strength to resist evil and baseness. As Nadia trudges away, the atmosphere suddenly changes. The poignant music that has accompanied Nadia's weeping is interrupted, and only diegetic sounds are heard during Simone's and Rocco's dialogue. This is the turning point of the entire film. Rocco says that Simone disgusts him. Simone is driven into a new rage. He savagely beats his little brother, who reluctantly returns his blows. The scene is prolonged, and its increasingly expressionistic overtones begin to reverberate as the brothers continue striking each other in the dark, desolate city.

In allowing himself to be humiliated in this way, Rocco seems a Myshkin-like "holy idiot": he refuses to condemn Simone, accepts his claim to Nadia, and assumes all guilt. He meets Nadia at the top of Milan Cathedral and tells her to return to Simone, who "cannot manage without her." She does so, but only to accelerate his – as well as her own – downfall. Rocco's attitude stems partly from his sense of guilt, partly from a deepseated association with the role models of the south. His apparent goodness turns out to be destructive for the three of them. By persuading Nadia to return to Simone, he sacrifices them all on the altar of anachronistic traditions.

Nadia is as much a victim of the tragedy as she is its catalyst. When she first appears in the story, she is a shrewd survivor. She is cynical and guards her independence jealously. When telling Simone about her childhood, she avoids giving too much of herself by making up certain details. Only Rocco's idealism and faith in human interaction makes her come out of her shell, enabling her to receive and to express tenderness. Nadia's idealism is short-lived, however, as it clashes head on with Simone's mercilessly egoistic possessiveness. It now has a shattering effect on her, for it utterly destroys her ability to find joy and hope. For one brief moment, she was able to experience something of true value. The return to her old life signals her entry into a spiritual vacuum. Now she sticks provocatively to Simone and settles down in the house of his mother, Rosaria (Katina Paxinou). The mother–whore opposition is thus brought under the same roof. Rosaria does not dare throw the girl out as she fears losing Simone. Nadia finally leaves after Simone makes an utter mess of his life by stealing from Morini, the boxing manager.

The Simone–Morini relationship has sadomasochistic overtones as well. When they first meet, Morini examines Simone as if he were an animal. A little later, Morini looks intently at Simone and Rocco as they are having a shower. Toward the end of the film, Simone comes to beg for money from him, but having lost his more charming masculine appeal, the rapidly deteriorating boxer is unable to persuade the rich man to help him. The scene, shot in a dark room, is given a surreal touch by the television in the background, which is showing images of divinities by the Renaissance painter, Il Giorgione. The only sound to be heard is the quiet, strange music floating from the television. The conversation between Morini and Simone could almost be a commentary on the program: "When I first saw you, you were like Apollo, a real Apollo," says Morini. He goes on to tell Simone how much he now despises him. The desperate boxer becomes aggressive, knocks him down, and steals money from him.[33] To stop Morini from going to the police, Rocco offers to compensate for everything, but to do so he has to sign a ten-year contract.

Just as Rocco is preparing for his first international match, Simone hears that Nadia is receiving clients in a park area on the outskirts of the town. He goes to meet her, but she, too, says she now despises him. She makes a brief attempt to escape – Rocco is seen in the ring. Simone is now losing his contact with life as it turns out that Nadia no longer has the will to live. As if in a dream, they yield to their fate. Their bodies momentarily form a cross as Nadia lifts her arms, as if to put them around Simone – Rocco knocks down his opponent. In a deathly embrace, Simone and Nadia engage in sadomasochistic writhing on the mud of the river bank, as he repeatedly strikes her body with his knife.[34] She finally dies, and Simone escapes – the audience around the ring screams ecstatically.

The parallel action between the murder and the match is reminiscent of the final scene of Bizet's *Carmen*, in which José stabs Carmen just as Escamillo triumphs in the bullring. Rohdie compares the passage with the cross-cutting patterns of the last-minute rescue passages of traditional melodrama. The irony of it is, of course, that in this case there is no hope of a last-minute rescue. The hero is not only unaware of Nadia's peril, but the way his blows in the ring are shot and intercut with Simone's blows to her body actually suggests his complicity: he, too, is an agent of her death.[35]

Paradoxically, Rocco's saintliness stems in part from his ability to discharge his aggressions in the ring. Hate has made him a champion and made him obsessively pursue family unity. It is his spiritual center, but it also implies an inability to accept the facts of life, to move ahead to what might be a less pleasant but at least a feasible future. In the party arranged to celebrate his victory, he gives a poignant speech about the south – with the family photograph behind him, of course – which makes the others, who in their hearts have betrayed the south, look almost embarrassed. Rocco's all-embracing craving for unity reaches its climax when Simone returns to the family as a murderer. Rocco wants to help and protect him, to put family ties before the norms of the social environment they live in. When he realizes what has happened, he and Simone, brothers united by a pain that pierces their entire being, embrace in a state of hysteria.[36]

There is an interesting analogy between Rocco and the protagonist of Mann's *Joseph and His Brothers*, although it occurs through an inversion. Whereas in the novel the brothers sell Joseph to get rid of him, thus inadvertently serving a divine plan, in the film Rocco's act of self-sacrifice for the benefit of the family is futile and destructive. The point is not just that Joseph lives in a world governed by divine Providence, whereas in the modern urban world God would be dead or simply silent. Mann's Joseph has a remarkable ability to live in the present, to have no regrets of the past, and to reach toward the future step by step. Being illuminated by God, he is able to conceive of time passing majestically over singular events and individual lives, including his own. He is able to encounter time unproblematically. He is, in Kierkegaardian terms, a child of both time and eternity. The tender, simple Rocco is not a man of such spirit; he is a man of the past. He has the innocence of a pure fool, but he is at the mercy of time. He can bring momentary consolation to Nadia, but because she yearns for a permanent change in her life, a different kind of future, the fleeting moment of hope and happiness with him leads her to ever deeper spiritual desperation and destruction.

On the "epic" level of the film, while his passionate elder brothers have been fighting their way through life, Ciro has become a skilled laborer at Alfa Romeo factories. Simone sinks into a criminal life and puts all that Ciro has achieved into jeopardy. Whereas Rocco embraces Simone in ecstatic forgiveness, Ciro rushes out to save the family by denouncing him. He chooses to conform to society instead of preserving family solidarity.

He realizes how dangerous Simone can be in an environment in which the moral code is determined basically by law and order instead of the values of the south. The stormy triangle has been resolved tragically, and a calm and sunny coda follows, with a promise of hope and new life. Ciro defends himself to the suspicious Luca. He tells the little boy that it was Simone who taught him that there was no returning to their old life. In the south they were at the mercy of the local landlords, but now they will have to learn to shoulder their responsibilities and to demand their rights. It is as if Simone had been diseased and was close to contaminating them all. Ciro acknowledges Rocco's saintliness but points out that in a man-made society there is no room for saints.

Ciro has started a family and formed a circle of friends. That his brother has turned out to be a murderer will probably not jeopardize his position as this is offset by the international success of the other brother. In the words of the director, Ciro might become "a petit bourgeois, perhaps even a haute bourgeois."[37] His life will be more even and boring than Rocco's and Simone's, but at least he is assured of some kind of family continuity. At the very end of the film, Luca shouts to him, inviting him to visit their old home. The conflict between old and new is not entirely antagonistic.

Whereas the lives of the three men are used to explore the different strategies of adaptation, the two main female characters, mother Rosaria and Nadia, embody the dangers of the past and the present, respectively. Some scholars view the two as destructive forces.[38] It would be more accurate to say that men and women are equally the exploiters and the exploited when it comes to emotional and sexual relationships, all guilty victims in the web of human relationships. The basic problems are the rigid role models – by no means confined to the traditions of the south – and the boundless possessiveness manifested in all emotional relationships. A lot of the trouble here springs from the mother's desire to control her sons. At Vincenzo's engagement party Rosaria asks him: "Can you afford to marry, now that you have to support the entire family?" Later on she writes to Rocco while he is doing his military service, asking him to send money because "you don't have any need for money there in the army." She jealously guards her sons and leaves them little room to grow up and form relationships with the opposite sex based on equality.

In the end Rosaria is, of course, unable to control the tide of events. In certain issues she represents the traditional values of the south, which are of little relevance in the industrialized modern world. She is the hand to which the five fingers belong. But she has not even the foggiest notion of her sons' needs or the temptations the new environment offers them. Thus at the end of the day she is completely powerless in the face of the tragedy that threatens the family. She rejoices at her sons' success as boxers without understanding how short-lived and costly such victories are. Yet thanks to the marvelous performance of Katina Paxinou, she also has a humorous side. Her wonderfully quaint attitudes make even her excessive motherliness appear in a positive light.

When Vincenzo tries to explain to his bride the traditional male and female roles of the south as taught to him by his mother, she slaps him on the face. Ginetta is a family girl and prepared to assume the role of a housewife, but not at any price. She, too, has an exasperatingly supportive family, who will not allow her standard of living to sink too low because of marriage. Vincenzo is all too aware of the economic prerequisites of marriage in Milan. He has left boxing. As the film moves on, he gradually becomes integrated into the urban society through a more conventional lifestyle. He succeeds also in another respect in which Simone fails: after Rosaria has more or less overcome her dislike of Ginetta, he is able to maintain his positive relationship with his mother and his brothers.

Though Visconti's attitude toward the characters in his films with contemporary settings is not on the whole ironical in the way it was in *Senso*, he brooks neither uncritical nostalgia nor utopianism in the social or in the private sphere. Uncritical hopes and more or less deliberate ignoring of present facts are shown to be destructive despite the best of intentions. Rocco's adherence to the traditional values of the south is blatantly discordant with the situations that develop in the north between Simone, Nadia, and him. Yet Visconti is by no means unsympathetic toward him. On the contrary, as Sam Rohdie has suggested, this sense of nostalgia for a past way of life might be one of the major points of contact Visconti personally had with the emigrants of the poor south. And once again he succeeded in combining his aesthetic sensibility with his social commitment, articulating his crucial themes by means of audiovisual narration.

The temporal structure of *Rocco* contrasts sharply with that of, say, *The Leopard*. Whereas in the second Risorgimento film the sense of time passing is conveyed in Chekhovian fashion, by a few long scenes in which the essence of a period in time is crystallized both on the individual and on the social level to a particularly revealing moment in time, here the story moves along somewhat hectically in fairly short scenes (in Visconti's terms, that is), which follow one another often without much indication as to how long a stretch of time separates them. This helps to create a sense of the beat of the modern city. The sense of time passing is created

by the changes that take place in people's relationships and social status
– the marriages of Vincenzo and Ciro, the careers of Ciro and Rocco.

The contrasts in lighting in this black-and-white film are considerable.
In very general terms, it can be said that the film progresses from dark
nocturnal scenes to bright sunlit ones. When the family arrives at Milano's
railway station, the *chiaroscuro* created by the smoke and fog increases
the sense of helplessness of the family. In contrast, the film ends in full
sunlight after most of the family members have found a place in their new
environment. For Simone, the lighting moves in the opposite direction. In
the early parts of the film he is quite often seen in bright light, but his later
scenes become increasingly dark. The dialogue between him and Morini is
shot with very little light. On the other hand, the scene that follows with
Ciro and Rosaria is almost blinding. Most of the shots in the flat the family
has been able to secure are also fairly bright. Particularly toward the end,
this appears to reflect Ciro's improved prospects in life.

Also Nino Rota's music has a thematic function. During the credit sequence, the instrumental "main theme" is first heard briefly in a dark,
foreboding mode, followed by the poignant folk melody *Paese mio*. At the
end of the film, the latter is associated with Luca and the possibility of
his returning to the south. The first tram ride of the family is accompanied
by jazzy music characterized by pizzicato on the double bass. The "tram"
theme is heard a few times during the first half of the film and is related
to the promises the big city appears to offer – one of them being Nadia.
Folk melodies are heard when references are made, sometimes only
briefly, to the past in the south and all it stands for.

But what makes the use of music in this film different from most other
films is the almost Wagnerian use of the main theme, Wagnerian not so
much in terms of harmony and orchestration, but in the highly sophisticated use of Leitmotif technique. That is, it is not used in the blunt
Hollywood fashion of simply equating a theme with a character, mood,
or situation, but in the sense of developing a motif in correspondence with
the dramatic situations and with the characters and their relationships.
In other words, both the theme and its functions vary subtly throughout
the film. The first part of the theme appears in two variations, one dark,
the other light, corresponding roughly to Simone and Rocco, respectively.
The former is first heard briefly on two occasions, when Simone is seen
stealing items at the laundry. The second part of the theme, more melodic,
first appears when Nadia returns to Rocco the stolen jewelry she has received from Simone. The theme appears in full for the first time in the
next scene, in which Simone and Rocco are talking about Nadia. By far

the most important manifestation of the theme is heard when Nadia and Rocco talk after she has been released from prison: the first half appears in its lighter version, after which the music seems to gently shake off its chains and become an expression of hope.

This light version reappears when the new couple in love are seen traveling together on a tram through Milan, and it is dexterously combined with the jazzy tune just mentioned. A little later, the dark version returns and is woven into the tension-building music to suggest Simone's malice as he creeps toward the lovers. After he has raped Nadia, the theme returns in its entirety, now infinitely sad: the music of hope has become a poignant expression of hope lost. The theme is heard a couple of times in this mode and function, most dramatically when Rocco rejects Nadia at the top of the Milan Cathedral. When Simone meets her at Idroscalo, the light version is heard changing into the dark one, and finally it blares forth in its most magnificent and tragic rendition, just as she succumbs to his knife – only to disappear with the cut to the boxing ring. The theme is heard for the last time when Ciro rushes off to report Simone to the police.

Despite its audiovisual refinement, its cast of international stars and all its melodramatic qualities, *Rocco and His Brothers* suggested a kind of return to neorealism. The way in which the shooting (in black and white) captured the relationship between the characters and their social environment was reminiscent of the great postwar Italian cinematic tradition. Almost all of the contradictions of neorealism can also be found in it. In some quarters the film was praised for its accurate depiction of social reality; in others it was denounced for doing the very opposite. There were those who saw in *Rocco* significant social criticism and an expression of class struggle; others saw in it a mere triangle drama that was an insult to the workers who had emigrated from the south.[39] The differences of opinion were closely connected with the question of the relationship between melodrama and realism, the keystone of Visconti's creative output.

Melodrama as nostalgia and a social commentary

As Nowell-Smith suggests, the exceptionally long time spent in writing the script for *Rocco* created a discrepancy between the epic and the tragic elements of the film: "*Rocco and His Brothers* is not an entirely satisfactory film. It is really two films in one, an epic and a drama. . . . As heroes, Rocco and Ciro are in no way comparable. They stand for the two ways in which the film has been interpreted, the drama and the tract."

Ciro's function in the story, as Nowell-Smith is of course aware, is "to put Rocco's tragedy into perspective" and "the epic and the drama are deliberately counterpointed." What he is worried about is that "it is not possible to see the conflict or its resolution as directly or exclusively representative of Visconti's *conscious intentions*" (italics added). Furthermore, in his films "in the final realization nostalgia prevails over progress." The reason for all this Nowell-Smith traces to Visconti's "intellectual belief in the cause of progress and an emotional nostalgia for the past that is being destroyed."[40] He points out that in the director's oeuvre as a whole, nostalgia overcomes progress since all those who try to rise up against history are defeated: 'Ntoni, Rocco, Franz, don Fabrizio, and Gianni in *Sandra*.[41]

It is true that the increasing emphasis on the nostalgic element in Visconti's late works indicates a shift from predominantly social to more psychological and existential issues. But although the characters of his late films are exceptional and alienated from their community, in one way or another they function as metaphors for that community and for its spiritual state at a given moment in history.

A crucial feature of Visconti's anthropomorphic cinema was his charting of the dialectical relationship between an individual and his or her environment, which was an attempt to crystallize the essence of a given social situation into the story of a few individual characters. The melodramatic aspects of his style have to be related to this. Visconti was heir to the nineteenth-century Italian operatic tradition, which in its curious ways has been a consistent feature of Italian culture and politics. Yet, says Guido Aristarco, the melodramatic aspects of Visconti's films do not overwhelm the need to make a social statement since "art is borne out of a national culture. And [Italy's] national culture is melodramatic. Not melodramatic in the negative sense of the word. But it is a culture characterized by the works of the great Verdi, not of the plots [of the operas] but of the great inspiration he provided."[42]

As Rohdie has also pointed out, "it was an extraordinary accomplishment to have taken the best of bourgeois culture and translate it successfully to the screen, not only for mass diffusion, but particularly to social groups relatively alien to what was then regarded as culture." In fact, it was the "operatic" or "melodramatic" qualities that made the film so popular: "It was sound, rhythm, melody, tone, colour, volume, intensity, dance, romance, passion: that is, it went to the body, not the head."[43]

The melodramatic strain in Visconti's films derives from emotional and existential extremes that tend to go beyond the socially acceptable, as well as beyond the rational faculty of the individual. Something emerges that cannot be articulated by symbolic means such as language, something that manifests itself in the intensity of emotions and that easily leads to gestures and actions unacceptable both to society and often also to oneself. By depicting such transgressions and the situations from which and to which they lead, Visconti's films reveal an entire social situation, with its norms and restrictions in all their oppressiveness. Other directors, too, such as Vincente Minnelli and Douglas Sirk, have been able to use melodramatic means to represent complex psychological conditions and relationships in a way that might be difficult to capture by other forms of expression. For example, Thomas Elsaesser notes, the way *all* characters appear to be victims means that

the critique – the questions of "evil," of responsibility – is firmly placed on a social and existential level, away from the arbitrary and finally obtuse logic of private motives and individualized psychology. This is why the melodrama, at its most accomplished, seems capable of reproducing more directly than other genres the patterns of domination and exploitation existing in a given society, especially the relation between psychology, morality and class consciousness, by emphasizing so clearly an emotional dynamic whose social correlative is a network of external forces directed oppressingly inward, and with which the characters themselves unwittingly collude to become their agents.[44]

This applies to a great extent also to Viscontian melodrama, above all to *Rocco*. In his analysis of this film, Sam Rohdie emphasizes that melodrama addresses otherwise (socially or psychologically) repressed questions:

Melodrama, by theatricalising reality, reveals it while at the same time revealing the impossibility, the unlivability of the emotions it calls up, except within melodrama – that is, not in life but in art. The overheated fiction of melodrama becomes simultaneously revelation of the real, protest against it, and salvation from it, the place where the values denied by reality, or defeated by reality, can still survive. . . . Melodrama is the means for making reality speak, for making history come alive, for giving ideology its "human," psychic sense.[45]

This statement goes quite far in emphasizing the melodramatic quality of *Rocco*, and it is the cornerstone of Rohdie's entire argument regarding this film. In his view, "the excess of feelings is signified in the film, not by language, but by gestures, or by grunts, screams, gnashing of teeth, well beyond the prosaic reality being presented." Movements are carefully "choreographed," he goes on to say, and "character is expressed more as cinematic, dynamic quality than as a psychological one, or rather, and more precisely, the psychic inside of the characters is translated to the outside. To the glide and sweep of their bodies, to the hesitancies of glances, to the intensity and power of their gestures."[46]

Visconti does indeed use music, color, and lighting to convey and emphasize emotions, to make the spectator sympathize and identify with the characters. But there is also another critical and distancing element. On the level of the plot, the characters might behave melodramatically – give themselves up to their emotions, refuse to accept facts – but in addition to identifying with them, the spectator is also invited to view them and their actions against a historically determined social background. Although the melodramatic triangle in *Rocco* occupies the foreground for a considerable part of the film, the oldest brother, Vincenzo, and the two younger ones, Luca and Ciro, though apparently left somewhat marginal, do have an important function in displaying one by one different ways of adapting to their new environment. Their contribution is essential in providing the epic, or rather, the thick and rich novelistic texture from which the melodrama arises and gains its full significance. But there are also other reasons why the brothers should not be considered mere adjuncts or the continuity from one brother to another, or "a hangover from the literary structure with which Visconti started," as Nowell-Smith and, in slightly different words, Rohdie suggest.[47]

As has already been pointed out, Visconti's characters are – just as Lukács expected of the characters of a novel – types rather than average personalities. In Christopher Prendergast's words, the "characteristic or 'essential' features of the social process are picked out and gathered into a single expressive moment of a peculiarly intense and concentrated kind."[48] On the other hand, as was expounded in connection with neorealism (Aristotle also made the same point about tragedy), in this kind of aesthetics, at least, it is the *plot* rather than the characters that has to be typical or representative; the plot universalizes the characters. To shed light on a social situation, a work must emerge from the wealth of details of practical life and make a statement by means of – to use Paul Ricoeur's terms – metaphorical *configuring* of past events, by means of *emplotment*.

In many of his films Visconti succeeds in creating a happy marriage between these two narrative principles. His preoccupation with (re)-creating in excessive detail the environment of his characters is not an example of mere surface naturalism but of providing the context in which behavior and dialogue become – in the Bakhtinian sense – truly dialogical, representative not only of the character as an individual but of a rich social texture in a certain place at a certain point in time. In all his films, whatever the social class he portrayed, Visconti succeeded in capturing convincingly the *social gestus* or the patterns of behavior of people belonging to a particular class. Everything his characters say or do echoes the contradictions and tensions of their social environment, of their communal as well as personal history. Thus even a singular event depicted can be recognized as a configuration of various factors that structure human behavior; generalization is, perhaps somewhat paradoxically, achieved by contextualizing the individual.

The social background never disappears in *Rocco*, nor is it relegated to a mere backdrop of the melodrama. The characters emerge as individuals and not as stock types of melodrama because they are seen as belonging to and being conditioned by their environment, a socially dynamic community. They are given certain opportunities and live under certain restrictions. Depending on their personal history, their immediate concerns and drives, and their future aspirations, the characters are – or are not, as the case may be – able to exploit these opportunities. They may be crushed by their restrictions, they may learn to live with them, and a few might just be able to overcome them – if only to encounter new ones. All this is the novelistic or epic aspect of the film. What the dramatic aspect does in *Rocco* is to bring forth the universal dimension in the events that take place in this particular environment, this class, this point in Italian history as represented in this film.

Thanks to all this, *Rocco* is neither an abstract thesis that can be followed without emotional involvement nor a melodrama without social and human relevance. In some ways the central melodrama, with its basically good but weak people sinking into the urban sewage, is reminiscent of the popular novels of the nineteenth century, but with the moralizing tone expurgated and replaced by a critical social perspective. Without becoming utopian, this provides an uplifting effect unusual in Visconti's films. It is supported by the masterly interplay of comic and tragic elements. The first chapter is predominantly warmly humoristic, but gradually the dark and tragic elements take over, until at the end there is a return to light, hope, and continuity.

SANDRA

The story and the characters

While Visconti was still shooting *The Leopard*, Franco Cristaldi offered to produce his next film on the condition that the main role be given to Claudia Cardinale. Another starting point was d'Amico's and Visconti's idea of locating the story in the Tuscan city of Volterra. The film was to be a kind of modern *Electra*, and instead of the Trojan War, the collective trauma overshadowing the drama was to be the archetypal horror of our century, the concentration camps. The plot mechanism is based essentially on ambiguity regarding the events of the past. Sandra (Cardinale) suspects her mother (Marie Bell) and the mother's lover Gilardini (Renzo Ricci) of betraying her Jewish father to the Nazis. Gilardini, who has subsequently married the mother, in turn accuses Sandra and his brother Gianni (Jean Sorel) of incest. Neither suspicion is given much substance, not to speak of determining the degree of guilt or complicity. Perhaps the mutual distrust has simply made everyone interpret everyone else's motivations and actions in the worst possible way. Sandra's husband Andrew (Michael Craig), who is encountering the rest of the family and all its internal conflicts for the first time, observes the family with amazement. While the film was still under production Visconti commented:

All the characters are ambiguous except Andrew. He would like to find a logical explanation to everything, instead of which he finds himself in a world dominated by the most profound, contradictory, and inexplicable passions. . . . It's along the same lines as those thrillers in which everything appears very clear at the beginning and very obscure by the end, as always happens when people attempt the difficult task of understanding their own reactions, feeling absolutely sure they have nothing to learn but ending up face to face with agonizing existential problems.[49]

In the precredit sequence, Sandra is hosting a cocktail party, when her attention is suddenly captured by the pianist playing César Franck's *Prelude, Chorale and Fugue*. The music carries her back into an abyss of memories, as is clearly evident from the piece being heard while the credits appear over images of roads leading to Volterra. Sandra and Andrew go to Volterra to attend a ceremony that will turn part of the gardens of her ancestral home into a public park dedicated to the memory of her father, who died in Auschwitz. Sandra has apparently structured her most cherished childhood memories around the image of her father. During their first night in Volterra, she goes to the garden to see his statue, which is to be unveiled during the ceremony. She embraces it ardently. Just then, her brother Gianni makes his first appearance in the film.

Later Sandra goes to see her mother in a mental home, and there the meaning of Franck's piano piece becomes evident: the mother used to be a concert pianist and the piece was once in her repertoire. Sandra enters her room just as she finishes playing it. She apparently sees her daughter enter but begins to play it again. She grows confused and ends by banging the keys of the piano in mad desperation.

Gianni's interest in his sister is undoubtedly erotically colored. He has written a book titled *Vaghe stelle dell'Orsa*, after a poem by Leopardi. It is based on his childhood memories and apparently incest looms large in it, but perhaps he is just out to shock people? Sandra has great affection for her brother and hopes to enlist him as an ally against those she thinks are their enemies. But are there any real enemies? On one level, internal conflicts have simply distorted the relationships within the family and destroyed all possibility of communication. In the background is the complex question of the actual persecution of Jews and the paranoia which it has created. In the mind of the mentally unbalanced mother, this confusion gives rise to a violent burst of hatred as she encounters her daughter: "You're afraid, aren't you? Your father? Do you want to hear the truth about your idol? You have Jewish blood like him. . . . You are corrupt, like him! Small, dirty vices. Secret vices!"

The victims of violence and injustice are known to become guilt ridden. In *Sandra* the fate of the Jews in the Second World War functions as a metaphor for the entanglement of victimization and groundless accusations practiced in the end by Jews and non-Jews alike. Sandra has participated in a committee set up to investigate why her father was turned in to the Nazis. Auschwitz represents the abyss of history that has engulfed innumerable lives and that still serves as a reminder of crimes people have committed against one another. Yet the memories of the concentration camps are already sinking to the depths of people's subconsciousness, only to be transmitted into feelings of guilt and revenge. Everyone in turn plays the role of the accuser and the accused.[50]

In the end the characters are unable to communicate even with those they consider to be their allies. Regardless of whether the mother and Gilardini have denounced the father, they have lost touch with other people, the mother because she lost her grip on reality and Gilardini because he became firmly entrenched in his position between the mother and the children. According to Sandra, Gilardini keeps bringing up Gianni's attempted suicide, by which he avoided being sent to boarding school. Sandra puts great emphasis on this event for she sees it as an attempt by the mother and Gilardini to keep her and Gianni apart. Her fruitless and possibly unfounded attitude finally leads her to to say to Andrew, as he is leaving the house in exasperation: "I don't want to be forgiven because I won't forgive anyone." Yet she is referring to something that according to her is mere slander against her and Gianni.

Andrew loves her and tries to understand her, but he lacks the sensitivity and the neurotic bend of mind required to see what is going on – he does not even notice that his wife is in tears just after they have arrived at the family palace. He is a sober man of the modern world and represents for Sandra an opportunity to break her ties with her past. But the way he plays with his camera early in the film suggests that he is able to capture only the surface of things – in contrast to Gianni, who has written a book that is apparently full of references to culture and the past. This impression is strengthened by pop music heard from the transistor radio in the camera scene. In the first shot of Sandra through Andrew's viewfinder, she is seen surrounded by a black frame – which forms a visual parallel with the first shot of Gianni, seen through the grid of the garden gate. Sandra's uneasiness anticipates her subsequent unwillingness to let Andrew form an objective view of her past and mediate a reconciliation between her and her supposed enemies. It is as if Sandra were not truly willing to have things recorded with any degree of objectivity, as if she feared that the suspicions she prefers to entertain might not be confirmed.

In one way or another, it appears to be in everyone's interest not to have the old disputes really sorted out. This need to maintain ambiguity is echoed in the subtly elliptical narrative style of the film itself. It is left unclear how much the characters know about one another at any given point in the film. We are not, for example, privy to what Gilardini tells Andrew about what he thinks has happened between the siblings, but this is made apparent toward the end of the film. While the conflicts between the characters further complicate their relationships without bringing any clarity to the situation, either for them or the spectators, interest focuses on the way Sandra and Gianni attempt to cope with the past, which turns out to be deception of various kinds.

Gianni accuses Sandra of driving their mother mad through her obsession with the memory of their father. Even as she continues to accuse their mother of betraying their father, she herself becomes enmeshed in deception. As a child, she and Gianni had formed an alliance against their mother and Gilardini, but that relationship was betrayed, he feels, when she married Andrew. In a sense, both men compete for her as a woman, but more important to the film's discourse is what they symbolize for her. The relationship with Gianni signifies a potentially regressive turning to the past. On the psychological level, allying with him would be an infantile attempt to restore the purity if not the entire unity of the idyll of their childhood. On the practical level, it would mean returning to a deadlock from which she has almost succeeded in extricating herself.

Andrew, on the other hand, represents the future. Again and again he tries to help Sandra form a rational relationship with her past. Gianni does his best to subvert this effort through misleading innuendos. For example, he introduces Andrew to Pietro, Sandra's first love and the mother's present doctor, suggesting that Sandra's relationship with Pietro had been more significant than it really was. Even more than Andrew, Pietro is a mere observer. He might well know better than anyone else what has really gone on in the family, but he has obviously learned to keep his distance from this tormented family. As Nowell-Smith points out:

He is not so much above as below the action, the hapless victim of Sandra and Gianni's complicity, Andrew's jealousy, Gilardini's mistrust and the mother's rages. His role is in fact the exact obverse of Andrew's. Pietro withdraws where Andrew rushes in. Where Andrew has power without understanding, Pietro has understanding but no power.[51]

For quite some time, Andrew does not even appear to be fully aware that he might have to struggle to keep Sandra. Yet already during their first night in the palace, she tells Andrew that she is going to sleep in her old room and later on locks the door to keep him (and/or Gianni?) out. About midway through the film, Sandra shows Andrew all the places where she and Gianni used to hide messages. They discover a note hidden in a clock decorated with a statue of Amor and Psyche. By being associated with the intimate relationship of Sandra and Gianni, this representation of forbidden love that literally cannot bear the light of day suggests that there has been an element of trespassing in the relationship of the siblings as well.[52] Perhaps also significant is the fact that the clock is at the bottom of the family labyrinth, that is, in the bedroom of the mother.[53]

Sandra appears to believe that the message has been in the clock since her childhood and jokes about how useless the words "most important, most urgent" have turned out to be. But after having diverted Andrew's attention, she goes to the meeting place mentioned in the note, an ancient cistern, and finds Gianni there. Once again, with the perennial chiming of church bells in the background, her past courts her present.

The contrasts between light and darkness are at their most subtle in this haunting scene. Gianni's attempt to make Sandra lend him her wedding ring triggers a flashback of their mother calling her children monsters.[54] The physical proximity of her brother in this scene and the thought of the possible revelations in his book make Sandra increasingly uneasy and afraid. She fears that the book might give "their enemies" reason to believe that something untoward has actually taken place between them. Gianni makes it clear that he is not prepared to assist Sandra in her battle against their mother and Gilardini. The scene is visually one of the most astounding in the entire film. It ends with a shot in which the siblings are seen as a reflection in the water with Sandra leaving and walking up a spiral staircase – but since she is seen as a reflection, she appears to be moving downward. Finally the camera zooms in on the reflection of Gianni's face in the water, which makes him appear to be fading into darkness.

Andrew arranges a dinner party in order to achieve a reconciliation between Sandra and Gilardini. The attempt ends in disaster when Gilardini tells the shocked siblings that their mother intends to attend the dedication ceremony. A quarrel ensues in which Gilardini finally openly accuses the two of incest. When Gianni does not deny it, Andrew flies into a rage. In a cruel burst of anger, he tries to squeeze the truth out of the brother, who escapes only with his sister's help. Realizing that the book alienates Sandra from him, Gianni in desperation burns the manuscript. Thus what has perhaps been a sincere attempt to come to terms with the past ends up in flames. It is as if he were relinquishing all hope of communicating his innermost feelings to anyone.

Meanwhile Sandra tries to persuade her husband that her relationship with her brother is based simply on a common love for their father and on belonging to the same race. Nevertheless, she also tells him that she is going to stay in Volterra for the time being. And so Andrew leaves the ancient city, Giovanni burns his book, and Sandra appears to sink into the shadows of the past. But the last meeting of the siblings changes everything. She refuses his almost violent approaches. He tries to persuade her:

You have hidden your tenderness toward me behind a sacrificial mask. You have created a moral code for yourself, with which you have given yourself the right to persecute a poor sick woman and a petty thief. And because of this noble goal you have let your loving husband go. . . . I may be a cynic . . . mediocre . . . depraved . . . but at least I am capable of one gesture.

He takes a bottle of poison from a drawer under the Amor and Psyche statue. He tries to blackmail Sandra by threatening to commit suicide, but she crushes him with her response: "To me you are already dead, Gianni."

Sandra has all the while been on the brink of deceiving Andrew by falling into her brother's arms. In the end, she betrays both Gianni and the entire family by not stopping his suicide attempt. Thus she once again betrays herself, by committing a crime analogous to the one she still lays at her mother's door. Sandra has performed a kind of lobotomy on herself. It might have been necessary to save the patient's life, but inasmuch as the richness of human life can only spring from one's personal history, her future now promises to be emotionally and intellectually barren.

In the last scene three letters are heard in voice-overs by their writers as Sandra washes herself and prepares for the dedication ceremony. In the first, Andrew assures Sandra of his love and asks her to return to him. In the second, which she does not read, Gianni issues a last desperate cry for help. While Sandra is preparing for the ceremony, Gianni, realizing too late that she is not coming to rescue him, suffers an agonizing death. As Sandra dresses – in white – we hear her letter to Andrew, in which she says that she will return to him. Gianni dies on the floor of their mother's bedroom.[55]

When Sandra arrives at the park, the ceremony has already started. The rabbi recites Isaiah 26:19: "Thy dead men shall live, together with my dead body shall they arise. Awake and sing, ye that dwell in the dust: for thy dew is as the dew of the herbs, and the earth shall cast out the dead."

Style and themes

Sandra epitomizes some of Visconti's most constant concerns. The past appears more ambiguous and suspect, the family more internally destructive than in any of his earlier films. Works of art are used more self-consciously and suggestively as reference points and metaphors than anywhere else in his cinematic oeuvre. The crucial issue is neither history nor social or economic dialectics in relation to the individual, but rather the question of a person trying to cope with her own somewhat exceptional past. Thus the film marks a turn in Visconti's career toward a more interiorized, existential direction.

The film is structured to a great extent around musical, literary, visual, and even geographical metaphors.[56] The setting, the city of Volterra, has a definite metaphorical function, although some of its aspects are likely to escape a viewer unfamiliar with the relevant cultural or historical details. Volterra is located on the site of an Etruscan city built around 800 B.C. The city stands on a slowly eroding slope. The ancient necropolis and a part of the Etruscan wall have already disappeared, and the Christian monastery is now close to the abyss. Thus the city itself can be seen as a metaphor for the transience of both nature and culture. In the film, this transience serves as a metaphor for the need to settle accounts with the past before falling helplessly into the abyss of memories.

Perhaps even more symbolically significant are two works of art, Giacomo Leopardi's *Vaghe stelle dell'Orsa*, taken from his collection *Ricordanze* (Remembrances, 1829), and César Franck's *Prelude, Chorale and Fugue* (1884). Franck's late romantic piece for the piano is often said to reflect the tragic struggle between God and humanity, spiritual quest, and the battle between darkness and light.[57] These themes can readily be associated with the film, but the memories that the piece seems to evoke in Sandra's mind are far more significant.

Almost the entire Prelude is heard at the opening of the film, first as diegetic and then as background music during the credits. Subsequently, the Prelude and the last section of the Fugue (from *Come una cadenza* onward) are heard as Sandra becomes immersed in the memories of her youth during the visit to her ancestral home, particularly to her mother's empty rooms. In these scenes the music heightens the sense of sinking into her memories and could even be thought of as subjective diegetic music. Extracts from the Prelude and the final section of the Fugue are also heard during the long scenes that show the siblings together or that evoke their memories of childhood. The extracts are often quite long and in the cistern scene the entire Prelude is heard. Similarly, during the last, violent encounter between Sandra and Gianni, an extract from the Fugue is heard starting from *Come una cadenza* and ending, significantly, with the work's final chords.

In an earlier scene, in which Gianni washes himself in front of Sandra and Andrew, and talks about donating the garden to the municipality and perhaps selling the entire house, the beginning of the Chorale is heard. It is heard again toward the end of the film when Sandra is preparing for the dedication ceremony and Gianni is dying. This extract from the Chorale is longer than the previous one (up to the *Poco allegro*) and also covers the dedication ceremony itself. The final chords of the Fugue are first heard when Sandra arrives to see her mother and first addresses her. Up to this point it appears that the music during the scene has been nondiegetic, but now it suddenly becomes distinctly diegetic as it turns out that the mother is playing the piece – apparently over and over again.

The final chords are heard again when Sandra speaks her last words to Gianni. They appear a third and final time at the very end of the film, when Sandra finally turns her back on the past, and her father receives his last honors during the dedication ceremony.[58]

Thus Franck's music is used to reflect what is going on in Sandra's mind. The Prelude and the Fugue seem to draw her into her memories, except for the final chords of the Fugue (and of the piece as a whole), which emphasize the scenes in which she turns away from the three members of her family.

In contrast to the Franck piece, pop music, metonymically connected with Andrew, is a reminder of the everyday modern world. These pieces are entirely diegetic, except that in the night scene in the garden, the sound of the radio – with the words "Let's go" repeated again and again – carries unrealistically far. This, together with the sound of the wind, gives the garden scene a slightly uncanny quality. This is when Gianni first appears in the film, just as the singer reaches the words: "I want you to come back."

The church bells have a somewhat different function. They, too, serve as a reminder of the "real" world – particularly as they are heard twice through diegetic pop music – but of course they also serve as a symbol of timelessness. They are first heard at night, when Andrew comes to the garden where Sandra and Gianni have just met and embraced in a somewhat suggestive manner. The bells peal again when Andrew and Gianni return from their nocturnal sightseeing tour, when Sandra locks her door, and when each is seen lying alone and awake in bed. The hushed words of a song are now also heard in the background: "Io che non vivo senza te" (I who cannot live without you). And again the music not unequivocally diegetically motivated. Finally, at the end of the film, the chiming bells accompany Sandra's "purification rites," as if to announce Gianni's death and her sterile rebirth.

The reference to Leopardi's poem resonates with a richness equal to that of the music. *Vaghe* means vague, hazy or pretty, or charming, but also desirous or even wandering, errant; *stelle dell Orsa* is the constellation of the Bear, which Heraclitus called an "immortal witness" of human affairs because it never disappears below the horizon.[59] Leopardi was a rational, systematic thinker whose work was infused with romantic passion and a sense of desperation. He had a problematic relationship with his dominating father and an emotionally cold mother. The crucial theme that reverberates in his poetry pertains to the struggle between *eros* and *thanatos*. Love generates life but turns out also to be an omen of death. This theme is particularly evident in the poem *Sopra il ritratto di una bella donna, scolpito nel monumento sepolcra della medesima* (About a portrait of a beautiful woman carved on a sepulchre, 1835), inspired by the illustrations in Giuseppe Micali's *Storia degli antichi popoli italiani* (The history of the ancient people of Italy, 1832). In one of the illustrations, the angel of death appears in the form of a young woman, an Etruscan Lasae.[60]

Sandra's plaited hair in the scene in the ancient Roman underground cistern resembles that of the female figures in the Etruscan frescoes of funeral rites in Tarquinia.[61] Thus to Gianni she looks like a Lasae, an unattainable object of love who leads her wooer to spiritual destruction and death. Leopardi's poetry, which Gianni at one point recites, reflects not only the poet's infatuation with the past but also his own, his intoxication with his memories and his romantic escape from the present and its complexities and responsibilities. Thus Leopardi's poetry acts as a symbol of Gianni's wish to lose himself in the shadows of the past, just as Franck's piano piece appears to draw Sandra and their mother toward memories so painful and laden with guilt that they have the power to drive one mad. The associations aroused by the music and the poem, combined with the possibility of incest, all present a turning inward, away from the world, into a sheltered nook of unconscious fantasy in the depths of primal family unity.

The visual realization, both in terms of mise-en-scène and camera work, enriches this figurative progression. The film is shot in black and white, often with extreme contrasts between light and darkness. In Nowell-Smith's apt expression, "The light dazzles and the darkness obscures. There is no middle term, no possibility of nuance in assessing the scene."[62] The pull of the past is repeatedly manifested whenever Sandra enters the dark rooms of her mother's apartment, in most encounters with Gianni around their childhood home, and above all in her descent into the womb-like cistern where she is to meet him. These are all shadowy scenes, always accompanied by Franck's evocative music. In contrast, Sandra and Andrew usually meet in well-lit surroundings. In general, the film moves from darkness to light, from a sinking into memories to the resolute denial of those memories and all that they have stood for.

The contrast between darkness and light is particularly evident in two of the film's most striking shots. One of these shows Sandra going to the park for the first time. White cloth covers the statue of her father and the trees around it are lit from below. It is nighttime. Together with the sound track, the image creates a strange atmosphere. The other, shot at the end of the film, shows the same place during the daytime and in full sunlight, but with the people hidden among the shadows under the trees. Perhaps because of the contrast with the earlier, nocturnal shot, this image, too, has a disturbing quality.

The contrast between black and white also appears in the clothing Sandra and her mother wear. At times, the way Sandra dresses does not fit the situation. At the diplomatic reception she appears to be the only woman in black. In most of the film she wears a black-and-white dress topped with a wide brimmed black hat that often leaves her face in shadow. Inside the palace she often wraps a large white shawl around her shoulders, easily associated with the cloth covering her father's statue. The shawl gains in significance as Gianni repeatedly fondles it. In the dinner scene Sandra is again dressed in black, whereas in the dedication ceremony, as if to demonstrate her new resolution (about which no one present knows anything), she wears white whereas everyone else is in black.

In *Sandra* Visconti employs cinematic devices such as the zoom in a more pronounced way than in any of his other films. The zoom, says Suzanne Liandrat-Guigues, almost seems to represent time: "The *zoom* 'traces' a vector of temporalization and gives a sensible depth to the shot. It mimes an interior journey through a thickness of time."[63] This applies particularly to the crucial zoom back when Sandra enters the rooms in which her mother used to live and to the two zooms to the Amor and Psyche statue. Also, the quiet zoom to Gianni and the sudden, striking zoom away from him when he first reveals he is writing a book based on his childhood memories (and is fondling Sandra's shawl) suggests the gravitational pull of the past.

Yet Liandrat-Guigues's account is somewhat unsatisfactory in explaining at least one of the most prominent uses of this device, namely, the six zooms back and forth within the single shot showing Sandra putting out the lights and locking her door to keep Andrew out. If anything, this seems to express Sandra's uncertainty about her feelings for Andrew (and perhaps for both men). A little later, the rocking movement continues in the three shots of the three characters lying awake in their beds: toward Andrew, away from Gianni, toward Sandra. Here the zoom seems to create both a parallel and a contrast between the two men in Sandra's mind. Thus the device is used throughout the film for various expressive purposes, mainly connected with character subjectivity, but always with a considerable degree of ambiguity.

Indeed, it is essential to accept the ambiguity and avoid overinterpreting *Sandra*. The ramifying cultural references thinly buried under its surface point to suppressed psychological problems, pathological human relations, and the inability to come to terms with the past. But all in all, the film is so packed with vague cultural references that the network they form is more significant as a whole than are the individual references as such. Liandrat-Guigues has aptly compared this to Pierre Boulez's aesthetic: "The superimpositions are at certain moments so dense that they annihilate each other and produce a global impression."[64]

Liandrat-Guigues has suggested that the key to *Sandra* is the notion of "scintillation." This term captures the ideas of "modification of intensity or luminosity, distance traveled over varying periods of time, appearance and obliteration, the interval between emission and perception, the sensation of something already disappeared, such as the perception of the light of stars already dead."[65] Indeed, it captures perfectly the tone of the film and unifies the multiplicity of its metaphors: showing how truly difficult it is to determine to what extent the distant past influences the present; and to recognize the vagueness and the relativity that all too often limit human perception and understanding.

THE WITCH BURNED ALIVE

After *Sandra*, Visconti had many ideas for other films, among them an adaptation of Robert Musil's *Young Törless*. However, his next work for the screen was an episode in the film *Le streghe* (The witches, 1966). The directors of the other episodes were Mauro Bolognini, Pier Paolo Pasolini, Francesco Rosi, and Vittorio De Sica.

Visconti's *Le strega bruciata viva* is about a film star, Gloria (Silvana Mangano), who visits her friend Valeria at the Austrian holiday resort Kitzbühl. There she also meets Valeria's husband, Paolo, and some guests. In the evening Gloria dresses in a glittering gown that resembles golden armor. The camera adoringly follows Gloria's seductive dance until she suddenly faints. The women withdraw, Gloria is freed from her armor, and it turns out that she is pregnant.

Gloria is enthusiastic, but when she tells her producer husband the news in a transatlantic telephone conversation, he reminds her that she is scheduled to make a film soon. She tries to postpone the shooting so that she can have the baby. But he refuses, and Gloria gives in. Out of her armor, she is a woman, but now she "puts it on" again and resumes the role of a diva. The next morning, surrounded by a flock of journalists, Gloria leaves on a helicopter.

Being a diva means being a part of a highly organized assembly line. At a party in the evening, an old industrialist says to her: "You are a product. A sublime product, extraordinary surely, but a product. . . . If you don't maintain your quality, have the same flavor, the same calories, you have a true and a proper disaster on your hands. . . . In my canned meat I always use the same ingredients. I am very scrupulous, I can assure you. One mustn't jeopardize an industry." Later, he adds: "You artists are a peculiar branch of industry . . . precarious, unlikely, all it takes is a draft or a love affair and all the capital goes up in smoke."[66]

On one hand, Monica Stirling suggests that Visconti sees the screen actress as not just an erotic symbol, but as a kind of witch who can influence people by playing on their emotions. And like a witch she risks losing her soul.[67] On the other hand, Le strega has been seen as Visconti's comment on the role of women in society as a whole: As Visconti's friend Suso Cecchi d'Amico has noted: "One thing which only a few know and which hardly anyone has brought up is that Luchino's concept of the family was completely patriarchal." Visconti himself has remarked:

A woman can be an artist – I am talking about a woman such as Callas, a painter, an author, or other great artist – but at some moment she realizes she is something else, a woman, that is, the guardian of the family. As she was originally. Women used to have a noble and an irreplaceable role in the home that no one would dream of disparaging.[68]

According to Visconti, men and women no longer have a clearly defined role in the household. That is why families everywhere are disintegrating and why society has been engulfed in chaos. But whatever opinion Visconti might have had about the role of women, it should be noted that the women in his films seldom succeed in maintaining their traditional roles. Not even the strongest mother of all, Rosaria, is able to prevent her family from falling apart. But what is perhaps even more noteworthy is that Visconti neither idealized nor disparaged the women he depicted any more than he fell into the trap of offering simplistic solutions for social or existential problems.

There are certain autobiographical elements in Le streghe both from Silvana Mangano's and Visconti's side. It was in Kitzbühl, in 1934, that Visconti met Irma Windisch-Grätz, the only woman he is ever known to have proposed to. The relationship between the film star and the producer in turn vaguely reflected that between Mangano and her husband, the

film's producer, Dino De Laurentiis. She was close to Visconti's idea of
an ideal diva in that her family life was stable and she was "dedicated to
her family and an elegant, austere professional, who shunned public-
ity".[69] The problem was her husband. He demanded that the episode be
shortened considerably. When Visconti refused to do so, Laurentiis had
it edited to his specifications. Visconti disowned the resulting film.[70]

CONVERSATION PIECE

Just before *Ludwig* (1973) was completed, Visconti had a heart attack. He never really recovered, and after being released from the hospital, he found it difficult to move about. His earlier plans, all on a grand
scale, had to be put on hold. This state of affairs led Enrico Medioli, Suso
Cecchi d'Amico, and Visconti to develop an idea that had struck Medioli
when reading Mario Praz's book, *Conversation Piece*. The title refers to
a term "used in England for paintings, usually not of large dimensions,
which represent two or more identifiable people in attitudes implying that
they are conversing or communicating with each other informally, against
a background reproduced in detail." [71]

In the early 1970s, Italy experienced one of its worst crises since the
war. Many extremist groups, fed up with parliamentary democracy, had
begun resorting to terrorism. The trouble started when right-wingers reacted to the student riots of 1968. When the riots failed to achieve their
objective, the left-wingers launched their own attacks. Many unemployed
and foreign workers were easily recruited to fight the establishment. Some
of them had fathers who had been members of the resistance and they
now felt they were facing a similar task. For some time, the terrorists had
quite a few sympathizers and a good deal of money at their disposal.[72]

Ten days before the shooting of *Conversation Piece* was due to begin,
the neo-Fascist group Ordine Nero (Black Order) threw a bomb into the
middle of a demonstration held in Brescia that killed six and wounded
ninety. Three weeks after the film was completed, a bomb planted by the
same group on a train between Florence and Bologna killed twelve and
wounded forty-eight. Although the police were given extended powers,
this did not help curb the violence. There were constant rumors of a
possible coup, and in December 1970 Prince Valerio Borghese, known as
the "Black Prince," had actually succeeded in occupying the Ministry of
the Interior for a short while. These events obviously served as the model
for the political intrigues referred to in the film.[73]

Perhaps because Visconti had great difficulty moving around now, the style of camera work and consequently also of the editing in *Conversation Piece* was somewhat different from that in his other films. That may also be why he avoided complicated shots, and why there are no particularly long takes, no narrative-audiovisual *tour de forces* of the kind featured in some of his earlier films. The conversations are often captured in series of fairly short close-ups. The film consists of about 770 shots, while in *Ludwig*, which is twice as long, there are only about 900 shots.[74] But again the sets are luxurious, their wealth of detail is abundant, and the sense of time and its passing is remarkably captured.

The film is about an old professor living alone in his big house and a group of people, a family of a kind, who rent an apartment in his attic. The central tension in the film is built around the cultural orientation of the professor (he is never given a name) and the relationship with the past this involves, on the one hand, and the intensive "living-in-the-present" of his tenants. The professor had used culture – primarily his art collection and his library – to build a barricade against the external world. The younger generation of the family live only in the present, and their opinions about society and their general philosophy are as trendy as those of the terrorist groups of the 1970s.

The gently pessimistic tone of the film derives from the failure of the professor to present new perspectives to the youngsters. They see in him only a quaint old collector of cultural objects of little significance beyond their decorative value. However, one of these young people, Konrad, has been an art student and is able to make perceptive comments about paintings and classical music. But his knowledge is superficial and has very little affective extension, although ironically enough Konrad is able to correct the professor on a point of fact concerning a painting. Art vibrates intensively in the mind of the professor, but he has let it become a timeless substitute for real life. As the film progresses, the "family" he has reluctantly accepted as his tenants gradually pulls him back into the exasperating flux of time – starting with a drastic refurbishing of the flat they have rented. But in the last instance, it is the professor's own longing that compels him to interact with the youngsters. Time mercilessly breaks through the walls he has built around himself.

During the film, the professor (Burt Lancaster) gradually gets to know Signora Bianca Brumonti (Silvana Mangano); her daughter, Lietta (Claudia Marsani); Lietta's fiancé, Stefano (Stefano Patrizi); and Bianca's kept boyfriend, Konrad (Helmut Berger). The crucial relationship in the film turns out to be that between the professor and Konrad, partly because at one point they perceive the others as their opponents. But their contact is, in the last instance, as insubstantial as the similarities that the terrorists saw between their own activities and the battle fought by the resistance. The professor – who on his mother's side is Italian, and on his father's American – came to Italy with the U.S. Army during the Second World War. For his part, Konrad was involved in the 1968 riots in Berlin.

Like Franz in *Senso*, Konrad sells himself to a woman and hates himself for doing so. The special relationship between him and the professor is signaled by a slight zoom toward his face when he first appears. For a passing moment, the professor and Konrad are on the brink of making contact. The young man succeeds in impressing the older with his knowledge of art and music and the older one has a chance to take care of the younger when one night he is beaten in the flat. The professor takes him into a small, secret, windowless room in which the professor's mother once offered asylum to partisans and Jews during the war – it is as if the professor, assuming the role of a father, was taking the boy to the safety of a mother's womb. They have both suffered disillusionment as the great battles they participated in did not lead to a better world – they have both experienced the *trasformismo* of their times – but that is where the similarity ends. Konrad has become an egoistic cynic, while the professor has at least remained considerate and sympathetic – but then of course, he was born into a class that offered him the comforts of life without struggle and compromise.

Konrad forbids the professor to report the beating to the police, arguing that they would not be interested, in his case. He also feels humiliated and does not want anyone to know what has happened. Although the cause may have been gambling debts, as Lietta and Stefano say, Konrad at least tries to give the impression that the beating had a more important, perhaps political, connection. In any case, the reason for the mugging is never made clear either to the professor or to the audience.

Despite these strict limits, the professor's relationship with Konrad offers him a chance to experience art and beauty as a means of reaching out to another human being rather than as a wall to keep them at a distance. At the same time, he is now thoroughly accustomed to enjoying experiences mediated by art rather than through direct experience. When the youngsters go out sailing, he is momentarily taken by the idea of the sea: "The sea is always lovely, colours of the sea, voices of the sea. . . . I can never understand how the Greek artists could concentrate on creating so many wonders when they had before their eyes always that haunting spectacle, fascinating, spellbinding." The youngsters invite him to come sailing with them, but he prefers to remain among the wonders inspired by the sea. "You live among people; you must think about people instead of their works, to become involved, to suffer because of them," the professor explains, "and besides, as someone said, crows fly in flocks, the eagle soars alone." Konrad answers him by quoting the Bible: "Woe to him that is alone when he falleth, for he hath not another to help him up."[75] And so the crows fly away and the eagle remains alone once again.

The *Conversation Piece* is very much about solitude, at once comforting and terrifying. The professor has learned to cope with loneliness, but the sudden penetration of his life by the youngsters instills in him the hope that he might still create around him the family of which life and his own character have deprived him. Although the wish remains unfulfilled, it awakens in him a sensitivity that at least metaphorically becomes the cause of his death. This is foreshadowed in three brief flashbacks representing a few of the most crucial moments of his life. We see his first visit, as a small boy with his mother, to the old house in Rome that is now his permanent residence. The second flashback, consisting of just three shots, shows his veiled bride arriving at that house, then complaining about their inability to communicate with one another. This flashback – framed by painterly images of the professor in his bed listening to Mozart's E flat major Sinfonia Concertante – is interrupted by the youngsters playing the hit tune, "La mia solitudine sei tu" (You are my solitude).

In the third flashback, presented as a dream, the professor hears his mother say: "You aren't at all nice to your grandfather. He is so happy to have us here. He's alone so much. It's terrible to be left alone. When you are alone and ill." The flashback turns out to be a fantasy in which the professor is defending not his present life but his behavior as a little boy: "Alone? He's not alone. He has a cook, a maid, he's even got a cat. I don't have a cat." Again, his reminiscence is interrupted by music being played by the youngsters and by Lietta's phone call inviting him to come upstairs. None of the three flashbacks shows the professor, and thus it takes some effort (and perhaps also repeated viewings) to grasp who the other characters are and how they are connected to the professor. What is obvious, however, is that throughout his life he has been drawn to solitude.

The professor's relationships with those other than Konrad remain shallow. In her arrogance and inability to take into consideration other people, Bianca is, after Sophie of *The Damned*, the most egocentric woman in Visconti's cinematic oeuvre. In its cruelty, the portrait is of the same class as Proust's images of Parisian high society. Bianca's relationship with Konrad is extremely intense, but nevertheless shallow; it is a love–hate relationship colored by furious jealousy. Konrad has to keep lying to her just to get a moment's peace from her, even if these lies inevitably lead to ever new dramas.

Lietta has an abundance of youthful charm, but it is only of moderate appeal to the professor. Perhaps Lietta's mother reminds him too much of what charming girls might turn into, or perhaps he simply has turned away completely from male–female relationships after his unsuccessful marriage. Lietta represents liberated sensuousness, living innocently for the pleasure of the moments. When the professor discovers the three youngsters engaged in a small orgy, she recites W. H. Auden's poem: "When you see a fair form/ Chase it/ And if possible embrace it/ Be it a girl or a boy/ Don't be bashful, be brash, be fresh/ Life is short, so enjoy/ Whatever contact your flesh/ May at the moment crave/ There is no sex in the grave." Lietta proposes a kiss for the professor, but he asks: "Do you think of me as one of those characters in a comic opera, the old man who is mocked and betrayed? The only love story that would suit a man of my age is King Lear's, by his love for his children."

Stefano's father is an industrialist, whose workers are on strike. Stefano's function in the story is mainly to bring out questions about Konrad's obscure activities and make equally ambiguous and unreliable political references. When the dinner toward the end of the film, to which the professor has invited the entire "family," ends in a quarrel, Stefano at first tries to calm everyone down. But soon he becomes agitated himself and accuses Konrad of hypocrisy, of condemning the society that enables him to live in luxury. Konrad defends himself by claiming that the people among whom Bianca and her husband move are murderers planning a coup. He tells Bianca to ask Stefano about this, and the expressions on his face suggest that there might be some truth in this – we never get to know how much, and the accusations remain as obscure as in *Sandra*. In any case, Stefano answers Konrad in angry tones, accusing him of being an informer and a slanderer. Konrad haughtily admits this to be true. The two start fighting. The exasperated professor tries to intervene. Finally, Konrad marches away.

And so ends the professor's attempt to build a family around himself, to place himself within his own conversation piece; a family of strangers far too restless to be contained within a fixed image. He summarizes the events that have now taken place and the effect it has had on his life:

If ever a landlord had difficult tenants, I believe I had. Yet I found myself thinking, as Lietta once said, that you really have been my family. A family that turned out well or badly, absolutely different. Since I love this wretched family, I want to do what I can for it, as it unawares has done something to me. There is a writer whose books I keep by my bed and read from time to time. He tells of a tenant who moves stealthily to the apartment above. The writer hears the tenant moving above, walking – and suddenly he seems to vanish. For a long time he is not heard again. But he comes back. Gradually his absence becomes more rare, his presence more constant. He's death, the awareness that [the writer] has reached the end of his life, announced to him in one of death's deceitful disguises. Your presence above me has meant just the opposite to me, and I don't believe I have been deceived. You have awakened me from a sleep as profound and as insensitive . . . as death itself.

The speech is made subtly touching by Burt Lancaster's fine, sensitive performance and Franco Mannino's discreetly sentimental music. During the last sentences, the camera pans in a graceful arc over the paintings on the wall, ending so that the professor can be seen in front of a window with his back toward the camera. This is already the beginning of the next scene.

A message arrives from Konrad, a simple farewell, signed: "Your son, Konrad." An explosion is heard. The professor rushes to the apartment and finds the unconscious, perhaps already dead, Konrad. In the last scene the professor is seen lying in a bed, attached to a cardiograph. Bianca and Lietta come to visit him. Bianca believes that Konrad committed suicide. She thinks he did it because he wanted to have the last word. But she also argues that he was doomed to fail because "grief is as precarious as anything else." Lietta, however, thinks that Konrad was liquidated. Her opinion is substantiated by the fact that when he died Konrad had in his grasp Stefano's scarf. After the women leave, the professor hears the sound of steps from above and collapses.

Some time before the film was completed, Visconti issued a statement in which he complained about the world "becoming more and more alienated, cruel and callous. Impossible to govern. And in Italy things are going worse than elsewhere. Italy is a country where they can't even form a cabinet."[76] References to political life in Italy are not too clear in *Conversation Piece*, but this very vagueness creates the sense that the country has no political or ideological, not to mention spiritual, center. Above all, the "family" the professor momentarily acquires seems to embody the director's feelings about the dissolution of the family as an institution and about the precariousness of love and friendship. Because Visconti's own life – particularly with respect to family – in many ways exemplifies these tendencies, the film appears to be an attempt to sort out some of the contradictions of his personality. In essence, the professor appears to be an image of the filmmaker himself, as the lonely carrier of tradition and high culture – culture not just as works of art such as these that both the professor and Visconti surrounded themselves with, but as an internalized code of behavior and a certain way of life. This projection is probably the reason for the almost unbearable contrast between the sympathetic professor and the crude and cruel caricature of the family he is given. It is as if Visconti wanted to show that family life is really not the right alternative for a man of culture dedicated to beauty and art.

4

Visconti and Germany

VISCONTI, THOMAS MANN, AND TWO ASPECTS OF EUROPE

Visconti liked to boast about his connection with German culture by claiming that he had partly German ancestry – after all, the Viscontis of the Middle Ages had been Langobards. But though Germany always fascinated him, in his youth he was drawn more to France. His life in Paris in the thirties had had a decisive influence on his development both as a person and an artist. Yet of all his films only *The Stranger* is based on a French subject. In contrast, three consecutive films were not only set in Germany but were also closely tied to the history and culture of that country – these films have often been called Visconti's German trilogy. The connection with Germany is also a significant factor in the episode film *The Job*.

To Visconti Germany meant above all culture: the works of Goethe, Thomas and Heinrich Mann, and Richard Wagner; also the Austrian variety of German culture – Gustav Mahler and the evocations of the dying Austro-Hungarian Empire by Franz Werfel, Stefan Zweig, and Robert Musil. Reading Karl Krauss and Joseph Roth probably helped give an edge to this nostalgia. But like a shadow behind this interest in German culture was Visconti's fascination with its negation, its plunge into ruthless barbarism. After seizing power in 1933, the Nazis began introducing a new order of their own making. Visconti decided to go and see what was happening with his own eyes.[1]

In later life Visconti seldom spoke of this journey. He was probably somewhat ashamed because at that time he had to some extent admired the Nazis. The features of the new order that fascinated him in particular could also be found in his own personality: orderliness, determination, and efficiency. He saw Leni Riefenstahl's celebrated film, *The Triumph of the Will* (1935), and could not help admiring not only its artistic and technical quality but also its idealization of youth, health, power, and order. On a few occasions Visconti went to see Hitler's magnificent displays in front of exuberant masses. Quite probably, he was also fascinated by the handsome blonde young men in their menacing black uniforms.[2]

Soon after the visit to Germany, Visconti got to know Horst, who helped him both accept his own homosexuality and break away from the enchantment of Nazism. In the eyes of the Nazis and the Fascists alike, he was now a pervert; in Paris, he became a socialite. About this time news of the terror and persecution practiced by the Nazis was spreading to the West, and Visconti's uninformed admiration began to turn into revulsion. Even so, a touch of inadvertent admiration for the Nazis remained with him throughout his life. Visconti's two closest German friends, Horst and the composer Hans Werner Henze, thought that he did not really understand Germany and Nazism and that he tended to mythify them. Henze strongly disapproved of the treatment of the rise of Nazism presented in *The Damned* (1969). Horst did not go to see the film at all.[3]

In the 1960s Visconti grew more and more alienated from the Contemporary political struggle. Neither Marx nor Gramschi seemed able to properly explain the anarchy and terrorism that followed the 1968 riots. What he found especially disconcerting about the new situation was that it reminded him of the years immediately preceding the Fascist era. He began to identify more and more with Thomas Mann, whom he saw as one of the last protectors of humanism at a point when Germany was falling into barbarism.[4] This admiration had its roots in Visconti's artistic sensibilities. In an interview with Gaia Servadio, he stated: "After Goethe I love Thomas Mann. In one way or another, all my films are dipped in Mann."[5] Many of the questions Mann probed were familiar to Visconti, and both sought a balance between art and life, beauty and truth, sensuality and intellect, passion and control, pathos and irony. Although one was by birth and breeding a sophisticated aristocrat and the other a cultivated bourgeois, both believed the artist played an important role as a member of society and of a certain class, on the one hand, and as their outside observer, on the other.

To Mann, Italy and its spirit, *latinitas*, was a necessary counterweight to Germany and its *germanitas*. For quite some time he thought that only Germany could produce real "culture," based on the manly spiritual quest, as opposed to mere "civilization," exemplified in Italian feminine sensuousness and sensitivity. This opposition paralleled a crucial distinction in Nietzsche's philosophy. In his *Die Geburt der Tragödie aus dem Geiste der Musik* (The birth of tragedy from the spirit of music, 1871), Nietzsche pits Dionysian, ecstatic sensuality against Apollonian rational control and the ideal of classical unity. Mann strove to reconcile these opposites – just as he sought to find a middle path in most ideological issues – but he never ceased to be suspicious about *latinitas*, or Dionysian abandon, for that matter. In Mann's oeuvre, the south, the Mediterranean, and Italy in particular radiate sensuousness that can only too easily throw the calm northern mind off balance. It may serve as a source of artistic expression, but inasmuch as it does so, it also implies that art and life cannot be reconciled. It is no coincidence that Adrian Leverkühn in *Doktor Faustus* encounters the devil on his journey to Italy.

During the First World War, Mann felt that only German culture could save European culture. Only gradually, particularly after the German defeat, he became aware of the contradictions and tensions that threatened the country and its culture from within. In *The Magic Mountain* (1924) and *Doctor Faustus* (1947), the two traditions and mentalities are pitted against each other through the opposition of representative characters (Settembrini versus Naphta and Zeitblom versus Leverkühn, respectively) in order to explore their complementarities. In the latter work, in particular, Mann hopes to articulate his own thoughts, his desperation and weakness in the face of what Germany and German culture had become in the 1930s. While in a sense paying respect to modernity in art, Mann in effect opposes it to culture. For him, the German tragedy was that the country had forgotten and distorted its profound cultural heritage. To some extent, this seemed inevitable to him in an era of worn-out forms. According to Dominick LaCapra: "German history has for Mann perhaps the most concentrated and forceful expression of the problems and paradoxes of modern civilization – the paradoxical meeting of the best and the worst."[6]

Visconti no doubt felt a close association with Thomas Mann because of Mann's position as a "late-comer," an essentially conservative and far from avant-garde author, who had many ties to the preceding cultural era. Visconti might well have seen himself, with his Germanic affiliations, as an Italian counterpart to the German artist haunted by his scarcely suppressed Latin leanings.

The difference between Italian and German cultures is reflected in an interesting way in the different forms that romanticism assumed in these two countries. After the 1815 restoration Italy developed its own brand of romanticism. In particular, it sneered at the emphasis on the "fantastic" that was thought to be typical of German culture and at the use of mythological themes. Instead, Italian artists concentrated on historical subjects, which were well suited to the needs of a people – or rather, an ascendant social class – that was striving to achieve national unity. The *Weltschmerz* type of romanticism had little appeal for the Italian educated classes either. The role of the artist was to express the deepest feelings and aspirations of the nation. These trends found their most powerful expression in the field of opera, particularly in the works of Giuseppe Verdi.[7]

Visconti fell right into step with Italy's great operatic tradition for his melodramas are deeply rooted in a conception of social and historical reality. Although the internalization of his late works definitely reflects a German influence, the tone derives from Thomas Mann, who was aligned with the nineteenth-century realistic tradition in literature rather than the fantastic or mythological romanticism epitomized in the operas of Karl Maria von Weber and Richard Wagner, respectively.

Visconti's first adaptation of Mann was a ballet-fantasy based on the novella *Mario und der Zauberer* (Mario and the magician, 1930). Franco Mannino wrote the music. After several postponements, the work had its premiere in 1956, under the title *Mario e il mago*. The magician of the novel is a hypnotist and a conjurer who is able to manipulate people in his audiences to make them act against their principles and natural patterns of behavior. The novella was obviously anti-Fascist, and it appeared in Italy only after the war. According to Micciché, Visconti gave Mann's text a very explicit rendering, except that where Mann used various metaphors to explore people's subconscious motives, Visconti emphasized the realistic elements and sensuality of the characters. Whereas in Mann liberation from the power of the magician signified the restoration of reason, in Visconti it appeared more like the victory of the power of *élan vital*.[8]

In addition to the two direct adaptations – the second being *Death in Venice* – Mann's influence can be seen particularly in *Rocco and His Brothers*, which was inspired in part by *Joseph and His Brothers* (1933–43), and in *The Damned*, which in some respects resembles *Buddenbrooks* (1901). But perhaps even more important are the parallels and contrasts between Italy and Germany that appear throughout Visconti's oeuvre – almost as if to suggest a kind of alternative way of being a European.

THE JOB

The Job is Visconti's contribution to the episode film *Boccaccio '70* (1962). It is about the daughter of a rich German industrialist, named

Pupe (Romy Schneider). She is married to an Italian count (Tomas Milian) just discovered by the tabloids to be involved with prostitutes. Not only does this ruin his reputation, but it puts a freeze on his bank accounts, which, for taxation purposes, have been set up in Switzerland in the countess's name. As the count's lawyers remind him, he is completely dependent on his wife financially. Her father, though apparently pleased with the prestige the marriage has brought to him, would now like his daughter to divorce the penniless count and keeps telephoning her from Germany to see how things are progressing.

Pupe says she has always known that theirs was just a marriage of convenience, but she has grown tired of being nothing more than high-class merchandise and wants to become financially independent. She has decided to support herself by going out to work and has even made a bet with her father that she is capable of doing so. The count strongly objects to the idea and tries to talk Pupe out of it by having a servant tell her how boring ordinary work can be. Pupe has to admit she does not know how to do anything that she could be paid for. She says she respects money, but apparently she is so used to it that it has never occurred to her that actually earning it might be a problem. She is also innocently dependent on her servants bringing her whatever she happens to desire.

Pupe prepares to have a shower and inadvertently undresses in a provocative fashion. As she is drying herself the count looks at her and is overtaken by desire for her – perhaps the fear of losing her has made him see her with hew eyes. He might have had his escapades and she might be hurt, but they are still beautiful people attracted to each other. It is only a question of time before they will reach some sort of reconciliation – as the servants, who obviously know their masters better than they do themselves, are well aware. Pupe realizes that there is a profession she can take up: the same one practiced by the women her husband recently "employed." By entering into a similar arrangement with Pupe, the count will not have to pay "Madame" Imola any more. At first, the count is taken back by this proposal but then finds the idea quite appealing. There is yet another telephone call from Pupe's father, but she refuses to take it on the excuse that she is just about to start in her new job. She has won her bet, but it is a sad victory. This deceptively charming, bittersweet film ends with the disconcerting image of a husband approaching his wife's bed with a check in his hand.

This film has some autobiographical elements, the most obvious of which is the countess's pet name, Pupe, which Visconti had used for the love of his youth, Irma Windisch-Grätz. Then, too, the count is in part

an ironic self-portrait of Visconti as a young man, while the efforts of
Pupe's father to control events from afar parallel those of Irma's father,
who did whatever he could to prevent her relationship with the Italian
aristocrat from developing into a serious affair. Visconti has even said
that the Austrian Romy Schneider bore a slight resemblance to the real
Pupe of his youth. The film is very much a vehicle for Schneider; poor
Milian has little chance of matching the performance of his exuberant
leading lady.

In his customary fashion, Visconti created a luxurious milieu down to
the smallest glamorous detail. The film's producer was Carlo Ponti, who
pointed out that although the episode was shot in a single apartment, it
was the most expensive episode of the entire film. The sumptuous setting
furnishes the perfect context for Schneider's delightful, glittering, cham-
pagne-like performance. All the action takes place in the count's palace,
in which Pupe has built her own feminine island. Whereas the count's
enormous dogs roam around the other parts of the palace, Pupe's rooms
are inhabited by innumerable cats. Pupe's entire existence appears to be
tied to the objects around her, for she is never seen anywhere else and all
the emphasis is on her feline ability to enjoy the comforts that surround
and dominate her. The idea of having to relinquish these wonderful objects is a threat to her very being. She has to own in order to exist because
she can only exist in high and glamorous style – and to do that, she needs
an aristocratic husband.

As in most of Visconti's films, sexuality and material possessions are
depicted in a hopeless tangle, as they are, for example in the relationship
between Angelica and Tancredi in *The Leopard*. But this time even the
illusion of love is shattered, perhaps because Pupe has almost accidentally
fallen out of love. Her uncontrolled laughter toward the end of the film
is telling: at some level she has grown aware that her life is shallow and
that her *haute-bourgeois* marriage is based on petty bourgeois commercial values. The count has no such problems. Since all that he wants is
what money can buy, he has nothing to lose except his income from his
father-in law.

THE DAMNED

The inverse side of Germany

After the Second World War, Thomas Mann lamented the spiritual
deterioration in Germany:

There are not two Germanies, a good and an evil, but only a single one, which turned its best by devilry into bad. Evil Germany, that is the good which has festered, the good in misfortune, in guilt and decline. For this reason it is so impossible for a German-born mind to disown the evil, guilt-laden Germany and to declare: "I am the good, the noble, the righteous Germany in white, the evil I leave to your extermination." Nothing of that which I have said to you about Germany or tried fleetingly to point out, came from knowledge dissociated, cool or uninvolved; I have it also in me, I have experienced it in my own body.[9]

The conflict that Mann knew so well both in himself and in Germany in general was familiar to Visconti, too: it was a deeply felt understanding of the destructive forces that are part and parcel of both the human mind and society as a whole. *The Damned* is a description not only of a diabolical power struggle but also of the misappropriation and utter negation of German culture.

The Damned was produced by the Italnoleggio, a state agency created in the sixties to distribute films with limited release possibilities. In this case, it had to resort to international cooperation. Against Visconti's wishes, the film was given the English title *The Damned* because the American producers thought that it would attract a wider audience than *The Twilight of the Gods*. In any case, *The Damned* become both a critical and a popular success, and it is the only Visconti film that ever made a significant profit. It broke box-office records in many major Italian cities and also enjoyed considerable success in the United States. The reasons were obviously not only artistic. The numerous murders, the atmosphere of perversity, and the scene of the night of the long knives attracted a large audience, and the film was followed by a wave of films about Nazism.[10]

When Visconti was asked why he wanted to make a film about Nazism and not about Fascism he answered:

Because of the difference between tragedy and comedy. Of course Fascism was a tragedy in many, many cases . . . but as the perfect archetype of a given historical situation that leads to a certain type of criminality, Nazism seemed to me to be more exemplary – because it was a tragedy that, like a hideous bloodstain, seeped over the whole world. . . . One could make thousands of films about Italian Fascism . . . about Matteotti . . . Mussolini's Republic of Salò . . . the death of Gramsci . . . but Nazism seems to me to reveal more about a historical reversal of values.[11]

Although Suso Cecchi d'Amico had only a small hand in the making of the German trilogy, she helped formulate the idea of *The Damned*:

[Originally,] we wanted to make a sort of *Macbeth*, placed in modern times. There was at the time the Profumo scandal in England, and that gave us the milieu for the story based on *Macbeth*. And when we were writing it . . . [I saw] in a magazine a big article with beautiful photos about the Krupp family. And so I called Luchino to say that I thought it offered a much better milieu than the one we had thought about. And so he started to read about the Krupp family.[12]

Nevertheless, something of the original idea remained. The story of Alfred Krupp merely intensified these traits in the script and gave them the perfect setting. Hitler had placed the economic organization of the war in Krupp's hands, and he was the one who masterminded the use of forced labor in many of his own as well as in other factories. The youngest of these prisoners were six-year-old children. It is said that toward the end of his life Krupp – like Macbeth – suffered frightful hallucinations.[13]

Visconti wrote the script together with Nicola Badalucco and Enrico Medioli. He had for some time toyed with the idea of filming a family chronicle along the lines of Mann's *Buddenbrooks*. Originally, he had planned to set it in Milan, but this would probably have brought the subject too close to home. He also began to feel that the subject was more closely connected with Germany. It was as if he wanted to treat the love–hate relationship both in his family background and in Germany in the same film. Just as *Buddenbrooks* is clearly about Mann's family, *The Damned* reflects certain features of Visconti's own family background as if seen through a grotesquely distorting mirror.

In addition to Shakespeare and Mann, the influence of Dostoyevsky, Musil, and Wagner can be detected in this film. Visconti also read masses of literature about the Nazi leaders, the *Sturmabteilung* (SA), and the *Schützstaffel* (SS). William L. Shirer's *The Rise and Fall of the Third Reich* turned out to be a particularly important source of information, as did Lorrain Kempski's novel, *The Night of the Long Knives*.[14]

Visconti decided to concentrate on the phase in which the Nazis seized control of the governmental institutions of Germany. The film begins on February 27, 1933, when the Reichstag building burned down in Berlin. The Nazis used this event as a propaganda weapon and an excuse for the persecution of the Communists. During the same spring, they purged the German government and society of anti-Nazi groups and liquidated all democratic and decentralizing institutions. The first concentration camps were founded.[15]

Now began the last great internal struggle for the control of the Nazi party. The were two main factions. One of these was the SA, which was founded in 1920 and consisted of soldiers, veterans, and hooligans. The

SA was the most important faction of the Nazi party in the early stages of its rise. Subsequently, however, Hitler decided that SA leader Ernst Röhm was not sticking close enough to the official party line, and he created for his own protection a new elite corps, the SS. Members were carefully picked for their racial purity and pronounced loyalty to Hitler.[16]

By the time the Nazis had seized control over the nation, the SA had become a serious problem for the party leadership in that it wanted to attack all the institutions connected with the old establishment. Although they had done most of the dirty work, the SA members gradually realized that they were as poor and as excluded from political power as they had always been. Meanwhile Hitler sought to secure his control over the nation by making pacts with industry and the military. In fact, there was not much need to exert pressure on industry as it was already prepared to cooperate. The SA leaders wanted their squadrons to assume the duties of the army and to create a new kind of military institution. This did not suit Hitler's plans, and so he probably made a deal with the military: if he did away with the SA and let the military maintain its position, in return it would support him after the death of President Paul von Hindenburg.[17]

The SA troops had been ordered to go on holiday in July 1934. Röhm himself happened to be convalescing in the Bavarian Alps. A group of SA leaders were already arrested on the night of June 29; Röhm and his closest men were apprehended the following morning. Some were shot on the spot, others the next day. In Berlin, SA leaders were rounded up in barracks and shot in groups by SS firing squads during the next day and night. In addition, many known anti-Nazis were assassinated summarily. The whole operation was carried out quickly and effectively. There was some panic and uncertainty, but many Germans only gradually realized what had happened. Visconti, who was in Germany at the time, was unaware of these events, although he did sense the ominous atmosphere that prevailed after "the night of the long knives." Hindenburg died on August 2, 1934, and Hitler took over the offices of the chancellor (prime minister) and of the president and assumed the supreme command of the armed forces. Now he had full dictatorial power and was referred to simply as *der Führer* (the leader).[18]

Visconti originally thought of using photographs and documentaries in order to connect the events of his film with historical reality. He also considered dividing it into four distinct "acts." The historical references would have provided a contrast with the melodramatically colored fiction, centered around the "Macbeths," Friedrich and Sophie. Their death would have provided a cathartic ending: With the death of the devil-like protagonists, culture would have had a new chance.[19]

This ending would obviously not have coincided with the historical events (unless the time span was extended to the end of the war). But Visconti's interest was now shifting from Friedrich and Sophie to the latter's son, Martin. This change transpired because more emphasis was now being placed on the Freudian aspects of the film: Martin's abuse of his young cousin and the little girl living next door to the room he has rented, as well as his oedipal relationship with his mother. As the characters increasingly became metaphors for the historical and political situation, the use of documentary material seemed superfluous.[20] Also, many of the historical references had faded into the background, so that in the end the story was centered on the struggle within the Essenbeck family over the control of the steelworks, modeled now on the struggle within the Nazi party. Visconti stated that *The Damned* was not a historical film, but a description of the family dynamics seen against a certain historical background:

The political atmosphere is a main factor in the Essenbecks' rush toward crime. It is not by chance that the film starts in 1933: that was a decisive year for Germany. . . . The Weimar Republic died and the Assassin State was born. The German middle class was finished, while the aristocracy of capital and of industry gave up their powers to the new arrivals or tried to share it with Hitler: a new leading class of criminals, of perverted men, was born.[21]

A descent to hell

The family relationships in *The Damned* are extremely complicated and quite difficult to work out even after repeated viewing. Part of the difficulty is that many of the characters represent somewhat schematically certain interest groups and reflect the power struggle in Germany. Before the film begins, the son of Baron Joachim (Albrecht Schönhals), the head of the Essenbeck family and steelworks, has died in the First World War. The war hero and his wife, Sophie (Ingrid Thulin), have had a son, Martin (Helmut Berger), who is now Joachim's sole heir. Joachim's second son, Konstantin (René Koldehoff), an SA leader, is also a widower and has a son, Günther (Renaud Verley). Other members of the family include Joachim's niece, Elizabeth (Charlotte Rampling); her politically liberal husband, Herbert Thalmann (Umberto Orsini); and their daughters, Thilde and Erika. Among regular visitors to the magnificent Essenbeck villa are Sophie's cousin, SS captain von Aschenbach (Helmut Griem), and Friedrich Bruckmann (Dirk Bogarde), who is the vice president of the steelworks and Sophie's lover.

A shadow of the original idea of the four "acts" remains, in that the action moves through four fairly distinct phases, defined by the changes in the balance of power between the characters and the groups that they represent. The first phase is a brilliantly constructed exposition during which the audience is acquainted with the characters, their mutual relationships, and their political stands. But soon enough the plot is driven forward with tremendous power. In the beginning the family is about to have an annual dinner together to celebrate Joachim's birthday: Konstantin is having a bath, assisted by his valet, who tells him what the other members of the family are doing; Günther is practicing on his cello, and Thilde comes to see him in eager anticipation of the party; the Baron is seen kissing a photograph of his son; Herbert grumbles to Elizabeth about Joachim's weakness under political pressures; in a car on their way to the villa, Bruckmann and Aschenbach discuss the future of Germany, the steelworks, and certain key people. Each of these scenes introduces different aspects of the complicated pattern.

In a family theater, the little girls recite poetry, Günther plays Bach, and Martin – the last of the major characters to appear – shocks the family with a Marlene Dietrich parody in drag. His performance is interrupted when news is brought that the Reichstag in Berlin is on fire. Political tension mounts after the meal when Joachim announces that he will name Konstantin the new manager of the steelworks – in assumed compliance with the wishes of "a certain Herr Hitler." Herbert is infuriated and marches out in protest. After the meal, Aschenbach is seen inciting Sophie and Bruckmann to take action in order to secure their position in the leadership of the steelworks; in parallel, we see Martin playing hide-and-seek with the Thalmann girls and Herbert preparing for an escape. The first phase reaches its climax when it is discovered that Joachim has been shot, Herbert Thalmann has been framed for the assassination, and, it is suggested to the audience, Martin has abused Thilde. Finally, in a family meeting, Martin, coaxed by his mother and to Konstantin's great surprise, announces that he will nominate Bruckmann to be the general director of the steelworks.

The second phase depicts daily life in National Socialist Germany: how books are being burned; how Sophie and Friedrich, with the assistance of Aschenbach, gain control of the steelworks; how Martin molests a little Jewish girl called Lisa;[22] and how Elizabeth implores Sophie to arrange the necessary documents for her and her daughters to leave Germany.

The third phase begins after Martin's approaches have driven Lisa to suicide and Konstantin starts to blackmail him in order to gain control of the steelworks. To prevent this, Friedrich and Sophie seek the help of von Aschenbach. It is apparent that though Sophie and Bruckmann think they are in control of the situation, almost without noticing it, they have became mere puppets of the SS. In the night of the long knives, SA troops, taken by surprise after their drunken and partly homosexual orgy, are quickly and effectively butchered by the SS. Bruckmann is forced to participate by killing Konstantin with his own hand. Bruckmann and Sophie have turned out to be far too attached to their personal ambition to be reliable partners for the SS. And so Aschenbach decides he must destroy them. This he will accomplish neatly by transforming Martin's mother fixation into venomous hatred.

The last phase forms a parallel with the first one, as it begins with a family meal at the same table featured in the first phase. Again the meal ends in a row, momentarily interrupted by the inexplicable appearance of Herbert. He says that Elizabeth has died in the concentration camp at Dachau, where she ended up with their daughters on their way to exile. Now he has come to give himself up to the Gestapo in exchange for the liberation of his daughters. He then disappears as suddenly as he appeared. Martin tells the rest of what has happened and his view of its implications to Günther, and Aschenbach completes the brainwashing: With the collapse of all values, even the gentle Günther is transformed into a Nazi. As all the underlying traumas surface and take new forms, Martin rapes his mother; then she and Friedrich marry, only to take poison immediately afterward.[23] The film ends with Martin raising his arm in the Nazi-salute and with an image of the furnace of the steelworks superimposed on him.

From the point of view of narrative strategy, *The Damned* occupies a special position among Visconti's films. In contrast to *The Leopard* and *Ludwig*, in particular, its structure and strategy of representing a period of history are dramatic rather than novel-like; in contrast to the Verdian melodramatics of *Senso*, it is Shakespearean in tone; as opposed to the slices of life in *Death in Venice* or even *The Innocent*, it presents a torrential flux of events in which the characters desperately try to pursue their ambitions or simply to master the course of their lives.

There are many details reminiscent of Shakespeare. Sophie and Friedrich are the ambitious Macbeths, with Sophie goading Bruckmann: "Even if I will never know how to push you enough, go, go, and go to the limit!" In this scheme, Aschenbach has the role of the three witches, who stand

for fate – in this case, the fate of Germany, which falls helplessly into the
hands of the Nazis. This is paralleled by the triangle of Sophie, Friedrich,
and Martin, presented in almost too obviously Freudian terms, which
resembles the situation between Hamlet, his mother, and his uncle – although the character of Martin has been inspired by Nikolay Stavrogin
of Dostoyevsky's *The Possessed*. Finally, there is Herbert's ghostlike appearance during the last meal, on the eve of the final battle.

But above all – and in strong contrast with all Visconti's other films –
the narrative structure, with its parallel lines of development, is reminiscent of Shakespeare's historical and Roman plays. The dramatic element
in *The Damned* emanates from the tight interrelationships between the
characters as functions of the plot. This is made manifest not only in the
multiple ways in which they act as foils to one another, but also in the
narrative strategy, which constantly forms contrasts and parallels between events and characters as the plot moves from one thread of the
story to another. For example, Sophie says she will throw a bait to Martin,
and then Martin is seen playing with Thilde; Elizabeth and the girls leave
to find what they erroneously think is liberty, and in the next shot the
little feet swinging gently in the air reveal that Lisa has killed herself.

But the analogy should not be pushed too far. There are crucial differences in the dramaturgy of theater and film. It has often been pointed
out that cinema is much closer to the novel than to drama as a narrative
genre. Georg Lukács has compared the nature of Shakespeare's tragedies
to the tradition of the nineteenth-century novel:

Shakespeare portrays in the relations of Lear and his daughters, Gloster [*sic*] and
his sons, the great typical, human moral movements and trends, which spring in
an extremely heightened form from the problematicalness and break-up of the
feudal family. . . . This psychological richness of the contending characters
grouped around the collision, the exhaustive totality with which, complementing
one another, they reflect all the possibilities of this collision, produces the "totality
of movement" in the play.

What, however, is *not* included here? The entire life surrounding parents and
children is missing. One need only compare this play with the great family portraits depicting the "problematic" of the family in an epic manner – e.g. Thomas
Mann's *Buddenbrooks*, Gorky's *House of Armonov*. What breadth and abundance
here of the real circumstances of family life, what generalization there of the
purely human moral qualities, the wills which can be brought into collision.[24]

There certainly is not as much "breadth and abundance here of the real
circumstances of family life" in *The Damned* as there is, say, in *La Terra*

trema, Rocco and His Brothers, or *The Leopard.* Yet already the quality of the film medium – its capacity to show rich and detailed images exploited to the full in the reconstruction of a way of life in a certain historical situation that in various ways determines the characters, their aspirations, and possibilities – gives a dimension to the film that could be described as novelistic in the sense Lukács understood it. So although the historical events, the diachronic dimension, are presented metaphorically – in Ricoeur's interpretation of *mimésis* – by means of the tightly knit tragic plot, the synchronic dimension of the film inevitably brings novelistic features into play.

This narrative scheme, this balance between dramatic and novel-like elements, allows for an extraordinarily powerful presentation of certain general factors or trends as manifested in certain instances. The plot closely follows the historical events of the rise and internal strife within the Nazi party, the fight for the steelworks connecting the historical public and the fictional private sphere. In the scenes in which the control of the steelworks is discussed, the conversation oscillates constantly between the different competing factions – SA, SS, the army – and the characters who embody or oppose them.

While the historical development proceeds by its own weight, it appears to be grounded in a swamp of ruthlessness, perversion, and ignorance of spiritual, cultural, and all human values, exemplified by the characters and their relationships. It is not as if Visconti were explaining the rise of Nazism in terms of sexual perversions, as he was accused of doing when the film opened and even later.[25] Rather, he is using the historical context as an example of a situation that has the power to reveal the most horrific aspects of humanity.

The relationships between the private and the public spheres are also made manifest in many figurative ways. These are centered on the Shakespearean elements: the "Macbeths" and the "Hamlet triangle." These configurations do not stand for actual historical factions, but the perversions they manifest grow into a metaphor for the prevailing spiritual state. There is a kind of Oedipal drama in operation. As in almost all Visconti's films, the father is dead. Martin's father has died on the battlefield in the Great War, but the murder of his grandfather, the Baron Joachim von Essenbeck, stands for the destruction not only of the Weimar Republic but of patriarchy in general. All these have guaranteed an order – however repressive and pretentious – which has at least offered the possibility of a civilized and cultured life. Historically, that order was replaced by a far more oppressive one, but what is at issue here, of course, is the metaphorical annihilation of all moral order. This begins with "the Macbeths" killing the old ruler, which coincides with Martin abusing Thilde, continues with the endless chain of murders and Martin seducing the little Jewish girl and driving her to suicide, and culminates in Martin raping his mother and leading her and Friedrich to their deaths immediately after their wedding.

Meanwhile, the best of European literature is being burned on a bonfire, and the most impressive victory of SS officer Aschenbach is the conversion of Konstantin's sensitive son, the cellist Günther, into an instrument of hate. Aschenbach is like a diabolical puppeteer, although he usually only has to give a slight impetus to his victims to make them act in a way that serves the purposes of the Nazis. Aschenbach is also the tempter, who teaches people not to be afraid of the evil inside them and to realize their potential for it to the full. This, he emphasizes, must be done for the benefit of the Reich. He destroys without hesitation all those who do not submit to his control, who seek their own advantage and not that of the state.

The plot configurations together with the melodramatic turns of events repeatedly remind one that the film is not to be interpreted too much in terms of realistic motivation, although the wealth of visual details, the sumptuous settings, the reconstruction of an era, constantly tempt one in that direction. The implausibility of many of the twists of the plot – Bruckmann's participation in the night of the long knives and Herbert's ghostlike appearance, in particular – emphasize the unpredictability of the tortuous flow of events and the exceptional nature of the historical context. Maurice Jarre's music[26] and the at times expressionistic use of colors serve the same purpose. In many scenes the intensity of the colors, particularly the glowing orange – the main color both in the home theater and at the steelworks – give emphasis to the towering ambition and perverted desires of the main characters. But eventually they fall quietly into the icy embrace of either pale shades of blue or the blackness of the SS uniforms. Visual stylization reaches its peak in the grotesque wedding scene, in which Sophie's face is like a linen-white mask through which her eyes stare in inane wonder.

The weird colors along with the camera work help to create an atmosphere of claustrophobia and nervous tension. Long shots tend to be short takes and the camera is almost constantly on the move, often panning and zooming dramatically. Characters are separated rather than united in the images, because they are seen one by one either in traveling shots or in separate close-ups – all of which is in accordance with the narrative structure of the film, with its many parallel story lines. This camera style is fully apparent for the first time when Günther is playing the Bach solo piece (the Sarabande from the C-minor cello suite): the camera moves calmly from one character to another, as if to show them all in their loneliness. Here, as in many similar scenes, the camera does not always distinguish between the situations of the characters during the particular event being shown. For example, when Joachim makes his announcement after his birthday meal, the camera has time to glide over the little Thalmann girls, surely ignorant of the implications and significance of the message, with the same steady speed with which it passes all those who know that their lives might depend on what he is about to say. This is not the sort of uninvolved gazing into the fictional world from a slight distance that we find in *The Leopard* and later in *Ludwig*. Here the audience is brought much closer to the heat of the events.[27]

It is essential that the motivations of the characters not be understood as an explanation of the historical chain of events. Rather, those events should be seen as a manifestation of more general and deeply buried traits of the human mind and Western civilization. In a sense, *The Damned* is more than a purely historical analysis of the events that led to the rise of the Third Reich. The way the fictional and historical levels are interwoven ensures that the film is not confined to its setting, the specific circumstances in Germany in the 1930s, and suggests that the forces that precipitated the rise of the Nazi party can be unleashed anytime and anywhere.

The crucial contrast between German culture and its negation is at its most pointed in the bonfire scene, where works by the masters of European literature are declared decadent and destroyed: "Thomas and Heinrich Mann, Remarque, Stefan and Arnold Zweig, Gide, Keller, London, Shaw, Zola, Proust." This contrast is apparent throughout the film, particularly in the conflict between the oafish Konstantin and his sensitive and cultured son, Günther. The other major polarity is that between Günther and Martin, as is seen in what they perform in the family theater at the beginning of the film. Neither of them is interested in the steelworks or politics, but during the film they both gradually become Nazis. Günther has got a long way to go, and his conversion – however weakly motivated in terms of character psychology – stands as a metaphor for the collapse of an entire culture. The society is morally dead, no firm ethical points of reference remain.

Upholding certain cultural standards is not enough – in this the Nazi regime, in its own limited way, succeeded remarkably well. It is meaningless without a spiritual core. Products of culture can reflect and develop spiritual standards but they cannot support them on their own as they are always in danger of being reduced to "mere" art. In Visconti's film, the bonfire represents intolerance and thus barbarism at the deepest level within a culture, which at the same time holds up the loftiest of cultural traditions. Günther might well play his Bach with new enthusiasm as a Nazi, hearing it as his final victory over his uncivilized father, and we as spectators might easily share his complicity in detesting the father and admiring the Bach. A lot has to be kept out of the mind to play and listen to something like Bach's cello suites really well.[28]

The very aesthetic quality of *The Damned* suggests this painful paradox. The most beautiful and pure – the Thalmann family – are among the first to perish. And though Konstantin might look fat and ugly, the majority of the SA men butchered during the night of the long knives are handsome young men made to look almost childlike and vulnerable in their nakedness and total incomprehension in suddenly waking to their deaths. Of course, the "Shakespearean" characters are beautiful too, as is Aschenbach and the rest of the SS men in their shining black uniforms and with their impeccably correct behavior. There is a great sense of a cult of beauty and death, perhaps even of idealizing racial purity in this, all of which further reinforces the disturbing quality of the film. The subject, it seems, is impossible to tackle without sharing in the corruption. It is not simply a question of a director visiting Germany just when the Nazis seized power and admiring more or less involuntarily the order and determination displayed by the new regime, the cult of youth and power, or the handsome blond men in black uniforms. Rather, it is the difficulty for the spectator of resisting the sinister beauty of this film.

DEATH IN VENICE

Adapting Mann and Mahler

Thanks to its meticulous reconstruction of a bygone era, its exquisite cinematography, and the considered use of Gustav Mahler's music, Visconti's adaptation of Thomas Mann's novella, *Death in Venice* (1911), is by general consent an extraordinarily beautiful film. Nevertheless, at times, it has also given rise to an almost savage diatribe. Neil Sinyard has pinned down the central dilemma as follows:

The film of *Death in Venice* (1971) represents a meeting of minds of three great European artists of the twentieth century: writer Thomas Mann, composer Gustav

Mahler, and filmmaker Luchino Visconti. The conjunction is almost too rich, a well-nigh indigestible cultural pudding from a writer who, in D. H. Lawrence's phrase, 'feels vaguely that he has in him something finer than ever physical life revealed'; from a composer who felt he was carrying the whole history of music on his shoulders; and from a massively cultured and aristocratic director seeking to make the ultimate art movie in an industry given over to commerce. Consequently, we have a movie almost insufferable in its self-importance, top-heavy with significance, which somehow compels respect and attention because the artists involved have the genius to justify this massive pretension.[29]

Sinyard also aptly notes that the film involves "the kind of artistic interchange that was, in fact, one of the most glorious aspects of the pre–First World War arts, and that, in Visconti's words, saw a 'whole complex of cultural change and revolution and that one must understand to follow our own history'."[30] Nowell-Smith, however, treats the question of how the film relates to established works of art more unkindly, not to say viciously:

Culture is present, particularly in the flashback, . . . but it is not seen problematically, only as a passively assimilated "value." By abolishing the structured discourse of the novella, with its twin foci in the mind of Aschenbach and in Mann's commentary on his cultural and sexual dilemma, Visconti has in a sense brought the story out of the clouds and down to earth and exposed the material, or rather the pseudo-ontological, content of Aschenbach's obsession. . . . The reason why Mann's discourse as opposed to that of some other writer should be important and worth reproducing is totally and irrevocably lost. The film trades upon, and helps to perpetuate, respect for the values of art while offering no reason why this Art should be taken even remotely seriously.[31]

Visconti had indeed set himself a formidable task, and he had to pay for it. Elaborating on Sinyard's observation, one might say that he was a giant climbing on the shoulders of two other giants. Maintaining balance turned out to be well-nigh impossible, although the Mahler connection actually derives from Mann himself. He had seen in the composer the cultural hero of the early nineteenth century. While Mann was on vacation in Brion in Dalmatia together with his wife, Katja, and his brother, Heinrich, he followed the daily medical reports on the composer's physical condition. When Mahler died on May 18, 1911, Mann cut out and kept the newspaper item announcing this. That same week they moved to Venice. *Death in Venice* was inspired by this trip, and the main character, Gustav von Aschenbach, was given many of Mahler's personal traits.[32]

By making the protagonist of his novella an author, Mann apparently wanted to connect the story with his own experiences both as a man and an artist. Lodging in the hotel in which he stayed in Venice was a Polish family with a thirteen-year-old boy, often dressed in a blue sailor's suit. Mann could not help but admire the boy's serene beauty. The Manns also visited Bolzano, and when they returned the Polish family was still in the hotel, and the author found himself following the youth with his eyes. One evening an "obscene" Neapolitan singer with a yellow, leering face entered the grounds of the hotel and caused some confusion. There were rumors of cholera, and a clerk at Cook's travel agency recommended that they leave Venice. A number of people had already died, he said, although the municipal officials preferred to remain silent about it. These and many other details of the Manns' stay in Venice found their way into the novella.[33]

In many ways, Aschenbach's character connects with Mann himself. The fictitious author resembles Mann's portraits of Schiller and La Fontaine, and his works are Mann's own projects. Some of the comments about Aschenbach's works echo Mann's statements about his own output. A hint of his sexual orientation also emerges in the novel. Mann acknowledged his interest in prepubertal boys in his diaries. He was undoubtedly fascinated by discovering this trait in himself, and to some extent it stimulated his creative work. On the other hand, he might have exaggerated this trait just as he exaggerated his minor physical ailments.[34]

Mann saw the artist as an exceptional individual, an overripe representative of his culture, who is able to create something new but has to pay a high price for it. A bourgeois artist, in particular is unable to detach himself from his social background, yet is hopelessly alienated from it. Because of this dilemma, he is unable to find personal happiness and his artistic achievements are simply its poor substitutes. Often the artistic impulse masks and even springs from a weakness or a sickness caused by some kind of spiritual or physical contamination. The noblest qualities in man cannot be separated from his tendency toward corruption.

In *Death in Venice* Mann sought to clarify his relationship with eros and ethos, the sensuous and the spiritual, art and life. The novella is about the difficulty of reconciling these oppositions. It is about an artist seized by the will to die, a cultivated human being trying to maintain his dignity in the face of inevitable physical decay. Death appears to him in the form of immoral and seductive love. An adventure that defies bourgeois morality, an attempt to achieve a unity of the spirit and the senses, only heightens the contradiction of life and spirit in his mind. Nevertheless, the value of art is strongly confirmed. According to Roger Wiehe, the central theme seems to be that "Aschenbach as an artist must be made to rely no longer on balance, harmony, and control; he must be challenged by the impulse toward chaotic plenitude and, in surrendering to that impulse, be re-integrated as an artist with the understanding that artistic illusions are painful yet corrective and necessary for human survival."[35]

Aschenbach's artistic development, the narrator suggests, has helped Aschenbach achieve "an almost exaggerated sense of beauty, a lofty purity, symmetry, and simplicity, which gave his productions a stamp of the classic, of conscious and deliberate mastery."[36] As the novella proceeds, Aschenbach finds himself encountering all those aspects of life and art he has tried to keep out of his mind and above all outside his art. On arriving in Venice, he is repulsed by the pretense of an old man dressed and made up to look like a youth, but immediately before his own death he has himself made up for the same purpose. What leads him to this inversion? On the beach Aschenbach sees a young boy, Tadzio. To the old writer he is "beauty's very essence; form as divine thought, the single and pure perfection which resides in the mind, of which an image and likeness, rare and holy, was here raised up for adoration."[37] About midway through the novella, he is enchanted by the sun, elevated into an oneiric fantasy of old Socrates instructing young Phædrus:

For beauty, my Phædrus, beauty alone, is lovely and visible at once. For mark you, it is the sole aspect of the spiritual which we can perceive through our senses, or bear so to perceive. Else what should become of us, if the divine, if reason and virtue and truth, were to speak to us through the senses? Should we not perish and be consumed by love, as Semele aforetime was by Zeus? So beauty, then, is the beauty-lover's way to the spirit – but only the way, only the means, my little Phædrus.[38]

When the fantasy returns toward the very end of Aschenbach's life, the shrewd Socrates takes the role of a poet, a man whose "return to detachment and to form" is sure to "lead to intoxication and desire." This way is sure to end in the pit, but what is the alternative for "us who are poets – who by our natures are prone not to excellence but to excess"?[39]

This latter fantasy and the desperate attempt to regain youth by cosmetic means are preceded by a violent Dionysian nightmare: the suppressed "Stranger God" has returned with vengeance in the guise of a beautiful youth. As expressions of Aschenbach's mental universe, the Socratic fantasy and the nightmare represent the opposite poles of classical order and chaotic delirium, respectively. Yet, as the Socrates of his mind points out to him, the former may easily lead to the latter, the Platonic adoration of beauty to sensuousness and abandon, presenting themselves as the only true way toward fulfillment. In the first instance, his interest in the boy may well be purely aesthetic, but fundamentally it is nevertheless desire aestheticized. This allows the erotic impulse surreptitiously to take over his ordered mind. Indulging in the Socratic fantasy leads Aschenbach inevitably to the destruction of the balance he has achieved through his escape into his aesthetic spheres. He ends up foolishly imagining that what really belongs "only" to the realm of the spirit can actually be encountered in flesh. After such a misstep, the pursuit of the fulfillment can only lead to the nothingness of death.

Mann's *Death in Venice* is firsthand evidence of the cultural and spiritual situation in Europe before the First World War. At the turn of the century, European art and intellectual life were moving toward new conceptions, ranging from sobriety and constraint to excess and the radicalization of expressive means: there was Arnold Schönberg's atonality and Igor Stravinsky's revolution of rhythm in music; Vasili Kandinsky's abstractionism, Paul Klee's expressionism, and Pablo Picasso's and Georges Braque's cubism in painting; the various theatrical experiments and theorizations of Edward Gordon Craig, Adolphe Appia, Vsevolod Meyerhold, and many others. With cinema moving at tremendous speed to occupy vast areas of the field of narrative art and entertainment, the avant garde in literature and theater, relieved of the burden of naturalism, began to explore more stylized and abstract means of expression. All this more or less coincided with philosophical and scientific developments such as Ludwig Wittgenstein's philosophy of language, Albert Einstein's theory of relativity, and Sigmund Freud's psychoanalysis; social progress in the form of the rise of the workers' movement; the impending catastrophe built into the system of nation-states organized into blocks with unprecedented destructive power at their disposal. There was plenty of utopianism about, enthusiasm about the new vistas that scientific and technical development appeared to open for human pursuits; but there was also the fear of the destruction of culture, the very basis of life and values as they were known. For many people, European civilization was decadent and worn out and its future a spiritual void.

Death in Venice, then, is about decadence in the sense of relating to a situation in which, to quote Dominick LaCapra, "traditional forms are not only displaced from any origin but [are] on the verge of sterility and exhaustion."[40] The danger, the waning of Western civilization itself, is expressed first of all in the weariness of the hero, second in the "Asiatic cholera" eroding the very basis of life itself. The hero, as well as the authorities, fail to take adequate measures against the disease as they prefer to indulge in sensuous yearning and the hope of gaining immediate profit, respectively. Having established this context, Mann focuses on the inability of the bourgeois artists to truly confront life and the indissoluble mixture of intoxicating immediacy and vertiginous transitoriness. Aschenbach has reached what the narrator calls the "Wunder der wiedergeborenen Unbefangenheit." LaCapra has analyzed this concept as follows:

Unbefangenheit is a doubly negative term. *Un* designates a lack or an absence. *Befangenheit* signifies constraint, self-consciousness, and also prejudice. I would suggest that the word *Unbefangenheit* does not refer to a lost original innocence but to an absence of constraint or of self-consciousness that is *achieved* and always subject to challenge or loss. It is a spontaneity derived in paradoxical fashion in and through culture and art. And whether one judges the quest for it to be yet another illusion or a higher-order naiveté will affect one's response to Mann in general.[41]

This concept is a manifestation of the romantic ideal of an artist, able to create spontaneously and effortlessly, carried on the wings of tradition and his own genius. Novalis wrote about what he called "intentionally random creativity," for "what appears to be inspired by the moment, extempore, sudden and fortuitous, is . . . the product of the highest, conscious artistic intent."[42] This ideal haunted countless artists. Mann no doubt also aspired to the condition of an artist free of the constraints of consciousness, but he lived in an era increasingly hostile to what Schiller called naive, as opposed to sentimental, artists. The former are those who experience no division between themselves and their community and to whom art is natural self-expression; the latter are those who are incurably alienated, to whom art is a means of criticizing life and community as it is known to exist and is a way of articulating yearning for a lost unity.

Mann – a sentimental artist, if anyone – was reflecting on a point in cultural history through which he had himself lived and that he had the audacity as well as considerable justification to think he was actually forming himself. But his path to this status had little to do with modernism in the arts. It was not in him to be an avant gardist; he had the role of a latecomer. His greatest gift – at least from the point of view of the present argument – lay in being aware of this position combined with the ability to derive from this conflict both the content and the form of some of his major works. And thus, through self-inspection and examination of his own role in the cultural historical situation, Mann himself actually succeeded in reaching a kind of "miracle of regained detachment" or "reborn unconstraint." It appeared to him in the only possible guise that the situation allowed, that of intricate irony, which he employs in putting his story and themes, himself and his situation, into perspective. Asking whether Mann "succeed[s] in where Aschenbach seems to fail," LaCapra comes to the conclusion that

ironic and parodic gestures seem close to unwitting themselves and suggesting a reborn unconstraint that is not a naive return to some original state but a cultural achievement. . . . The text of *Death in Venice* does not totally transcend the problems it explores, but neither does it replicate them in a fully symptomatic manner. In a double movement it enacts certain limiting possibilities and becomes a counteragent or antidote to them, for it shows how a complex use of irony and parody may both touch extremes and not be altogether consumed by them. In this sense, irony and parody are neither the figures of absolute impasse nor negative cultural items to be transcended in a refound innocence or state of salvation. Used in a certain way, they may, however problematically, be parts of a "reborn unconstraint."[43]

Transforming literary into audiovisual splendor

Death in Venice, the film, should obviously be taken above all as Visconti's own statement about life, art, and death in the making of which the novella and Mann's aesthetic and philosophy in general have not been the only important source of material and inspiration. Considering the cultural status of the novella, this is not easy. Nevertheless, it is somewhat surprising that even to some highly sophisticated commentators the problem with Visconti's film appears to have been the transformation of this particular literary text to an audiovisual discourse as such, as if the novella had some divine right to be left in its verbal-philosophical excellence. Nowell-Smith, on the other hand, thinks Visconti was captured by the excellence of the novella to the point where it prevented him from attempting any discourse of his own.

For many critics, the main problem of the film is closely connected with the fact that Tadzio has had to be visualized and thus particularized instead of appearing more or less just as a projection of Aschenbach's mind. Visualization has brought with it other problems. In Geoffrey Wagner's opinion:

The real difficulty is the appearance of Bogarde, looking like an absent-minded professor who is in reality a lecherous fag. . . . This happens because Visconti has no time to insinuate Tadzio into Aschenbach's consciousness as deftly and delicately as does the original author. Visualizing has made everything too explicit, and quoting Paul Zimmermann, "He [Aschenbach] and the boy exchange lengthy glances, whose explicitness turns Aschenbach into a foolish dirty old man, and the boy into a pretty little tease."[44]

Joy Gould Boyum more or less agrees with this but is even more disturbed by Tadzio's androgynous appearance and find his glances back at Aschenbach "so unequivocal that it's impossible to read them (as we might in the novella) as a function of Aschenbach's imagination."[45] As Nowell-Smith has also suggested with merciless irony: "Maybe this tetchy old man has a mental and fantasy life richer and more intelligible than can be deduced from merely watching him lech after a pubescent boy in a provocative bathing costume."[46]

Someone reading such comments before seeing the film and thus expecting to see a "foolish dirty old man" "lech after a pubescent boy in a provocative costume," "a pretty little tease," would surely be surprised. The vigor of these attacks and their moralizing tone suggest that Visconti's film has at least been profoundly disturbing. But these writers make little mention of the splendid audiovisual realization of the film, and none of them discuss the extraordinary use of Mahler's music.

First of all, it should be noted that the rich audiovisual reconstruction has merit in itself. Visconti was consciously recreating sceneries and situations from his own youth, when his family used to spend their holidays at the Lido. He was, in effect, once again doing in audiovisual terms what Marcel Proust had done in words: giving the people and environments of his past a new lease on life in a work of art. And although in the space of a single film – or even a few films – Visconti could not possibly achieve the monumentality and the wealth of the temporal cross-relations of *La recherche*, the value of the shear authenticity of the audiovisual reconstruction can only be neglected from a puritan viewpoint that measures cultural achievements solely in terms of literary values.

It should also be noted that even audiovisualization as such is likely to have philosophical implications. Despite the splendor of the film, paradoxically, at least in one important sense, considerable restraint has been exercised: there is very little indulging in the picturesque aspects of Venice. Hardly any of its distinguished monuments are seen during the film. Instead, Venice is turned into a metaphor for Western culture at the turn of the century. Its glorious and sensuous artistic achievements based on ruthless materialism are but memories of the past, and the city is relegated to a glorious leisure resort. Its labyrinths are exhausting, and it appears to be dying of its own filth; yet it is where earth, sea, and sun meet to form a uniquely intoxicating mixture – all this splendidly captured by Pasqualino De Santis's exquisite camera work.

In addition, the film contains its own web of cultural references, largely independent of the novel but in a crucial way related to it. The protagonist's connections both with certain Mannian fictive characters as well as with Mahler are made fairly evident in nine flashbacks, although appreciating these allusions does require considerable background knowledge. The Mannian themes emerge mainly in the second, third, fourth, and fifth flashbacks, while the first, fifth, and ninth flashbacks refer to the crises Mahler experienced in his life around 1907.[47] His elder daughter died of scarlet fever and he himself was diagnosed to have a weak heart. After protracted quarrels and disputes, he lost his position as the director of the Vienna State Opera. At the same time, public recognition continued to elude him as a composer.

Perhaps more so than any other composer, Mahler marked the ending point of a certain chapter in the history of Western music. He brought the classical-romantic symphonic tradition to its peak in terms of grandeur of form, harmony, and orchestration. In doing so, he provided his students with a starting point from which to totally renew that tradition. This was accomplished mainly by Arnold Schönberg and his students Anton Webern and Alban Berg. Schönberg and Mahler used to have endless debates about the nature of art and music, often ending in furious quarrels. Their mutual respect, however, always ensured reconciliation. In public, Mahler always defended the widely despised Schönberg, although in private he admitted that he did not always understand his music.

Inasmuch as the protagonist of the film is associated with Mahler, it is difficult not to see his colleague Alfred as a reflection of Schönberg, although Visconti expressly denied the connection and emphasized that Alfred should be thought of simply as Aschenbach's alter ego.[48] And true enough, Alfred's diatribes clearly articulate Aschenbach's own doubts and fears. Furthermore, the connections between the real-life composers and the characters in the film are muddled by the conversations Aschenbach and Alfred have concerning art and music. The dialogue has been patterned to a great extent after passages in Mann's *Doctor Faustus* (1947). The main character of the novel, Adrian Leverkühn, is, in Lino Micciché's words, like "an Aschenbach survived," whose art has involuntarily become an expression of the demonic, forming a curious parallel with German history up to the Second World War. The description of the musical system he employs is modeled on Schönberg's twelve-tone system[49]

– the book even concludes with an acknowledgment of this. Schönberg was infuriated.

In the film, however, Alfred is the spokesman of the demonic in art; and Aschenbach, the Mahler character, is the proponent of pure spirituality. Alfred accuses him of sterility in his pursuit of "pure beauty, absolute severity, purity of form, perfection, the abstraction of the senses."[50] Unfortunately, though this might conceivably be said about Schönberg's music, it absolutely does not apply to Mahler's. He could be intoxicated by the beauty and charm of nature, but he was also aware of its comical, grotesque, and terrifying aspects – and all this he sought to express in his music. In his Third Symphony his aim was to capture Being in all its multiplicity, to "embrace the whole world." According to his own statement, the first movement expresses the panic horror of a midsummer noon that had struck him in his solitude in the stillness of a summer's day. The fourth movement, set to Friedrick Nietzsche's text and known as *Zarathustra's Night Song*, is about wakening into humanity. However, Mahler was able to exercise Apollonian reserve, too. Perhaps he could not always be bothered to do so, but it is certainly apparent in the Adagietto of the Fifth Symphony.

It has obviously been necessary to distance the protagonist from the real Mahler in order to maintain the basic pattern of the novella. An erotic reaction precipitated by the aesthetic contemplation of the beauty of a young boy confuses Aschenbach, who apparently has never been able to reconcile spirituality and sensuality. His decision to leave Venice is followed by a flashback in which Alfred accuses him of being alienated and lacking feelings. According to the young colleague, health, particularly that of the spirit, is dry and sterile. Referring to spirituality in art, Aschenbach says that "reality only distracts and degrades us" and that "the creation of beauty is a spiritual act." But Alfred assures him that "beauty belongs not to the sense, only to the senses." To him, art is basically demonic. In trying to reach some extreme purity, art loses its contact with real life and becomes self-sufficient. And at least in his own recollections, Aschenbach's attempt to convey spiritual beauty to his audience has failed. In the present of the film, his old ideals appear dead to him, they have led him to an impasse. This failure has been complemented by the death of his daughter and apparently also of his wife.

The conversations about aesthetics between Aschenbach and Alfred are at times almost embarrassingly pretentious and facile. In this they are in accord with the notion Aschenbach, the author, makes in the novel after indulging in aesthetic speculations while having his first dinner at the hotel. He soon comes to the conclusion that "what seemed to him fresh thoughts were like the flattering inventions of a dream, which the waking sense proves worthless and insubstantial."[51] Visconti has stated that he attempted to render the ironic tones of Mann's novella through the excessively cultivated and intellectual tones of these conversations.[52] Unfortunately, this intention does not really come across in the film as the flashbacks might all too easily be taken as a pathetic attempt to create a lofty cultural discourse. But what the film does suggest quite clearly is that the flashbacks need not be thought of as objective renderings of past events, but rather as Aschenbach's increasingly distorted memories. Thus understood, platitudes such as "it is only by the complete domination of the senses that you can ever achieve wisdom, truth and human dignity," or, in answer to this, "genius is a divine gift . . . or no . . . a divine affliction, a cynical morbid flash of natural gifts," could be thought of as vague recollections of what might have been much more substantial arguments or even fantasies of debates that have never actually taken place.

However, the Mahler connection as a cultural reference as such is not its most relevant aspect. It is by far more significant that the background music is taken from the Adagietto movement of his Fifth Symphony and the Nightsong of the Third Symphony. The Adagietto expresses at the most direct level a yearning for a unity of serenity and sensuousness, but what makes its use in this film special is that it is heard in four exceptionally long stretches during which relatively little is said. The film evolves as a leisurely spectacle inviting the spectator to enter into a mode of reception in which the audiovisual quality of the film emerges as a major theme in itself, thus giving this adaptation its own unique quality independent of the literary source.

The opening music starts before the credits and continues until the boat carrying Aschenbach to Venice lands and about three-fifths of the movement has been heard. The second stretch begins when Aschenbach, just about to leave Venice, encounters Tadzio. Apart from a short interruption at the railway station, the music continues through his return and settling down in the hotel again right into the flashback with him and his family. The flashback begins beautifully at the point where an arpeggio on the harp announces the return of the main theme. Altogether, about four-fifths of the movement is heard. It is soon followed by the Nightsong, which continues about halfway through. The third stretch of the Adagietto begins with the flashback of the daughter's coffin and continues through the scene at the barber's and the long walk with Aschenbach following the Polish family through Venice. This time the movement reaches its climax in a shot showing Aschenbach reduced to hysterical laughter; the music is suddenly interrupted by the flashback in which the closing chord of a piece Aschenbach is conducting is heard. Finally, the Adagietto is played at the end of the film, starting from the point where Aschenbach is following Tadzio with his eyes for the last time. The music continues over the final credits until the return of the main theme.[53]

Not only are the musical stretches exceptionally long, but there are five long sequences that are almost wordless or that contain only words in a foreign language (Polish, French), which Aschenbach presumably does not understand and/or which are narratively and thematically irrelevant:

1. Aschenbach settles down to his hotel room (1.5 minutes), watches the Polish family in the lounge (8 minutes) and goes and takes a seat in the dining room (1 minute) (total almost 11 minutes).
2. Aschenbach hears that his luggage has gone astray at the railway station and returns to the hotel (5 minutes), goes to the beach again (6 minutes), and listens to Tadzio play the piano (1 minute) (total over 12 minutes, in addition to which the short interlocution at the railway station is preceded by a 1.5 minute long wordless scene).
3. Aschenbach's first "chase" after the Polish family through the streets of Venice lasts 3 minutes, preceded by a 0.5 minute long wordless scene in the cathedral.
4. The second "chase" lasts 7 minutes (interrupted only by the governess calling for Tadzio) and is followed by the concert flashback, which goes on for about 1 minute before Alfred speaks.
5. The wordless "finale" at the beach lasts for more than 10 minutes.

Sequence 2 is accompanied throughout first by the Adagietto and then by the Nightsong, Sequence 4 by the Adagietto, and 5 first by Mussorgsky's *Nenia* and then by the Adagietto. Already these amount to three-quarters of an hour, in addition to which there are, of course, many other relatively long wordless scenes. All this is hardly counterbalanced by the wordy flashbacks with Alfred. Thus the purely audiovisual quality of the film, the Adagietto often furnishing the only obvious unifying element, is strongly foregrounded.

Music is also used to make certain points. Once diegetic music is used as a bridge from one scene and diegetic level to another – as when Aschenbach hears Tadzio try Beethoven's *Für Elise* on the piano and this leads to a flashback in which he goes to meet a prostitute playing that same piece – the music continues without interruption, even though before the actual flashback we see that Tadzio has already left. This is, in a sense, just a conventional "cue for a flashback," but it also serves to create a metonymic connection between Tadzio and the prostitute and thus to emphasize the precariousness of Aschenbach's feelings toward the boy. Since neither "pianist" plays particularly well and Aschenbach is ill at ease with both of them, the scene also suggests the feebleness of his passion. Besides, the similarity only frames a difference: while the encounter with the prostitute looks almost like a weak attempt to become "contaminated" and thus to make more carnal contact with the world, the relationship with Tadzio represents an attempt to overcome carnality and contamination and thus to live and love in the spirit only. Aschenbach ends up failing both in the sphere of flesh and of the spirit.[54]

The diegetic music in two other flashbacks has a more referential meaning. Alfred plays on the piano first an extract from the Adagietto and later on a theme from Mahler's Fourth Symphony, saying to Aschenbach: "This is your music!" Here the Adagietto accompanies Aschenbach's hourglass monologue, which ends: "To our eyes it appears that the sand runs out only at the end. Until it does it is not worth thinking about. The last moment, when there is no more time . . . no more time left to think about it."[55]

The very opposite of the serenity of the Adagietto is heard in the music of the street players. Led by a grotesque figure of a singer, they visit the balcony of the hotel. Their racy performance mocks the decorum of the fine guests, not to speak of Aschenbach's refined sensibilities. As Tadzio, standing near him, appears to react similarly, there is a faint suggestion of a momentary connection between them. More generally, Aschenbach's attitude toward the boy is contrasted with his encounters with various ominous men. He is able to admire the boy's chaste beauty only from a distance, whereas every now and then he is pathetically unable to keep away from these rather unpleasant people. They vary from grotesque and intrusive (the old man on the boat and the street singer) to haughty and manipulative (the gondolier and the hotel manager). When encountering them, Aschenbach attempts to display strength and determination but always ends up appearing rather silly.

The camera work is based on long takes that constantly create relationships between people looking and people being looked at. Gazes appear to have the power to make the music sound, as when the Adagietto begins the moment Tadzio's and Aschenbach's eyes meet as they pass each other. Looks set things going and lead to flashbacks. The uneasy game of gazes between Aschenbach and Tadzio, in particular, is one of the crucial elements of the film. It is true that the looks they exchange are much more explicit than they are made to appear in the novella, mainly for the obvious reason of being realized in a visual medium. Nevertheless, even in such an extremely slowly paced film as *Death in Venice*, things must proceed quickly enough to prevent the film from descending into the languor of some of the more extreme avant garde works. These glances are not quite as intrusive as some critics have claimed. For example, when the boy and the man pass each other in the nocturnal scene, Aschenbach hardly stops, Tadzio slows down only slightly, and the glance they exchange is but a fleeting one.

On the whole, Tadzio certainly does not appear to be a "pretty little tease." Every now and then he simply turns to face the gaze he realizes has been fixed on him for some time. The only point at which he looks at Aschenbach in the film, but not in the novella, is when he leaves the lift fairly early on. In the film, he seems to be staring directly at Aschenbach; in the novella, he leaves "with his eye cast down."[56] From Aschenbach's point of view, it is apparent that looking is not so much leching as it is a sad acknowledgment of the distance that must remain between his desire and its object, of his inability and perhaps even fundamental unwillingness to overcome his detachment and his alienation. He is doomed to experience the tantalizing ecstasy of forbidden, impossible, and unrequited love.

More generally, the camera work has a subtle role in expressing character subjectivity. The scene in the lounge before the first meal after Aschenbach has arrived is a tour de force of camera work producing an intriguing play of points of view. Pasqualino de Santis's pan-and-zoom style of shooting is at its most elaborate and expressive. First the camera pans extremely slowly from right to left, reaching Aschenbach about midway and following him to the extreme left and then again across the lounge to the right, after which the camera stops on him for a brief moment. The same take continues with a slight zoom backward and a movement toward the left. In the second shot, Aschenbach's gaze catches the Polish family, and in the third the camera moves from one family member to another and ends on Tadzio. This shot can be taken as subjective, that is, from the point of view of Aschenbach, as it is framed by shots of Aschenbach looking. There is a shot of the salon orchestra and a new shot of Aschenbach. He interrupts his reading, and his gaze wanders until it is fixed on the Polish family again. The next shot begins from Tadzio, and at first it appears to represent Aschenbach's visual point of view, but as the camera pans gently it ends up showing him. Still later in the same scene, there is a shot that again appears to be from his point of view, but the slow zoom (possibly combined with tracking) back reveals Aschenbach from behind until it is beyond what can be properly considered an actual point-of-view shot.

At points in the lounge scene, it appears as if the degree of subjectivity of the shots depended on how attentive Aschenbach happens to be. The objectivity/subjectivity of the shots is at times left ambiguous, so that the points of view of the spectator and of Aschenbach coalesce and separate seamlessly. This ambiguity extends to the level of overall narration. As already pointed out, it is not clear whether the flashbacks show events from Aschenbach's life "as it really happened," or whether the flashbacks are at least to some undefined degree distorted memories. Similar ambiguity appears when a clerk at a travel agency tells Aschenbach about the epidemic and he is seen warning the Polish family. The spectator might at first assume that this is "really" taking place, but a new shot of Aschenbach back at the travel agency reveals that he has only been imagining what his next act might be.

The most disconcerting feature about an audiovisual adaptation of *Death in Venice* is that a story about looking and reflection inevitably becomes much more a discourse on looking than on reflection. The attention of the literary Aschenbach constantly oscillates between his reflections on beauty, morality, or whatever, on the one hand, and being aware of his immediate surroundings and the one object there that really inspires him, on the other. Instead, the visualized Aschenbach, the composer, being seen in his physical environment appears much more tied down to earth, much nearer to the object of his desire. This becomes conspicuous in the scenes in which Aschenbach follows Tadzio and his family through the Venetian labyrinth with all the passion and energy he has left in him. Finally, he is overwhelmed by exhaustion, mixed with a growing awareness of the town suffocating in dirt. The experience of the splendor of the glittering sea and the colorful life on the beach have become inextricably intertwined with the cold and unnatural blue and white hues of the streets and channels of Venice.[57]

The range from splendor to squalor sets the tone for Aschenbach's attraction toward Tadzio. It is romantic longing for something sufficiently idealized and ambiguous as never to be consumed, not even in fantasy. But the combination of spiritual and physical exhaustion has left Aschenbach too weak to cope with even a spark of spontaneity. It kindles a fire in him that at first makes him glow and then consumes him. An attempt to escape the illicit impulse, to leave Venice, fails almost by design – a "happy," manipulated coincidence – and Aschenbach is left with an excuse to stay close to his temptation. But internalized codes of morality rapidly start corroding the attempt at pure contemplation of the object of forbidden love. Aschenbach is destroyed by the mere temptation of shaking off his constraints.

In the sequence accompanied by *Zarathustra's Night Song*,[58] the music creates an almost magical effect as it emerges ever so gradually from the sounds of the beach. It is full of that same exasperated sensuality that the late sexual reawakening together with the *sirocco* wind has induced in Aschenbach. There is a shift to the limits of consciousness where perceptions and sensations become inseparable from dreams and memories. On this level, the boy represents desires and needs beyond the erotic and even the aesthetic. Somewhat like the professor in *Conversation Piece*, Aschenbach tries to awaken from a deep sleep that is alienating him from the world and his fellow men. And very much like the professor, Aschenbach discovers that he has been awakened by an angel of death in the form of a beautiful youth. Tadzio stirs in Aschenbach certain spiritual and sensuous processes that lead him to an abyss, on the other side of which all that is worth pursuing appears to be located.

Toward the end, Aschenbach lets himself be made up to look young, but he only finds himself ever more pointedly incapable of throwing himself into the stream of life. As the barber inadvertently aptly says, "In the end we are just as old as our mind and heart feel they are." Once more, Aschenbach follows the Polish family through the streets of Venice, but eventually he falls down by a fountain in helpless, almost hysterical laughter. There follows the last flashback, which is really a dream, a nightmare, which stands for both the nightmare and the soliloquy on *eros* and *ethos* in the novel. A concert Aschenbach has just conducted ends in whistling and booing. Having survived the audience's howls, he is immediately attacked by Alfred announcing him the end of "wisdom, truth, human dignity" and telling him that "now there is no reason why you shouldn't go to your grave with your music."

After waking up once more, still uneasily trying to keep up his new appearance, Aschenbach returns to the desolate beach. There he sees a group of Russian tourists, one of them singing Mussorgsky's *Nenia*, a cradle song. Aschenbach's arrival is seen from high up, from an "impossible" angle to which the camera returns in the very last shot of the film. Here the pretense behind Aschenbach's new appearance becomes even more evident than in the novella. The stream of black dye running down

Aschenbach's cheek on the hot beach is like putrefied blood: it's an agonizing image of the life force finally expiring.

In his final moments, Aschenbach turns his attention to Tadzio and his friend, who have a falling out and begin to fight. Finally, Tadzio succeeds in getting rid of his friend and, refusing a gesture of reconciliation, walks into the sea. The shocked Aschenbach sees him just as a distant figure amid the elements, raising his arm toward the sun. Like a stiff puppet, Aschenbach repeats his gesture but then collapses. Many commentators have been reminded of a poem by August von Platen, lines that Mann often used to quote: "Who has observed beauty eye to eye/ Is already dedicated to death."[59] Youssef Ishaghpour writes:

This attachment to the visible, to the sensible appearance, to the physical splendour of life which does not find completeness in life itself, easily brings about a separation between life and form. As the tie between appearance and idea, between body and soul, "beauty" reaches us through the senses but is not solely sensuous. As the feminine remains tied to the reproduction of existence, "love" of beauty becomes guilty in respect of life, something useless, sterile, mournful: this, the intervolvement of eros and death in passion, dominates Visconti's oeuvre. And evil, immorality, death, attached to this passion for beauty, can not be redeemed except by beauty itself, sacralized by the love for works which have become a new religion: art as other than life in the existence of a bourgeois artist, and art in the life of the decadent. *Conversation Piece, Death in Venice, Ludwig* center entirely round the refusal–recognition of homosexual desire and its relationship to art: the way of death.[60]

Aschenbach projects on the object of his vision . . . what? The only cue the film provides is the Adagietto. It is significant that the three long stretches of the Adagietto that begin while the story is already under way are connected with a farewell: as Aschenbach encounters Tadzio, just when preparing to leave Venice; with the flashback of the coffin of his daughter; when he sees Tadzio getting involved in the fight and succumbs to death. In all these instances, it is as if the music brought consolation at a moment of sadness and pain, helped to make life appear worth living despite the inevitable losses and frustrations, even despite the transience of life itself. The nondiegetic music, thanks to the connection established with the protagonist, at the moment of his death becomes a symbol of the transcendental power of art.

If one takes into account the audiovisual merits of the film, starting from the considered use of the Mahler Adagietto – itself an epitome of this miracle of reborn unconstraint if any and made emphatic by the minimal narrative tension, which creates the sense of attempting to stop time, overcome death and old age by stepping out of time into the eternal spheres of beauty of forms – *Death in Venice* does indeed achieve a kind of spontaneity of expression "derived in paradoxical fashion in and through culture and art." There is a truly Apollonian balance in the way the Dionysian sensuality is indulged in while being constantly kept in check by the presence of death and decay. The genuine achievements of the spirit through the creation of beauty are counterbalanced by the decadence that seems to be eroding the basis of the civilization that has produced it.

But while the spirit may continue to exist in works of art, biological and social corruption inevitably take their toll. The contrast between the tragedy of Aschenbach's inability to accept this and the way his story is rendered through the serene and sensuous splendor of the film becomes a metaphor for the basic paradoxes of our relationship to art and to life: inasmuch as art can be a way of transcending the contingencies of life and even overcoming its fundamental transience, inasmuch as art can be a path toward resignation, it also runs the risk of becoming alien to life. Art as the purest and truest manifestation of the human spirit cannot be separated from the exploitation of art as an escape, withdrawal, illusion.

LUDWIG

The battle for *Ludwig*

Visconti first got the idea of making a film about Ludwig II, King of Bavaria, when he was hunting for locations for *The Damned*. In 1971 an even grander project he was working on, adapting *Remembrance of Things Past* for the screen, was postponed for financial reasons, and Visconti thought the time was ripe for *Ludwig*. Both the Wittelsbachs, the ancient ruling house of Bavaria, and the Bavarian civil service turned out to be very helpful. He got permission to shoot in all the royal palaces he wanted and to use the family treasures to create the right setting. But after the shooting of *Ludwig* had been completed on July 27, 1972, Visconti suffered a severe heart attack while he was dining with Cecchi d'Amico and a couple of producers in a restaurant in Rome.[61]

During his convalescence, Visconti was sent to Kantonsspital in Zurich, the same hospital where Thomas Mann had died on June 12, 1955. This connection rekindled a dormant idea of adapting Mann's *Magic Mountain* (1924). He also thought of working on another novel by Mann, *Der Er-*

wählte (The holy sinner, 1951), which was based on a poem by the medieval poet Hartmann von Aue. Together with Cecchi D'Amico, Visconti also developed some other ideas, but none of them were realized. His greatest concern at this time, however, was the need to complete *Ludwig*. The production company, Mega Film, had just signed a contract with MGM stipulating that the film was not to run longer than two hours. This was about half the length Visconti had planned.[62] According to Cecchi D'Amico:

> If Luchino had been in good health, he would never have accepted, never. He was such a strong character. He never wanted to see *Ludwig* as it was distributed. But although he made the montage with Ruggiero Mastroianni under the obligation for it to remain within two hours, he succeeded in making it about two and a half hours long. . . . After he had died I read in the papers that they were selling the material at an auction. I called to the people who had worked with him [among others Mario Garbuglia, Franco Mannino, Armando Nannuzzi, Piero Tosi] and so we went to the office and bought it. I went first to check whether they had kept all the material. They had and so we bought it and restored the film.[63]

The producer's attitude is perhaps understandable, if not forgivable, when the excessiveness of Visconti's conception is considered. Actually, the director himself had already cut scenes during the shooting: a scene in which Ludwig's cabinet secretary finds Wagner and hands him the royal gift of a ruby ring; Ludwig listening to a private performance of *Tristan und Isolde*; Wagner's death in Venice and his funeral cortege through Munich, accompanied by the funeral marches from Beethoven's *Eroica* and Wagner's own *Twilight of the Gods*; a scene in which Elizabeth hears about Ludwig's death and cries: "They have killed him! Traitors! Assassins!"[64] But now many scenes that had been shot had to be shortened or completely deleted.

The ending Visconti originally conceived was based on a rumor that had been spread after Ludwig's death, according to which someone had seen a bullet hole in the king's coat and his clothes had disappeared almost immediately after he had been dragged out from the lake in which he had drowned. In the final scene of the script, an old servant tells a younger one that he knows the king was murdered, because he saw a bullet hole in the king's coat. This was shot, but it was left out even from the reconstructed version. Cecchi D'Amico did not think it was "good to end like that. . . . Someone takes a cloth that belonged to Ludwig, and they see that there is a hole. But this scene would have needed something more, I don't know what. I don't think that Luchino would have wanted to put it into the film."[65] One shot that was left out although Visconti had included it in the first version was an image of the dead Empress Elizabeth under a white veil following the scene in which Elizabeth, after the premiere of *Tristan*, tells Ludwig that he must behave like a king and that one of the privileges of kings and queens is that they might be murdered. Cecchi D'Amico thought that this one flashforward did not add anything to the film and that it would simply not have been understood.

A film about Ludwig II

In Visconti's film the story of Ludwig II occurs between the waning of German romanticism and the formation and implementation of Bismarck's *Realpolitik*. Ludwig's most cherished dreams are crushed by a political reality that subsumes everything under a single goal: the unification of Germany into a single modern nation-state.

In 1806 Napoleon declared the ancient principality of Bavaria a kingdom. His aim was to create a buffer state to protect France from Austria. After his downfall, Bavaria's ruling house, the Wittelsbachs, was able to show its respect to its true idols, the Bourbons. The second king of Bavaria was named after Ludwig IX of France, and his grandson was given this name in homage to Ludwig XVI.[66]

The young Ludwig received a good training in the arts but not in administrative duties. This was partly because he was crowned at the age of nineteen when his education had not yet been completed. Nor was he mature enough to assume his duties. His heart was more in the romanticized German Middle Ages than in the Europe of the age of *Realpolitik*. Ludwig's views of life and art were influenced to a great extent by the works of Richard Wagner. Ludwig's heraldic animal was the swan, and after seeing Wagner's *Lohengrin* (1848) he identified with the knight in shining white armor and with his loneliness. Ludwig's attempts to act like a true ruler within the banal reality of Bavarian bureaucracy, having to cooperate with petty-minded civil servants and scheming politicians, soon shattered his illusions about being a king.[67]

In the war of of 1866 Ludwig agreed with his ministers that the kingdom should form an alliance with Austria against Prussia, but he did not want Bavaria to join in. When the war began, Ludwig withdrew to the castle of Berg. Austria, Bavaria, and the principalities allied with them lost the war and only a few years later Bavaria joined with Prussia to fight France. No war could have been more unpleasant for Ludwig, who knew full well and appreciated the fact that Bavaria owed a debt of gratitude to Napoleon for helping it become a kingdom. Under pressure from his ministers, he finally had to give the order to mobilize the Bavarian troops. He did it in French and signed the decree using the French form of his name, Louis.[68]

The king was needed, however, when German unification was finally achieved in the fervor that followed the victory over France. Bismarck wanted to consolidate Prussian leadership, and the best way to do so, he thought, was to persuade the king of the largest Germanic state, namely Ludwig, to invite the Prussian king to become the emperor of Germany and ask that his kingdom be accepted into the new empire. Fearing that his own troops in Paris might participate in proclaiming Wilhelm the emperor in any case, Ludwig acquiesced.[69]

After unification, Ludwig preferred to spend his time in the castles of Berg and Hohenschwangau and retreated deeper and deeper into a world of romantic fantasy. He began pouring money into Wagner, to support the construction of the Bayreuth Festspielhaus – not to mention the composer's luxurious lifestyle – as well as into the building of fabulous castles in southern Bavaria. The Bavarian government tolerated the king's enormous expenses as long as the funds came from his own purse. But when he tried to blackmail the government and the parliament in order to restructure his debts and solicit some new funds, a plan was set in motion to depose him. A Professor von Gudden, who was already in charge of the king's demented brother Otto, undertook an inquiry, at the end of which he issued a statement: the king was mentally unbalanced and unfit to rule. Since Otto was obviously in no better mental condition, their uncle Luitpold was invited to act as regent.[70]

Ludwig was forced to leave the castle of Neuschwanstein and was taken to the older castle of Berg, which was much closer to Munich. Some time after he arrived there, he and Professor von Gudden left for a walk. They did not return. The following night their bodies were discovered in Lake Starnbergersee nearby. According to the official explanation, Ludwig had tried to commit suicide and in the attempt also drowned von Gudden. Ludwig was formally succeeded by the deranged Otto.[71]

As is typical of "biopics," *Ludwig* selects certain details from the biography of a historical personage in order to present a coherent story. The film is exceptional, however, first of all because its narration has been structured around statements supposedly made in connection with the inquiry into the king's mental health by politicians, civil servants, and Ludwig's valets, among others. According to the first statement, which follows the short opening scene of the film, the reason for this "difficult and painful inquiry is to determine whether our king is fit to rule our unhappy, despised, and tortured Bavaria." In the last statement von Gudden relates his final assessment: the king is unfit to rule. The statements have been shot as close-ups of the witnesses looking more or less straight into the camera. The background is dark, and the little that is seen of their clothes makes clear the historical period they represent. At times there are slow track-ins toward slightly closer framings, and some are lit by a strong sidelight. Thus they form a clear contrast with the otherwise full-blown historical reconstruction.

The statements consist of more or less objective facts about Ludwig's life, presented, however, from different points of view and obviously selected, if not actually distorted, to the benefit of the various interests of the witnesses. Through them, the sad end to Ludwig's aspirations, the collapse of the world of romantic illusions, is present right from the beginning, even before the coronation scene. This makes the film appear less tragic and emphasizes its melancholy and elegiac elements.[72] Furthermore, the contrast between the two narrative levels gradually reveals Ludwig's alienation from political and social reality. History proceeds on its inevitable march and is given a voice through the mouths of messengers, as if in a Greek tragedy. A new political order is being forged in Europe – a system that will almost destroy the world and culture Ludwig has cherished and patronized.

The film begins with a scene in which Ludwig (Helmut Berger) confesses to the family priest his determination to make his court a center for the arts and sciences. This scene introduces one of the leading motifs of the film, namely, Ludwig's relationship to religion (and the church), the state, and his own responsibilities. The first statement is followed by the coronation scene, filled with all the pomp that can be mustered by both mundane and spiritual institutions. It is one of Visconti's most splendid reconstructions of a historical era. A new statement opens a sequence showing the relationship between Ludwig and Elizabeth (Romy Schneider) developing in the wintery landscape of Bad Ischl. Ludwig's youthful, romantic sensitivity is immediately contrasted with Elizabeth's mature sense of responsibility, thinly disguised under a veil of gentle irony and humor.

A search for a politically opportune spouse for Ludwig continues, but Minister Pforz[73] states that at least the meeting with the Russian tsarina did not help to make the king forget his dear Wagner. The next scene confirms Pforz's accusations: Wagner appears totally unscrupulous in exploiting both the king and the young conductor Hans von Bülow, whose wife Cosima is already Wagner's lover. Ludwig, in the meantime, tries in vain to elicit in Elizabeth some enthusiasm for Wagner's art. But she grows more and more distant from him and endeavors to interest him in her little sister Sofie. The king prefers to seek comfort in art. According to the next statement, the premiere of *Tristan und Isolde* cost the state a fortune.

Ludwig continues to try to win Elizabeth over to the splendors of opera, and Elizabeth to convince Ludwig of the madness of Wagner's project. She understands that the sole purpose of the royalty is to parade before the public and that their attempts to interfere in state affairs might well lead to their assassination. But Ludwig still clings to his romantic ideals about the role of the king. Wagner and Cosima do not hesitate to ask for even greater sums from Ludwig in order to finance their sumptuous way of life. Only when Ludwig's police bring him a host of evidence against Wagner and the Bülows does he cease to betray himself and signs the order to expell them from Munich.

During the war of 1866, Ludwig stays in seclusion in the castle of Berg, refusing to receive any messages from the battlefields. He agrees to see only his dear brother Otto, but even he fails to persuade Ludwig to attend to his kingly duties. After this conversation, he goes out for a nocturnal walk and encounters his valet secretly taking a swim. He is naked, and this appears to make Ludwig uneasy. After the valet has gone, he prays: "Help me, help me!"

There follows a long conversation with his trusted Colonel Dürkheim, and then a scene in which Ludwig tells his mother that he intends to marry Sophie. The mother immediately starts the necessary preparations. The families of the bride and the groom are seen in a meeting in which Elizabeth also participates, stealing the show from her sister, as it were. Later, in a short and otherwise wordless scene, Sophie is at the piano, her young voice stumbling through Elsa's aria, "Einsam in trüben Tagen" (Lonely in troubled days) from *Lohengrin*. Ludwig's tortured face indicates that the chasm between reality and ideals in his mind is deepening.

The next statement is about the tremendous cost of building the king's castles and a pathetic attempt to instruct Ludwig in traditional heterosexual behavior. Ludwig obviously finds this arranged meeting with a society prostitute repulsive, and so the prospects for the union with Sophie begin to look even worse. Ludwig introduces her to Wagner and claims that she likes to sing his music. This is a cruel irony, and the relationship between Ludwig and Wagner appears to be much warmer than that between Ludwig and Sophie. The next scene with the valet, Hornig, implies that Ludwig is increasingly seeking the company of men.

Sophie complains to Elizabeth about Ludwig's indifference, but the little advice she can give comes too late and would probably have been of no use anyway. In the next scene, Ludwig announces in his confession that he will not marry Sophie. As we hear the end of the confession, Ludwig is seen entering a room where Hornig is sleeping. Ludwig kisses him.

The next statement is about the breaking of the engagement, the incurable mental illness of Otto, and the Queen Mother's embracing of the Catholic faith. The war against France is reaching its end, and Ludwig, on the excuse of having a toothache, once again withdraws into seclusion. Count von Holnstein intrudes and demands that he sign a letter addressed to the king of Prussia asking him to become the emperor of the unified Germany. An almost hysterical Ludwig tries to refuse, but he must yield to his fate. He visits Otto, now a raving maniac, in a mental institution and succeeds in calming him down. As a contrast to the sad meeting of the brothers, the next scene shows Wagner bestowing a Christmas present on Cosima, who has by this time become his wife: the *Siegfried Idyll*, played by a full orchestra on the stairs of Wahnfried, their new home.

The next two statements relate to the expenses incurred in building the castles and the gifts that Ludwig has bestowed on beautiful valets and artists. The actor Kainz is Ludwig's newest protégé. The sequence showing their relationship is one of the most enchanting in Visconti's entire cinematic output: Ludwig glides in his swan boat through the "Venus Grotto" at the palace of Linderhof accompanied by Wolfram's song for the evening star from Wagner's *Tannhäuser;* the castle itself is magnificent, with its vast bedrooms and tables that sink through the floor and down to the basement so servants can clear and refill them; there is a magical sleigh ride through the wintery landscape; the enchanting nocturnal travel seems endless. The sequence is followed by two further statements, the first of which reports what subsequently happened to Kainz; the second is once again about building the castles.

In the next sequence Elizabeth is seen examining the palaces Ludwig has had built, starting with the rococo-style Linderhof, continuing to the Versailles-like Herrenchiemsee, and finally ending at the mock-medieval Neuschwanstein where Ludwig resides. On the excuse of illness, he refuses to meet her. But the pain that torments him is not primarily physical. In yet another statement, one of the servants tells us that he heard the king weeping behind a locked door and repeating the name of Elizabeth. The scene ends with a shot of Elizabeth driving away in her carriage.

An emotionally shocking cut leads to a shot of Ludwig, now physically deteriorating, with a bandage over his eyes, fooling around in a Bavarian inn. The scene implies once again that he is giving in to his homosexual tendencies (the scene is disturbingly reminiscent of the SA revelry in the *The Damned*). Meanwhile the government is already planning to depose him, and their representatives are seen asking Prince Luitpold to act as regent. The last statement follows, Professor von Gudden's final diagnosis that Ludwig is suffering from incurable paranoia and is unfit to rule.

The last sequence relates most of what is actually known about Ludwig's last day and night: Colonel Dürkheim's vain attempts to persuade him to save himself and his position; his arrest and arrival in Berg; his departure for the walk with Professor Gudden. When it becomes apparent that they have been away for too long, a search party is sent out. In the darkness and rain, two bodies are found floating in the lake. Count von Holnstein announces what is to be the official explanation of their death, and the film ends with a shot of Ludwig lying on the wet ground.

Thematic concerns and narrative structure

Youssef Ishaghpour has called *Ludwig* "one of the few cinematic novels" ever produced.[74] This is to a great extent an effect of the narrative structure. The statements do not mark any particularly important points of narrative development or the perimeters of clearly defined sequences. Instead, they form fairly coherent sequences together with the actual scenes. The fact that the narration is somewhat elliptical, in that the sequences connect with each other fairly loosely, enriches the psychological portrait of Ludwig and prevents the film from falling into the trap of trivial psychologizing. Some actual events taken from the life of the real king, are presented; and the way they follow one another suggests that there may be connections between them. However, no claims are made about the strength of these possible causal links.

If the information given in the statements had been rendered by voice-overs, they would have resembled the omniscient narrator of a Balzac novel. Instead, the statements appear almost subordinate to the enacted part of the narration. Though their factuality is not questioned, they are shown to be reductive and ignorant of or indifferent to the human tragedy as well as the cultural and spiritual values at issue. On the other hand, the statements reciprocally put the narrative into focus, as they remind the audience of the political and social constraints that ultimately determine the king's fate. Thus the crucial theme of the film is actually built into its narrative structure. *Ludwig* is a story about an individual whose kingly status makes it possible to magnify out of all proportion certain idiosyncratic traits and to realize certain excessive ideas. But it is also about a sensitive and artistic personality made distraught by an oppressive culture and society. As the narrator of Thomas Mann's *Doctor Faustus* observes about the real king:

But to the form of royal existence, which is sovereign and surrounded by great respect, to a large extent free from criticism and responsibility, the display of noble status has become a style unlike anything even the richest private person can indulge in – royalty gives the nervous desires and antipathy of its bearer certain leverage, the proud and complete exploitation of which may easily appear like madness.[75]

Ludwig is free of the constraints that ordinary individuals face in their daily lives. Ordinary mortals use these constraints as an excuse for not trying to realize their aspirations. At first, Ludwig's royal status deludes him into thinking that he can fulfill his dreams – but he quickly discovers the limits set by politicians, civil servants, and ultimately by Bismarck's *Realpolitik*, implemented with the aid of iron and blood. Whereas in *Senso* the story of a few individuals served as an allegory of historical events, now the story of the king becomes a manifestation of the abyss between having to live in historical time, within the severe constraints of the real world, and the difficulty of experiencing life as something meaningful, maintaining faith in the dignity and value of human activity. Instead of melodrama, the predominant mode of expression is now contemplation and interiorization.

The governing theme of *Ludwig* – the perverse opposition of life and art – conforms with the historical situation well enough for the theme to serve not just as a generalized metaphor but also as a comment on a specific cultural and historical situation depicted through the fate of an extraordinary individual in a highly privileged position. No other character rises to play a crucial role in Ludwig's drama. This reflects the king's central problem: he is unable to interact with other people, not to mention the world at large. To him the reality represented by his ministers, civil servants, and ordinary people at large is anchored in cynicism and banality. Yet, for all his efforts to escape to a more beautiful reality, by building fabulous castles and subsidizing art of unprecedented proportions, he is unable to realize his deepest desires, just as he is unable to keep up his public role. To achieve the former, he would have to interact with his fellow men; to achieve the latter, he would have to submit to the laws of politics. Unable to relinquish the desire for what he cannot obtain,

Ludwig is doomed never to mature. He clings desperately to his ideals and becomes increasingly alienated from reality, until that reality refuses to tolerate him anymore.

Ludwig's suppressed homosexual drives appear to be a partial cause of his idealized love for Elizabeth. It is a safe love for Ludwig, which grows stronger the more impossible it is. For a long time, he is afraid of his homoerotic tendencies, and the engagement with Sophie is obviously an attempt to deny them. But, in one way or another, all women disappoint the king. His relationship with his mother is cold and detached, Elizabeth is hopelessly unavailable, and Sophie by far too available. Ludwig yearns for idealized, rather than real, relationships with women.

Homoeroticism offers Ludwig an even better opportunity to sublimate his desires, to realize at least partially his romantic dreams by sponsoring art. His relationships with Wagner and Kainz are paralleled by his relationships with Elizabeth and Sophie, respectively. But even with these men he is not interested so much in the living persons as in the different mythical figures they create and, in their different, ultimately unsatisfactory ways, embody. Inevitably, they, too, disappoint him, but at least these relationships lead to the production of wonderful art. Ludwig's later relationships with stable boys and valets appear to subdue the frustrations caused both by sexuality and its sublimation. Forbidden as these affairs are, they also become a protest against the prevailing norms of society and the straightjacket that royalty turns out to be. But Ludwig is unable to shake off those norms, and they eventually crush him.

Ludwig's bravest attempt to overcome his inclinations and to bear his responsibilities as a king follows a conversation with Colonel Dürkheim after the 1866 war. A servant tells his king:

My Lord thinks he has made a brave choice, pretends to himself that he can find happiness outside the narrow rules imposed on men. He who really loves life, your Majesty, has to exercise the greatest care. Also a monarch. The monarch's great power is limited always by the human community to which he himself belongs . . . Doesn't a person who has life before him want to find for his existence some other purpose? A humble, exasperating purpose, in a real community among simple people – however mediocre. It demands great courage from someone who has great aspirations which are not from this world to accept mediocrity, I know it. But it is the only way to save oneself of a filthy solitude.

The scene is one of the most moving in the entire film, and it forms one of its important turning points. It is followed by the sequence in which Ludwig tries to assume his responsibilities and becomes engaged to So-

phie. The sequence ends in the confession, which addresses issues similar
to those that arise in Dürkheim's tactful admonition, but now they are
discussed in a much more vulgar and straightforward fashion:

PRIEST: How can you be so haughty as to imagine you know the Lord's plans?
Today you are asked only to marry and have children. Listen to me, Ludwig.
You have to turn the Devil's temptations against him. Use them to the glory of
the Lord. In the darkness of the chamber, with the help of sinful imagination,
the warmth of one body feels the same as that of another.
LUDWIG: Father, you are teaching me new things.
PRIEST: Because of your country and people, you have to be one of them. Mightier,
more privileged, touched by Providence but still one of them. They will never
forgive if you try to be different. Wagner was expelled from Munich because he
was a genius. In this sense he was a stranger. Different. Ludwig, you are the
Lord's chosen, because more than others you are exposed to sin and can therefore
give the Lord proof of your love. I know you have said that until now you have
had the power to resist sin.
LUDWIG: Yes.

The difference in the register of these two speeches is not due simply to
Dürkheim's greater tact. The sexual nature of the problem has become
increasingly obvious, although it is still not addressed directly. The confession scene is interrupted by a chronologically obscure insert, which
shows the king approaching the sleeping Hornig – it could be a flashback,
a flashforward, or just fantasy – and the scene ends in an image of the
king and Hornig kissing. Also the mention of Wagner in this connection
is significant as a sign of otherness that cannot be allowed. The only
remaining possibility for Ludwig is to yield to the inevitable. This becomes apparent in the sequence following the confession in which Ludwig
finally signs the appeal to King Wilhelm.

As if in revenge, he gives way to his homoerotic desires and gradually
gathers round him a princely court of young men. He becomes even more
excessive in his spending. Soon the problem is not just one of bourgeois
morality; it becomes a necessity of state to dispose of him. Because Ludwig has remained popular, he must be imprisoned surreptitiously. But
Ludwig has already become utterly frustrated in his attempts to forge a
new world – or his kingdom, at least – in accordance with his own image.
For him, art and myth have now ceased to be a means of communicating
and entering into a relationship with the world and other people. Instead,
they become a means of retreating from the world, a way into an endless
night of melancholy solitude. *Tristan und Isolde,* that ecstatic celebration

of night, is eminently suited to portray this nocturnal mentality, this turning away from the world – a connection made earlier by Thomas Mann in his famous essay, *The Sorrows and Grandeur of Richard Wagner*, in which he compares the romantic thought and sensibility, so well epitomized in *Tristan*, with Linderhof, Ludwig's castle. The largest and most elaborately decorated room in that structure is the bedroom, "the real stateroom of the royal residence, consecrated to the night."[76]

Because the king prefers to live for something better than historical reality, the tremendous political event that is taking place, the formation of the German Empire, is denied the sense of burning immediacy, or even of glorification: there are no battle scenes, victory celebrations, or even lengthy dialogues or meditations on the historical process that is taking place. The tone is somber and reflects a total disillusionment with nationalistic fervor, with any kind of political activity, in fact. This allows this story of a singular individual to grow into a metaphor for the psychopathological conditions of European civilization. In Visconti's earlier film *The Damned*, the gap between cultural aspirations and political reality led to a total perversion of spiritual values. *Ludwig* retraces one critical phase in the development of European culture that led to that situation. By being relieved of the petty necessities of everyday life, a king is granted the power to completely substitute art for reality and ignore the necessity of transforming aspirations to action, lest they be reduced into mere illusions that will mask reality instead of providing a way of engaging in a dialogical relationship with it.

The king can be seen as a metaphor denoting the elevated but potentially sterile and destructive condition of art toward the end of the Romantic era. He has palaces built in which no one will ever live; his life is the epitome of romantic ideals and for that very reason alienates him from reality and its contingencies. In Wagner he subsidizes one of the most equivocal and contradiction-ridden artists of all times, a man who poses as a prophet of higher spiritual truths and whose art will haunt and inspire the dominant figures of German culture and politics from Thomas Mann to Adolf Hitler. Indeed, the entire contradiction is embodied in the mendacious and avaricious Wagner, whom the king insists on appreciating in terms of his art – the sublimity of which is rendered in the background music – instead of seeing that he, too, is "intolerable and despicable," just like the rest of the world the king so hates. Wagner's art sets the tone of the film, but without the ironical twist that the reference to the art of Verdi – in his revolutionary phase – gives to *Senso*. *Tristan und Isolde* (1859, first performance 1865) is characterized by the pessimistic philosophy of Schopenhauer and is a move away from historical time, set in the timeless spheres of myth.

Although the film can be said to reflect the disillusionment of the time of its making (1973), and particularly that of its director, it also affirms and embodies the continuity and vitality of the cultural tradition it depicts. In his two films immediately preceding *Ludwig (The Damned* and *Death in Venice)*, Visconti had already shown that he was profoundly and painfully aware of what the future had in store for the culture Ludwig sponsored and for the system of nation-states that Bismarck, among others, created. The formation of another state, Italy, had furnished the settings for Visconti's two earlier historical films. Created over almost three decades, these works display a change of attitude, if not of basic analysis. The theme of betrayal and the ironic touch in depicting it that characterized *Senso* recedes to the background while pessimism and resignation compete for predominance in *The Leopard* and *Ludwig*.

Audiovisual style

The dominant color of *Ludwig* is blue, the king's favorite color, a symbol of romanticism and, together with white, the color of the Bavarian flag. Combined with the constantly foggy and rainy landscapes, the blue makes the world the king inhabits appear cold, however much it is contrasted with the splendid gold and sensuous red of many of the interior scenes. Visconti has by no means exploited to the full the possibilities for spectacle that Ludwig's castles have offered. The style of the film is more like chamber music than symphony or opera.

As in *The Leopard*, the camera style is slightly distanced and objective. Montage is leisurely used, and Visconti often pans and zooms instead of cutting. Narration is seldom deeply focused on any of the characters, though the framing and camera movements have been structured around the characters roughly along the lines of classical cinema. Scenes often start before an event and sometimes continue for quite some time after. Correspondingly, many shots continue beyond the needs of telling a story. This becomes increasingly evident toward the end of the film with the long, almost wordless sequences with first the actor Kainz and then Empress Elizabeth gazing in wonder at Ludwig's palaces and the Venus grotto at Linderhof. Finally, the detaining of the king, his stay in the palace of Berg, the final walk with Professor Gudden, and the search for the bodies make up a considerable part of the film, although the number of events is relatively small. Thus, as in *The Leopard*, the narrative tempo becomes increasingly slow toward the end, though perhaps with slightly less justification. Together with the color scheme, this creates a somewhat chilly overall effect, especially in comparison with the Sicilian film.

The music is mainly Wagner, and it is used in a subtle manner, avoiding excessively grand gestures. The most important extract is an instrumental adaptation by Franco Mannino of the *Liebesnacht* (Night of love) from the second act of *Tristan und Isolde*, beginning from (where the words would be) "So stürben wir um ungetrennt" – echoing Isolde's *Liebestodt* (Love death) at the end of the opera. It is first heard as we are introduced to Wagner and learn of his interest in money. The connection with the shameless pursuit of self-interest and deception are further strengthened when the orchestral music fades away and von Bülow plays another extract from the *Liebesnacht* on the piano, while further away his wife, Cosima, tells Wagner that she is pregnant again – with his child, though the point is not made explicit in the film. In immediate contrast to all this, a particularly long stretch of the *Liebesnacht* music accompanies Ludwig and Elizabeth on their nocturnal ride. As the film unfolds, the music becomes ever more associated with the gradual shattering of Ludwig's illusions as a king, a patron of the arts, and a man.

The beginning of the overture of *Lohengrin* also connects with disillusionment, particularly in reference to Wagner, and as if by inversion of Sophie. It is first heard when Ludwig, in his first royal act, demands that his minister search for Wagner and bring him to Munich. It is heard again much later when Ludwig talks to Wagner about postponing his wedding with Sophie. He has been trying to project the image of *Lohengrin*'s Elsa on the poor girl, and the disparity has been made manifest both to the King and to the spectators as the poor princess makes a pathetic attempt to sing Elsa's aria, "Einsam in trüben Tagen," in an otherwise wordless scene.

"O du mein holdes Abendstern," Wolfram's song for the evening star from *Tannhäuser*, is heard at times, mainly as diegetic music. When Otto visits Ludwig during the 1866 war, the music issues forth from a mechanical music box, while another device projects the night sky on the ceiling. At the end of the film, Ludwig listens for a moment to the same musical box. The theme is also heard, again in an instrumental adaptation, when first Kainz and then Elizabeth visit the Venus grotto at Linderhof. Here the music is quasi diegetic, the orchestra is not seen but presumably the characters do hear it.[77] The theme is heard also as Ludwig and Kainz travel on a sleigh through the dark, snowy landscapes. In this scene the music is obviously nondiegetic. This ambiguity between diegetic and nondiegetic music foreshadows the way the *Liebesnacht*-music continues over a statement by one of the valets when Ludwig refuses to meet Elizabeth, who has come to see him at Neuschwanstein. In this instance, the way the music becomes manifestly independent of the different diegetic levels produces a particularly strong emotional effect – only to be shockingly contrasted with the transition to the drunken revel.

During the credits, the spectator hears a rare unpublished piece, reputed to be a composition dedicated by Wagner to Cosima.[78] It moves in the harmonic sphere of *Tristan* and it appears at times on the piano, at times as an orchestral adaptation by Franco Mannino (who has also conducted all the orchestral music). During the film it is first heard when Wagner receives the king's letter expressing his regret for having to exile him from Munich. Next it is briefly heard in its orchestral version when Ludwig adorns Sophie with some of the crown jewels. Toward the end of the film, the piece is heard after Colonel Dürkheim has made his last, useless, effort to save his king. Finally, it appears in the last scene as the bodies are retrieved from the lake, and from here on the music continues uninterrupted until the final credits, during which it changes from the piano to the orchestral version. The poignancy of this music sets the tone for the entire film.

One more piece by Wagner is heard, namely, *Siegfried Idyll*, which Wagner presents as a gift to Cosima and their baby son, Siegfried, played by a string orchestra to awaken them on Christmas morning.

Schumann's *Kinderszenen* is first heard, presumably as diegetic music, early on in the film, when Elizabeth is practicing riding. The association between the music and her is emphasized by a straight cut from Ludwig's face and the *Lohengrin* overture to her and her music. Later, the *Kinderszenen* music appears in other scenes in which she is at the center of events – again there is a seamless movement toward the nondiegetic. The tone of the music in this context is not too serious, and thus it has the effect of mocking Ludwig's passion for Elizabeth – particularly when it is heard just as a chambermaid tells him that Elizabeth will not go for a ride with him.

The scene with the prostitute is backed by Offenbach's overture to *La Périchole*, and in another scene Wagner plays an extract from an operetta by the same composer, *La vie parisienne*. The securely German composer says in disgust: "This is what the Germans like, not my music." In addition to these brief passages, there is some diegetic music such as bold brass music in the coronation scene and folk music in the revel scene.

Ludwig has been accused of being a cold film lacking clear intellectual structure, a vision of history, and emotional drive.[79] It has also been seen as a symptom of autobiographical existential crisis.[80] These assessments have been made on the basis of the short version of the film, which does not convey Visconti's historical, social, cultural, and psychological ideas.[81] There are so few statements in this version that they do not stand out in clear counterpoint to the rest of the film. They do not even properly guide the spectator through the narrative. Either completely missing or severely mutilated are such crucial scenes as Dürkheim's and the priet's speeches to Ludwig, a scene recounting the events that have taken place within the royal family, and the meeting between Luitpold, Dürkheim, and certain ministers of state. There is even somewhat less music than in the four-hour version, and it is used in a different way. The "So stürben wir" theme is not heard at all, and it is replaced by a much more lyrical – and in this context less effective – extract from the *Liebesnacht* music.

There is also an extremely interesting difference between versions dubbed in different languages. In the short English language version, quasi-"foreign" accents result in the typically silly effect this practice so easily produces, whereas in at least the Italian four-hour version the language is beautiful and unpretentious. And what is quite staggering is the difference between Helmut Berger speaking his own lines in English and Giancarlo Giannini giving Ludwig his beautiful Italian voice. The former makes the king appear bickering and unsympathetic; the latter's interpretation makes Ludwig sound tender and vulnerable.

The difference between the short versions and the complete film emerges also in the editing and rhythm. The short versions are jerky and uneven, and the flashback structure only muddles the temporal organization of the film; the long version lets the two-tier structure unfold calmly and majestically. Again, the careful choice of leisurely evolving scenes creates the sense of a long stretch of time passing, which is used here more to draw a picture of psychological development than to depict historical change as such. Only in this form can *Ludwig* be appreciated as an intellectually and emotionally satisfactory work in which Ludwig's singular destiny is universalized and elevated into the sphere of art.

5

Visconti as an Interpreter of European Literature

EXPERIENCING LITERATURE AND CINEMA

Visconti's literary ideals

Throughout his life Visconti was an avid reader. His first great love was Shakespeare, and having read in *The Tempest* Prospero's words to Miranda, "Twelve years since, Miranda, was your father duke of Milan," he wondered whether she might have been one of his ancestors. The next great object of admiration was Stendhal, followed soon by Proust and his *A la recherche du temps perdu*. Proust's monumental work became a lifelong source of inspiration for Visconti. For years he planned to adapt it for the screen, and it clearly influenced many of his films. Even after losing all hope of realizing his dream, Visconti found great comfort in Proust during his illness in the last years of his life.[1] Like the narrator of the novel, he might have thought: "Life as it passes is but Time lost: but all can be transfigured, found again, presented under the aspect of eternity, which is that of art."[2] And what André Maurois has written about Proust applies equally well to Visconti: "Proust loved to study . . . the historical formation of various social environments, and the way in which they grow old and worm-eaten, until at last they break down altogether."[3]

But there is more to the literary background of Visconti's aesthetics than just Proust. In Guido Aristarco's view, Visconti is the only filmmaker who has truly succeeded in perpetuating literary tradition of the eighteenth and nineteenth centuries. For Visconti, it was to a great extent a question of achieving a certain kind of realism. The nineteenth-century novel offered a model for working out plots in terms of the motivations of the characters conditioned by natural, social, ideological, and psychological factors. According to F. W. J. Hemmings:

A feeling for history, in its broadest sense, is a feeling for the changes that time brings about; and for those who, like Stendhal, had been borne on the eve of the French Revolution and were in middle age when the romantic revolution was subverting all the old literary canons, nothing was more evident than that everything was subject to change. A sense of the entirely provisional nature of laws, customs, and social institutions, of the impermanence of men's most cherished beliefs and most settled convictions, marked the romantic generation as it had no previous one.[4]

The nineteenth-century realist author could think of himself as a conservationist, wanting to preserve something of the life of the community threatened with extinction. From this arose the more crucial feature of the way realism was understood, not as imitation of reality as such, but as social criticism.

Of the great authors of the nineteenth century, Dostoyevsky probably had the most influence on Visconti's artistic ideals – although of all his works Visconti adapted only the novella *White Nights*. There is an enormous tension in the output of this artist, a revolutionary turned conservative, suspended between the desire to change everything and the deeply felt need to have everything remain the same. This conflict was familiar to Visconti, although he arrived at it from the completely opposite direction. The nineteenth-century Russian author saw the universe as ordained by God; the twentieth-century Italian filmmaker analyzed society in terms of history – but of history appearing at times almost like fate or a vengeful god. In any case, the works of both these artists are illuminated by their faith in the ability of the human mind to grasp, articulate, and perhaps in some way even transcend the human condition, a faith manifested in the very persuasiveness of these works themselves.

The means Visconti used in his films to create a rich portrayal of individuals, societies, and the multifarious interconnections between them resembles Dostoyevsky's achievement in his novels. The ideological state of societies is manifested by pitting characters against one another, as well as by depicting their internal conflicts. In Dostoyevsky, the moral and psychological world is often centered around a problem to which the protagonist, as if by a leap, gains a crucial insight that enlightens his entire existence. Something similar can be seen in the awareness Gino acquires in *Ossessione*, 'Ntoni in *La terra trema*, Maddalena in *Bellissima*, and Franz in *Senso*.[5]

But more significantly, very much like the main characters of the Russian master – each of whom has his or her obsession (nihilism, being

superman, love or hate, whatever), which leads him or her to agonizing
solitude, inability to communicate with fellow human beings – many of
the characters in Visconti's films, particularly in the late ones, become
victims of their own sensitivity and ideals and thus succumb to loneliness,
alienation, and finally to death. In both cases, the ideals may be lofty or
degraded, truly idealistic or decadent, but in their shameless subjectivity
they are indicative of a refusal or an inability to enter into genuine dialogue and interaction. Nevertheless, there is often a sense of the upbeat
because of the way continuity is manifested in the increased understanding of the social and psychological implications of the events that have
occurred. This at least suggests the possibility of development and ma-
turing both for the individual and the community.

Of all the major nineteenth-century writers, Stendhal is probably the
one who would most closely match Visconti in character and background.
Like him, Visconti had the worldview of a political revolutionary but was
an aristocrat by character and aesthetic orientation.[6] As time passed, both
began emphasizing their aristocratic heritage, although by no means un-
critically. Isaiah Berlin's comments on certain major nineteenth-century
intellectuals applies also to them:

they belonged to the class of those who are by birth aristocratic, but who themselves go over to some freer and more radical mode of thought and of action.
There is something singularly attractive about men who retained, throughout
their life, the manners, the texture of being, the habits and style of a civilized and
refined milieu. Such men exercise a peculiar kind of personal freedom which
combines spontaneity with distinction. Their minds see large and generous horizons, and, above all, reveal a unique intellectual gaiety of a kind that aristocratic
education tends to produce. At the same time, they are intellectually on the side
of everything that is new, progressive, rebellious, young, untried, of that which
is about to come into being, of the open sea whether or not there is land that lies
beyond. To this type belong those intermediate figures . . . who live near the fron-
tier that divides old from new, between the *douceur de la vie* which is about to
pass and the tantalizing future, the dangerous new age that they themselves do
much to bring into being.[7]

"Intellectual gaiety" could almost be used to describe Visconti's undog-
matic relationship with Marxism. To him it was a tool of analysis, which
had to be adapted creatively and integrated with one's cultural and historical heritage. Although in his late films he confined himself to depicting
the upper classes, he never lost his critical perspective of them. He was
convinced that they were doomed to perish because by their very nature
they were unable to change. His nostalgic feelings about the waning social

order did not blind him to its iniquities. The result was often something that could be described as a *critical elegy*.

In his attitude toward society as well as in the way he depicted it, Visconti came close to Balzac, particularly as seen by Georg Lukács:

The basis of Balzac's realism is the way he constantly reveals social being as the basis of all social consciousness; especially in and through all those contradictions that inevitably take place between the social being and consciousness within each social class. Thus Balzac is fully justified in stating in his novel *Les paysans*: "Tell me what you own and I will tell you what you think."[8]

Like Balzac, Visconti was able to "bring out the specifically individual and the class-bound typical features of every single character," and simultaneously to focus on the "capitalist community, which manifests itself in different people of different levels of the bourgeois society."[9] This is the core of Visconti's marxism: just like the great French realist, he was able to depict social reality so that it could be grasped as unity in diversity, a dialectical relationship between individuals and the community, as a structure in process. George Lukács's description of Balzac's characters applies also to those of Visconti:

Every "tooth" in [Balzac's] plot "mechanism" is a fully rounded living person with his own specific interests, passions, tragedies and comedies etc. *One* element of this total complex of being and consciousness connects him with the given plot complex of the novel, but entirely in terms of the pursuits of his life. As this connection grows organically from the character's own interests and passions it is alive and indispensable. The deep internal necessity gives the characters fullness of life, makes them more than just parts of a plot mechanism.[10]

Balzac and Visconti have in common not only their realistic bent but also their considered use of melodramatic elements. But the way they work out this element differs slightly.

The attempt to capture reality can also be seen as a way of processing certain subconscious configurations. According to Christopher Prendergast, Balzac's *Comédie humaine* project can be seen as an attempt to secure the trinity of God-Father-Artist. All these roles are about governing by word in an attempt to determine what reality is. From this point of view, the artist is the ruler of the realm of meanings: "Lord and master of intelligibility, the artist is the figure who transacts nothing less than 'reality' itself to the reader."[11] In this sense, mimésis, understood as the imitation of reality, is indicative of an attempt to satisfy an infantile need to control. But then again, all attempts to imitate reality as well as the very social construction of reality itself take place within a tradition and are therefore historically determined. Hence the realist artist is more or less unwittingly kneeling before a higher authority. Perhaps the only way for an artist to avoid it even in part is to reject conventional realism. Balzac achieves this by melodramatic means, by introducing "a margin of excess, the element of the unexpected, the implausible, the inexplicable, dislodging the 'father,' undermining the *doxa*, subverting the official history, challenging the conventions of representation and intelligibility posited by the text itself."[12]

As pointed out earlier in connection with *Senso*, melodrama in Visconti's films is not about coincidence or other narrative devices that would counter the aim of portraying characters as historically and socially determined individuals. He did not seek to "challenge the conventions of representation and intelligibility"; he was never interested in following the streams of the avant garde. While Jean-Luc Godard sought to shatter traditional illusionist forms of cinematic representation as a manifestation of bourgeois ideology by radically new cinematic means, Visconti adhered to mimésis and cinematic verisimilitude. He wanted to perpetuate the Western narrative tradition – an emphatically mimetic tradition – in the most splendid fashion conceivable, and in some respects, at least, this inevitably meant holding fast to certain acquired forms of representation. Was this adherence to mimésis and refusal to address the questions of representation in works of art themselves an indication of succumbing to the "father's voice"? Did the figure of the father, which Visconti had so carefully eradicated from almost all of his films, hold its own by becoming thoroughly internalized into the discourse?

As the overtly social element in Visconti's films receded, it was replaced by a more internalized understanding of growing old and of the transitoriness of all beings. The main characters of the last four films are all lonely men, who in their various ways are emphatically not, or are no longer, fathers. Inasmuch as their attempts to gain or to maintain the status of the father fail or have failed, Visconti is also questioning patriarchy and the culture it hosts. Thus although neither the trinity of God-Father-Artist nor the basic faith in the possibility of representing reality is undermined on the level of discourse or expression, at least the power of the father is challenged as if from within. Like Visconti himself, the male characters of his films do not fail as fathers; as a rule they fail in becoming fathers. Like children, they seek comfort by escaping into the spheres of art or mad exaggeration of the ego, as if to regain at least symbolically the ground they have lost. As a result, they enter into an ever deeper solitude.

The problems of adapting

John Ellis has defined adaptation as "a process of reducing a pre-existent piece of writing to a series of functions: characters, locations, costumes, actions and strings of narrative."[13] Obviously, a literary work in which these functions or agents are set out fairly clearly, that is, a work that could be classified as a classical realistic text, is more susceptible to adaptation than a novel in which literary devices are foregrounded. This kind of mainstream adapting is governed to a considerable extent by economic and social constraints. A filmmaker is likely to be much more dependent on his audience and the goodwill of a producer in getting his ideas realized than an artist working in almost any other sphere. This has its inevitable consequences. Carolyn Anderson, writing about the relationships between literature and film, classifies the typical changes that occur when fiction is adapted to film as a "condensation of plot and character; emphasis on dialogue and action; attention to emotion rather than reflection; a heightening of love interest; a pull toward [a] happy ending, and so forth."[14]

But adapting literary classics might well have at least slightly different aims and results, even though the decision to adapt in the first place may be made because it offers the chance to "replicate in another work of art" some of the qualities that accounted for the greatness of the original work. As Jay Gould Boyum argues, one must take into consideration the quality of the reading when assessing adaptations. Furthermore, "in the case of a classic literary work, at least, there seems to be something else at stake: that an adaptation will be considered faithful to the extent that its interpretation remains consistent with those put forth by the interpretive community; with the interpretation (or possible interpretations) of that classic work, then, that made it a classic in the first place."[15] But a valid reading of a text "will generally tend to be one that itself has a coherence and inner consistency."[16]

Though Boyum clings to the concept of fidelity, she acknowledges that an adaptation must achieve a kind of aesthetic autonomy in order to be worthy of the original, however great its prestige or popularity might be. In his *Filming Literature*, Neil Sinyard goes even further to suggest that because film adaptation inevitably involves a process of selection and emphasis, it is implicitly a form of literary criticism. At its best, an adaptation involves stressing what is believed to be the main theme of a given text, selecting certain episodes and excluding others, offering preferred alternatives, focusing on specific areas of the original, expanding and contracting details, having imaginative flights about some characters. Through this process, new light is shed on the original.[17] Adaptation can even become a form of ideological criticism. Paying tribute to the original work of art in adapting it does not require literal fidelity – in terms of plot, character motivation, dialogue – or even assumed spiritual fidelity, as much as it does the ability to exploit the potential of the new medium to rearticulate what are seen as the salient features of the original in respect of new sensibilities and intellectual concerns.

Béla Balázs writes in his *Theory of the Film* about how in the case of adaptations it is possible that "while the subject, or story, of both works is identical, their *content* is nevertheless different."[18] He mentions as an example Friedrich Hebbel's plays based on the *Nibelungen Saga*, pointing out that though Hebbel kept the mythical foundation as the skeleton of the story, he gave it a different interpretation:

The actions and events remained largely the same, but were given other motives and explanations.

Thus the same event, being given quite different emphasis was turned into a different theme. . . . The same external action has quite different inner motives, and it is these inner motives which throw light on the hearts of the characters and determine the content which determines the form. The material, that is the external events, serve merely as clues, and clues can be interpreted in many ways.[19]

Balázs thinks that such reinterpretation of motives and inner states is at the heart of all artistically serious adapting. It is a kind of refiguring that makes adapting a form of cultural regeneration. Familiar situations are constantly repeated, reinterpreted, and refashioned through adaptation. Thus new links are forged with the past and all the experiences it can offer, and new insights are suggested to the related attitudes and patterns of behavior. Such repetition is not redundancy; it is what makes these patterns resonant and resounding.

A classification that takes into account most of the observations presented above and opens up a whole gamut of the art of adapting can be found in Dudley Andrew's *Concepts in Film Theory*. Andrew treats adaptation as one of the key concepts that helps elucidate the role of art in society. According to Andrew, "The matching of the cinematic sign system to prior achievement in some other system, can be shown to be distinctive of all representational cinema." This is because representation itself is essentially a practice of articulating and appropriating already existing concepts and texts. In adaptations, the relationship to a previous text is foregrounded, sometimes to the extent that the new work cannot be properly appreciated without some knowledge of the previous one and its cultural status. Andrew divides adaptations into three categories, according to their relationship with their models: *borrowing, intersecting,* and *fidelity of transforming.*[20]

Borrowing is undoubtedly the most common form of adaptation. In this category, "the artist employs, more or less extensively, the material, idea or form of an earlier, generally successful text." The definition is broad and includes cases such as symphonic poems, in which the listener is invited to enhance the listening experience by "basking in a certain pre-established presence." In some cases a pattern rather than a definite precedent can be perceived in this presence.[21]

The concept of *intersecting* covers all those adaptations in which "uniqueness of the original text is preserved to such an extent that it is intentionally left unassimilated in adaptation." Andrew mentions as an example Bresson's adaptation of Bernanos's novel *Diary of a Country Priest,* which in André Bazin's words presents Bernanos "as seen by the cinema." In other words, the director has, in a sense, "refused to adapt" and preserved the distinctiveness of the original, thereby, according to Andrew, "initiating a dialectical interplay between the aesthetic forms of one period with cinematic forms of our own period." The study of such adaptations requires giving "attention to the *specificity* of the original within the *specificity* of cinema."[22] Finally, *fidelity of transforming* implies "the reproduction of something essential about an original text."[23]

In addition to the elements Ellis lists – characters, locations, costumes, actions, and strings of narrative – Andrew points out that motivations, consequences, context, viewpoint, imagery, and other such details can be produced equally in two works. Thus "if a novel's story is judged in some way comparable to its filmic adaptation, then the strictly separate but equivalent processes of implication which produced the narrative units of that story through words and audio-visual signs, respectively, must be studied."[24] Inasmuch as all signifying systems change in time and from society to society, adaptation cannot be understood without investigating the different signifying practices, the various styles and periods in film and in literature. Andrew mentions as an example the way Zola and Maupassant influenced Jean Renoir to "muscularly reorient the style of world cinema in the 1930's" and how this "naturalistic impulse" was further developed by Visconti in his adaptations of Cain and Verga.[25]

As an aspect of telling and retelling stories within a culture, then, adapting is a way of negotiating cultural heritage. All the cases of Andrew's classification of adaptations can be seen as a form of continuing and transforming tradition, taking part in a game of "sedimentation" and innovation that reflects and enhances changes in social, political, ideological, and spiritual climates – the adaptation of the community to ever new situations. The interplay of sameness and difference between the adaptation and the original opens up new interpretative possibilities regarding both the original work and life in general. From this point of view, adaptations can be thought of as standing in a metaphorical reaction to the original – although this point can obviously be fully appreciated only by those acquainted with the work that has been adapted.

The aim of adapting, then, is to find and justify an "alternate statement." The artist has to face tradition with a combination of reverence and radicalism, take into possession his or her cultural heritage, and engage in a dialogue with it in order to be able to rearticulate it convincingly in his or her own terms. In George Steiner's words: "The 'abler soul' of the great precedent, the proximity of the rival version, the existence, at once burdensome and liberating, of a public tradition, releases the writer from the trap of solipsism. A truly original thinker or artist is simply one who repays his debts, in excess."[26]

Guido Aristarco has emphasized that one of the crucial characteristics of Visconti's art is the way he was able to combine "cultural experience" with "original experience," that he had the ability to integrate inspiration gushing forth from cultural history, on the one hand, and life and the problems of existence, on the other.[27] Another Italian film scholar, Gian Piero Brunetta, has remarked about the inferiority complexes filmmakers sometimes appear to have in respect of literary authors: "It was totally different with Visconti. All authors, whose works he adapted from Verga to Proust and Mann, were a part of himself. It was a kind of cultural communion. His adaptations were transformations of the original into a new medium in the spirit of the original."[28] Similarly, it has been pointed out that, to Visconti, "to adapt" was almost synonymous with "to adopt." He would take the texts he was working on into his possession in order to produce a discourse that was his own, worked out in properly cinematic means, and that would have its own "coherence and inner consistency" (Boyum). Adaptation was for Visconti, in Youssef Ishaghpour's words, "simultaneously a labour of invention and conversion."[29]

Most of Visconti's films are more or less based on novels, novellas, or plays – sometimes more than one of them, as is the case in *Rocco and His Brothers* (1960). Depending on the task at hand, the degree of fidelity could range from using the original merely as a starting point, as in *Senso*, to the high degree of fidelity of *The Leopard*. In adapting a modern classic such as Mann's *Death in Venice*, Visconti could pursue what Andrew called intersecting, reproducing the "*specificity* of the original within the *specificity* of cinema."

While this adherence to tradition and the past may be seen as succumbing to patriarchal values, it must also be appreciated from exactly the opposite point of view. Reworking tradition is, after all, doing it for the future, with the intention of creating a link in a chain from the past to the future. It is thus a question of acknowledging the fact that creative activity can only be based on preexisting signifying systems. According to Mikael Enckell:

Contrary to what we in progressive delirium may imagine, tradition does not mean stiffness and unadaptability; in fact it gives us guidelines, patterns and alternative formation possibilities. The importance that the traditional ways of thinking attribute to the past and to ideas, liberates the individual from the unlimited captivity in himself and in his own perspective, and thus tradition stimulates increased mobility.[30]

WHITE NIGHTS

In 1956 Visconti started planning another film, fully aware that after *Senso* he now had the reputation among producers of being an extravagant spender. Thus the new film was to be made on a small scale. The idea to adapt Dostoyevsky's novella, *White Nights*, came from Suso Cecchi D'Amico's father, Emilio Cecchi. Since it was not possible to do the shooting in St. Petersburg – or Leningrad, as it was called at the time – Visconti decided to set the film in Livorno. But then it became apparent that production costs would be lower inside a studio, and a stylized Livorno was built in the Cinecittà studios. Even so, the costs were far beyond anyone's estimates, and Visconti's cofinanciers were horrified by his recklessness in financial matters. He thought he was being careful, but in fact he was hopelessly impractical. He appeared to have an intuitive talent for choosing the most expensive materials.[31] Fortunately, the film won the Silver Lion at the Venice film festival in 1957 – otherwise Visconti may not have been able to find financing for his next film, *Rocco and His Brothers*.

For many critics, *White Nights* was the final evidence that Visconti had forsaken neorealism. Most later commentators, however, considered the film a charming interlude in the director's career.[32] True enough,*White*

Nights is an extreme point in Visconti's cinematic oeuvre. It lacks all those historical, geographical, and social determinants that define the characters in most of his films. Everything takes place, even more than in the novel, in a peculiarly oneiric setting. The geographical center of the film's world is the bridge on which Mario (Marcello Mastroianni) finds Natalia (Maria Schell) weeping at the opening of the film. The bridge divides the city into two parts, one representing Natalia's private and timeless world actualized in her dreams and memories, the other the public and temporal, concrete, and disillusioned world.[33] Thus Mario and Natalia quite obviously stand for the worlds of reality and of dreams, respectively. The events fluctuate constantly between these two worlds corresponding to very subtle modulations of feeling. The film has a theatrical quality in that the characters stand out from the self-consciously stylized sets. At the same time, some of the secondary characters seem almost a part of the sets. They lurk in the shadows, emerging momentarily now and then to encounter Mario and Natalia.

Although the story line has been changed but little, Visconti's audio-visual recreation of course reflects his own times and mores. The main difference between Dostoyevsky's novella and Visconti's adaptation is the setting. The gentle lyricism of the northern white summer nights has been transformed into the darkness of Mediterranean winter nights, where only the occasional fog and snow are white. In the novella, the milieus are not made specific; we learn only that the events take place in St. Petersburg in the summer, when people have left for their villas in the countryside. The lonely dreamer-narrator walks through the streets in the hope of finding someone he might know at least by sight. The nocturnal world of the film is subtly stylized so that even the apparently "natural" elements have symbolic functions. Alessandro Bencivenni has written about "the fog which obfuscates all relationships between the protagonists; the rain which accompanies Natalia's tears, the wind which underlines Mario's exasperation; the snow which appears to dress up the city for a feast, emphasizing the illusion of happiness of the protagonist."[34]

The narrator of the novella is a pathetic, dreamy romantic whose main problem appears to be that he lacks self-confidence. Thoroughly involved with her own feelings as she is, Nastenka is drawn to him only because she is unable to perceive that the dreamer is painfully in love with her. Her love, like that of her filmic counterpart, is thoroughly narcissistic: she sees other people only in terms of her own feelings. Both girls innocently exploit their admirers' emotions – they are innocent in that they probably are genuinely unaware of the pain they are inflicting because they are blind to all other love but their own.

The literary dreamer is far more willing to throw himself into romantic illusions than is the Mario of the film. This trait enables him to enter into a relationship with Nastenka, but only on her terms. The dreamer is doomed to frustration. The illusory quality of love is further highlighted by the conspicuous absence of the tenant, whose character is filtered entirely through the enamored consciousness of Nastenka. In the film, he is at least seen in a flashback and is heard talking. He seems quite forward in his manners, but Jean Marais's tacit performance ensures that he retains his mystic aura. His appearance on the bridge at the end of the film suggests a kind of fate figure.

Mario lives in a real, banal little world, he is a clerk of some sort, he catches a cold, argues with his landlady. He is a sympathetic, bored, unhappy, petty bourgeois unable to discover how he might become happier – except by finding a sweetheart. Nadia appears to open up new possibilities for him, but he wants love in the real world – in great contrast to Dostoyevsky's "hero." Mario finds Natalia's story absurd and tries to convince her that it is silly to expect the tenant to return. The difference between Natalia and Mario is emphasized in the scenes in which they are not together: Natalia's reminiscences and Mario's mornings in the boardinghouse.

When Natalia tells Mario about the tenant and how she fell in love with him, a series of dreamlike flashbacks take place suggesting that her feelings are genuine, if not all that strongly related to reality. The interchangeability of different levels of reality in her mind is made manifest by the first flashback, which begins with a shot that transcends time and space by panning from the street to the grandmother's carpet service. Many of the flashbacks also create a sense of unreality because, in contrast with the rest of the film, they bathe in light and because Nadia does not utter a word in them. Her voice is heard only as a voice-over, as she relates the events to Mario. Only the last line of the flashbacks, as Natalia tells how she met the tenant for the last time, appears to be uttered in the past. But the shot that at first appears to belong to the flashback turns out to belong to the present: she seems to be flinging herself into the arms of the tenant, but in fact there is only Mario.

Natalia's fairy-tale–like grandmother patches oriental carpets, of which there are piles in their little workshop. Grandmother has her suspicions about handsome tenants but is overjoyed when he takes her and

Natalia to see Rossini's *The Barber of Seville*. She even sings a few phrases
from Rosina's aria, "Una voce poco fa," in which she says she can change
from a gentle little girl into an asp that will think of a hundred tricks
rather than yield against her will. Perhaps this is indicative of the grandmother's idea of how women should treat men.

In Dostoyevsky's novella, too, the tenant takes the women to see *The
Barber of Seville*. There is a charming parallel with the plot of the opera
and the events of the novella when the narrator realizes he has inadvertently played the part of Figaro by suggesting that the girl should write
a letter to her beloved, only to discover that she has already done this.
The point is not lost on the characters. In the film the parallel is made
apparent only in that the tenant and the ladies are seen in the opera house
just as the performance is reaching this point.[35] A far more crucial difference is that the film's Mario angrily tears up the letter Natalia has left
for him to deliver.

The next day, Mario rather comically pretends to himself that he has
no pangs of conscience. That evening he sees Nadia as he wanders through
the town, tries weakly to escape, but ends up accompanying her, supposedly until it is time for her to go and meet her beloved, summoned to
the bridge by the letter. Now the night at the opera is contrasted with a
scene in a bar that Natalia and Mario enter. Soon they are drawn into
dancing to Bill Haley's *Thirteen Women*. The opposition between high art
and popular culture is a part of the symbolic structure of the film,[36] but
it also offers a new point of view into the conflict between dreams and
reality. The dance is like their relationship in miniature: at times it flings
them apart toward the other dancers; at times it throws them into each
other's arms. At first Mario draws back, frightened by the vigor of the
young man leading the dance. But he plucks up his courage, dances an
irresistibly silly solo, and appears to win Natalia for himself. As they
continue to dance a slow piece, there appears to be a genuine possibility
for a relationship between them. Both the merrymaking and the tenderness are spontaneous and genuine, born on the spur of the moment. Mario
and Natalia have shared a moment of innocent happiness with each other,
in a real world – or as real as it could possibly be for them.

But suddenly the enchantment is broken by a banal cry from the street
indicating how late it is. Natalia realizes she is late and rushes to meet
her beloved. He is not there, of course, and Natalia is distraught, not only
because the beloved has not arrived but also because she has in her own
terms been unfaithful to him. Mario follows, but she tells him to go away.

Mario is unable to break the spell of Natalia's love, but there is an alternative available to him in the form of a raven-like prostitute (Clara Calamai). She already happened to pass by on the first night, just as Mario first succeeded in making contact with Nadia. She appears every four evenings in which the action takes place, each time making further contact with Mario until finally, after having been rejected by Natalia, he becomes flushed with frustration and makes an attempt to go with her. But before anything happens, he changes his mind and the woman screams in pathetic disappointment. Men suddenly appear and Mario finds himself involved in a street brawl. The contrast between the two women is a reflection of the virgin–whore dichotomy, and Mario wants only the virgin. Even at the moment of his greatest frustration he cannot reduce his aspirations to mere sexual desire. In his own everyday sort of way, he yearns for pure, idealized love. This is in accord with the novella, in which sex as such plays no part. In both cases, albeit in quite different ways, sublimation brings out the mechanisms of love; that is to say, sexuality is bracketed in order to facilitate concentration on the workings of feeling and idealization.

The reality–fantasy opposition is explored mainly from the point of view of Mario. To him Natalia is an object of idealized love, something that by definition could never work out in real life. Tearing Natalia's letter up is an attempt to shatter a deceptive illusion, but of course it is also self-serving in that it keeps her and the tenant apart. Thus Mario accepts the possibility that the tenant might actually have been serious in courting Natalia, and this thought obviously gnaws at him. But he is passive. Just before he meets Natalia on the last evening, a very attractive woman offers him a chance to make her acquaintance, but he ends up with Natalia.

It is Natalia's turn to be frustrated by love. Mario is willing to exploit the opportunity that appears to open up for him, and he is suddenly very willing to entertain flights of fantasy. Natalia, made at least momentarily a bit more wise by her disappointment, yields slightly, but she still has her reservations. Now she talks about letting time pass before they start anything together. Nevertheless, she accepts his invitation to go on a boat trip on the canal with him, as if in an attempt to reconcile reality and dreams. Mario tries to pose as a romantic lover. In the boat, as snow falls on them, as they glide through the channel that separates Mario's reality and Natalia's fairy tale world, they are literally between two worlds. They rejoice at the sudden snowfall and hardly notice the homeless by the banks of the channel, shivering in the cold.

Morning dawns and bells ring as they get back to the street. They play and walk in the snow, until suddenly Natalia hears her true self calling to her in the figure of the tenant, who has suddenly appeared on the bridge. For Mario, ideals and reality have shown themselves to be hopelessly separated. They can interact and enrich each other, but only by remaining separate. Natalia can be herself and the object of Mario's love only by remaining on her side of the channel. Thus, in keeping with the logic of the story, the tenant must return and Mario must remain alone. He must be satisfied with the company of the little stray dog he met at the beginning of the film. It is as if everything that has happened is but a dream. The story ends with Mario's words: "I bless you for the moment of happiness you gave me. . . . It is not little even for a whole lifetime."[37]

THE STRANGER

Being French in Algeria

Albert Camus's roots were deep in the soil of French Algeria. His childhood memories were inextricably connected with this country, scorched by the mercilessly blazing sun, refreshed by the blue Mediterranean. Better than most of his compatriots of European extraction, he understood how explosive the situation in Algeria was in the 1940s. He had already demanded social reforms in the 1930s and was well aware of the squalor in which the Arab population lived. These themes are crucial in L'étranger (The stranger 1942), his most celebrated novel. But it also conveys the feeling of an existential vacuum, of a consciousness thrown into a world that has no God or any other absolute point of reference. The only "meaningful" goal appears to be to try to regain unity with Being. Meursault, the protagonist, is characterized above all by indifference. His condition is apparent right from the beginning, in his reaction to his mother's death and her funeral. He has not been in touch with her for some time and treats the event as if it did not really concern him.

Meursault gets on well with his fellow men, but because he lacks the capacity to be genuinely interested in them he is unable to fathom their motives. He keeps on making weak attempts to understand why things are as they are or happen as they do. He might tell us that he understands someone else's point of view, too, but this appears to be only because he never becomes really engaged in the kind of heated situations in which most people are left stuck with their own limited point of view. Moreover, Meursault simply cannot be bothered to think out the reasons, not to speak of the moral implications of why people act as they do. If he is asked for help, he usually acquiesces because refusing would require more effort and involve more complications: "As I usually do when I want to get rid of someone whose conversation bores me, I pretended to agree," he tells us when describing his interrogation by the magistrate.[38]

Because of his alienation, Meursault is unable to resort to those stereotypical reactions that usually guide people's behavior, and often thinking, and make them conform to expectations of the community and society at large. He must act according to some motivation or another, but to him the established patterns of behavior and expected emotional responses are merely conventions to which he is in no way personally attached. When Marie asks him about love or marriage, for example, he notes:

> Marie came that evening and asked me if I'd marry her. I said I didn't mind; if she was keen on it, we'd get married.
> Then she asked me again if I loved her. I replied, much as before, that her question meant nothing or next to nothing – but I suppose I didn't.[39]

The story is kept in motion mainly by agents other than Meursault. He merely drifts with the flow of events and his own haphazard sensations and displays neither initiative nor involvement. He suffers and enjoys without inhibition all the sensations stirred up by his natural environment, the resplendent and exasperating Mediterranean.

A series of disconnected events follow that lead to Meursault's execution. He ends up killing an Arab as a result of mounting circumstances as well as psychological and physiological factors that he is unable to keep in check because he is so underrehearsed in thinking out the consequences of things. He kills the Arab in a state of exhaustion because the Arab is his competitor in the pursuit of indifference and unity with Being, because they have ended up on the opposite sides in a conflict with which he thinks he has nothing to do, because the Arab appears to be between him and the refreshing brook, because there happens to be a gun in his pocket, and finally because at the fatal moment "a shaft of light" shoots from the knife the Arab is holding, and Meursault feels "as if a long, thin blade [had] transfixed [his] forehead."[40] His ramshackle framework of temporal perspectives collapses, he is at the mercy of a moment's impulse, his grip closes on the revolver.

But the fact that Meursault has killed a native is not the important question for the French court of justice. It is his indifference to established social values that is the true crime against this society, his inability to even pretend that he sees them as absolute. Nevertheless, in the courtroom, sensing the hate of all those around him, even Meursault himself finally becomes convinced of his guilt. He is condemned to death.[41]

In prison, waiting to be executed, Meursault is able to view his life in its entirety. Finally, significantly enough after an exhausting encounter with a priest during which he asserts his love of earthly life, he is finally able to reconcile his strong bodily urge to live with the inevitability of death: "It was as if that great rush of anger had washed me clean, emptied me of hope, and, gazing up at the dark sky spangled with its signs and stars, for the first time, the first, I laid my heart open to the benign indifference of the universe."[42] At the very end, he can only hope that the people gathered to watch his execution will greet him with "howls of execration."

The Stranger as film and literature

When L'étranger was released in June 1942, it was first seen as a rather pessimistic type of realism, as a study of the moral decadence of France under the Vichy regime. It was even seen as a revolt against a society that prevented people from looking after their mothers properly. A few years later it was suggested that Meursault was a schizophrenic.[43] Since then, the novel has been seen, with various degrees of emphasis, as an existentialist statement and a comment on the situation of the French in Algeria.

From an existentialist perspective, Meursault's attitude can be considered a critique of European bourgeois mentality, of existence confined by convention. The only way to be true to oneself is to shake off the shackles imposed by society, the empty customs, and the learned patterns of behavior. It is a path marked by solitude, in the course of which one must balance lucidity and self-deception, and, as Terry Keefe observes, "face up squarely and unequivocally to our metaphysical state and somehow . . . come to terms with it, rather than try to evade it or cover it up in some manner." This pursuit cannot but end in isolation because society and all that it stands for represent its very opposite. As Keefe points out, Meursault's "truthfulness has little to do with a desire to communicate the right things to other people."[44]

Visconti first read The Stranger not long after it was published, in 1942. Later, in 1965, he described the experience:

I could have made a film out of it already then, but I would have done it very differently from the way I will do it now. In 1942 we were in the dawn of existentialism; people and artists were intent on asking about the reasons for their destiny, and Camus was one of the first to provide a precise answer. He indicated that it is possible to live outside ordered society, avoid its laws, to lock oneself up into indifference, to confine oneself into absurdity. This was the message of The

Stranger. In this book there is above all one great intuition: In the apparently casual gesture of Meursault, exhausted by eating fried fish and drinking too much wine, blinded by the sun, the way he points a revolver toward the Arab seen as if he were a hologram, toward "the shining blade," there is something more that can be seen today: the fear of the *pied noir* brought up in this country, who feels he is an intruder and who knows he has to go and to leave the land to those it belongs to.[45]

That Visconti intended to adapt *The Stranger* had already been announced in 1962. At first, he talked about remaining faithful to the original work, about wanting "to have the book in my hand and shoot it as it's written."[46] But he did not actually begin working on this film until after *Le streghe* was completed in 1966. Now he scoffed at his original ideas. Together with Cecchi D'Amico, he prepared a script in which they took some license with the novel. But Camus's widow rejected it and demanded strict fidelity.[47] Visconti later remarked on the constraints this created:

The written page is only a starting point. And it is nonsense to ask a director of a film to be faithful to a literary text. Really, I prefer the authors to be dead in order to avoid conflicts. And I hope in any case that their families are as small as possible. When the authors are gone, the widows remain! *The Stranger* became a fiasco because Albert Camus' widow demanded objective, absurd fidelity. In order to honour our contract I was forced to renounce the film I had always wanted to do and to confine myself strictly to the text.[48]

Visconti had other problems, too. He still intended to "render manifest, to visualize the psychology of the protagonist, to give a face to what for Camus is above all an idea and a protest."[49] Originally, the face was to have been that of Alain Delon. This hope was dashed owing to a series of misunderstandings and disputes about remuneration. In the end, Marcello Mastroianni was given the main role. It was arguably not a bad choice but inevitably brought a different tone to the film. Unable to release himself from his contract with the producer, Dino De Laurentiis, Visconti found himself making a film that he could not shape to his liking.

The Stranger was a particularly difficult novel to adapt faithfully because its innermost quality and excellence are inseparable from the literary devices used to render the story. In the words of Bruce Morrissette:

The "double I" of Proust, the laconic/elliptical first person of Meursault in Camus's *L'Etranger* (reinforced by the systematic use, in French, of the passé composé to fragment the presentation of time) . . . the not always apparent fact, first enunciated by Sartre, that every novelistic technique implies a metaphysical attitude on the part of the author. The choice of narrative mode, far from being a mere "formal" feature of fiction, conditions its whole structure and determines to a great extent the receptive stance and aesthetic involvement of the reader.[50]

Proust's and Camus's narrative modes are not easily transposed into the means and narrative strategies available to the filmmaker. Meursault's inability to perceive coherence in the world is rendered to a great extent by literary devices themselves, mainly by the use of free indirect speech with its vagueness concerning whose point of view is being presented. Tenses are used to the same effect, says Patrick McCarthy:

> Camus does not use the simple past – "I did" – which is the usual tense of the French novel. The simple past depicts a succession of events and implies that they have a coherence which the narrator can perceive. Camus uses the perfect tense – "I have done" which links the experience more directly to the narrator but does not organize it.[51]

Nevertheless, to express the experience of meaninglessness and lack of motivation, Camus must call on a structure in which motivation and meaning would normally be important, namely, the narrative. According to McCarthy, all three of Camus's novels appear to be "attempts to tell a story while leaving out an essential part of it." In *The Stranger* he succeeds in "writing from the viewpoint of this emptiness instead of merely writing about it."[52]

It was obviously naive to assume that the excellence of the novel could be translated to another medium by adhering faithfully to its "characters, locations, costumes, actions, and strings of narrative." Visconti could not help but lose the elusive essence of the original because he was unable to explore cinematic equivalents that would have had the same effects as the literary devices used by Camus.

Yet it is difficult to envisage precisely how he would have tackled the philosophical aspects of the novel even if he had had the liberty to proceed as he wished. His cinematic style is characterized by objectivity, a kind of omniscient narration that is almost totally contrary to the implications of Camus's novel, particularly in its first half, which paved the way for the *nouveau roman* of Alain Robbe-Grillet, Michel Butor, Claude Simon, and others. The idea of doing away with the kind of literature that sought to reject the conventional aspects of the novel found its cinematic equivalent in the films of Jean-Luc Godard, Alain Resnais, and Chris Marker, to mention but a few. On the other hand, on the eve of May 1968 adapting

The Stranger was not exactly a revolutionary choice – the young radicals thought of Camus as an "impostor" and a "bleating boy scout" – but Visconti might have felt an affinity with Camus's insistence that left-wing utopias only too often serve as pretexts for bloodshed.[53]

In any case, being forced to copy the novel, Visconti was left with very little scope to explore new modes of adapting. As Visconti's statement about giving a face to Camus's creation suggested, the film is about the fate of an individual rather than about an existential condition as such. Mastroianni as Meursault is as sympathetic as ever, tenderly melancholy and lovable even in his indifference. His fate is touching and sad: something irretrievably valuable is lost when this individual is executed. The audience is denied the luxury of detachment. Also, the way Mastroianni speaks his internal monologues suggests that his condition is much more of a problem for him than it is for his literary counterpart. And whereas the way that the Meursault of the book renders the court scene is full of subtle irony, in the film the overdone gestures and statements by the judge and the members of the court are seen as if from an objective point of view and appear excessively melodramatic and grotesque. One could, of course, claim that this scene is rendered from Meursault's point of view, but it is not cued to be so. Rather, every now and then the camera also observes his reactions by quickly zooming to his face.

Meursault would appear to fit quite well the gallery of characters in Visconti's films. From *Ossessione*'s Gino to Tullio in *The Innocent*, Visconti's main characters are in one way or another lonely wolves, "keepers of distances," to use Alfred's admonition to Aschenbach in *Death in Venice*. Meursault is an extreme case, however, in that on the psychological level he almost succeeds in tearing himself from the collective consciousness of his society. Unfortunately, the film does not quite succeed in portraying the benign existential detachment that Meursault of the book assumes in the face of death. Meursault's ponderings in the film appear unconvincing in their assumed indifference.

Taken simply as a film in its own right, *The Stranger* can be seen as a fairly subtle, sensuous, and unpretentious film. Its controlled beauty, the mainly grey-blue, white, and brown-red color scheme, the atmosphere of tortuous tension created by Piero Piccioni's music, the opposition between the suffocating blaze of the sun and the refreshment offered by water – the brook and the sea – create the setting in which Meursault lives and enjoys life, sweats, and exhausts himself. All this becomes a vibrant manifestation of a certain experience of life, of a life that has to end because of a chance accumulation of unconnected causes: there is a sense of tragedy and loss in the film, the absence of which was really the gist of the novel.[54]

REMEMBRANCE OF THINGS PAST

In the preface to the printed script for *Remembrance of Things Past*, Suso Cecchi D'Amico recalls that Visconti used to say that adapting *La recherche* for the screen would be his last film project. According to her, the director was haunted by an almost superstitious fear of this project. Visconti's other principal screenwriter, Enrico Medioli, agrees, but thinks it was also a question of uncertainty:

He knew very well, that one could not possibly make Proust into a film. Because, I mean, unless you make thirteen or fifteen episodes. . . . Even a film of four hours wouldn't correspond to the volumes of *La recherche*. You wouldn't have the *temps perdu*, which is so fascinating in the novel: you see the character you have met at the beginning completely transformed by time at the end of this work.[55]

Visconti's dream of making his Proust film came closest to realization in 1971. The rights belonged to the French producer Nicole Stéphane. She originally wanted René Clément to direct it, but Visconti succeeded in persuading her that he and no one else should direct Proust's colossal work. Cecchi D'Amico prepared the script that had lived in their minds for long.

Visconti spent weeks hunting for locations in Paris and in Normandy. The prospective cast was breathtaking: Silvana Mangano as Oriane de Guermantes; Alain Deloin or Dustin Hoffman as Marcel, the narrator; Helmut Berger as Morel; Charlotte Rampling as Albertine; Marie Bell as la Berma; Marlon Brando or Laurence Olivier as Charlus; Simone Signoret or Annie Girardot as Madame Verdurin. According to the most exciting rumor, Greta Garbo, thirty years after having left the screen, had considered accepting the part of the queen of Naples. Many actors were enthusiastic about the idea of participating in the film, and some even contacted Visconti to offer their services.[56]

But then trouble began. When the final budget turned out to be enormous, Stéphane asked Visconti to postpone the shooting for four months so that she could find more money. But the impatient Visconti had to start working on something. So, to allow himself to do *Ludwig* first, he demanded that the Proust project should be postponed even further. Stéphane thought Visconti had let her down and sued him. In her fury, she ordered a new script from Harold Pinter and invited Joseph Losey to direct it. To make matters worse, Visconti's heart attack after the shooting of the *Ludwig* left him incapable of assuming tasks on this scale. But for various reasons, Losey did not get to do his film, either. There was still not enough money for the ever more expensive project, there were innumerable personality conflicts, Stéphane had doubts about Pinter's script, Losey would have directed in English.[57]

Visconti would have started his film from the second volume of the novel, *A l'ombre des jeunes filles en fleurs* and made *Sodome et Gomorrhe* the nodal point. In this scheme, the total length wold have been about four hours. According to Visconti himself, he wanted to adapt Proust as if he were Balzac, to treat the changes in French society before the First World War and leave the questions of time and memory in the background. As many critics have pointed out, it is questionable whether such a film could have been called a true Proust adaptation.[58]

Perhaps Visconti would have succeeded in harnessing this subject to serve his own artistic and philosophical vision. This might have happened because of the deep affiliation he felt with the author. In an essay focusing mainly on *The Innocent*, Mikael Enckell writes:

Suffering and brutality as prerequisites for tenderness and yearning connects Visconti's sensuality to that of Proust's. . . . Visconti and Proust distinguish a feature which they see as typical of their main characters' relationships to the beloved and to life in general, namely their tortured and tireless quest for perfect safety, to guard themselves from the danger of ending up in loneliness, and the equally unavoidable result of this quest, misfortune, in love because of jealousy and in life because of death.[59]

The basic concept of Pinter's script is almost the exact opposite of Cecchi D'Amico's. Whereas the latter proceeds primarily linearly, the former is utterly fragmented, with the narration moving constantly back and forth in time and associations of varying strength connecting the different levels. The film would have ended with a return to the opening scene and the words, "It was time to begin."

The film would undoubtedly have been fascinating, but probably also extremely difficult to follow without prior knowledge of the novel. Proust's narration proceeds in long sentences that create webs of associations, reminiscences, and foreshadowings. But behind this, the main line of the story proceeds majestically. The passing of time becomes apparent mainly through the surprises the narrator experiences in meeting his old

acquaintances again and realizing how they have changed. These encounters give the impetus to the workings of his memory.[60]

The crucial idea of the novel is really a literary device: that is, the first
person narrator is simultaneously Marcel experiencing these events and
Marcel relating these events with the advantage of hindsight. He is seen
experiencing life in all its intoxicating, frustrating immediacy, but its
meaning is revealed to him only in retrospect. Proust uses the distance
between these two points of view to work out a balance between the spontaneous reactions of the protagonist and to focus on them from a distance.
Finally these two "I"s join when the novel comes to its end.[61] This fusion
signifies the regaining of time, for just as Marcel matures and is about to
begin his work, the narrator is finishing his. Time has been conquered as
the past is seen in all its richness from the point of view of the present,
when memories have been harnessed to serve art, when death has been
overcome by taking one's life fully into possession.

The two Proust scripts differed not only in their basic approaches and
narrative structures but also to some extent in their handling of the characters. Because Cecchi D'Amico's script does not begin until the second
part of the novel, Charles Swann, Odette, and their daughter Gilberte
remain fairly marginal characters.[62] Along with them, a great many of
Marcel's childhood memories and his youthful love for Gilberte are left
aside. Instead, Morel and his homosexual relationship with Baron de
Charlus is quite prominent. The script ends with a scene at the time of
the First World War, in which Morel, now a deserter, is sent back to the
front line. After this, Marcel begins to write his book, and childhood memories return to him. A visit to the Princess de Guermantes, which Pinter
uses as a frame in his version, is absent.

The scripts are so different that both could have had a place in film
history. In fact, they would have complemented, explained, and enriched
each other. Inasmuch as the interplay of time and memories would have
been realized in Pinter's version, Cecchi D'Amico's script would have
enabled Visconti once again to recreate a bygone era; to dramatize people's fixity in time, place, class, historical and social situation; and show
them in the penetrating yet tender light of critical nostalgia. The two
taken together would have created a kind of analogy with the tension
between Proust's two "I"s.

Although Visconti never made his Proust film, there are many traces
of the French author in his works. The ball scene in *The Leopard*, beach
life in *Death in Venice*, and the concerts in *The Innocent* probably give
some idea of what Visconti's *La recherche* would have been like. On the

whole, perhaps even more than any of the earlier films, his last work, *The Innocent*, is a similar nostalgic but critical evocation of things past, as is Proust's masterpiece.

THE INNOCENT

D'Annunzio and Visconti as decadents

In 1975, after having completed *Conversation Piece*, Visconti, Cecchi D'Amico, and Medioli started to explore the possibilities of adapting one of Gabriele D'Annunzio's novels for the screen. Because the rights for *Il piacere* had already been sold, they began working on *L'innocente*.

Gabriele D'Annunzio (1863–1938) was one of the key figures of decadentism. This turn-of-the-century trend was an outgrowth of romanticism and carried certain of its features to and past their breaking point. However, the word "decadent" can be used in two ways. On the one hand, it is a fairly neutral term referring to a certain postromantic trend in the arts running parallel and partly covering styles ranging from Pre-Raphaelitism to symbolism, expressionism, surrealism, and so on, and including artists such as Charles Baudelaire, Jovis Huysmans, Paul Verlaine, Arthur Rimbaud, and Stéphane Mallarmé in France, Oscar Wilde and William Butler Yeats in Britain, Gerhard Hauptmann and Stefan George in Germany, and D'Annunzio and Luigi Pirandello in Italy. Sometimes the term has been extended to include even Proust, Mann, and James Joyce.

On the other hand, the word "decadence" has pejorative connotations. Thus works considered to be decadent can only too easily be considered to actually promote the excesses they depict in such loving detail. And true enough, at its most excessive, decadentism could lead to indulgence in shameless subjectivity and sensuality, a wallowing in the forbidden and the perverse, morbid interest in sickness and death, a flaunting of moral and social values, fierce antireligiousness and arrogant faith in the rights and possibilities of men supposedly elect because of racial or cultural superiority and threatened only by undecipherable and pernicious women.

In any case, decadence in the arts obviously cannot be separated from its social context: bourgeois society heading toward a crisis at the turn of the century. From this point of view, decadentism can be seen as a symptom of an overcultivated civilization with a relatively narrow class basis trying to block out awareness of the unavoidable increase in social dynamism by escaping into interiority and overrefined sensibility. Decadentism was also a reaction against nineteenth-century positivist ideology and its manifestation in the arts, naturalism and verism. Conversely, this interpretation has been used mainly by old-style marxist critics, to label almost all works flaunting the codes of classical realism as decadent.[63]

D'Annunzio, instead of depicting the geographical and social environment of poor people, as the verists did, preferred to describe the pretentious, shallow, and boring way of life and mentality of the Italian upper class. This he did with accuracy but without much ironic distance. Even when he appears to be condemning the lifestyle and ideals of his protagonists, this does not convince the reader because he, in the disguise of the narrator, so obviously identifies himself with and idolizes his characters. In a style that could be described as naturalism turned decadent, he evokes with his stifling verbal luxuriance the innermost feelings and the subtlest shades of sensations of his characters, usually at the cost of psychological depth.[64]

D'Annunzio was not always original, but he was capable of fusing various sources and giving them new force. Many of the provocative elements in his works derive from certain features of late romantic literature. For example, erotic love between siblings became a popular theme in nineteenth-century sensational literature. D'Annunzio's heroes often desire their sisters of project brotherly feelings on their wives.

Mario Pratz has defined D'Annunzio as a *parvenu* whose semibarbaric sensuality provided a fruitful ground for the decadent profaning of all communal values. Pratz summarizes his view in the statement: "D'Annunzio is a barbarian and at the same time a decadent, and there is lacking in him the temperate zone which, in the present period of culture, is labeled 'humanity.' "[65] In many of his works this leads to a lack of critical perspective and to the idea of a superman. The feeling of racial, cultural, and physical prowess convinces his characters of their right to fulfill their desires irrespective of all limits and makes them scorn customs and institutions that they think belong only to the masses. Such a character can already be found in D'Annunzio's first novel, *Il piacere* (1889), and in a more fully developed version in *L'innocente*, which appeared three years later.[66]

The Innocent is written in the form of a confession. Tullio Hermill begins his story by revealing that he has committed a crime, that he has killed "a poor creature" "with perfect clarity of mind, with precision and maximum security."[67] This has taken place a year earlier, and now Tullio is asking himself whether he should confess everything to the judge. He decides that he cannot and will not, because no tribunal on the earth would know how to judge him. Thus he has to accuse himself. He has to reveal his secret to someone, but to whom? The implied answer is, of course, to the reader. Through the novel Tullio describes in detail his innermost feelings and the wealth of his sensations, while the external reality is revealed only inasmuch as it directly affects him. His love for his wife Giuliana is metonymically marked by incest for she has been taken into the family almost as a substitute for Tullio's sister, who died at the age of nine. By adopting a brotherly attitude toward his wife, he has been able to reconquer his "primitive liberty with Giuliana's consent, without hypocrisy, without subterfuge, without degrading lies."[68] He thinks that she recognizes the superiority of his intelligence: "Thus she too – I thought – understands that being different from others and having a different conception of life, I can justifiably shirk the duties that others would impose on me, I can justifiably despise the opinions of other people and live in the absolute sincerity of my elected nature."[69] These thoughts have been presented in the past tense, and at first a modern reader, at least, could easily assume that the aim is to throw critical light on them. However, the mild self-irony that one might sense in Tullio's narration does not suffice to put his ideas into a critical perspective. In the last instance, the function of any self-reflection appears to be to prove that Tullio is genuinely capable of assessing himself and his motivations. His states of mind, his sensations, and feelings are described thoroughly and colorfully, and so in his own terms D'Annunzio does succeed in making his attitudes and behavior appear understandable. But this is countered by the killing of an innocent creature, the baby Giuliana has had with another man. At the end, Tullio is genuinely horrified by his deed; nevertheless, he does not repent it. In his own view, he could not have acted otherwise. Because he is completely imprisoned by thoroughly internalized codes of honor, tradition, and love, as well as by his excessive sensuality, this can in a sense be accepted as the truth.

As the novel proceeds, a chain of associations is built between depravity, sickness, and Giuliana's baby. Tullio appears to have feelings for his wife only when she is ill and weak. When she recovers, her husband loses his interest and returns to his lover. When after giving birth Giuliana does not appear to regain her strength, Tullio believes the very existence of the child constitutes a threat to her life and comes to the conclusion that his love for his wife compels him to kill the child. Tullio tells how he committed the crime, exposing the innocent to the winds of winter, in cold consideration, even feeling relieved of his earlier feelings of repulsion for the child. Apparently he receives no other punishment but his own feelings of guilt, which he almost appears to boast about.

There were critics who thought that adapting this novel by the arch-decadent D'Annunzio was a logical ending for Visconti's career. His late works, sometimes starting as early as *Sandra*, have often been labeled decadent. These films have been seen as an expression of an aging director's morbid fascination with the themes of sickness, decay, and death. On the whole, however, it has not always been clear whether the label of decadence is a reference to the subject matter, the style, or both, or whether it is used simply as a pejorative term. Guido Aristarco sought to define the nature of Visconti's decadence in his article *Critic or Poet of Decadence?*

There is in him "a sense of the decline of culture and of a profound crisis," the awareness of "finding himself at the conclusion of a historical cycle and approaching the end of a civilization" and a profound "sense of death." . . . Is it not true that beginning from *The Leopard* he showed sympathy for "ultra-refined and exhausted old times" and that the "sensation of being at a turning point" was accompanied by "a profound lament" and that death truly became "romantically desired"?[70]

Visconti made *The Innocent* at the time he was facing his own death (he died on March 17, 1976, just when the film was in its editing stage). In it, Visconti reconstructed the era and the class into which he had been born – as he had already done in *Death in Venice*. Adapting D'Annunzio's novel implied a return to something familiar, remembered with bitter nostalgia and detachment, with an awareness of its weaknesses and even depravity. So whereas D'Annunzio epitomized the transition from verism to decadentism, with *The Innocent* Visconti rounded out his career in the cinema by completing his own trajectory from neorealism to his own critical brand of decadentism, which really serves as a vehicle for giving expression to certain psychological concerns. According to Enckell:

The Innocent's facade is dominated by erotic complications, triangle patterns in a painfully heavy, brutal and at the same time over-cultivated, baroque-like frame. The more the spectator goes into the film and into his/her own complementary reactions to it, the more obvious it becomes that Visconti's last work is rather an expression of deep sorrow than those events which appear to dominate its surface.[71]

The power of adapting

During the opening credits, Visconti's own hand is seen turning the pages of D'Annunzio's *L'innozente*. A beautiful society woman, Teresa Raffo (Jennifer O'Neill), is blackmailing Tullio (Giancarlo Giannini) in order to persuade him to show more attention to her and to ignore his wife. He decides to give in and openly tells his wife, Giuliana (Laura Antonelli), that he is going to do so. Soon after, Giuliana meets the author D'Arborio (Marc Porel) at a small dinner party arranged by Tullio's brother, Federico (Didier Haudepin). Later they notice each other at a concert just as a soprano is singing the aria "Che faro senza Euridice," from Gluck's opera *Orfeo ed Euridice,* a song about the pain of losing a beloved through death. Tullio appears but does not realize what is going on for his only concern is to attract Giuliana's attention to fulminate about Teresa's infidelity. Against this background, Giuliana's adultery can be seen as a justified attempt to claim for herself the same rights that her husband has assumed.

Tullio begins to suspect that something has happened when he hears Giuliana sing "Che faro senza Euridice." He happens to see a book by D'Arborio on her table with a dedication to her. A casual conversation about his literary talents appears to lead Tullio's thoughts in the right direction. But it is not until Teresa mildly mocks Tullio about the affair his wife is having that he actually faces the fact. He meets D'Arborio in a fencing hall and they engage in a match – one of the ever-occurring "duels" in this film. His discovery of the affair leads Tullio to leave Teresa and return to Giuliana. She has retreated to the countryside, to her mother-in-law's villa, and Tullio follows her – there is a striking cut here from luscious red, black, and gold to wonderful green and white. Nothing incites Tullio's love as much as the fear of losing the object of his love to someone else. Now he calls Giuliana "my wife, my sister, my lover." She invents an excuse as to why they should have separate rooms, but when her husband begins his attempts to rekindle her love she finds it difficult to resist his approaches. But we never really know at which point her possibly renewed love becomes a strategy with which to protect herself and the child she is carrying. Antonelli's acting is too subtle to permit any simple interpretations.

Finally, Tullio's mother reveals to him that Giuliana is pregnant. However much he pretends to allow his wife the same liberties he enjoys himself, he seems to have an almost infantile fear of being left alone, being excluded from the sphere of love and caring. This fear is actually justified and increased by his own inability to experience such feelings toward others. Perhaps it is the idea of a mother's love for her baby, doubly alien to the man who has forced his wife to seek love and caring from another man, that makes Tullio see the baby as his archenemy. This fear grows into hate, which has the effect of making the objects of passion and love truly unapproachable.

Tullio is unable to meet his beloved on equal terms and tends to experience human relationships as confrontations. He projects his own anxieties on others. At one point, when discussing the situation with Giuliana, he suddenly hears a voice challenging him to another match. He turns around and to his utter amazement sees a man in a white fencing suit with a visor over his face – just like D'Arborio when Tullio first laid eyes on him. But it is not Giuliana's knight in shining white armor, it is Tullio's brother, Federico. They have a match, which puts Tullio in a state of rage, as if he were engaged in actual combat. Both D'Arborio and Federico are Tullio's competitors in love, the one in relation to his wife, the other to his mother – and tellingly enough, when the latter appears at the gym, Tullio lunges furiously at Federico, as if he were fighting for his life. Enckell suggests that "the masked antagonist is not only a living rival, he is in this, Visconti's last film, also a symbol of death, that victorious competitor who overcomes us all and forever deprives us of all that we cherish."[72]

D'Arborio dies of a fever before Tullio has had a chance to exact his revenge. When Giuliana does not yield to his atheistic temptations to "cancel the results of our errors, be independent of the conditions of our existence, of the uncertainty caused by anxiety and losses," when she refuses to get rid of the "intruder," Tullio is left alone. The only course he sees for himself is to destroy the enemy that appears to take his place in the sphere of love. While the others are attending the Christmas mass in the family chapel, Tullio exposes the child to the winter air. The parallel with the Christ child is made emphatic and poignant by the parallel editing and the music of the service being carried to the room where Tullio is waiting for the baby to catch his death. But killing the innocent merely seals Tullio's fate: expulsion. Giuliana finally renounces the "holy" sacrament of marriage that has bound them:

Not for a moment – listen carefully – did I want to be free of it [the child]. Not in order to follow the rules of my consciousness but because I loved it, my poor little creature, whom I denied a thousand times in my words. Respect for the laws of religion and morality, which I now curse, have brought me back to you. The

sacrament of marriage. What holiness can there be in the disgusting ties that have
kept us together during these last few months? I cannot explain it. Yet it has
happened because of that sacrament. Because of it I have suffered and caused
pain. . . . What folly . . . what folly!

Later, Tullio confesses to Teresa Raffo what he has done, ending his story
with the words with which his literary counterpart begins, claiming that
no tribunal on the earth would know how to judge him. Teresa fails to
be impressed, however, and points out that through death Tullio's opponents have now become truly invincible. Finally, she says: "On the day
when I could convince myself of being the only judge of my life, I would
like to be worth it. Let me go."

Having killed the innocent creature, Tullio has proved to himself that
he really is able to live up to his total amorality. He cannot but face the
spiritual void he has created for himself. By posing as the sole judge of
his morality and ethical conduct, by creating his own solitary sphere of
right and wrong, love and hate, he has excluded himself from the company of his fellow human beings. Human life is essentially about interaction with other people, and having deprived himself of it, Tullio realizes
he has no future. He ends his life without much further ado, although not
without a melodramatic gesture: he does it in Teresa's presence. In a
sense, this feature makes it, as Visconti pointed out, a truly D'Annunzian
addition to the book.

The actual plot has been altered in many ways partly because of narrative economy. For example, the early scene in the book dealing with
Giuliana's illness has been omitted, and the relationship between the couple is rendered in a conversation in which Tullio demands Giuliana's
complicity against the society that would condemn his relationship with
the beautiful Teresa Raffo.

But by far more important is the rethinking of the motivations of the
character in the sense that Balázs defined as the essential feature of good
adapting. The very audiovisualizing of the literary text as such points the
way to this. First of all, Tullio has lost his position as the narrator – he
is not even given the benefit of presenting his own views through voice-
over narration. Because all the characters are actually seen by the spectator, their appearances and behavior are not confined to Tullio's point
of view. They have become full, rounded characters, and correspondingly
Tullio's spiritual void is made more explicit. D'Arborio is not the unpleasant man that the Tullio of the book describes, but a sympathetic, quiet,
and tactful individual who is considerate of other people. Giuliana is no

more the weak inane creature of Tullio's description, who says she is prepared to commit suicide to save Tullio from shame. In D'Annunzio's world, a woman who has gone astray is tainted, whereas a man may enjoy promiscuity as his natural right. In the film, Giuliana's transgression is made to appear a legitimate demand for her rights as a woman living with a blatantly unfaithful husband. She pretends to acquiesce to Tullio's ideas and to hate her baby only to protect it. She also has the courage to refuse to have an abortion – in the book the abortion is not carried out for medical reasons.

In a sense, the relationship between the literary original and the filmic adaptation has been reversed: D'Annunzio and his shallow narrator offer only a surface view, whereas Visconti's characters are interiorized. Giuliana, in particular, develops and changes as the narrative proceeds. Thus this film, more than any other of Visconti's adaptations, can be seen as a form of literary criticism in the way Neil Sinyard has suggested. And whereas *Death in Venice*, because of the difference in the two media, could not explore the same range of thought and sensibility as the novella, the film made on the basis of D'Annunzio's novel penetrates right into its moral and intellectual core and turns it upside down. Thus the novel as well as the period, society, and culture it reflects are put into a critical perspective. A new, remarkable "coherence and inner consistency" is imposed on the diegetic material as it is refigured in terms of the motivation of the characters and the point of view from which it is told.

The Innocent is one of Visconti's most beautiful films. Its peacefully evolving plot and the gentle montage create a quiet and elegiac atmosphere. The camera work is designed to show as much as possible of the sumptuous settings, but Visconti does not hesitate to cut and even to zoom to close-ups. The color scheme has an important role in giving accents to the milieu. Intensive red and luscious gold, together with some black and white, dominate most of the interiors in which the high society of Rome resides. In contrast, Giuliana's boudoir, as well as Federico's apartment, have delicate pastel colors and shades. The villas in the countryside, amid their greenery, are mainly creamy yellow and pure white. In each case the colors correspond to the sensitivity of the person to whom the place is principally related.

In addition to the music in the concerts – where so many in the audience, as in the musical soirées Proust describes, cannot be bothered by music – three kinds of background music by Franco Mannino are heard. Quiet, poignant music mainly on the piano accompanies the scenes with Tullio and Giuliana together. It is gradually replaced by similar music for the strings, which is increasingly associated with loneliness and sorrow caused by the sense of loss. It is also heard in a scene in which Tullio tries to rekindle Giuliana's love and in a scene in which she has apparently just refused to have an abortion, and again when they discuss the situation. From the latter scene the music continues as two shots of D'Arborio's memorial vitrines are seen. Most tellingly, this theme is heard when Giuliana goes to see her baby. It is interrupted violently when Tullio discovers her as she is leaving the room and slaps her on the face. However, it soon continues as Giuliana tells him how she hates the child – the tenderness of the music suggesting that she is not being honest with her husband.

A third, tormented theme for piano and strings accompanies scenes in which Tullio faces his most painful inner conflicts. It is first heard as Federico asks him to come fencing, then during Tullio's atheistic "credo" with the piano music heard ever so faintly through it. In later scenes the themes mix ever more, as they do when Giuliana is giving birth and when Tullio exposes the baby to the outside elements. On the whole the music is used quite differently from the way it functions in *Senso, Sandra, Death in Venice*, or even *The Leopard*, in that it remains more constantly in the background and does not emerge as an almost autonomous level of meaning.

But the beauty of the film does not imply mere indulging in sensuality, as in D'Annunzio's novel. Instead, it functions as a representation of an aesthetisized way of life, devoid of spiritual substance. Not only are the concertgoers indifferent to the music, but pure beauty on the whole has become such an abundant commodity in this society that it is accepted as self-evident, not as an achievement related to tradition, culture, history, and society at large. Both the diachronic and the synchronic dimensions of culture are ignored, thus permitting the outgrowth of solipsism and immoral hedonism. When Tullio renounces God, he is in fact renouncing all responsibility in the face of anyone else except himself. He is the very opposite of the other protagonists of Visconti's late films: he flaunts their tormenting spiritual aspirations and seeks fulfillment in immanence, the good things of the earth. His almost infantile pursuit of the satisfaction of his own desires at the expense of all true consideration for others leads him into a spiritual vacuum, or rather, an awareness of it, which is something that his literary counterpart could not conceive of.

The persuasive power of Visconti's rethinking of *The Innocent* derives from the sensitivity and nuance with which the characters are realized through their acting and their relationship with the decor. The way the bygone period has been lovingly recreated, together with the unfolding of this plot of cruelty and anguish, create an atmosphere of sorrow and loss inextricably linked to what it is to be a human being, yearning for the unconditional love that only an idealized mother can offer her baby. The inability to come to terms with the inevitable frustrations of life can become a destructive force, all the more frightening when it stems from the basic human trauma of having to grow independent from that basic security. Behind the mask of the deprived superman, there is something deeply touching in Tullio's childlike panic at the thought of being left alone and unloved.

Mikael Enckell – a psychoanalyst by profession – suggests that the crucial features of *The Innocent* cannot be separated from the fact that Visconti was dying when he made this film. Once again, he was drawing a self-portrait. As in *The Leopard*, in which the prince of Salina and Tancredi together mirror Visconti's personal history, the autobiographical trait in this film is built around the joint fate of Tullio and the baby. The events depicted in the film can be assumed to take place at the time of Luchino's birth, and whereas Tullio's character can be said to represent Visconti's awareness of the decadence of his own social class, the baby can be considered a protest on behalf of innocence. The murder committed by Tullio is a self-destructive act to which the suicide is only a logical follow-up. Everything he does can be judged from the point of view of this decision. The superman turns out to be the most pitiable of all people. He is like a child who in his absolute self-centeredness only wants to have his desires fulfilled and to be loved by everyone – or at least by all women. He is a tragic figure who, after a violent struggle, suddenly capitulates when he realizes he has destroyed everything worth fighting for.

The Innocent would be a gloomy end for Visconti's career were it not – thanks to its beauty, nuance, and psychological penetration – such a perfect work of art. It is a manifestation of the possibility of finding at the extreme moment of anguish a way of reconciling life and death in and through art.

Notes

INTRODUCTION

1. Proust, *Remembrance of Things Past*, p. 60.
2. Enckell, "Slutsatsen av Viscontis rekviem." Published in the collection *Eko och återsken*, p. 52. Translations from this as well as Enckell's other essays are by the present author.
3. Ishaghpour, *Visconti*, p. 26.
4. Ibid., p. 145.
5. Enckell, "Slutsatsen av Visconti's rekviem," p. 85.
6. Mann, *Schopenhauer*, p. 16. Translation by the present author.

CHAPTER 1, "VISCONTI AND NEOREALISM"

1. Rondolino, *Visconti*, pp. 44–6; Servadio, *Luchino Visconti*, pp. 40–3.
2. Servadio, *Luchino Visconti*, pp. 56–8.
3. Durgnant, *Jean Renoir*, p. 99.
4. Renoir, *My Life and My Films*, p. 154.
5. Andrew, *Mists of Regret*, p. 206.
6. Renoir, *My Life and My Films*, pp. 156–7.
7. Rondolino, *Visconti*, p. 55.
8. Servadio, *Luchino Visconti*, pp. 52–3.
9. Ibid., pp. 61–3.
10. Rondolino, *Visconti*, pp. 62–4.
11. Ibid., pp. 70–2.
12. René de Ceccatty, Introduction to Luchino Visconti's *Angel*, pp. x – xi.
13. Stirling, *A Screen of Time*, pp. 47–8; Servadio, *Luchino Visconti*, pp. 64–5.
14. Stirling, *A Screen of Time*, pp. 48–9.
15. Servadio, *Luchino Visconti*, pp. 67–9.
16. Ibid., p. 69; Durgnant, *Jean Renoir*, p. 215.
17. Servadio, *Luchino Visconti*, pp. 68–9.
18. Clark, *Modern Italy*, p. 246.
19. Bondanella, *Italian Cinema*, pp. 12–13.

20. Hay, *Popular Film Culture in Fascist Italy*, pp. 245–6. The term "white telephone films" is derived from American films such as Cecil B. De Mille's *Male and Female* (1919) in which white telephones appear as one of the symbols of a leisurely upper-class style of life (Liehm, *Passion and Defiance*, p. 21, fn. 56).
21. Hay, *Popular Film Culture in Fascist Italy*, pp. 71–2.
22. Quoted in Armes, *Paths of Neorealism*, p. 50.
23. Ibid., p. 51.
24. Bencivenni, *Luchino Visconti*, p. 20.
25. Carsaniga, "Realism in Italy." Quoted in Overbey, *Springtime in Italy* (introduction), p. 19.
26. Pacifici, *The Modern Italian Novel*, pp. 8–12; Whitfield, *A Short History of Italian Literature*, pp. 244–5.
27. Visconti, *"Tradizione ed invenzione."* "Stile," Milano, vol. VII, inverno 1941. Published in Aristarco, *Su Visconti*, pp. 115–18. Translations from this work by the present author.
28. Rondolino, *Visconti*, p. 104.
29. Revel, *On Proust*, pp. 142–3.
30. Visconti, "Il cinema antropomorfico." Cinema prima serie, Roma, a. VIII, n. 173–4, 25 settembre–25 ottobre 1943. Published in Aristarco, *Su Visconti*, pp. 119–21.
31. Doniol-Valcroze & Domarchi, "Entretien avec Luchino Visconti," p. 2; Servadio, *Luchino Visconti*, pp. 68–72.
32. Rondolino, *Visconti*, pp. 107–10; Servadio, *Luchino Visconti*, p. 75.
33. Servadio, *Luchino Visconti*, pp. 77–8; Villien, *Visconti*, p. 35. The two American adaptations of the novel, directed by Tay Garnett (1946) and Bob Rafelson (1981), rely much more on the appeal of their star actors – Lana Turner and John Garfield, Jessica Lange and Jack Nicholson, respectively – as does to some extent the very first adaptation of the novel, Pierre Chenal's *Le dernier tournant* (1939), with Corinne Luchaire and Fernand Gravey.
34. Schifano, *Luchino Visconti*, p. 196; Servadio, *Luchino Visconti*, p. 79.
35. Rondolino, *Visconti*, pp. 115–16. Serandrei was to edit all of Visconti's films right up to his death in 1966, the last one being the episode *La strega bruciata viva*. Subsequently, all of Visconti's films were edited by Ruggero Mastroianni, brother to the actor Marcello Mastroianni.
36. Ibid., pp. 115–17. There are many conflicting versions of the incidents in Visconti's life during this period. The one usually most different from the rest is that of De Santis.
37. Ibid., pp. 118–19.
38. Ibid., pp. 120–3.
39. Liehm, *Passion and Defiance*, pp. 327–8, fn. 35. After the Fascists were expelled from government in 1943, Italy was occupied by the Germans and became a battlefield for them and the Allies. Cinecittà's as well as Centro Sperimentale di Cinematografia's equipment was moved to Germany or to Venice, where the Fascists started a new film studio called Cinevillaggio

(Film village), as opposed to the Cinecittà (Film town, in Rome). Twenty-one films were made, mainly on the lines of the "white telephone films." Only one has an explicitly fascist message (ibid.).

40. It could hardly have been otherwise. According to De Santis: "At Fondi the donkey and the bicycle still prevailed; the roads were no wider than a couple of ditches; of insurance we only knew the one given by a handshake between buyers and sellers; vagrants were allowed to circulate only on the occasion of the annual fair; and, finally, postmen did not knock on any door nor could they be expected to ring non-existent doorbells so that it was considered a great privilege if they peeked in your window to call you aloud." (De Santis, "Visconti's Interpretation of Cain's Setting in *Ossessione*," p. 27.)

41. This, apparently, was one of the changes Visconti made to the original script. According to Alicata, Spagnuolo was to have been "a positive hero," "he should have been the critical consciousness of the film." (Quoted in Baldelli, *Visconti*, p. 130.) William van Watson calls the way Visconti changed what was to have been a socialist positive hero into a homosexual "an exquisite move of sublime perversity" ("The Underclass as Object of (Homosexual) Desire in Visconti's *Ossessione* and *Senso*"). A paper at Convegno internazionale di studi Viscontiani 1994. Published as "Il sottoproletario come oggetto del desiderio" in Bruni and Pravadelli, *Studi Viscontiani*, pp. 100–1.

42. Van Watson has argued that the whole scene is shot as if the two were lovers preparing for a kiss rather than a fist fight (Watson, "Il sottoproletario come aggetto del desiderio," p. 91). I am not entirely convinced, but Watson is right in pointing out that many times the way the two are shot parallels the way Gino and Giovanna are shot, as in the scene of Gino and Spagnuolo by the river bank, or Gino and Giovanna on the roadside only a bit later.

43. The plot function of the insurance is completely different in the novel and the two American adaptations. In the novel, Katz, a crafty lawyer, devises a complicated arrangement between two insurance companies with the result that only Cora is sentenced for manslaughter and let out on probation – Frank is made to appear an innocent victim. This means that she cannot be tried for murder again, whereas Frank can, as she reminds him after discovering he has had an affair with another woman. In *Ossessione* it is left unclear how Giovanna could denounce Gino without implicating herself. This could be due to a deficiency of the copy – perhaps the one I have studied – but this does not appear likely.

44. Possibly because of overexposure in some copies, this scene appears surreally bright. Since all known copies derive from a duplicate negative, this might be due to technical problems rather than expressive needs.

45. In Cain's novel and in Garnett's film, the couple go for a swim when Cora says she wants to give Frank a chance to get rid of him if he wants.

46. Watson, "Il sottoproletario come oggetto del desiderio," p. 87.

47. Micciché, *Visconti e il neorealismo*, p. 60.

48. Bohne, introduction to De Santis's article "Visconti's Interpretation of Cain's Setting in *Ossessione*," p. 24; Sorlin, *Sociologia del cinema*, pp. 188–90.

49. Giuseppe De Santis, "Visconti's Interpretation of Cain's Setting in *Ossessione*," p. 30.
50. Micciché, *Visconti e il neorealismo*, pp. 61–3, 67.
51. Deleuze, *Cinema 2*, p. 4. This can be seen as a realistic effect created by the so-called code of extraneous detail. See, e.g., Andrew, *Concepts in Film Theory*, pp. 64–5.
52. I am taking a slight risk with this statement in that the copies I have been able to study are slightly shorter than the reputedly longest extant copies.
53. Quoted in Armes, *Patterns of Realism*, pp. 66–7. Further reference: *Film and Filming*, April 1959.
54. Lucia Bohne writes in her introduction to Giuseppe De Santis's article, "Visconti's Interpretation of Cain's Setting in *Ossessione*": "In a curious way, the silence imposed by the makers of *Ossessione* over facts known to the public of 1942, namely the defeats of the fascist armies in Albania, Africa, and Russia – a ghostly silence over crucial, contemporary events which the protagonists second – is a silence that is overdetermined and bodes revolt." I find nothing "curious" in the lack of references to contemporary events in Italian foreign policy. In addition to the problem of censorship – which Bohne acknowledges – it just is not that kind of film. One of the liberties fiction enjoys is to relieve itself of the burden of reference according to its own structure of relevance.
55. Quoted in Overbey, *Springtime in Italy*, p. 29.
56. Bondanella, *Italian Cinema from Neorealism to the Present*, p. 35.
57. See, e.g., Nowell-Smith, *Luchino Visconti*, p. 32.
58. Chiarini, "Tradisce il neorealismo," *Cinema nuovo*, 55, March 25, 1955. Published as "Neo-Realism Betrayed," in Overbey, *Springtime in Italy*, p. 208.
59. Ibid., p. 209.
60. Zavattini, "A Thesis on Neo-Realism." Published in Overbey, *Springtime in Italy*, p. 71.
61. Chiarini, "Discorso sul neorealismo," *Bianco e nero*, XII, July 7, 1951. Published as "A Discourse on Neo-Realism," in Overbey, *Springtime in Italy*, p. 145.
62. Morlion, "Le basi filosofiche del neorealismo cinematografico italiano." Published as "The Philosophical Basis of Neo-Realism," in Overbey, *Springtime in Italy*, p. 121. It should be noted that when Morlion speaks of "a magic window which opens to the real," he is, of course, speaking metaphorically. The critics of realism in cinema have only too often picked on such phrases to construct an easy target for their criticism.
63. Bazin, *What Is Cinema?*, vol. II, p. 97.
64. Bazin, "William Wyler, or the Jansenist of mise en scène." Published in Williams (ed.), *Realism and the Cinema* p. 44.
65. Ibid., p. 21.
66. Bazin, "De Sica et Rossellini." Published in Bazin, *Qu'est-ce que le cinéma?* vol. IV, p. 114.

67. According to neoformalist terminology, the spectator may justify a given textual element in terms of four categories of *motivations*: relevance in terms of story necessity is *compositional* motivation; plausibility, accordance with one's conception of the real world, is *realistic* motivation; recognition of a typical way of presentation such as genre conventions is *transtextual* motivation; and artistic motivation in turn justifies the foregrounding of some component of the work of art for its own sake (Bordwell, *Narration in the Fiction Film*, p. 36).

68. Ricoeur, *Time and Narrative*, p. 67.

69. Ricoeur, *The Rule of Metaphor*, p. 39.

70. In the semiology of C. S. Peirce, a sign is either an *icon* (it resembles the object it refers to), an *index* (it has some kind of existential connection with the object; e.g., the photographic image has a photochemical connection with the object), or a *symbol* (it refers to something through established convention). These categories are usually not considered to be mutually exclusive (Peirce was somewhat ambiguous on this point), but their relevance, say, for the study of cinema might vary according to the point of view. In Peter Wollen's opinion, "It is this awareness of overlapping which enabled Peirce to make some particularly relevant remarks about photography" (*Signs and Meaning in the Cinema*, p. 123).

71. The beauty of this interpretation of the mimetic process (Ricoeur's scheme being naturally far more elaborate than what has been presented here) is that it legitimately subverts the knotty question of realism in its full philosophical depth: the focus is on pitting different discourses or narratives against one another, not on the question of the existence of an objective reality and its knowability. Yet it could be argued that these are implied in the faith in modeling human experience as a meaningful activity.

72. De Santis and Alicata, "Verità e poesia: Verga e il cinema italiano," *Cinema*, 127, October 10, 1941. Published as "Truth and Poetry: Verga and the Italian Cinema," in Overbey, *Springtime in Italy*, pp. 131–2.

73. Rondolino, *Visconti*, pp. 152–5; Servadio, *Luchino Visconti*, pp. 104–5; Schifano, *Visconti*, p. 230–1.

74. Servadio, *Luchino Visconti*, pp. 106–7; Schifano, *Visconti*, pp. 237–40.

75. Stirling, *A Screen of Time*, p. 64. In connection with the Hemingway production, Visconti became acquainted with Suso Cecchi d'Amico, who had translated the play into Italian. She was to work on the scripts for almost all of Visconti's subsequent films, and they became lifelong friends.

76. Castello, "Luchino Visconti," p. 185.

77. Schifano, *Luchino Visconti*, pp. 252–4.

78. Baldelli, *Luchino Visconti*, pp. 16–18.

79. Stirling, *A Screen of Time*, p. 72.

80. Doniol-Valcroze & Domarchi, "Entretien avec Luchino Visconti," p. 7; Villien, *Visconti*, p. 56. Based on a statement by Antonino Arcidiaconi, who played the part of 'Ntoni.

81. Analyzed with his customary thoroughness by Miccichè, *Visconti e il neo-realismo*, pp. 155–60.

82. Interview with Enrico Deaglio, "Ritorno ad Acitrezza," September 1, 1990. For an account of the method of producing the language and its function, including the voice-over commentary, see Parigi, Stefania: "Il dualismo linguistico."

83. Baldelli, *Luchino Visconti*, pp. 91–2.

84. Parigi, Stefania: "Il dualismo linguistico." Published in Miccichè, *La terra trema di Luchino Visconti*. pp. 142–8.

85. Doniol-Valcroze & Domarchi, "Entretien avec Luchino Visconti," p. 7. Zeffirelli himself claims to have coached the actors while Visconti was not watching (Zeffirelli, *The Autobiography of Franco Zeffirelli*, p. 85).

86. Armes, *Patterns of Realism*, p. 110; Baldelli, *Visconti*, pp. 93–100. The synopsis of the original script was published in *Bianco e nero* XII, nn. 2.3, febbraio–marzo 1951. A version of the synopsis can also be found in Miccichè, *La terra trema di Luchino Visconti*, under the title, "Quoando gli episodi erano tre: scaletta del progetto." This work, with its many excellent articles, frame enlargements, drawn sketches and written drafts relating to various aspects of the film, is invaluable for any future study of this film.

  The scene in which the Mafia shoot at the peasants was based on a real incident. A group of bandits led by Salvatore Giuliano started, possibly accidentally, a massacre at Portella della Ginestra on May 1, 1947. The incident features both in Rosi's *Salvatore Giuliano* (1962) and Michael Cimino's *The Sicilian* (1987).

87. Miccichè, "Verso La terra trema," published in Miccichè (ed.), *La terra trema di Luchino Visconti*, pp. 38–41 (Rosi quotation in fn.6, p. 59). In this article Miccichè makes a thorough examination of the various drafts of the project.

88. Marcus, *Filmmaking by the Book*, p. 37.

89. Lino Miccichè has pointed out, as an example of the perfection of Visconti's design, that the storm scene is not only narratively but also formally the center of the film: it is preceded and followed by 58 sequences, the former consisting of 251 shots and lasting for about 1 hour, 10 minutes, the latter consisting of 258 shots and lasting 1 hour, 25 minutes – the scene itself lasts for about 5 minutes (Miccichè, *Visconti e il neorealismo*, p. 103).

90. Visconti, "Il Cinema anthropologico." Originally published in *Cinema*, prima serie, Roma, a. VIII, nn. 173–4, 25 settembre–25 ottobre 1943, pp. 108–9. Published also in Aristarco, *Su Visconti*, p. 116.

91. Ibid., pp. 119–21.

92. "Implied author" is used here to distinguish between the actual historical author and the mental construct one might form of the author of a work of art on the basis of that work only.

93. Verga, *I Malavoglia*, p. 198. Don Michele is the chief of the local customs office.

94. Ibid., p. 199.

95. Ibid., p. 192.
96. Micc-iché, *Visconti e il neorealismo*, pp. 175–7.
97. Brian Henderson has discussed the question of the pseudo-iterative in cinema in his essay, "Tense, Mood, and Voice in Film (Notes after Genette)," *Film Quarterly*, XXXVI, no. 4 (Summer 1983), pp. 11–12. Marsha Kinder has further developed the idea in her article, "The Subversive Potential of the Pseudo-Iterative," *Film Quarterly*, XXXXIII, no. 2 (Winter 1989–90), pp. 2–16.
98. Marcus, *Filmmaking by the Book*, pp. 41–2.
99. Villien, *Visconti*, pp. 60–1. Villien mentions also an inscription on a rock: "W il re" (Long live the king), a reference to the 1946 referendum concerning the form of government. It has never caught my eye.
100. In the novel, it is 'Ntoni who has not got the courage to stay in Aci Trezza, and it is left for the grandfather to stay and fight for the survival of the family.
101. Micc-iché, *Visconti e il Neorealismo*, pp. 123–5.
102. Verga, *I Malavoglia*, p. 28.
103. The director of photography was G. R. Aldo (Aldo Graziani), who after the war brought wide-angle and deep-focus techniques to Italy. His brilliant career was cut short by a car accident while he was shooting Visconti's *Senso*.
104. Marcus, *Filmmaking by the Book*, p. 39.
105. E.g., Baldelli, *Visconti*, pp. 81–2. Baldelli thinks the entire scene is contrived both in terms of content and realization. According to Aristarco, Dario Natoli went as far as comparing the film more precisely with *The Battleship Potemkin* (1925) ("Cinema e mezzogiorno," *Cronache Meridionali*, nuova serie, Napoli, a VIII, n. 6, dicembre 1961).
106. Ishaghpour, *Visconti*, p. 33.
107. Aristarco, "Esperienza culturale ed esperienza originale in *Luchino Visconti*." Published originally as an introduction to the script of *Rocco e i suoi fratelli*, subsequently in Aristarco, *Su Visconti*, p. 26.
108. Ibid., p. 27.
109. Marcus, *Filmmaking by the Book*, p. 27.
110. Micc-iché, *Visconti e il neorealismo*, pp. 108, fn. 83; 180.
111. Nowell-Smith writes of the use of the two levels: "Considered simply as a technique the juxtaposition of the two levels is not necessarily an aid to realism at all. It does nothing to solve the problem of content, whether of the images or of the text, nor does it prescribe any necessary relation between the two" (Nowell-Smith, *Visconti*, p. 50). Because I do not see realism as being an issue in the juxtaposition, fail to see any problem of content to be solved, and see the two levels as intricately interwoven, I could not disagree more. Marcus, however, does agree with Nowell-Smith: "This intrusive, anticinematic device [the voice-over] serves to frame and contain the film, distancing us from its documentary immediacy and announcing

an authorial presence that paternalistically manipulates the representation from above and presumes to interpret it for us" (Marcus, *Filmmaking by the Book*, p. 29). Again, why intrusive, why anticinematic, and above all, why antirealistic (as Marcus also labels it)? Though the device does deviate from the most naive ideals of neorealism (or of what Bill Nichols has called observational mode of documentary film), i.e., the idea of capturing reality unmediated by an authorial subject, the use of voice-over commentary as such can hardly be accepted as a criterion of realism.

112. Micciché, *La terra trema di Luchino Visconti*, p. 44.

113. Nowell-Smith sees this issue differently, if not exactly the other way around. He thinks the "lyrical exaltation" does violence to the "documentary" aspects Visconti was initially after: "His initial scenarios have an ideological clarity and purity about them which is then systematically betrayed in the final elaboration" (*Visconti*, p. 40). The resulting films are indeed elaborated in respect of the original scenarios, but I do not see their clarity being betrayed except inasmuch as the process of elaboration brings into focus the weaknesses of the original concept. Neither do I see what Nowell-Smith calls the "conceptual" (the voice-over commentary) and the "pure" (pictorio-musical) elements to be in any way in conflict with each other.

114. Ishagpour, *Visconti*, p. 52.

115. Zeffirelli, *Autobiography*, p. 88.

116. Bruni, David, "La fortuna critica del film" (an account of the critical reception of the film up to the 90s). Published in Micciché, *La terra trema di Luchino Visconti*, p. 17; Rondolino, Visconti, pp. 219–20.

117. Visconti, "Sul modo di mettere in scena una comedia di Shakespeare." *Rinascita*, dicembre 1948. Quoted in Rondolino, *Visconti*, p. 248. Translation by the present author.

118. Ibid., p. 255.

119. Ibid., pp. 339–42; Stirling, *Luchino Visconti*, pp. 115–16. This production is discussed further in chapter 4, "Visconti, Thomas Mann and two aspects of Europe."

120. Bondanella, *Italian Cinema*, pp. 86–7.

121. Quoted in Overbey, *Springtime in Italy*, p. 29.

122. Liehm, *Passion and Defiance*, pp. 92–3.

123. Bondanella, *Italian Cinema*, p. 37.

124. Liehm, *Passion and Defiance*, p. 142.

125. Stirling, *A Screen of Time*, p. 85.

126. Baldelli, *Luchino Visconti*, pp. 111–12.

127. In the original treatment, Spartaco was to have been a petit bourgeois watchmaker but ended up being a worker of unidentified skills (Micciché, *Visconti e il Neorealismo*, p. 199).

128. Doniol-Valcroze & Domarchi, "Entretien avec Luchino Visconti," p. 6. Translation by the present author.

129. Nowell-Smith, *Luchino Visconti*, p. 63.

130. Lagny, "Visconti et al, 'cultura populaire.'" Published in Bruni and Pra-vadelli, *Studi Viscontiani*, p. 247. Translated by the present author.

131. Micchiché reads this as a return to the "authoritarian and phallocratic" patriarchal Italian family (*Visconti e il neorealismo*, pp. 198–9).

CHAPTER 2, "THE RISORGIMENTO FILMS"

1. Villien, *Visconti*, p. 71; Rondolino, *Visconti*, pp. 272–3. For a long time all copies were lost, but one has recently been found and is being restored at this writing.

2. Servadio, *Luchino Visconti*, p. 132; Stirling, *A Screen of Time*, pp. 88–9; Villien, *Visconti*, p. 84.

3. Tulloch, *Chekhov*, p. 104.

4. Pitcher, *The Chekhov Play*, pp. 130–1.

5. Tulloch, *Chekhov*, pp. 105–7.

6. Rondolino, *Visconti*, pp. 265–70.

7. Apparently Visconti himself grew a bit fed up with this explanation. In an interview he stated: "To me, when someone writes an article, he feels the need to pigeonhole me as 'an aristocrat and a revolutionary' or 'a count and a communist.' I am an aristocrat, that is true, but as such I can't do anything. . . . I think I am sufficiently committed to activity; that I have asserted myself by taking a stand on various issues, that I have for about twenty years given myself to thinking and creating" ("Chekhov, Shake-speare e Verdi." *Cinema Nuovo*, Milano, a XIV, n. 173, gennaio – febbraio 1965. Quoted in Aristarco, *Su Visconti*, p. 84).

8. Ishaghpour, "L'art et la vita: L'unità dell'opera e l'impuro." Published in *Studi Viscontiani*, p. 184. The expression "Film in the aura of art" is from Dudley Andrew's book by that title.

9. An interview with Henri Chapler, *Arts* magazine 1958. Quoted in Rondol-ino, *Visconti*, p. 334. Translation from Italian by the present author.

10. Stassinopolous, *Maria Callas*, p. 134.

11. Rondolino, *Visconti*, pp. 352–3.

12. Stirling, *A Screen of Time*, p. 95.

13. Partridge, *Senso*, p. 45.

14. Boito, *Senso*. Reprinted in Cavallaro, *Senso*, p. 12. Translations by the present author.

15. Ibid., p. 18.

16. Ibid., p. 37.

17. Ibid., p. 10.

18. Ibid., pp. 43–57.

19. Ibid., p. 72. According to D'Amico, however: "One dialogue is by Tennessee Williams, and then he disappeared. And nobody could find him anymore. It is the one in the villa, where she says, 'It isn't Venice, it isn't Venice'" (Cecchi D'Amico, interview with the author).

20. Doniol-Valcroze & Domarchi, "Entretien avec Luchino Visconti," p. 9.

21. I am left somewhat perplexed by certain critics who find Granger's performance to be weak. According to Marcus: "Granger is utterly unconvincing
as the inspirer of a passion great enough to destroy the virtuous Livia" (*Italian Film in the Light of Neorealism*, p. 166). But, surely, Livia is not virtuous.
Right from the beginning she is weak and obviously feels the great need to
experience all the emotions that neither her marriage to the old Serpieri nor
her dealings with the idealist Ussoni can offer. Partridge, in turn, writes:
"His performance is static, not rippling; his stiff postures and still body suggest stubborn – almost puritanical – constraint, not the manned ferocity of
seductive hedonism" (*Senso*, p. 104). I suspect that "rippling sensuality"
(which Partridge does find in Valli's performance) and "manned ferocity"
would have worked against some of the most interesting strains in Visconti's
film, one of which is the tension between Franz's cynicism and his ultimate
vulnerability.
22. Cavallaro (ed.), *Senso*, pp. 73–4.
23. Rotunno remained Visconti's main cinematographer until *The Stranger*
(1967).
24. Cavallaro (ed.), *Senso*, pp. 202–3.
25. Doniol-Valcroze & Domarchi, "Entretien avec Luchino Visconti," p. 10.
26. Ibid.; Ranvaud, *Masterpiece as Minefield*. The execution was shot at the
Castello San Angelo in Rome because it would not have been practical to
return to Verona with all the equipment.
27. Cavallaro (ed.), *Senso*, pp. 197–201.
28. Lisi, Umberto, "Paura della storia." *Cinema nuovo*, no. 52.
29. Mack Smith, *Victor Emanuel, Cavour and the Risorgimento*, p. 322.
30. Taylor, *The Hapsburg Monarchy* 1809–1918, p. 127.
31. Mack Smith, *Victor Emanuel, Cavour, and the Risorgimento*, p. 305.
32. Mack Smith, *Italy*, pp. 79–80.
33. Ibid., pp. 80–2.
34. Ibid., pp. 81–2.
35. Mack Smith, *Victor Emanuel, Cavour, and the Risorgimento*, pp. 322–33.
36. For general information about the different factors that shaped the Risorgimento, see Mack Smith, *Italy*, pp. 2–9.
37. Doniol-Valcroze & Domarchi, "Entretien avec Luchino Visconti," p. 10.
Translation by the author.
38. Schifano and Tonetti emphasize the similarities with the traumatic defeat in
Caporetto during the First World War. This, however, was a catastrophe of
quite different proportions from that at Custoza: 40,000 killed, 91,000
wounded, 293,000 captured, and the rest of the army retreating in complete
chaos. But, of course, even on this occasion the Italians managed in the end
to be on the side of the winners (Schifano, *Visconti*, pp. 99–100; Tonetti,
Luchino Visconti, p. 68).
39. Kogan, *A Political History of Italy*, pp. 23–4.
40. Clark, *Modern Italy* 1871–1982, pp. 324–5.
41. Aristarco, interview with the author.

42. Cecchi D'Amico, interview with the author.
43. Cavallaro (ed.), *Senso*, pp. 175–7. According to Aristarco, the scene had a precise historical referent in an episode related by Caronti in his *Memorie* and reported by Gramschi in his notes about the Risorgimento. Caronti had met with success in the 1848 uprising against the Austrians and in 1866 formed a company of volunteers to do so again. His offer of help was refused by the Piedmontese minister Balbo with the words: "It is useless to arm yourselves, as the regular army is strong enough to rout the enemy" (Aristarco, *Su Visconti*, p. 44).
44. Lisi, "Paura della storia."
45. Ranvaud, *Masterpiece as Minefield*. I have been fortunate enough to have seen and studied what are probably the longest existing copies.
46. Visconti has stated that the character of Livia was influenced by la Sanseverina in Stendhal's *The Charterhouse of Parma* (1839) (Doniol-Valcroze & Domarchi, "Entretien avec Luchino Visconti," p. 5).
47. The date being May 27, 1866, and the film ending in the morning after the battle of Custoza, i.e., June 27, 1866, the events of the film take place within a month. Boito is not as precise but conveys the impression of a longer time passing, in addition to which the narrative frame extends the time span to 1882.
48. Godefroy, *The Dramatic Genius of Verdi*, vol. I, p. 230.
49. Marcus, *Italian Film in the Light of Neorealism*, p. 181.
50. It may be difficult for us, infected by postmodernism, not to see the contrast between the situations of the end of Act III and the beginning of Act IV of *Il trovatore* as profoundly ironical. For the contemporary audience with its romantic sensibilities (even if of an Italian variety), this opera completed in 1852, with the defeats of the 1848 uprising still fresh in memory, was probably a powerful symbol of oppression overcoming even the bravest of men.
51. Thanks to the cinematic realization, the spectator can grasp the parallel even without knowing or being able to follow the words she is singing.
52. Cavallaro (ed.), *Senso*, p. 109.
53. Ibid., p. 171.
54. Ishaghpour, *Visconti*, p. 74. Ishaghpour is punning with the meanings "color" and "flavor" in the French word *couleur*. He even goes so far as to claim that "*Luchino Visconti* remains in the history of cinema as the creator of colour film: before there were only 'coloured' films" (p. 75).
55. Cavallaro (ed.), *Senso*, p. 121.
56. Najder, Zdzislaw, "Joseph Conrad's the Secret Agent or the Melodrama of Reality." Printed in Gerould (ed.), *Melodrama*, p. 160.
57. Ibid., pp. 175–6.
58. Bermel, Albert, "Where Melodrama Meets Farce." Printed in Gerould (ed.), *Melodrama*, p. 174.
59. Ishaghpour, *Visconti*, p. 79.
60. Dalle Vacche, in her *The Body in the Mirror*, demonstrates the influence of the *Battle of Custoza* (1876–8) and certain other paintings by Giovanni

Fattori on the way the battle scene has been shot. The influence is not purely visual but involves also the way people in their different tasks are captured in the images (*The Body in the Mirror*, pp. 108–12). Visconti himself has expressly denied having copied the paintings and suggests that similarities arise from a common pursuit of truth (Doniol-Valcroze & Domarchi, "Entretien avec Luchino Visconti," p. 4). Influence might take place unintentionally, of course. Micciché also mentions several other "references" to paintings by Francesco Hayez, Silvestro Lega, Telemaco Signorini (*Luchino Visconti*, p. 84).

61. At times, Visconti takes the risk of having one of his characters actually spell out the moral of the story: 'Ntoni's "speech" to the little girl at the end of *La terra trema*, Ciro's self-justification at the end of *Rocco*, don Fabrizio's ponderings in *The Leopard*, and so on. They are usually saved from appearing overtly didactic because the idea has been worked out and elaborated narratively in a way that is far richer than the statements themselves and thus it serves to contextualize them – not necessarily so as to make them appear realistic but rather by presenting them just as threads in a complex web of meanings.

62. As pointed out earlier, the role was already reduced before the film was censored. Visconti has stated: "I always prefer to tell about defeats, to describe the victims, destinies crushed by reality" (interview with Visconti, in Micciché, *Morte a Venezia*, p. 124).

63. Aristarco, interview with the author.

64. Marcus, *Italian Film in the Light of Neorealism*, pp. 172–3.

65. Mack Smith, *Italy*, pp. 8–9, 13–14.

66. Ibid,. pp. 18–20, 39–42, 66–7.

67. Ibid., pp. 54, 71–3.

68. Clark, *Modern Italy 1871–1982*, pp. 18, 29; Mack Smith, Italy, pp. 2–4.

69. Kogan, *A Political History of Italy*, pp. 137–9.

70. Ibid., p. 133. This is a debatable issue. Comparing *Viva l'Italia* to earlier films featuring Garibaldi, José Luis Guarnier thinks that Rossellini has demystified his figure (Guarnier, *Roberto Rossellini*, p. 91).

71. Stirling, *A Screen of Time*, pp. 163–4.

72. Bencivenni, *Luchino Visconti*, p. 56; Stirling, *A Screen of Time*, p. 165.

73. Stirling, *A Screen of Time*, pp. 170, 177. Pio Baldelli has criticized the supposed realism of the film on the grounds that Visconti, as opposed to Lampedusa, has not taken into account the shabbiness of the Sicilian provincial aristocracy (Baldelli, *Luchino Visconti*, p. 229).

74. Servadio, *Luchino Visconti*, p. 178.

75. Quoted in Rohdie, "The Anglo-Saxon Response to *Il gattopardo*." Published as "Il giudizzio della critica anglosassone," in Micchiché, *Il gattopardo*, p. 218. Unfortunately, this piece of scholarship dedicated to this single film did not appear until after I had completed my manuscript. Therefore I was unable to make full use of it, apart from Rohdie's article, the English version of which I happened to receive in advance of publication.

It is often not appreciated how much dubbing can affect one's appreciation of a film, one's impression of the acting, and how subtleties such as social background, register, and tone are conveyed.

76. Servadio, *Luchino Visconti*, p. 178.

77. This is particularly emphatic in the American version. In the Italian version, Tancredi plays a role in getting the prince and his train through.

78. This is partly because in the film he says many things to don Pirrone that in the book are just presented as his thoughts or as comments of the narrator. Don Fabrizio's superiority is emphasized by making don Calogero almost a clown.

79. The novel contains references to the future degradation of the Salina family, such as when the family arrives at Donnafugata: "For never before would he have issued so cordial an invitation: and from that moment, invisibly, began the decline of his prestige" (Tomaso di Lampedusa, *The Leopard*, p. 43).

80. It is a part of the art of mise-en-scène to be able to make such points, audiovisual metaphors within the diegetic world created for the film. For a perceptive account of the metaphorical use of mirrors and paintings in *The Leopard*, see Millicent Marcus's *Filmmaking by the Book*, pp. 56–61.

81. Lukács, *The Historical Novel*, p. 177.

82. Ishaghpour, *Visconti*, p. 34.

83. The proportional length of the ball sequence in the American version appears to have escaped the attention of some scholars. Millicent Marcus, for example, writes that in the film's original version the scene would have lasted for a full hour of the total length of 185 minutes, thus comprising one-third of the whole (Marcus, *Filmmaking by the Book*, p. 53 and fn. 38). I suspect, however, that the ball sequence lasted for a full hour only in the very first version, which was 205 minutes long. In Visconti's own final cut (185 minutes), the ball scene is shorter, yet it appears perfectly balanced and satisfactory. In the American version the sequence is shorter, but not as much as one would think, to judge by some commentators. What is more serious is that the order of some scenes has apparently been changed for some obscure reasons.

84. Genette, *Narrative Discourse*, p. 92.

85. Nowell-Smith, *Luchino Visconti*, p. 110.

86. Tomaso di Lampedusa, *The Leopard*, p. 154.

87. Rohdie, "The Anglo-Saxon Response to *Il gattopardo*." Published as "Il giudizzio della critica anglosassone," in Micchiché, *Il gattopardo*, p. 222.

88. LaCapra, *History, Politics, and the Novel*, p. 21.

89. Enckell, " 'Citizen Kane' and Psychoanalysis," p. 33. Enckell concludes his article with a reference to *The Leopard*.

90. Ricoeur, *Time and Narrative*, vol. III, p. 95.

91. Sorlin, *The Film in History*, pp. 133–7.

92. Ishaghpour, *Visconti*, p. 92.

CHAPTER 3, "THE FAMILY AND MODERN ITALIAN SOCIETY"

1. Stirling, *A Screen of Time*, pp. 7, 9; *Encyclopedia Britannica*, s.v. "Visconti."
2. Servadio, *Luchino Visconti*, pp. 6, 22; *Encyclopedia Britannica*, s.v. "Visconti."
3. Stirling, *A Screen of Time*, pp. 7–9.
4. Servadio, *Luchino Visconti*, pp. 16–17, 25, 37. At least on these main points, Servadio's account is in accord with that of Rondolino and Schifano.
5. Ishaghpour, *Visconti*, p. 129.
6. An interview with Lietta Tornabuoni in *L'Europeo*, April 10, 1969. Quoted in Servadio, *Luchino Visconti*, p. 17.
7. Enckell, "Slutsatsen av Viscontis rekviem." Published in Enckell, *Eko ock återsken*, p. 73.
8. Chekhov's letter to Meyerhold. Quoted in Tulloch, *Chekhov*, p. 108.
9. Servadio, *Luchino Visconti*, p. 153.
10. Brunette, interview with Suso Cecchi D'Amico.
11. Servadio, *Luchino Visconti*, p. 153; Brunette, interview with Suso Cecchi D'Amico, pp. 54–5.
12. Nor is Tullio the father of two older children, as is the protagonist of D'Annunzio's novel.
13. Rohdie, *Rocco and His Brothers*, p. 53.
14. Stirling, *A Screen of Time*, pp. 147–8.
15. Ibid., pp. 148–51.
16. Quoted in Rohdie, *Rocco and His Brothers*, p. 72. Originally from Guido Gerosa, "L'odissea censoria," *Schermi*, no. 28, December 1960.
17. Rondolino, *Visconti*, pp. 391–3; Stirling, A Screen of Time, pp. 151–2.
18. Clark, *Modern Italy 1871–1982*, pp. 357–9; Kogan, *A Political History of Italy*, p. 80.
19. Clark, *Modern Italy 1871–1982*, pp. 360–2.
20. Stirling, *A Screen of Time*, pp. 140–2.
21. Aristarco & Carancini, *Rocco e i suoi fratelli*, p. 47; Rondolino, *Visconti*, p. 396.
22. Stirling, *A Screen of Time*, p. 140.
23. Miller, *Collected Plays*, p. 379.
24. Cecchi D'Amico, interview with the author. It should be noted, however, that this statement was given almost a quarter of a century after the event. The prologue – the title of which would have been "mother" – would have shown the father's burial at sea, the toil of making a living in the south, and the mother giving her reasons for the emigration (Aristarco & Carancini [eds.], *Rocco e i suoi fratelli*, pp. 57–61). The prologue would probably have paralleled *La terra trema* – Visconti himself thought of *Rocco* as the never realized second episode of that film (ibid., p. 52). The comparison with the five fingers of the hand appears in Verga's *I Malavoglia*.

25. Nowell-Smith, *Luchino Visconti*, p. 163.

26. Aristarco & Carancini, *Rocco et i suoi fratelli*, pp. 47, 45, 53.

27. Ibid., p. 46.

28. Medioli, interview with the author. Collaboration between several screenwriters, with more or less all of them credited, is a fairly common practice in Italy, whereas in Hollywood for example, there is a tendency to credit only one or two screenwriters at the most, irrespective of the number of collaborators. According to Cecchi D'Amico, it does not matter if one of the writers has contributed more than the others, for within the industry such things are fairly common knowledge.

29. Aristarco & Carancini, *Rocco et i suoi fratelli*, p. 45.

30. See, e.g., Cecchi D'Amico, interview with the present author.

31. Originally, Ciro was to have had a much bigger role. As a trade unionist, he would have represented a socialist view and a positive class consciousness. At some stage of writing the script, it was planned that he would become an entrepreneur and start transporting olive oil from Lucania to Milan (Aristarco & Carancini, *Rocco et i suoi fratelli*, p. 46; Nowell-Smith, *Luchino Visconti*, p. 164; interview with Visconti in *Schermi*, December 28, 1960, pp. 331–5, quoted in Tonetti, *Luchino Visconti*, p. 85).

32. Rohdie points out that, since Rocco has just sent all his money to mother Rosaria, Nadia pays for their carriage ride and their coffee, thus reversing her role as a prostitute. There is added irony in this, as Simone has been getting himself in trouble in order to "afford" Nadia (Rohdie, *Rocco and His Brothers*, p. 34).

33. In the script published by Cappelli, this scene is missing and instead there is a much shorter scene in Morini's car.

34. In England this scene was censored, with the result that Simone is seen striking her only once. According to Nowell-Smith, this only helps to make the murder appear premeditated and cold-blooded (Nowell-Smith, *Luchino Visconti*, p. 178).

35. Rohdie, *Rocco and His Brothers*, pp. 35–6.

36. In the script stage, Rocco had two other alternatives. According to one scenario, he would have died in a match because his physical constitution would not have been suited to boxing. According to the other, he was to have been imprisoned instead of his brother. Visconti thought the former was too melodramatic, the latter too mechanical (Aristarco & Carancini, *Rocco et i suoi fratelli*, p. 53).

37. Baldelli, *Luchino Visconti*, p. 209.

38. Tonetti, *Luchino Visconti*, p. 90; As regards Nadia, also Nowell-Smith, *Luchino Visconti*, p. 176.

39. Baldelli, *Luchino Visconti*, pp. 193–6.

40. Nowell-Smith, *Luchino Visconti*, p. 177. Space does not allow me to enter into an extended criticism of these views; suffice it to say that, from a methodological point of view, I do not think the question of authorial intentions is of primary significance in assessing the final product. While the characters

may be overwhelmed by nostalgia, this cannot automatically be taken even
as the implied author's stand on this issue, not to speak of that of the historical author. Nowell-Smith wrote this as an early proponent of cine-
structuralism, and this probably led him to put inordinate emphasis on
authorial intentions.

41. Ibid., pp. 170–1. In the second edition of this work, the treatment is extended
to cover *Death in Venice*.

42. Aristarco, interview with the author. Also Pio Baldelli thinks *Rocco* is a valuable contribution to the tradition of Italian melodrama inasmuch as it is an
instance of an originally bourgeois cultural heritage having found an expression in a working-class context. In Baldelli's opinion, the film is at its
weakest when it does not stick to concise melodramatic symbolism but lin-
gers in naturalistic depiction of the environment (Baldelli, *Luchino Visconti*,
pp. 200–202).

43. Rohdie, *Rocco and His Brothers*, p. 56.

44. Elsaesser, *Tales of Sound and Fury*. Published in Nichols, *Movies and Methods*, vol. II, p. 185.

45. Rohdie, *Rocco and His Brothers*, pp. 23–4.

46. Ibid., p. 59. Rohdie sees this and several other features as being modeled on
"Verdian opera." The audiovisual richness of *Rocco* – as well as that of many
other Visconti's films, or many other Italian films, for that matter – can, in
a very, very general sense, be called "operatic" in that it conveys to most
people the idea of a style characterized by excess. But specifying it as being
Verdian is totally pointless. What is Verdian about the grunts, screams, and
the "orchestrated" use of other sounds? Music theater of the 1960s would
be a more plausible comparison. Nor does the idea that the "chapters" should
be called "acts" because they "correspond to the five acts of Italian grand
opera, the true source of *Rocco*," bear critical scrutiny. Grand opera with its
five acts is a French genre, and though Italian composers wrote them and
even had a major influence in the development of the whole genre, they did
so mainly for the Paris Opéra, rather than the stages of their home country.
The five-act format is a rarity among Italian opera. It is indicative that, when
Verdi wrote an Italian version of his *Don Carlo*, he reduced it to four acts.
(I write this as an irritated opera historian, not as a film scholar pretending
to engage in serious debate.)

47. Nowell-Smith, *Luchino Visconti*, p. 171.

48. Prendergast, *The Order of Mimesis*, p. 32.

49. Quoted in Stirling, *A Screen of Time*, p. 180. Original source not mentioned.
Visconti referred to incest as the last taboo in modern society. The theme
appeared also in other Italian films of that time, such as De Sica's *I seques-
trati di Altona* (The condemned of Altona, 1962), Bertolucci's *Prima della
rivoluzione* (Before the revolution, 1964), and Bellochio's *I pugni in tasca*
(Fist in his pocket, 1966) (Schifano, *Visconti*, pp. 385–6).

50. Laurence Schifano suggests that this pattern might have been influenced by

Arthur Miller's *After the Fall*, which Visconti directed the same year as *Sandra* (Schifano, *Visconti*, p. 381).

51. Nowell-Smith, *Luchino Visconti*, p. 144.

52. In Greek mythology Psyche was a beautiful maiden loved by Eros (Amor in Roman mythology), the adopted son of Aphrodite. Because he was immortal, he could not allow her to see him and thus visited her only by night. She, however, fearing that her lover might be an ugly monster, one night lit a lamp so as to gaze at him as he was sleeping. A drop of hot oil dropped on him and he fled in terror. For a long time Psyche looked for her beloved in vain, because Aphrodite did not approve of her and thwarted her search. Finally, however, they were reunited and married.

53. Referring to César Franck's symphonic poem *Psyché* and Antonio Canaletto's *Amore e Psiche giacenti*, Liandrat-Guigues argues that the statue is the "pivot round which the ensemble of aesthetic mechanism conceived by Visconti's turns" (*Les images du temps*, p. 212). I find these references rather weak and the notion somewhat exaggerated.

54. The ring scene is an indirect reference to incest also in that it is an obvious recollection of John Ford's play *'Tis Pity She's a Whore*, which Visconti had directed a few years earlier. In one scene Florio asks his daughter Annabella: "Where's the ring, That which your mother, in her will, bequeathed, And charged you on her blessing not to give't to any but your husband? Send back that." Annabella answers that she has not got the ring because "My brother in the morning took it from me, Said he would wear't to day" (II, 6). At the end of the play, the siblings, who are ardently in love, are destroyed, the sister through the hand of the brother (Dunn, *Eight Famous Elizabethan Plays*).

55. As Suzanne Liandrat-Guigues has pointed out (*Les images du temps*, p. 45), it is difficult to place Gianni's death struggle exactly in the diegetic time scheme. It is fair to assume that he died in the previous evening. In any case, what matters is the juxtaposition of this with Sandra's turning her back both on him and on their mutual past.

56. These have been painstakingly charted by Suzanne Liandrat-Guigues in her *Les images du temps*, although she prefers to talk about references "none of which has the role either of a symbol or a metaphor" (p. 187). Her book appeared only when I was already approaching the completion of my own study, and so space does not allow me to enter into full dialogue with her. I will, however, introduce below some of her notions that I have found particularly pertinent and that have helped me to develop my own views.

57. Seiller, text to Aldo Ciccolini's recording.

58. For a detailed analysis of the use of the music, see the chapter "L'évidement" in Liandrat-Guigues's *Les images du temps*. Liandrat-Guigues emphasizes the ternary structures of the piece as being parallel with the various triangular patterns between the characters. I do not find this entirely convincing as the ternary structures of the music are not really evident in the film and,

above all, are in no way mapped on the triangular structures of the story patterns.

59. For this latter observation I am again grateful to Liandrat-Guigues, whose source is Héraclite, *Fragments*, texte établi, traduit, commenté par Marcel Conche, coll. Epiméthée, PUF, 1986, p. 210. Athens is on the 38th northern latitude, a location where part of Ursa Major does actually go below the horizon. Further north, it remains higher. Similar celestial geometry applies, of course, to other constellations as well, but Ursa Major is the most prominent and well known (source: Astronomical Society Ursa, Helsinki).

60. Carsaniga, *Leopardi*, pp. 1–4, 49, 100, 106.

61. Schifano, *Visconti*, p. 383. Liandrat-Guigues points out that it also corresponds to Isabella's coiffure in D'Annunzio's *Forse que si forse que no*, p. 186 (*Les images du temps*, p. 182).

62. Nowell-Smith, *Luchino Visconti*, p. 155.

63. Liandrat-Guigues, *Les images du temps*, p. 241. Translation by the author.

64. Originally from Boulez's interview, "*Par volonté et par hazard.*" Entretien avec Célestin Deligé. Bd du Seuil, 1975, p. 64.

65. Liandrat-Guiges, "Lo scintillo" in "Vaghe stelle dell'orsa. . . ." Published in Bruni and Pravadelli, *Studi Viscontiani*, p. 121.

66. Villien, *Visconti*, pp. 172–3.

67. Stirling, *A Screen of Time*, p. 186.

68. Baldelli, *Luchino Visconti*, pp. 254–5. Translation by the present author.

69. Servadio, *Luchino Visconti*, p. 187.

70. Bencivenni, *Luchino Visconti*, p. 65.

71. Mario Praz, *Conversation Pieces* (London 1971), s. 33. Quoted in Tonetti, *Luchino Visconti*, p. 172. Praz is a scholar eminently suited to inspire Visconti. According to Alessandro Bencivenni: "With his characteristic diabolical levity Praz points out many times the subtle and morbid ties that run between the Soul (Anima) and its anagram, Mania" (Bencivenni, *Luchino Visconti*, p. 96).

72. Clark, *Modern Italy 1871–1982*, pp. 385–6; Kogan, *A Political History of Italy*, pp. 239–40.

73. Clark, *Modern Italy 1871–1982*, p. 385; Kogan, *A Political History of Italy*, p. 288.

74. This refers, of course, to the version restored after Visconti's death.

75. Ecclesiastes, 4:10.

76. *L'Europeo*, November 21, 1974, quoted in Baldelli, *Luchino Visconti*, p. 294.

CHAPTER 4, "VISCONTI AND GERMANY"

1. Servadio, *Luchino Visconti*, pp. 45–46.

2. Ibid., pp. 46–7.

3. Ibid., pp. 60, 193, 196.

4. Schifano, *Visconti*, pp. 400–401.

5. Ibid., p. 46. Originally in *Observer*, July 30, 1972.

6. La Capra, *History, Politics, and the Novel*, pp. 169–70.

7. Kimbell, *Verdi in the Age of Italian Romanticism*, pp. 9–15.

8. Miccihé, "Visconti e le sue ragioni." Introduction to the published script of *Morte a Venezia*, pp. 33–5.

9. Thomas Mann's speech, "Germany and the Germans," at the U.S. Library of Congress, Washington, D.C., May 29, 1945. Quoted in Hamilton, *The Brothers Mann*, p. 332.

10. Servadio, *Luchino Visconti*, pp. 194, 196.

11. Stirling, *A Screen of Time*, p. 191.

12. Cecchi D'Amico, interview with the author.

13. Schifano, *Visconti*, pp. 408–9.

14. Stirling, *A Screen of Time*, pp. 192–3.

15. Dill, *Germany*, pp. 344–7.

16. Ibid., pp. 299, 316–17.

17. Ibid., pp. 348–9.

18. Stirling, *A Screen of Time*, p. 192; Dill, *Germany*, pp. 349–51.

19. Baldelli, *Luchino Visconti*, pp. 262–3.

20. Ibid., pp. 264–5; Rondolino, *Visconti*, pp. 484–5.

21. An interview with Lietta Tournabuoni, L'Europeo, April, 10, 1969. Quoted in Servadio, *Luchino Visconti*, pp. 47–8.

22. The events connected with the little girl are almost the same as in Nikolai Stavrogin's confession in Dostoyevsky's *The Possessed* – in a chapter that during its time was censored in Russia. But whereas Tihon, to whom Stavrogin confesses his crime, represents at least some kind of possibility of salvation, Aschenbach, with whom Martin discusses the consequences of the death of the little girl, leads his victim into a free fall into the hell of Nazi atrocities.

23. The way they have been shot, with Sophie staring ahead and Bruckman lifeless on the couch, corresponds to a description of Eva Braun and Hitler after they had committed suicide after their wedding (Schifano, *Visconti*, p. 407; Tonetti, *Luchino Visconti*, p. 137).

24. Lukács, *The Historical Novel*, pp. 106–7.

25. Micciché, for example, writes: "the Nazi setting, rather than determining the climate of the family disintegration becomes a projection of it; all in all, rather than proposing a historicization of psychology it proposes a psychologization of history" (Micciché, "Visconti e le sue ragioni," published in Micciché, printed script of *Morte a Venezia*, p. 54).

26. Visconti's original intention had been to use Mahler. Jarre was forced on Visconti by the producers, and he was not very happy about it: "Bruckmann the Essenbecks and Aschenbach have nothing to do with [Doctor] Zhivago," he said to Franco Mannino, "and Jarre's music proceeds exclusively on those lines." Mannino, *Visconti e la musica*, p. 43.

27. Hannu Salmi has pointed out that one of the ways in which a film is coded to be historical is through the use of long shots that reveal wide landscapes,

huge sets, or masses of people – the heroes, the historical actors, are then picked out in close-ups (Salmi, *Elokuva ja historia*, pp. 225–6). It is notable that in *The Damned* Visconti has to a great extent relinquished such spectacular elements.

28. George Steiner has addressed this question in the television program "With Care and Desperation" (produced by NOS-Holland): "What happens is this: The cry of King Lear becomes louder and more real and more important than the cry in the street. If your brain, your nervous system, your imagination, your sensibility, your professional skills are completely and deeply invested in the great arts of the imagination and in abstract thought, speculation, instead of becoming more human, you may, unless you are terribly careful, become less human. . . . Unless we find a way to train the heart – I don't know how else to put this – to humanize the heart also, we may have this paradox of very high civilization, which is feeding inside itself the hunger for barbarism on the one hand and the indifference to barbarism on the other. So I began trying to understand how a man who tortured in a Gestapo cellar in the afternoon or helped to run Auschwitz or Belsen, could play very beautiful Schubert in the evening. And the liberal answer that he did not play well is a lie, a liberal lie! He played it very, very well. How a man could weep over Rilke, and they did. Know Elegies by heart and massacre a ghetto."

29. Sinyard, *Filming Literature*, p. 126. D. H. Lawrence quotation from "Thomas Mann," *Blue Review* (July 1913). Published in *Selected Literary Criticism* (Heinemann Educational Books, 1967), p. 265.

30. Sinyard, *Filming Literature*, p. 130. Visconti quotation from Servadio, *Luchino Visconti*, p. 211.

31. Nowell-Smith, *Luchino Visconti*, pp. 202–3. This was written in 1973. In a footnote, Nowell-Smith writes: "In general I would argue (also for a hundred and one other reasons not gone into in this book) that the Marxist artist, to be consistent, has to remove himself at some distance from the sphere of realism, however 'critical,' in order to establish and to clarify his relationship with reality" (ibid., p. 205). Since then, Nowell-Smith has confessed to being "a great admirer of Visconti's late films" (personal communication at the Convegno internazionale di studi viscontiani in 1994).

32. Rondolino, *Visconti*, p. 494; Hamilton, *The Brothers Mann*, p. 147.

33. Hamilton, *The Brothers Mann*, pp. 147–8.

34. Winston, *Thomas Mann*, pp. 268, 273–4.

35. Wiehe, "Of Art and Death," p. 210.

36. Mann, *Death in Venice*, p. 10.

37. Ibid., p. 38.

38. Ibid., p. 39.

39. Ibid., p. 63.

40. LaCapra, *History, Politics, and the Novel*, p. 118.

41. Ibid., p. 114.

42. Borchmeyer, *Richard Wagner*, p. 49.

43. LaCapra, *History, Politics, and the Novel*, p. 126.
44. Wagner, *The Novel and the Cinema*, p. 343.
45. Boyum, *Double Exposure*, pp. 186–7. Roger E. Wiehe expresses a similar view in his article, "Of Art and Death: Film and Fiction Versions of *Death in Venice*," p. 212.
46. Nowell-Smith, *Luchino Visconti*, p. 199.
47. Miccichè lists these in his excellent introduction to the published script, "Visconti e le sue ragioni," and adds as a ninth the fiasco at the concert hall that is followed by Alfred's invective. This is a kind of nightmarish culmination of both the Mannian and the Mahlerian themes.
48. Visconti's interview in the published script of *Death in Venice*, p. 121.
49. Mann, *Doctor Faustus*, pp. 191–3.
50. The discrepancy is not alleviated by the fact that a fragment of one of Aschenbach's answers to Alfred is taken directly from one of Mahler's letters to his wife, Alma Maria ("Sometimes I think that artists are like hunters aiming in the dark . . ."). From the point of view of parallels between different fictitious characters and real persons, it should be noted that in the novel it is the Faustian character Adrian Leverkühn who expounds ideas about aesthetics and theology and who is fascinated with the harmonic system as a system of mathematical combinations (Mann, *Doctor Faustus*, pp. 46–7 ff.). In the film, this point is made by Alfred. This makes sense, but it further emphasizes the discrepancy in having him accuse Aschenbach of being "a keeper of distances." In the novel, it is Adrian who has a "distaste for the too great physical nearness of people." He is "in the real sense of the word a man of disinclination, avoidance, reserve, aloofness" (ibid., p. 220).
51. Mann, Death in Venice, p. 29.
52. Visconti's interview in the published script, p. 114. More precisely, the idea might have been to imitate a literary effect that LaCapra detects in *Doctor Faustus*, which he sees as "written in intentional parody of a pompous, stuffy, academic style not up to the events it relates and the problems it treats" (LaCapra, *History, Politics, and the Novel*, p. 155).
53. Sinyard has criticized the use of the Adagietto, which in his opinion "not only . . . lose(s) much from being wrenched out of its context, seeming more sentimental and careworn than it actually is when heard in the full symphonic argument." He also thinks that "the Fifth Symphony itself charts a movement from tragedy to triumph, from darkness to light, which one could argue is exactly the reverse of what happens in *Death in Venice*." This, Sinyard thinks, is "crippling to film that prides itself on its cultural refinement" (*Filming Literature*, pp. 128–9). It could, however, be argued that the film, too, is about a progress toward light, light as consuming as the appearance of Zeus to Semele.
54. The name of the prostitute (as well as of the ship on which Aschenbach arrives in Venice), Esmeralda, refers to a similar character in *Doctor Faustus* (pp. 142, 154–6).

55. Adapted from the Devil's speech to Adrian Leverkühn in Mann's *Doctor Faustus*, p. 227.

56. Mann, *Death in Venice*, p. 29. One wonders whether these views might have been influenced by the production stills, which give a wholly different idea of the degree of explicitness of the gazes exchanged between Aschenbach and Tadzio than the film itself does. This effect could have been strengthened by the ubiquitousness of the picture of Aschenbach and Tadzio passing each other, the former with his back toward the audience and the latter looking intently at Aschenbach. It appears, for example, on the cover of the second edition of Nowell-Smith's book on Visconti.

57. At one point, Aschenbach follows Tadzio's family along a lane by a channel that appears to be the same one seen in *Senso*, along which Franz pursues Livia. The difference between the erotic simmering in that film and the pallor of *Death in Venice* is disturbing.

58. Since Aschenbach, soon after the beginning of this sequence, moves to pencil something on paper, it has been suggested that he has conceived the music we hear in his mind and proceeds to write it down. This parallels the hero of the novella, when he suddenly feels the urge to write an article "on a question of art and taste" (Mann, *Death in Venice*, p. 48).

59. Mann, *August von Platen*. Published in Mann, *Leiden und Grösse der Meister*, p. 138. Translation by the present author. Among the commentators of Visconti's films, Miccichè, for one, has used the quotation.

60. Ishaghpour, *Visconti*, p. 154.

61. Servadio, *Luchino Visconti*, pp. 205–6; Stirling, *A Screen of Time*, pp. 224–5, 237.

62. Rondolino, *Visconti*, p. 520; Stirling, *A Screen of Time*, pp. 238–41.

63. Cecchi D'Amico, interview with the author.

64. Stirling, *A Screen of Time*, p. 244.

65. Cecchi D'Amico, interview with the author.

66. Herre, *Ludwig II*, pp. 10–12, 22–7, 34.

67. Ibid., pp. 59, 65–6, 69–75, 86–8.

68. Of Prussia's enemies, Austria was successful on its other front, in its war against Italy. *Senso* refers to these events from the Italian side.

69. Dill, *Germany*, pp. 139, 145; Herre, *Ludwig II*, pp. 219; 223–4.

70. Herre, *Ludwig II*, pp. 270–2, 292–3, 297, 355–9, 362–3.

71. Ibid., pp. 375–6, 379.

72. The shorter versions contain proportionally fewer statements than the reconstructed version and the important opening statement, for example, is missing. Instead, after the coronation, there is a scene in which Ludwig's servant comes to Neuschwanstein with the message that people are coming to arrest the king. This is so also in the printed script (p. 72), but in the reconstructed version this scene is placed in chronological sequence.

73. The names of the witnesses at the inquest are not given, but some of them introduce themselves and yet others can be identified as they appear in the staged part of the film.

74. Ishaghpour, *Visconti*, p. 80.
75. Mann, *Doctor Faustus*, p. 430.
76. Mann, "The Sorrows and Grandeur of Richard Wagner." Printed in *Mann, Pro and Contra Wagner*, p. 125.
77. Music was played in the grotto in Ludwig's time, but the acoustics were appalling.
78. Phillips recording of the Music for *Ludwig*. In his book, *Visconti e la musica*, Franco Mannino says he heard about these thirteen bars for piano from Toscanini in 1945, who had discovered them when he had requested to see the original manuscript of *Parsifal* in Bayreuth. Mannino had some problems in getting hold of the music in time, but according to his fabulous account, it turned out that Suso Cecchi D'Amico's husband, Fedele D'Amico, happened to have a photograph of the sheet with its thirteen bars (pp. 49–50).
79. Tonetti, *Luchino Visconti*, p. 159.
80. Rondolino, *Visconti*, p. 508.
81. Several versions of this mutilated film are in circulation, at least one in German (130 minutes), and one in English (150 minutes). They are badly structured, have no rhythm, and are even somewhat difficult to follow.

CHAPTER 5, "VISCONTI AS AN INTERPRETER OF EUROPEAN LITERATURE"

1. Stirling, *A Screen of Time*, p. 30.
2. Maurois, *The Quest for Proust*, p. 186.
3. Ibid., p. 68.
4. Hemmings, "Realism and the Novel: The Eighteenth Century Beginnings." Printed in Hemmings (ed.), *The Age of Realism*, p. 43.
5. Renzi, the published script of *Le notti bianche*, p. 17.
6. May, Stendhal and the Age of Napoleon, p. 64.
7. Berlin, "Alexander Herzen." Published in Berlin, *Russian Thinkers*, p. 186.
8. Lukács, *Balzac und der französische Realismus*, p. 41. Translations from this work by the author.
9. Ibid., p. 42.
10. Ibid., p. 53.
11. Prendergast, *Balzac*, pp. 180–1.
12. Ibid., p. 183.
13. Ellis, "The Literary Adaptation," p. 3.
14. Anderson, Carolyn, "Film and Literature." In Edgerton, *Film and the Arts in Symbiosis*, p. 99.
15. Ibid., p. 77.
16. Ibid., p. 73.
17. Sinyard, *Filming Literature*, p. 117.
18. Balázs, *Theory of the Film*, p. 260.
19. Ibid., p. 264.
20. Andrew, *Concepts in Film Theory*, pp. 96–8.

21. Ibid., pp. 98–9.
22. Ibid., pp. 99–100.
23. Ibid., p. 100.
24. Ibid., p. 103.
25. Ibid., p. 105.
26. Steiner, *After Babel*, p. 460.
27. Aristarco, *Su Visconti*, p. 22.
28. Brunetta, interview with the author.
29. Ishaghpour, *Visconti*, pp. 43–5 (referring particularly to a statement by Antonioni).
30. Enckell, " 'Citizen Kane' and Psychoanalysis," p. 33.
31. Cecchi D'Amico, interview with the author; Stirling, *A Screen of Time*, pp. 116–7.
32. Stirling, *A Screen of Time*, p. 124.
33. Ibid., pp. 123, 125.
34. Bencivenni, *Luchino Visconti*, p. 41.
35. The performance is heard beginning from Rosina's line: "Now listen, how could I get a message through to Lindoro." A slight burst of laughter at the end of the (filmic) scene indicates that Rosina has taken out the letter she has written. The line quoted in the novella occurs just before this.
36. Nowell-Smith, *Luchino Visconti*, p. 127.
37. It is interesting to compare Visconti's interpretation to Bresson's adaptation of the *White Nights*. *Quatre nuits du un reveaur* (1971) is placed in modern Paris and its style is plain and suggestive. The girl, named Marthe, is quiet and stable in comparison with Natalia. The "madness" of her love lies in her stubbornness rather than in romantic illusions. When she reencounters the tenant and forsakes Jacques, the effect, in its everydayness, is less poignant than in Visconti's version. Jacques is more withdrawn and more of a dreamer than Mario. In Bresson's film, feeling emerges through an extraordinarily taciturn and thus superbly sensitive style of acting. It leaves a lot of scope for the spectator to assess the situation and to project his or her own feelings into it. While Visconti takes hold of Dostoyevsky's story by fantastic stylization, Bresson does so through restraint.
38. Camus, *The Stranger*, p. 96.
39. Ibid., pp. 52–3.
40. Ibid., pp. 75–6.
41. In the real French Algeria, it is unlikely that a European would have been sentenced to death for killing an Arab, particularly as it could have been explained away as self-defense. (McCarthy, *Camus*, p. 160; Thody, *Albert Camus*, p. 41).
42. Camus, *The Stranger*, p. 154.
43. McCarthy, *Camus*, p. 70; Thody, *Albert Camus*, pp. 18–19. The opinions expressed are, respectively, from *Le Figaro Littéraire*, July 17, 1942; *Nouvelle Revue Francaise*, October 1942; and *L'Arche* 1944.
44. Keefe, *French Existentialist Fiction*, pp. 32, 78.

45. *L'Espresso*, November 7, 1965. Quoted in Villien, *Visconti*, p. 177, translation by the present author. *Pied noir*, or "black foot," is a nickname the Arabs gave to the French.
46. *Cahiers du Cinema*, no. 171. Quoted in Villien, *Visconti*, p. 177.
47. Baldelli, *Luchino Visconti*, p. 257; Stirling, *A Screen of Time*, pp. 187–8. According to Stirling, Visconti intended to tell the story as reflected through the Algerian war and by using as additional material Camus's articles of the 1950s, thus taking into consideration that they were making a film for an audience that was aware of how things had developed in Algeria after Camus's death. Also, Baldelli emphasizes the idea of taking into account the change in the historical awareness, and Micciché, in his *Luchino Visconti –Un profilo critico*, mentions this as Visconti's pronounced initial intention (p. 57). According to Cecchi D'Amico, however, she and Visconti "never planned to use Camus' articles, or to add [references to the] political situation, as related to the Algerian war." The freedom they wanted was related mainly to the fact that they were primarily making a film for the Italian audience and that Mastroianni would play the part of Meursault. They also wanted, for example, to open the film with the trial scene and to put "a strong accent on Meursault's behaviour as seen by the judge, the priest etc." Unfortunately the first draft for the script is lost (a letter in reply to the author, January 9, 1996).
48. *Le Monde*, February 12, 1971. Quoted in Villien, *Visconti*, pp. 177–8. Translation from Italian by the author.
49. *Cinématographe*, n. 103, settembre–ottobre 1984. Quoted in Villien, p. 178.
50. Morrissette, *Novel and Film*, p. 108.
51. McCarthy, *Camus*, p. 156.
52. Ibid., pp. 153, 155.
53. Ibid., pp. 327–8.
54. The film has its notable admirers, though. In his *Movie and Video Guide* (1996), Leonard Maltin gives *The Stranger* a rating of three and a half stars (the maximum is four) and writes: "Excellent adaptation of Albert Camus' existential novel about a man who feels completely isolated from society. Mastroianni is perfectly cast in lead." Steven H. Scheuer makes a similar assessment in his guide. Both pan *Ludwig*, but neither has seen the restored version.
55. Medioli, interview with the author.
56. Villien, *Visconti*, p. 209; Rondolino, *Visconti*, p. 478. The information about the cast differs slightly in the various sources.
57. Cecchi D'Amico, interview with the author; Servadio, *Luchino Visconti*, pp. 200–201. For Losey's side of the affair, see Caute, *Joseph Losey*, pp. 337–42. The accounts differ on several minor details.
58. E.g., Rondolino, *Visconti*, p. 475.
59. Enckell, "Slutsatsen av Viscontis Rekviem." Published in Enckell, *Eko ock återsken*, p. 51. Translations from this work are by the author.

160. Revel, *On Proust*, p. 26.
 61. Shattuck, *Proust*, pp. 43–4.
 62. Their story has been rendered for the screen in Volker Schlöndorff's *Swann in Love* (1984), produced by Stéphane and based on a script by Peter Brook and Jean-Claude Carrière.
 63. Branca, *Dizionario critico della letteratura italiana*, s.v. "Decadentismo."
 64. Pacifici, *The Modern Italian Novel*, pp. 36–7, 41–4.
 65. Praz, *The Romantic Agony*, pp. 420–1.
 66. Pacifici, *The Modern Italian Novel*, p. 45.
 67. D'Annunzio, *L'Innocente*, p. 39.
 68. Ibid., p. 43.
 69. Ibid., p. 42.
 70. Aristarco, *Su Visconti*, p. 103.
 71. Enckell, "Film ock psykoanalys." Published in Enckell, *Spegelskrift*, p. 45. Translations from this work are by the author.
 72. Enckell, *Eko och återsken*, p. 50.

Filmography

The standard English name is given after the original title if the film has been commercially distributed in Great Britain or the United States. The duration given is that of the longest known standard version. When the duration of the version available for this study is shorter, it is indicated in parentheses. The main source: Rondolino, *Visconti*.

UNE PARTIE DE CAMPAGNE / A DAY IN THE COUNTRY

Director: Jean Renoir
Assistant Directors: Yves Allégret, Jacques Becker, Jacques B. Brunius, Henri Cartier-Bresson, Luchino Visconti
Source: Guy de Maupassant's novella, *Une partie de campagne*
Script: Jean Renoir
Director of Photography: Claude Renoir, Jean Bourgoin
Editor: Marguerite Houle-Renoir, Marinette Cadix
Costumes: Luchino Visconti
Music: Joseph Kosma
Production Company: Panthéon
Producer: Pierre Braunberg
Actors: Sylvia Bataille (Henriette), Georges Saint-Saëns [Georges Darnoux] (Henri), Jacques Borel [Jacques B. Brunius] (Rodolphe), Jeanne Marken (Madame Dufour), Gabriello (Monsieur Dufour), Paul Temps (Anatole)
First Performance: France, May 8, 1946
Length: 1,232 m
Duration: 40 min

LA TOSCA

Director: Jean Renoir, Carl Koch (Luchino Visconti)
Source: Victorien Sardou's play, *La Tosca*

Script: Jean Renoir, Carl Koch, Luchino Visconti
Director of Photography: Ubaldo Arata
Editor: Gino Bretone
Music: Giacomo Puccini; Adaptation: Umberto Mancini
Performers: Mafalda Favero, Ferruccio Taglivini
Production Company: Scalera Film
Actors: Imperio Argentina (Tosca), Michel Simon (Scarpia), Rossano Brazzi
(Cavaradozzi), Carla Candini, Juan Calvo, Adriano Rimoldi, Nicholas Per-
chicot
First Performance: Paris, August 30, 1942

OSSESSIONE

Director: Luchino Visconti
Assistant Directors: Giuseppe De Santis, Antonio Pietrangeli
Source: James M. Cain's novel, *The Postman Always Rings Twice*
Script: L. Visconti, Mario Alicata, Giuseppe De Santis, Gianni Puccini
Director of Photography: Aldo Tonti, Domenico Scala
Editor: Mario Serandrei
Scenery: Gino Franzi
Costumes: Maria De Matteis
Makeup: Alberto De Rossi
Music: Giuseppe Rosati
Performers: Fernando Previtali, Eiar's Symphony Orchestra
Production Company: Industrie Cinematografiche Italiane (ICI)
Producer: Libero Solaroli
Actors: Clara Calamai (Giovanna Bragana), Massimo Girotti (Gino Costa), Juan
De Landa (Giuseppe Bragana), Dhia Cristiani (Anita), Elio Marcuso (Lo Spag-
nuolo), Vittorio Duse (plainclothes policeman), Michele Riccardini (don Re-
migo), Michele Sakara.
First Performance: Ferrara, Italy, May 17, 1943
Length: 3,923 m
Duration: 135 min (124 min)

GIORNI DI GLORIA (DAYS OF GLORY)

Technical Coordination: Mario Serandrei, Giuseppe De Santis
Directors: Marcello Pagliero (Fosse Ardeatine), Luchino Visconti (the lynching
of Carretta and the trial and execution of Caruso)
Commentary Text: Umberto Calosso, Umberto Barbaro,
Commentary: Umberto Calosso
Director of Photography: Della Valle, De West, Di Venanzo, Jannarelli, Lastri-

cati, Navarro, Pucci, Reed, Terzano, Ventimiglia, Werdier, Vittoriano, Manlio, Caloz and the technical personnel of the Milan CLN
Editor: Mario Serandrei, Carlo Alberto Chiesa
Music: Costantino Ferri
Production Company: Titanus
Producer: Fulvio Ricci
First Performance: Italy, October 1945
Length: 1,956 m

LA TERRA TREMA / THE EARTH TREMBLES

Director: Luchino Visconti
Assistant Directors: Francesco Rosi, Franco Zeffirelli
Source: Giovanni Verga's novel, *I Malavoglia*
Script: Luchino Visconti
Commentary Text: Luchino Visconti, Antonio Pietrangeli
Commentary: Mario Pisu
Director of Photography: G. R. Aldo [Aldo Graziati]
Editor: Mario Serandrei
Coordination of Music: Luchino Visconti, Willy Ferrero
Production Company: Universalia
Producer: Salvo D'Angelo
Actors: The people of Aci Trezza
First Performance: Venice Festival, Italy, September 1, 1948
Length: 4,523 m
Duration: 160 min

BELLISSIMA

Director: Luchino Visconti
Assistant Directors: Francesco Rosi, Franco Zeffirelli
Script: Suso Cecchi D'Amico, Francesco Rosi, Luchino Visconti
Director of Photography: Piero Portaluppi, Paul Ronald
Editor: Mario Serandrei
Scenery Gianni Polidori
Costumes: Piero Tosi
Makeup: Alberto De Rossi
Music: Franco Mannino on the themes of *L'Elisir d'Amore* by Gaetano Donizetti
Performers: Franco Ferrara and the Symphony Orchestra of the Rome Opera House together with the orchestra and choir of RAI
Production Company: Film Bellissima
Producer: Salvo D'Angelo
Actors: Anna Magnani (Maddalena Cecconi), Walter Chiari (Alberto Annovazzi),

Tina Apicella (Maria Cecconi), Alessandro Blasetti (as himself), Gastone Renzelli (Spartaco Cecconi), Tecla Scarano (acting teacher), Lola Braccini (the wife of the photographer), Arturo Bragaglia (photographer), Linda Sini (Mimmetta), Vittorio Glori (as himself), Iris (Liliana Manicini), Geo Taparelli (as himself), Mario Chiari (as himself), Filippo Mercati (as himself), Nora Ricci, Vittorio Benvenuti, Giusella Monaldi, Amalia Pellegrini, Teresa Battagli, Luciana Ricci, Giuseppina Arena
First Performance: Italy, December 28, 1951
Length: 3,162 m
Duration: 113 min

DOCUMENTO MENSILE N. 2, APPUNTI SU UN FATTO DI CRONACA (MONTHLY REPORT N. 2, NOTES ON A NEWS ITEM)

Director: Luchino Visconti
Commentary: Vasco Pratolini
Producer: Marco Ferreri, Riccardo Ghione
First Performance: Italy, 1951

SIAMO DONNE / WE THE WOMEN, ep. ANNA MAGNANI

Distributed in the United States as an addition to the film *Questa e la vita*/ Of Life and Love

Director: Luchino Visconti
Assistant Director: Franco Maselli
Script: Suso Cecchi D'Amico, Cesare Zavattini
Director of Photography: Gabor Pogany
Editor: Mario Serandrei
Music: Alessandro Cicognini
Production Company: Titanus
Producer: Alfredo Guarini
Actors: Anna Magnani (as herself)
First Performance: Italy, October 1953
Length: 2,764 m
Duration: 18 min

SENSO / THE WANTON CONTESSA

Director: Luchino Visconti
Assistant Directors: Francesco Rosi, Franco Zeffirelli

Source: Camillo Boito's novella, *Senso*
Script: Suso Cecchi D'Amico, Luchino Visconti; Collaborators: Carlo Alianello,
    Giorgio Bassani, Giorgio Prosperi; Part of the dialogue: Paul Bowles, Tennessee
    Williams
Director of Photography: G. R. Aldo [Aldo Graziati], Robert Krasker
Editor: Mario Serandrei
Scenery: Ottavio Scotti
Costumes: Marcel Escoffier, Piero Tosi
Makeup: Alberto De Rossi
Music: Anton Bruckner: VII Symphony, 1st and 2d Movements
Performers: Franco Ferrara and the RAI Symphony Orchestra
Production Company: Lux Film
Producer: Claudio Forges Davanzati
Actors: Alida Valli (Countess Livia Serpieri), Farley Granger (Lieutenant Franz
    Mahler), Massimo Girotti (Marquise Roberto Ussoni), Rina Morelli (Laura),
    Marcella Mariani (Clara), Heinz Moog (Count Serpieri), Christian Marquand
    (officer), Sergio Fantoni (Luca), Tino Biacnhi (Meucci), Ernst Nadherny (The
    Commander of Verona), Tonio Selwart (colonel), Marianna Leibl (wife of a
    German general), Christoforo De Hartungen (the Commander of Venice), Go-
    liarda Sapienza (landlady)
First Performance: Venice Festival, Italy, September 3, 1954
Length: 3,250 m
Duration: 115 min (Finnish Film Archive copy 122 min)

LE NOTTI BIANCHE / WHITE NIGHTS

Director: Luchino Visconti
Assistant Directors: Fernando Cicero, Albino Cocco
Source: Dostoyevsky's novella, *White Nights*
Script: Suso Cecchi D'Amico
Director of Photography: Giuseppe Rotunno
Editor: Mario Serandrei
Scenery: Mario Chiari, Mario Garbuglia
Costumes: Piero Tosi
Makeup: Alberto De Rossi
Music: Nino Rota
Performer: Franco Ferrara
Songs (with Performers): "Scusami" (Colombo-Malagodi-Perrone), Cinico An-
    gelini's Orchestra, "O' Cangaceiro" (Nacimento), Luiz el Grande's Orchestra,
    "Thirteen Women" (Thompson-Gadda-Lidianni), Bill Haley and His Comets
Production Company: Vides, Rome / Intermondia Films, Paris
Producer: Franco Cristaldi, Jean-Paul Guilber
Actors: Marcello Mastroianni (Mario), Maria Schell (Natalia), Jean Marais (ten-
    ant), Clara Calamai (prostitute), Dick Sanders (dancer), Corrado Pani, Mar-

cella Rovena (landlady of the boardinghouse), Maria Zanolli (maid), Elena
Fancera (the cashier), Ferdinando Guerra (Mario's friend), Leonilde Montesi
(his wife), Anna Filippini (their daughter), Romano Barbieri (their son), San-
dro Moretti (young hooligan), Sandra Verani, Lanfranco Ceccarelli, Angelo
Galassi, Renato Terra
First Performance: Venice Festival, Italy, August 6, 1957
Length: 2,916 m
Duration: 107 min

ROCCO E I SUOI FRATELLI / ROCCO AND HIS BROTHERS

Director: Luchino Visconti
Assistant Directors: Rinaldo Ricci, Jerry Macc
Source: An idea developed by Luchino Visconti, Vasco Pratolini, and Suso Cec-
chi D'Amico on the basis of Giovanni Testori's collection of stories, *Il ponte
della Ghisolfa*
Script: Suso Cecchi D'Amico, Pasquale Festa Campanile, Massimo Franciosa,
Enrico Medioli, Luchino Visconti
Director of Photography: Giuseppe Rotunno
Editor: Mario Serandrei
Scenery: Mario Garbuglia
Costumes: Piero Tosi
Makeup: Giuseppe Banchelli
Music: Nino Rota
Performer: Franco Ferrara
Songs (with Performers): "E vero" (Nisa Bindi), "Tintarella di luna" (De Filippi-
Mibliacci), "Calypso in the Rain" (Luttazzi), "Il mare" (Pugliese-Vian), "La
più bella del mondo" (Marini), "paese mio" (?)
Production Company: Titanus, Rome / Les Films Marceau, Paris
Producer: Goffredo Lombardi
Actors: Alain Delon (Rocco), Renato Salvatore (Simone), Annie Girardot (Na-
dia), Katina Paxinou (Rosaria, the mother), Roger Hanin (Morini), Paolo
Stoppa (Cecchi), Suzy Delair (Luisa), Claudia Cardinale (Ginetta), Spiros Fo-
cas (Vincenzo), Claudio Mori (girl at the dry-cleaner's), Alessandra Panaro
(Franca, Ciro's fiancée), Corrado Pani (Ivo), Max Cartier (Ciro), Rocco Vi-
deolazzi (Luca), Becker Masoero (Nadia's mother), Franca Valeri (the widow),
Adriana Asti, Enzo Fiermonte, Nino Castelnuovo, Rosario Borelli, Renato Terra
First Performance: Venice Festival, Italy, September 6, 1960
Length: 4,973 m
Duration: 180 min

BOCCACCIO '70, ep. IL LAVORO / BOCCACCIO '70, ep. THE JOB

Director: Luchino Visconti
Source: Guy de Maupassant's novella, *Au bord du lit*
Script: Suso Cecchi D'Amico, Luchino Visconti
Director of Photography: Giuseppe Rotunno
Editor: Mario Serandrei
Scenery: Mario Garbuglia
Music: Nino Rota
Production Company: Concordia Compagnia Cinematografica, Cineriz, Rooma / Francinex, Gray-Films, Pariisi
Producer: Carlo Ponti, Antonio Cervi
Actors: Romy Schneider (Pupe), Tomas Milian (Count Ottavio), Paolo Stoppa (Attorney Alcamo), Romolo Valli (Attorney Tacchi), Amedo Girard
First Performance: February 1, 1962
Length: 5,412 m
Duration: 46 min

IL GATTOPARDO / THE LEOPARD

Director: Luchino Visconti
Assistant Directors: Rinaldo Ricci, Albino Cocco
Source: Giuseppe Tomaso di Lampedusa's novel, *Il Gattopardo*
Script: Suso Cecchi D'Amico, Pasquale Festa Campanile, Massimo Franciosa, Enrico Medioli, Luchino Visconti
Director of Photography: Giuseppe Rotunno
Editor: Mario Serandrei
Scenery: Mario Garbuglia
Costumes: Piero Tosi; Collaborators: Vera Marzot, Bice Brichetto
Makeup: Alberto De Rossi
Music: Nino Rota (and his arrangements from Verdi's *La Traviata*, as well as dance music including a previously unknown waltz by Verdi as diegetic music)
Performer: Franco Ferrara
Production Company: Titanus, Rome / S.N. Pathé Cinéma. S.G.C., Paris
Producer: Goffredo Lombardo
Actors: Burt Lancaster (Prince Fabrizio Salina), Alain Delon (Tancredi Falconeri), Claudia Cardinale (Angelica Sedara), Paolo Stoppa (don Colegero Sedara), Rina Morelli (Maria Stella, Princess of Salina), Romolo Valli (Father Pirrone), Leslie French (Chevalley), Ivo Garrani (Colonel Pallavicino), Serge Reggiani (don Ciccio Tumeo), Lucilla Morlacchi (Concetta), Mario Girotti (Viscount Cavriaghi), Pierre Clementi (Francesco Paolo), Giuliano Gemma (A Garibaldian General), Ida Galli (Carolina), Ottavia Piccolo (Caterina), Carlo

Valenzano (Paolo), Brock Fuller (a Prince), Anna Maria Bottini (Miss Dombreuil, the governess), Lola Braccini (donna Margherita), Marino Masè (the teacher), Howard Nelson Rubien (don Diego), Tina Lattanzi, Marcella Rovena, Rina De Liguro, Giovanni Melisenda (don Onofrio Rotolo), Valerio Ruggeri, Carlo Lolli, Olimpia Cavalli (Marianna), Franco Gulà, Vittorio Duse, Vanni Materassi, Giuseppe Stagnitti, Carmelo Artale, Anna Maria Surdo, Alina Zalewska, Winni Riva, Stelvio Rosi, Carlo Palmucci, Dante Posani, Rosalino Bua
First Performance: March 27, 1963
Length: 5,482 m
Duration: 205 min (180 min)

VAGHE STELLE DELL'ORSA / SANDRA

Director: Luchino Visconti
Assistant Director: Rinaldo Ricci
Script: Suso Cecchi D'Amico, Enrico Medioli, Luchino Visconti
Director of Photography: Armando Nannuzzi
Editor: Mario Serandrei
Scenery: Mario Garbuglia
Costumes: Bice Brichetto
Makeup: Michele Trimarchi
Music: César Franck: *Prelude, Chorale and Fugue*
Performer: Augusto D'Ottavi (piano)
Songs (diegetic) (with Performers): "Io che non vivo senza te" (Donaggio-Pallavicino; ed. Accordo), "Una rotonda sul mare" (Migliacci-Faleni; ed. La Busola), "E se domani . . ." (Giorgio Calabrese and Carlo Alberto Rossi), "Strip Cinema" (Pino Calvi), "Let's Go" and "If You Don't Want" (Le Tigri)
Production Company: Vides
Producer: Franco Cristaldi
Actors: Claudia Cardinale (Sandra), Jean Sorel (Gianni), Michael Craig (Andrew), Renzo Ricci (Antonio Giraldini), Marie Bell (mother), Amalia Troiani (Fosca), Fred Williams (Pietro Fornari), Vittorio Manfrino, Renato Moretti, Giovanni Rovini, Paola Pescini, Isacco Politi
First Performance: Venice Festival, Italy, September 3, 1965
Length: 2,878 m
Duration: 100 min

LE STREGHE, ep. LA STREGA BRUCIATA VIVA / THE WITCHES, ep. THE WITCH BURNED ALIVE

Director: Luchino Visconti
Source and Script: Giuseppe Patrone Griffi; Collaborator: Cesare Zavattini

Director of Photography: Giuseppe Rotunno
Editor: Mario Serandrei
Scenery: Mario Garbuglia, Piero Poletto
Costumes: Piero Tosi
Makeup: Goffredo Ricchetti
Music: Piero Piccioni
Production Company: Dino De Laurentiis Cinematografica, Rome / Les Productions Artistes Associés, Paris
Producer: Dino De Laurentiis
Actors: Silvana Mangano (Gloria), Annie Girardot (Valeria), Francisco Rabal (Valeria's husband), Massimo Girotti (a sportsman), Elsa Albani (friend), Clara Calamai (ex-actress), Véronique Vendell (young guest), Leslie French (industrialist), Nora Ricci (Gloria's secretary), Bruno Filippini (singer), Dino Mele (1st waitress), Marilù Tolo (2d waitress), Helmut Steinbergher
First Performance: February 28, 1967
Length: 3,050 m
Duration: 37 min

LO STRANIERO / THE STRANGER

Director: Luchino Visconti
Assistant Directors: Rinaldo Ricci, Albino Cocci
Source: Albert Camus's novel, *The Stranger*
Script: Suso Cecchi D'Amico, Georges Conchon, Luchino Visconti; Collaborator: Emmanuel Robbles
Director of Photography: Giuseppe Rotunno
Editor: Ruggero Mastroianni
Scenery: Mario Garbuglia
Costumes: Piero Tosi; Collaborators: Cesare Rovatti, Giuliana Serano
Makeup: Giuseppe Banchelli
Music: Piero Piccioni
Performer: Bruno Nicolai
Production Company: Dino De Laurentiis Cinematografica, Rome, Raster Film, Rome / Marianne Production, Paris, in collaboration with Casbah Film, Algeria
Producer: Dino De Laurentiis
Actors: Marcello Mastroianni (Meursault), Anna Karina (Marie Cardona), Georges Wilson (examining magistrate), Bernard Blier (Defense Council), Jacques Herlin (director of the home for the elderly), Georges Geret (Raymond), Jean-Pierre Zola (employer), Pierre Bertin (judge), Bruno Cremer (priest), Alfred Adam (Prosecutor), Angela Luce (Mrs. Masson), Mimmo Palmara (Masson), Vittoria Duse (lawyer), Marc Laurent (Emanuele), Joseph Maréchal (Salamano), Mohamed Cheritel (1st Arab), Saada Rahlem (2d Arab), Brahim Hadjadj (3d Arab), Paolo Herzl (Guard), Jacques Monod, Valentino Macchi

First Performance: Venice Festival, Italy, September 6, 1967
Length: 3,130 m
Duration: 110 min

LA CADUTA DEGLI DEI / GÖTTERDÄMMERUNG / THE DAMNED

Director: Luchino Visconti
Assistant Directors: Albino Cocci, Fanny Wessling
Script: Nicola Badalucco, Enrico Medioli, Luchino Visconti
Directors of Photography: Armando Nannuzzi, Pasquale De Santis
Editor: Ruggero Mastroianni
Scenery: Pasquale Romano
Costumes: Piero Tosi, Vera Marzot
Makeup: Mauro Gavazzi
Music: Maurice Jarre
Performer: Maurice Jarre
Production Company: Praesidens Film, Zürich / Pegaso, Italnoleggio, Rome / Eichberg Film, München
Producers: Alfred Levy, Ever Haggiag
Actors: Dirk Bogarde (Friedrich Bruckmann), Ingrid Thulin (Sofia von Essenbeck), Helmut Griem (Aschenbach), Helmut Berger (Martin von Essenbeck), Renaud Verley (Günther von Essenbeck), Umberto Orsini (Herbert Thalmann), René Koldehoff (Konstantin von Essenbeck), Albrecht Schönhals (Baron Joachin von Essenbeck), Florinda Bolkan (Olga), Nora Ricci (governess), Charlotte Rampling (Elisabeth Thalmann), Irina Vanka (Lisa Keller), Karin Mittendorf (Thilde Thalmann), Valentina Ricci (Erika Thalmann), Wolfgang Hillinger (police inspector), Howard Nelson Rubien (headmaster), Werner Hasselmann (Gestapo officer), Peter Dane (clerck at the foundry), Mark Salvage (police inspector), Karl Otto Alberty (1st army officer), John Frerick (2d army officer), Richard Beach (3d army officer), Claus Höhne (1st SA officer), Ernst Kühr (2d SA officer), Wolfgang Ehrlich (SA soldier), Esterina Carloni (1st waitress), Antonietta Fiorita (2d waitress), Jessica Dublin (nurse)
First Performance: October 16, 1969
Length: 4,296 m
Duration: 150 min

MORTE A VENEZIA / DEATH IN VENICE

Director: Luchino Visconti
Assistant Director: Albino Cocci
Source: Thomas Mann's novella, *Death in Venice*

Director of Photography: Pasquale De Santis
Editor: Ruggero Mastroianni
Scenery: Ferdinando Scarfiotti
Costumes: Piero Tosi
  Assistant: Gabriela Pescucci
Makeup: Mario Di Salvio, Mauro Gavezzi; Silvana Mangano's makeup: Goffredo
  Rocchetti
Music: Gustav Mahler's III Symphony, 4th Movement, and V Symphony, 4th
  Movement
Performers: Franco Mannino and the Orchestra of the Academy of Santa Cecilia,
  Lucretia West (contralto)
Production Company: Alfa Cinematografica, Rome / Production Editions Ci-
  nématographiques Francaises, Paris
Producer: Mario Gallo
Actors: Dirk Bogarde (Gustav von Aschenbach), Romolo Valli (manager of the
  hotel), Nora Ricci (Tadzio's governess), Björn Andersen (Tadzio), Silvana
  Mangano (Tadzio's mother), Mark Burns (Alfred), Marisa Berenson (Aschen-
  bach's wife), Carole André (Esmerelda), Leslie French (clerk of the travel
  agency), Sergio Garfagnoli (Jasciu), Ciro Cristofoletti (clerk at the hotel), An-
  tonio Apicella (tramp), Bruno Boscetti (clerk of the railway station), Franco
  Fabrizi (barber), Luigi Battaglia (old man on the boat), Dominique Darrel (the
  English tourist), Mirella Pompili (customer at the boardinghouse), Masha Per-
  dit (a Russian tourist)
First Performance: London, U.K., March 1, 1971
Length: 3,688 m
Duration: 135 min

LUDWIG

Director: Luchino Visconti
Assistant Director: Albino Cocci
Script: Enrico Medioli, Luchino Visconti; Collaborator: Suso Cecchi D'Amico
Director of Photography: Armando Nannuzzi
Editor: Ruggero Mastroianni
Scenery: Mario Chiari, Mario Scisci
Costumes: Piero Tosi; Collaborators: Gabriela Pescucci, Maria Fanetti
Makeup: Alberto De Rossi
Music: Robert Schumann, Richard Wagner, Jacques Offenbach
Performers: Franco Mannino and the Orchestra of the Academy of Santa Cecilia;
  Piano solo: Franco Mannino
Production Company: Mega Film, Rome / Cinétel, Paris / Dieter Geissler Film-
  production, Divina-Film, München
Actors: Helmut Berger (Ludwig), Trevor Howard (Richard Wagner), Silvana
  Mangano (Cosima von Bülow), Gert Fröbe (Father Hoffman), Helmut Griem

(Dürkheim), Isabella Telenzynstein (the Queen Mother), Umberto Orsini (Count von Holnstein), John Moulder Brown (Prince Otto), Sonia Petrovna (Sophie), Folker Bohnet (Joseph Kainz), Heinz Moog (Professor Gudden), Adriana Asti (Lila von Buliowski), Marc Porel (Richard Hornig), Nora Ricci (Countess Ida Ferenczy), Mark Burns (Hans von Bülow), Maurizio Bonuglia (Mayer), Romy Schneider (Elizabeth of Austria), Alexander Allerson, Bert Bloch, Manfred Furst, Kurt Grosskurt, Anna Maria Hanschek, Gerhard Herter, Jan Linhart, Carla Mancini, Gernot Mohner, Clara Moustawcesky, Alain Naya, Alessandro Perrella, Karl Heinz Peters, Wolfram Schaerf, Hennig Schlüter, Helmut Stern, Eva Tavazzi, Louise Vincent, Gunnar Warner, Karl Heinz Windhorst, Rayka Yurit
First Performance: Bonn, Federal Republic of Germany, January 18, 1973
Length: 5,170 m
Duration: 245 min

GRUPPO DI FAMIGLIA IN UN INTERNO / CONVERSATION PIECE

Director: Luchino Visconti
Assistant Director: Albino Cocci
Source: Enrico Medioli's original idea
Script: Suso Cecchi D'Amico, Enrico Medioli, Luchino Visconti
Director of Photography: Pasquale De Santis
Editor: Ruggero Mastroianni; Collaborators: Lea Mazzocchi, Alfredo Menchini
Scenery: Mario Garbuglia
Costumes: Vera Marzot; Silvana Mangano's costumes: Piero Tosi
Makeup: Alberto De Rossi, Eligio Trani
Music: Franco Mannino; also Wolfgang Amadeus Mozart, "Vorrei spiegarvi, o Dio!" and Sinfonia Concertante, E Flat Major, 2d Movement
Performers: Franco Mannino; Mozart extracts: Emilia Ravaglia (soprano), Prahan Chamber Orchestra, Josef Suk (violin), Josef Kodousek (viola)
Production Company: Rusconi Film, Rome / Gaumont International, Paris
Producer: Giovanni Bertolucci
Actors: Burt Lancaster (professor), Silvana Mangano (Bianca Brumont), Helmut Berger (Konrad), Claudia Marsani (Lietta), Stefano Patrizi (Stefano), Elvira Cortese (Erminia), Philippe Hersent, Guy Trejan, Jean-Pierre Zola, Umberto Raho, Enzo Fiermonte, Romolo Valli (lawyer), George Clatot, Valentino Macchi, Vittorio Fantoni, Lorenz Piani, Margherita Horowitz
First Performance: December 10, 1974
Length: 3,330 m
Duration: 120 min

L'INNOCENTE / THE INNOCENT / THE INTRUDER

Director: Luchino Visconti
Assistant Directors: Albino Cocci, Giorgio Treves
Source: Gabriele D'Annunzio's novel, *L'innocente*
Script: Suso Cecchi D'Amico, Enrico Medioli, Luchino Visconti
Director of Photography: Pasquale De Santis
Editor: Ruggero Mastroianni; Assistants: Lea Mazzocchi, Alfredo Menchini
Scenery: Mario Garbuglia
Costumes: Piero Tosi
Makeup: Goffredo Rocchetti, Gilberto Provenghi, Luigi Esposito
Music: Franco Mannino; Frederic Chopin: "Berceuse" and "Walze"; Wolfgang
    Amadeus Mozart: "Turkish March"; Frans Liszt: "Giochi d'acqua a Villa
    d'Este"; Christoph Willibald von Gluck: "Che farò senza Euridice" from *Orfeo
    ed Euridice*
Performers: Franco Mannino and the Orchestra of the Academy of Santa Cecilia;
    piano accompaniment and solos: Franco Mannino, Benedetta Pechioli (so-
    prano)
Production Company: Rizzoli Film, Rome / Les Films Jacques Leitienne, Paris /
    Société Imp. Ex. Ci., Nice / Francoriz Production, Paris
Producer: Giovanni Bertolucci
Actors: Giancarlo Giannini (Tullio Hermil), Laura Antonelli (Giuliana), Jennifer
    O'Neill (Teresa Raffo), Rina Morelli (Tullio's mother), Massimo Girotti (Count
    Stefano Egano), Didier Haudepin (Federico Hermil), Marie Dubois (Princess),
    Roberta Paladini (Mrs. Elviretta), Claude Mann (Prince), Marc Porel (Filippo
    D'Arborio); Philippe Hersent, Elvira Cortese, Siria Betti, Enzo Musumeci
    Greco, Alessandra Consorti, Filippo Perego, Margherita Horowitz, Riccardo
    Satta
First Performance: Cannes Film Festival, France, May 15, 1976
Length: 3,543 m
Duration: 130 min

Stage Productions

For fuller credits, see Caterina D'Amico de Carvalho (ed.) *Il mio teatro – Luchino Visconti*, or Rondolino, *Visconti*

THEATER

Carità mondana, Giannino Antona Traverso
Director: R. Caló and R. Simoni
Sets and Costumes: Luchino Visconti
Time and Place: Como, Teatro Sociale, 1936

Il dolce aloe / Sweet Aloes, Jay Mallory (Joyce Carey)
Director: R. Caló and R. Simoni
Sets and Costumes: Luchino Visconti
Time and Place: Milan, Teatro Manzoni, 1936

Il viaggio / Le voyage, Henry Bernstein
Sets and Costumes: Luchino Visconti
Time and Place: San Remo, Teatro del Casinó Municipale, 1938

Parenti terribili / Les parents terribles, Jean Cocteau
Director: Luchino Visconti
Sets and Costumes: Luchino Visconti
Time and Place: Rome, Teatro Eliseo, 1945

Quinta colonna / The Fifth Column, Ernest Hemingway
Director: Luchino Visconti
Time and Place: Rome, Teatro Quirino, 1945 (first performance in Italy)

La macchina da scrivere / La machine à ecrire, Jean Cocteau
Director: Luchino Visconti
Sets and Costumes: Luchino Visconti
Time and Place: Rome, Teatro Eliseo, 1945 (first performance in Italy)

Antigone, Jean Anouilh
Director: Luchino Visconti
Time and Place: Rome, Teatro Eliseo, 1945 (first performance in Italy)

A porte chiuse / Huis clos, Jean-Paul Sartre
Director: Luchino Visconti
Time and Place: Teatro Eliseo, 1945 (first performance in Italy)

Adamo / Adam, Marcel Achard
Director: Luchino Visconti
Sets and Costumes: Luchino Visconti
Time and Place: Rome, Teatro Quirino, 1945 (first performance in Italy)

La via del tobacco / Tobacco Road, John Kirkland after Erskine Caldwell's novel
Director: Luchino Visconti
Time and Place: Milan, Teatro Olimpia, 1945

Il matrimonio di Figaro / Le mariage de Figaro, Pierre A. Caron de Beaumarchais
Director: Luchino Visconti
Time and Place: Rome, Teatro Quirino, 1946

Delitto e castigo / Crime et châtiment, Gaston Baty after Dostoyevsky's novel
Director: Luchino Visconti
Time and Place: Rome, Teatro Eliseo, 1946

Zoo di vetro / The Glass Menagerie, Tennessee Williams
Director: Luchino Visconti
Time and Place: Rome, Teatro Eliseo, 1946 (first performance in Italy)

Vita col padre / Life With Father, Howard Lindsay and Russell Crouse after Clarence Day's novel
Director: Geraldo Guerriri; Visconti supervised the production
Time and Place: Rome, Teatro Eliseo, 1947

Eurydice / Eurydice, Jean Anouilh
Director: Luchino Visconti
Time and Place: Firenze, Teatro La Pergola, 1947 (first performance in Italy)

Rosalinda, O come vi piace / As You Like It, William Shakespeare
Director: Luchino Visconti
Time and Place: Rome, Teatro Eliseo, 1948

Un tram che si chiama desiderio / A Streetcar Named Desire, Tennessee Williams

Director: Luchino Visconti
Time and Place: Rome, Teatro Eliseo, 1949

Oreste, Vittorio Alfieri, adapted by Luchino Visconti
Director: Luchino Visconti
Time and Place: Rome, Teatro Quirino, 1949

Troilo e Cressida / Troilus and Cressida, William Shakespeare
Director: Luchino Visconti
Time and Place: Firenze, Giardino di Boboli, 1949 (first performance in Italy)

Morte di un commesso viaggiatore / Death of a Salesman, Arthur Miller
Director: Luchino Visconti
Time and Place: Rome, Teatro Eliseo, 1951 (first performance in Italy)

Un tram che si chiama desiderio / A Streetcar Named Desire, Tennessee Williams
Director: Luchino Visconti
Time and Place: Milan, Teatro Nuovo, 1951

Il seduttore, Diego Fabbri
Director: Luchino Visconti
Time and Place: Venice, Teatro La Fenice, 1951 (first performance in Italy)

La locandiera, Carlo Goldoni
Director: Luchino Visconti
Sets and Costumes: Luchino Visconti, Piero Tosi
Time and Place: Venice, Teatro La Fenice, 1952

Tre sorelle / Tri sestry, Anton Chekhov
Director: Luchino Visconti
Time and Place: Rome, Teatro Eliseo, 1952

Il tabacco fa male / O vrede tobaka, Anton Chekhov
Director: Luchino Visconti
Time and Place: Milan, Teatro di via Manzoni, 1953

Medea, Euripides
Director: Luchino Visconti
Time and Place: Milan, Teatro di via Manzoni, 1953

Festival, Age, Furio Scarpelli, Dino Verde, and Orio Vergani
Consultant: Luchino Visconti
Time and Place: Milan, Teatro Nuovo, 1954

Come le foglie, Giuseppe Giacosa
Director: Luchino Visconti
Time and Place: Milan, Teatro Olimpia, 1954

Il crogiuolo / The Crucible, Arthur Miller
Director: Luchino Visconti
Sets and Costumes: Luchino Visconti
Time and Place: Rome, Teatro Quirino, 1955 (first performance in Italy)

Zio Vanja / Djada Vanja, Anton Chekhov
Director: Luchino Visconti
Time and Place: Rome, Teatro Eliseo, 1955

Contessina giulia / Fröken Julie, August Strindberg
Director: Luchino Visconti
Sets and Costumes: Luchino Visconti
Time and Place: Rome, Teatro delle Arti, 1957

L'impresario delle smirne, Carlo Goldoni
Director: Luchino Visconti
Sets and Costumes: Luchino Visconti
Time and Place: Venice, Teatro La Fenice, 1957

Uno sguardo dal ponte / A View from the Bridge, Arthur Miller
Director: Luchino Visconti
Time and Place: Rome, Teatro Eliseo, 1958

Immagini e tempi di Eleanora Duse, Gerardo Guerrieri
Director: Luchino Visconti
Time and Place: Rome, Teatro Quirino, 1958

Veglia la mia casa / Look Homeward, Angel, Ketti Frings, after Thomas Wolfe's
   novel
Director: Luchino Visconti
Time and Place: Rome, Teatro Quirino, 1958

Deux sur la balancoire / Two for the Seesaw, William Gibson
Director: Luchino Visconti
Sets and Costumes: Luchino Visconti
Time and Place: Paris, Théatre Ambassadeur, 1958 (first performance in
   France)

I ragazzi della signora Gibbons / Mrs. Gibbons' Boys, Will Glickman and Joseph
   Stein

Director: Luchino Visconti
Time and Place: Rome, Teatro Eliseo, 1958

Figli d'arte, Diego Fabbri
Director: Luchino Visconti
Time and Place: Rome, Teatro Eliseo, 1959

L'Arialda, Giovanni Testori
Director: Luchino Visconti
Sets and Costumes: Luchino Visconti
Time and Place: Rome, Teatro Eliseo, 1960

Dommage qu'elle soit une p . . . / 'Tis Pity She's a Whore, John Ford
Director: Luchino Visconti
Sets and Costumes: Luchino Visconti
Time and Place: Paris, Théatre de Paris, 1961

Il tredicesimo albero / Le treizieme arbre, André Gide
Director: Luchino Visconti
Time and Place: Spoleto, Teatro Caio Melisso

Aprés la chute / After the Fall, Arthur Miller
Director: Luchino Visconti
Time and Place: Paris, Théatre du Gymnase, 1965

I giardino dei ciliegi / Višnëvyj Sad, Anton Chekhov
Director: Luchino Visconti
Sets and Costumes: Luchino Visconti, Ferdinando Scarfiotti
Time and Place: Rome, Teatro Valle, 1965

Egmont, Johann Wolfgang von Goethe
Director: Luchino Visconti
Time and Place: Florence, inner courtyard of Palazzo Pitti, 1967

La monaca di monza, Giovanni Testori
Director: Luchino Visconti
Time and Place: Cesana, Teatro Bonci, 1967 (first performance)

L'inserzione, Natalia Ginzburg
Director: Luchino Visconti
Time and Place: Milan, Teatro San Babila, 1969 (first performance in Italy)

Tanto tempo fa / Old Times, Harold Pinter
Director: Luchino Visconti
Time and Place: Rome, Teatro Argentina, 1973 (first performance in Italy)

OPERA AND BALLET

La Vestale
Libretto: Etienne Jouy
Music: Gaspare Spontini
Conductor: Antonino Votto
Director: Luchino Visconti
Time and Place: Milan, Teatro alla Scala, 1954

La Sonnambula
Libretto: Felice Romani
Music: Vincenzo Bellini
Conductor: Leonard Bernstein
Director: Luchino Visconti
Time and Place: Milan, Teatro alla Scala, 1955

La Traviata
Libretto: Francesco Maria Piave
Music: Giuseppe Verdi
Conductor: Carlo Maria Giulini
Director: Luchino Visconti
Time and Place: Milan, Teatro alla Scala, 1955

Mario E Il Mago (a choreographic work after Thomas Mann's novel)
Music: Franco Mannino
Conductor: Luciano Rosanda
Director: Luchino Visconti
Time and Place: Milan, Teatro alla Scala, 1956 (first performance)

Anna Bolena
Libretto: Felice Romani
Music: Gaetano Donizetti
Conductor: Gianandrea Gavazzeni
Director: Luchino Visconti
Time and Place: Milan, Teatro alla Scala, 1957

Ifigenia en Tauride
Libretto: Nicolas-Francois Guillard
Music: Christophe Willibald Gluck
Conductor: Nino Sanzogno
Director: Luchino Visconti
Time and Place: Milan, Teatro alla Scala, 1957

Maratona Di Danza
Libretto: Luchino Visconti

Music: Hans Werner Henze
Conductor: Richard Kraus
Director: Luchino Visconti
Time and Place: West Berlin, Städtische Oper, 1957 (first performance)

Don Carlo
Libretto: Joseph Méry and Camille du Locle
Music: Giuseppe Verdi
Conductor: Carlo Maria Giulini
Director: Luchino Visconti
Time and Place: London, Royal Opera House, Covent Garden, 1958

Macbeth
Libretto: Francesco Maria Piave
Music: Giuseppe Verdi
Conductor: Thomas Schippers
Director: Luchino Visconti
Time and Place: Spoleto, Teatro Nuovo, 1958

Il Duca D'Alba
Libretto: Eugene Scribe
Music: Gaetano Donizetti
Conductor: Thomas Schippers
Director: Luchino Visconti
Time and Place: Spoleto, Teatro Nuovo, 1959

Salome
Libretto: Hedwig Lahmann
Music: Richard Strauss
Conductor: Thomas Schippers
Director: Luchino Visconti
Time and Place: Spoleto, Teatro Nuovo, 1961

Il Diavolo in Giardino (a historical pastoral comedy by Luchino Visconti, Filippo
   Sanjust, and Enrico Medioli)
Music: Franco Mannino
Conductor: Franco Mannino
Director: Luchino Visconti
Time and Place: Palermo, Teatro Massimo, 1963

La Traviata
Libretto: Francesco Maria Piave
Music: Giuseppe Verdi
Conductor: Robert La Marchina

Director: Luchino Visconti
Time and Place: Spoleto, Teatro Nuovo, 1963

Le Nozze di Figaro
Libretto: Lorenzo da Ponte
Music: Wolfgang Amadeus Mozart
Conductor: Carlo Maria Giulini
Director: Luchino Visconti
Time and Place: Rome, Teatro dell'Opera, 1964

Il Trovatore
Libretto: Salvatore Cammarano
Music: Giuseppe Verdi
Conductor: Gianandrea Gavazzeni
Director: Luchino Visconti
Time and Place: Moscow, Bolshoi Theater, 1964

Il Trovatore
Libretto: Salvatore Cammarano
Music: Giuseppe Verdi
Conductor: Carlo Maria Giulini
Director: Luchino Visconti
Time and Place: London, Royal Opera House, Covent Garden, 1964

Don Carlos
Libretto: Joseph Méry and Camille du Locle
Music: Giuseppe Verdi
Conductor: Carlo Maria Giulini
Director: Luchino Visconti
Time and Place: Rome, Teatro dell'Opera, 1965

Falstaff
Libretto: Arrigo Boito
Music: Giuseppe Verdi
Conductor: Leonard Bernstein
Director: Luchino Visconti
Time and Place: Wien Staatsoper, 1966

Der Rosenkavalier
Libretto: Hugo von Hofmanstahl
Music: Richard Strauss
Conductor: Georg Solti
Director: Luchino Visconti
Time and Place: London, Royal Opera House, Covent Garden, 1966

La Traviata
Libretto: Francesco Maria Piave
Music: Giuseppe Verdi
Conductor: Carlo Maria Giulini
Director: Luchino Visconti
Time and Place: London, Royal Opera House, Covent Garden, 1967

Simon Boccanegra
Libretto: Francesco Maria Piave
Music: Giuseppe Verdi
Conductor: Josef Krips
Director: Luchino Visconti
Time and Place: Wien, Staatsoper, 1969

Manon Lescaut
Libretto: Marco Prago, Domenico Oliva, Giulio Ricordi, and Luigi Illica
Music: Giacomo Puccini
Conductor: Thomas Schippers
Director: Luchino Visconti
Time and Place: Spoleto, Teatro Nuovo, 1973

Unrealized Film Projects

This list includes only those projects that got as far as some script stage. The years are approximations and refer mainly to the time when the project was initiated. In cases in which the project was completed by another director, the script might not have been the one referred to here. Main source: Rondolino, *Visconti*.

L'amante di gramigna (Gramigna's Lover, 1942)
After Giovanni Verga's story. Directed by Carlo Lizzani in 1969.

The 2nd and the 3rd episodes for *LA TERRA TREMA (The Earth Trembles, 1947)*.

Pensione Oltremare (Boardinghouse Oltremare, 1949)
Story based on the experiences of Visconti and certain others at the end of the war.

Cronache di poveri amanti (The Story about Poor Lovers, 1949)
Free adaptations of Vasco di Pratolini's novel. Directed by Carlo Lizzani in 1953.

La carozza di santissimo sacramento (The Carriage of the Most Sacred Sacrament, 1949)
Adaptation of Prospèr Merimée's story. If realized, this would have been the first Italian color film. It was directed by Jean Renoir in 1952 under the title *La Carozza d'oro (The Golden Coach)*.

Marzio nuziale (The Wedding March, 1950)
Stories about different kinds of married couples, centered on a suicide that takes place in the beginning. Based on a news item.

Il ballo del Conte D'Orgeli (Count Orgel's Ball, 1963)
After Raymond Radiguet's novel.

La contessa Tarnowska (Countess Tarnowska, 1965)
A long-term plan based on a famous incident.

Il giovane Törless (Young Törless, 1965)
After Robert Musil's novel.

Vita di Puccini (Puccini's Life, 1969)
A project conceived in connection with *Death in Venice*. Presumably it would not have been a conventional "biopic."

A la recherche pour la temps perdu (Remembrance of Things Past)
After Marcel Proust's novel. A long-term plan that came close to realization in 1971.

La montagna incantata (The Magic Mountain, 1972)
After Thomas Mann's novel.

Bibliography

FILM THEORY AND HISTORY

Andrew, Dudley   *Concepts in Film Theory*. Oxford University Press, Oxford, 1984.

Mists of Regret – Culture and Sensibility in Classic French Film. Princeton: Princeton University Press, 1995.

Aristarco, Guido   *Su Visconti – materiali per una analisi critica*. Roma: La Zattera di Babele srl., 1986.

Armes, Roy   *Patterns of Realism – A Study of Italian Neo-Realist Cinema*. London: Tantivy Press, 1971.

Balázes, Béla   *Theory of the Film – Character and Growth of a New Art*. Translated by Edith Bone. New York: Dover Publications, 1970.

Baldelli, Pio   *Luchino Visconti*. Milano: Gabriele Mazzotta editore, 1982.

Bazin, André   *Qu'est-ce que le cinema?* Vol. IV – *Une esthétique de la réalité: le néo-réalisme*. Paris: Editions du cerf, 1962.

What Is Cinema? Translated by Hugh Gray. Berkeley: University of California Press, vol. I, 1967; vol. II, 1971.

Luchino Visconti. 2d ed. Milano: Il Castro Cinema, 1994.

Bondanella, Peter   *Italian Cinema from Neorealism to the Present*. New York: Fredrick Ungar, 1984.

Bordwell, David   *Narration in the Fiction into Film*. London, Routledge, (1985) 1988.

Boyum, Joy Gould   *Double Exposure – Fiction into Film*. New York: Universe Books, 1985.

Brunette, Peter   "An Interview with Suso Cecchi D'Amico." *Sight and Sound* (Winter, 1986–7).

Bruni, David & Pravadelli, Veronica (eds.) *Studi Viscontiani*. Venezia: Marilio editori, 1997.

Castello, Giulio Cesare   "Luchino Visconti." *Sight and Sound*, vol. 25, no. 4 (Spring 1956), pp. 184–90, 220.

Caute, David   *Joseph Losey – A Revenge on Life*. London: Faber and Faber, 1994.

Dalle Vacche, Angela   *The Body in the Mirror – Shapes of History in Italian Cinema.* Princeton: Princeton University Press, 1992.

Deaglio, Enrico   "Ritorno ad Acitrezza – Luchino e le sorelle." *La Stampa*, September 1, 1990.

Deleuze, Gilles   *Cinema 2 – The Time Image.* Translated by Hugh Tomlinson and Robert Galeta. London: Athlone Press, 1989.

De Santis, Giuseppe   "Visconti's Interpretation of Cain's Setting in *Ossessione*." Translated by Luciana Bohne. *Film Criticism*, vol. IX, no. 3 (Spring 1985).

Doniol-Valcroze & Domarchi, Jean   "Entretien avec Luchino Visconti." *Cahiers du Cinema*, no. 93 (March 1957), pp. 1–10.

Durgnant, Raymond   *Jean Renoir.* Berkeley: University of California Press, 1974.

Edgerton, Gary R. (ed.)   *Film and the Arts in Symbiosis – A Resource Guide.* New York: Greenwood Press, 1988.

Ellis, John   "The Literary Adaptation – An Introduction." *Screen*, vol. 23, no. 1 (May/June 1982), pp. 3–5.

Enckell, Mikael   " 'Citizen Kane' and Psychoanalysis" – Film and Psychoanalysis (III). *The Scandinavian Psychoanalytic Review*, vol. 8, no. 1 (1985), pp. 17–34.

Eko och återsken. Ekenäs: Söderström & C: o, 1979.

Spegelskrift. Ekenäs: Söderström & C: o, 1984

Guarnier, José Luis   *Roberto Rossellini.* Translated by Elisabeth Cameron. New York: Praeger, 1970.

Hay, James   *The Passing of the Rex – Popular Film Culture in Italy in the Fascist Era.* Bloomington: Indiana University Press, 1987.

Ishaghpour, Youssef   *Visconti – Le sens et l'image.* Paris: Editions de la difference. 1984.

Kinder, Marsha   "The Subversive Potential of the Pseudo-Iterative." *Film Quarterly*, vol. 43, no. 2 (Winter 1989–90), pp. 3–16.

Liandrat-Guigues, Suzanne   *Les Images du temps dans* Vaghe stelle dell'Orsa *de Luchino Visconti.* Paris: L'œil vivant, 1995.

Liehm, Mira   *Passion and Defiance – Film in Italy from 1942 to the Present.* Berkley: University of California Press, 1942.

Lisi, Umberto   "Paura della storia." *Cinema Nuovo*, no. 52, 1954.

Mannino, Franco   *Visconti e la musica.* Lucca: Akademos & Lim, 1994.

Marcus, Millicent   *Filmmaking by the Book – Italian Cinema and Literary Adaptation.* Baltimore: Johns Hopkins University Press, 1993.

Italian Film in the Light of Neorealism. Princeton: Princeton University Press, 1986.

Micciché, Lino   *Luchino Visconti – Un profilo critico.* Venezia: Marsilio Editori, 1996.

(ed.) *Il Gattopardo.* Rome: Centro Sperimentale di Cinematografia & Electa Napoli, 1996.

(ed.) *La terra trema di Luchino Visconti – Analisi di un capolavoro.* Torino:

Associazione Philip Morris Progetto Cinema, Centro Sperimentale di Cinematografia & Cineteca Nazionale, 1993.

Visconti e il neorealismo – Ossessione, La terra trema, Bellissima. Venezia: Marsilio editori, 1990.

Morrissette, Bruce *Novel and Film – Essays in Two Genres.* University of Chicago Press, Chicago, 1985.

Nichols, Bill (ed.) *Movies and Methods*, vol. II. London: University of California Press, 1985.

Nowell-Smith, Geoffrey *Luchino Visconti.* Norwich: Secker & Warburg/BFI, 1973.

Overbey, David (ed.) *Springtime in Italy: A Reader on Neo-Realism.* London: Talisman Books, 1978.

Partridge, Colin *Senso – Visconti's Film and Boito's Novella – A Case Study in the Relation between Literature and Film.* Lewiston: Edwin Mellen Press, 1991.

Ranvaud, Don "Senso: Masterpiece as Minefield." *Monthly Film Bulletin* (April 1983).

Renoir, Jean *My Life and My Films.* Translated by Norman Denny. London: Collins, 1974.

Rohdie, Sam *Rocco and His Brothers.* London: BFI Publishing, 1992.

Rondolino, Gianni *Visconti.* Unione Tipografio – Editrice. Torino: Torinese, 1981.

Salmi, Hannu *Elokuva ja historia.* Helsinki: Painatuskeskus Oy, 1993.

Schifano, Laurence *Luchino Visconti – Les feux de la passion.* Flammarion, (1987) 1989.

Servadio, Gaia *Luchino Visconti – A Biography.* London: Mondadori, 1982.

Sinyard, Neil *Filming Literature – The Art of Screen Adaptation.* London: Croom Helm, 1986.

Sorlin, Pierre *The Film in History – Restaging the Past.* Oxford: Basil Blackwell, 1980.

Stirling, Monica *A Screen of Time – A Study of Luchino Visconti.* New York: Harcourt Brace Jovanovich, 1979.

Tonetti, Clara *Luchino Visconti.* London: Columbia Books, 1987.

Villien, Bruno *Visconti.* Translated into Italian by Saverio Esposito. Milano: Vallardi, 1987.

Wagner, Geoffrey *The Novel and the Cinema.* London: Tantivy Press, 1975.

Wiehe, Roger E. "Of Art and Death: Film and Fiction Versions of *Death in Venice*." *Literature/Film Quarterly*, vol. 16, no. 3 (1988), pp. 210–15.

Williams, Christopher (ed.) *Realism and the Cinema.* London: Routledge & Kegan Paul, 1980.

Windeler, Robert *Burt Lancaster.* London: Comet, 1984.

Wollen, Peter *Signs and Meaning in the Cinema.* London: Secker and Warburg, in association with British Film Institute, (1969) 1972.

Zeffirelli, Franco *The Autobiography of Franco Zeffirelli.* London: Weidenfeldt & Nicolson, 1986.

LITERATURE, HISTORY, AND
CULTURAL HISTORY

Berlin, Isaiah   *Russian Thinkers*. Harmondsworth: Penguin Books, (1979) 1984.

Borchmeyer, Dieter   *Richard Wagner – Theory and Theatre*. Oxford: Clarendon Press, 1991.

Branca, Vittore (ed.)   *Dizionario critico della letteratura italiana*. Torino: UTET, 1973.

Carsaniga, Giovanni   *Leopardi*. Edinburgh: Edinburgh University Press, 1977.

Clark, Martin   *Modern Italy 1871–1982*. London: Longman, 1984.

Dill, Marshall, Jr.   *Germany: A Modern History*. Ann Arbor: University of Michigan Press, 1961.

Genette, Gérard   *Narrative Discourse – An Essay in Method*. Translated by Jane E. Lewin. Ithaca, N.Y.: Cornell University Press, (1980) 1990.

Gerould, Daniel (ed.)   *Melodrama*. New York: New York Literary Forum, 1980.

Godefroy, Vincent   *The Dramatic Genius of Verdi – Studies of Selected Operas*, vol. I. London: Victor Gollancz, 1975.

Hamilton, Nigel   *The Brothers Mann*. New Haven, Conn.: Yale University Press, 1979.

Hemmings, F. W. J. (ed.)   *The Age of Realism*. Harmondsworth: Penguin Books, 1974.

Herre, Franz   *Ludwig II*. Stuttgart: Deutsche Verlags-Anstalt, 1986.

Keefe, Terry   *French Existentialist Fiction: Changing Moral Perspectives*. London: Croom Helm, 1986.

Kimbell, David R. B.   *Verdi in the Age of Italian Romanticism*. Cambridge: Cambridge University Press, 1981.

Kogan, Norman   *A Political History of Italy*. New York: Praeger, 1983.

LaCapra, Dominick   *History, Politics, and the Novel*. Ithaca: Cornell University Press, 1987.

Lukács, Georg   *Balzac und der französische Realismus*. Berlin: Aufbau-Verlag, 1952.

   The Historical Novel. Translated by Hannah and Stanley Mitchell. Harmondsworth: Penguin Books, 1969.

Mack Smith, Denis   *Italy. A Modern History*. Ann Arbor: University of Michigan Press, 1959.

   Victor Emanuel, Cavour and the Risorgimento. London: Oxford University Press, 1971.

Mann, Thomas   *Pro and Contra Wagner*. Translated by Allan Budden. London: Faber and Faber, 1985.

   Leiden und Grösse der Meister. Baden Baden, 1974.

   Schopenhauer. Stockholm: Bermann-Fischer Verlag, 1938.

Maurois, André   *The Quest for Proust*. Translated by Gerard Hopkins. Harmondsworth: Penguin Books, (1950) 1962.

May, Gita   *Stendhal and the Age of Napoleon.* New York: Columbia University Press, 1977.

Mayer, Hans   *Thomas Mann.* Frankfurt am Main: Suhrkampf Verlag, 1980.

McCarthy, Patrick   *Camus.* London: Hamish Hamilton, 1982.

Pacifici, Sergio   *The Modern Italian Novel from Capuana to Tozzi.* Carbondale: Southern Illinois University Press, 1973.

Pitcher, Harvey   *The Chekhov Play – A New Interpretation.* Berkeley: University of California Press, 1973.

Praz, Mario   *The Romantic Agony.* Translated by Angus Davidson. London: Fontana Library (1933) 1966.

Prendergast, Christopher   *Balzac, Fiction and Melodrama.* New York: Holmes and Meier, 1978.

The Order of Mimesis – Balzac, Stendhal, Nerval, Flaubert. New York: Cambridge University Press, 1986.

Revel, Jean-Francois   *On Proust.* Translated by Martin Turnell. London: Hamish Hamilton, 1972.

Ricoeur, Paul   *The Rule of Metaphor – Multi-disciplinary Studies of the Creation of Meaning in Language.* Translated by Robert Czerny with Kathleen McLaughlin and John Costello, SJ. London: University of Toronto Press, 1978.

Time and Narrative. Translated by Kathleen McLaughlin and David Pellauer. Chicago: University of Chicago Press, vol. I, 1983; vol. II, 1984; vol. III, 1985.

Seiler, Jacques   Text to Aldo Ciccolini's recording of César Franck's *Prelude, Chorale and Fugue.* EMI C 069–10755.

Shattuck, Roger   *Proust.* London: Fontana/Collins, 1974.

Stassinopolous, Asianna   *Maria Callas – The Woman behind the Legend.* New York: Simon and Schuster, 1981.

Steiner, George   *After Babel – Aspects of Language and Translation.* London: Oxford University Press, 1975.

Taylor, A. J. P.   *The Habsburg Monarchy 1809–1918.* London, (1948) 1961.

Thody, Philip   *Albert Camus.* London: Macmillan, 1989.

Tulloch, John   *Chekhov: A Structuralist Study.* London: Macmillan, 1980.

Whitfield, J. H.   *A Short History of Italian Literature.* London, 1960.

Winston, Richard   *Thomas Mann, The Making of an Artist 1875–1911.* New York: Knopf, 1981.

EDITIONS OF THE NOVELS, SHORT STORIES, AND SCREENPLAYS

Aristarco, G. ja Carancini, G. (ed.)   *Rocco e i suoi fratelli.* Bologna: Cappelli editore, 1978.

Cain, James M. *The Five Great Novels of James M. Cain*. London: Picador, (1981) 1985.

Cavallaro, G. B. (ed.) *Senso*. Bologna: Cappelli editore, 1977.

Cecchi D'Amico, Suso, & Visconti, Luchino *A la recherche du temps perdu – scénario d'apres l'œuvre de Marcel Proust*. Editions Persona, 1984.

Camus, Albert *The Stranger*. Translated by Stuart Gilbert. New York: Vintage Books, 1954.

D'Annunzio, Gabriele *L'Innozente*. Milano: Arnoldo Mondadori editore, 1986.

Dostoyevsky, Feodor *Stories. White Nights*. Translated by Olga Shartse. Moscow: Raduga Publishers, (1971) 1983.

Dunn, Esther Cloudman *Eight Famous Elizabethan Plays*. New York: Modern Library, 1932.

Ferrara, Giorgio (ed.) *Ludwig*. Bologna: Cappelli Editore, 1973.

Mann, Thomas *Death in Venice and Other Stories*. London: A Landmark Edition, 1983 (1971) 1982.

—— *Doctor Faustus*. Translated by H. T. Lowe-Porter. London: Secker & Warburg, (1949) 1969.

Miller, Arthur *Collected Plays*. London: Secker & Warburg, (1958) 1974.

Micciché, Lino (ed.) *Morte a Venezia*. Bologna: Cappelli Editore, 1971.

Pinter, Harold *The Proust Screenplay*. London: Eyre Methuen, 1978.

Proust, Marcel *Remembrance of Things Past*. Translated by C. K. Scott Moncrieff and Terence Kilmartin. Vol. I. New York: Vintage Books, 1982.

Renzi, Renzo (ed.) *Le Notti Bianche*. Bologna: Cappelli Editore, 1957.

Tomaso Di Lampedusa, Giuseppe *The Leopard*. Translated by Archibald Colquhoun. London: Harvill, (1988) 1993.

Verga, Giovanni *I Malavoglia (The house by the medlar tree)*. Translated by Judith Landry. Sawtry: Dedalus, (1985) 1991.

Visconti, Luchino *Angelo*. Edited by René de Ceccatty. Rome: Editori Riuniti, 1993.

INTERVIEWS

Aristarco, Guido Helsinki, October 5, 1988. In Italian. Interpretation by Elina Suolahti.

Brunetta, Gian Piero Helsinki, February 4, 1992. In English. Published in *Filmihullu* 3/92.

Cecchi D'Amico, Suso Rome, September 14, 1988. In English. Published in *Filmihullu* 2/89.

Medioli, Enrico Orvieto, September 12, 1988. In English. Published in *Filmihullu* 2/89.

Index